Species of Origins

American Intellectual Culture

Series Editors: Jean Bethke Elshtain, University of Chicago
Ted V. McAllister, Pepperdine University
Wilfred M. McClay, University of Tennessee, Chattanooga

Species of Origins

America's Search for a Creation Story

Karl W. Giberson and Donald A. Yerxa

ROWMAN & LITTLEFIELD PUBLISHERS, INC.
Lanham • Boulder • New York • Toronto • Oxford

ROWMAN & LITTLEFIELD PUBLISHERS, INC.

Published in the United States of America
by Rowman & Littlefield Publishers, Inc.
A wholly owned subsidary of The Rowman & Littlefield Publishing Group, Inc.
4501 Forbes Boulevard, Suite 200, Lanham, Maryland 20706
www.rowmanlittlefield.com

PO Box 317
Oxford
OX2 9RU, UK

British Library Cataloguing in Publication Information Available

Library of Congress Cataloging-in-Publication Data

Giberson, Karl.
  Species of origins : America's search for a creation story / Karl W. Giberson and
  Donald A. Yerxa.
    p. cm. — (American intellectual culture)
  Includes bibliographical references and index.
  ISBN 0-7425-0764-5 (alk. paper) — ISBN 0-7425-0765-3 (pbk. : alk. paper)
    1. Religion and science. 2. Creation—Biblical teaching. 3. Creation—Mythology. 4.
  Evolution. I. Yerxa, Donald A., 1950– II. Title. III. Series.
  BL240.3 .G53 2002
  231.7'652'0973—dc21

                                                                    2002002365

Printed in the United States of America

⊗™ The paper used in this publication meets the minimum requirements of
American National Standard for Information Sciences—Permanence of Paper
for Printed Library Materials, ANSI/NISO Z39.48–1992.

Contents

Acknowledgments

In the course of writing this book, the subject matter of which has taken us both far beyond our professional training, we have relied heavily on the advice and input of countless colleagues and scholars who were generous in their assistance and encouragement. We have, to be sure, accumulated a great many debts, which we shall attempt to acknowledge, although it is impossible to do so properly.

Our documentation reveals our debt to the hundreds of scholars and intellectuals who have weighed in on aspects of the contemporary debate over cosmological and biological origins and who have made this discussion so lively and engrossing. Beyond that, we are grateful to the many people who responded to our various, and frequently inconvenient, requests. These include: Earl Aagaard, William A. Cirignani, William A. Dembski, Owen Gingerich, Shaun Henson, Phillip E. Johnson, Denis O. Lamoureux, James Mahaffy, David Raup, Jay Wesley Richards, James Skehan, SJ, Dennis Wagner, Larry Witham, and especially Michael Woodruff.

This book would not have been written without generous support from the John Templeton Foundation, which provided grant assistance to give us time to write and also sponsored our participation in the Templeton Oxford Seminars on Science and Christianity over the course of three years. (This program was an initiative of the Council of Christian Colleges and Universities.) This book was a product of those seminars, and we are most appreciative of the stimulation and interaction that occurred at Wycliffe Hall, Oxford University, during the summers of 1999–2001. In particular, we thank the seminar leaders Alister E. McGrath and John Roche, along with some of the foremost scholars working in the fields of the history of science and science and religion who gave us special encouragement. These include William Shea, John Hedley Brooke, Ronald L. Numbers, Ernan McMullin, and Howard J. Van Till. All of our fellow seminar participants were helpful, but none more than Rebecca Flietstra, Alexei Nesteruk, and Jitze Van der Meer.

We are grateful to our series editor Wilfred McClay, who suggested that we take our Oxford project and work it into a volume for Rowman and Littlefield's American Intellectual Culture Series. He provided unflagging support, timely advice, and a most memorable title.

At critical moments in our careers, we have benefited from the support, encouragement, and friendship of some special people, and we take this opportunity to acknowledge James Cameron, Lowell Hall, Kent Hill, Cecil Paul (deceased), Maxine Walker, and John Wilson.

We also thank those who read our manuscript and provided critical comments: Donald Christensen, Darryl Falk, Douglas Fish, John C. Greene, Alister E. McGrath, Paul Nyce, and Howard J. Van Till. Of course, none of them bear responsibility for the arguments we have advanced, though our outlook has certainly benefited from their input.

Walt Jones assisted us in research, and Janet Calhoun provided invaluable technical service in preparing the manuscript. Phil Davis designed our cover.

Last, but most importantly, we thank our wives and families for their patience and support. They sacrificed summer vacations and many quiet evenings at home, and for that we will always be grateful.

Note to the Reader

All biblical references are taken from the King James Version, which, although it has been largely supplanted by more recent translations, is the version whose prose dominated American religion throughout the twentieth century.

Introduction

In both science and religion, we seek creation myths, stories that give our lives meaning.

— George Johnson, *Fire in the Mind*

Human beings need creation stories. Cultures are defined, in part, by their common creation myths, stories that answer important questions about how things came to be and how meaning is to be found within the existing order. Creation myths clarify and mitigate the exhilarating, challenging, and terrifying patterns of life and death; they create the security of space and place; they address the need for meaning and purpose. Creation myths are "more than rational explanations of first causes of physical processes or justifications of existing social conditions." Creation myths must make evident the "*meaning* of the world's appearance, that is, the fact that the world has *appeared*."[1]

Creation stories both unify and separate. Cultures can be united by a creation story; disparate and incompatible creation stories, on the other hand, can split and alienate cultures from each other. The patterns of human history and the findings of social science confirm that a coherent human society must have agreement on fundamental issues if it is to cohere and endure. And the creation story that undergirds and supports the larger structures of meaning is certainly a central element in this agreement. There must be a shared common notion about how things came to be. Cultural historian and theologian Thomas Berry goes so far as to suggest that "[n]o community can *exist* without a unifying story."[2]

Cultures place great burdens on their creation stories. They are expected to account for generally accepted explanations of the origins of the visible universe, the genesis of human life, the sources of social and moral order, and the

1

grounding of meaning. Just about every culture generates creation stories that serve similar purposes, despite the often radical differences in the stories themselves. Philosopher and religious scholar Paul Brockelman puts it like this: "[V]irtually every human culture that has ever existed has developed creation stories which explains how reality has come to be just as it happens to be. These stories," he adds, "provide those cultures with a sense of a larger whole to which they belong."[3] From the highly theological Near Eastern creation stories of the Gilgamesh epic and the Hebrew Bible to the modern scientific accounts that invoke mathematical and physical laws, every creation story is pregnant with a particular worldview.

America is no exception. In fact, the foundational documents of its own political creation, the Declaration of Independence and the Constitution, are often treated in political discussions as "sacred texts," describing the "creation events" that gave birth to the United States. People expect these "creation accounts" to answer profound questions about who they are and how they should manage their social affairs. On a larger scale, Americans traditionally have believed that their political rights are ultimately grounded in the Judeo-Christian creation story that is invoked in the immortal phrase "all men are endowed by their Creator with certain unalienable Rights." In a curious and controversial sense, the creation of America is understood by many to be an extension of the creation described in the opening passages of the Bible. That is why so many U.S. flags hang in the sanctuaries of American churches.

Starting in the late nineteenth century, however, we have witnessed something in America that increasingly departs from the norm described earlier: there is no agreed–on creation story.[4] In contemporary America, a variety of creation stories circulate, reflecting a growing worldview "dyssensus." We have coined the term "species of origins"[5] to describe these diverse creation myths, playing off the title of the most controversial book in the origins debate, Charles Darwin's *The Origin of Species by Means of Natural Selection*.

One has only to pick up a newspaper or opinion journal to see America's ongoing worldview struggle as it debates issues like abortion, euthanasia, and evolution. The partisans in these interminable, strident, and occasionally even violent, cultural controversies often appeal, explicitly and implicitly, to different creation stories—different species of origins—to justify their positions.

Some of this disagreement no doubt reflects America's growing cultural and religious diversity. But most of it flows from the deeper reality that Americans continue to grant a large measure of cultural authority to two competing worldviews: modern naturalistic science and traditional Judeo-Christian religions, the latter often brought into sharp focus through the lens of biblical literalism. Religion was foundational for Western civilization until the nineteenth century, and remains central to American culture even today, despite the emergence of what some would suggest is a scientific alternative. The culture that so frequently defined itself as "*one* nation under God" found itself bifurcating along a previously undiscovered seam as a new scientific worldview, without a recognizable god, emerged to challenge the traditional perspective. So competitive have these two worldviews been that, for over a century, their tense and complex relationship has appeared to many as a sort of perennial warfare.

This confrontation intensified at the dawn of the twentieth century when a deeply Christian America found itself struggling against the same foe that had all but vanquished Europe's traditional Christianity—religious modernism. The modernization of Christianity was driven by a number of factors—chief among them were German biblical criticism with its conclusions that the Bible, including the New Testament accounts of Jesus, was historically unreliable, and biological evolution, with its conclusion that the Judeo-Christian creation story in Genesis was false. The removal of these two pillars—biblical authority and special creation—created a certain instability that had all but toppled European Christianity and threatened to do the same in America. Theological conservatives, among whom could be counted some of America's leading political and business leaders, perceived a real threat. As the twentieth century unfolded, the tension between competing "species of origins" became ever more apparent, as events conspired to create an increasing divergence between the traditional creation story and the new scientific account.

- From 1910 to 1915, California businessman Lyman Stewart financed twelve paperback volumes that he hoped would be a great "Testimony to the Truth," a counter to encroaching modernism. *The Fundamentals* was the centerpiece of an opposition to modernism that would soon drive many conservative evangelical Christians into the fundamentalist camp.[6] But what is most interesting, even unexpected, is the moderation and restraint evidenced in *The Fundamentals*, particularly with regard to the topic of biological evolution. A. C. Dixon, the series' first editor, confessed to harboring a feeling of "repugnance to the idea that an ape or an orang-outang was my ancestor," but he also was "willing to accept the humiliating fact, if proved." The editor of the last two volumes, Reuben A. Torrey, acknowledged that a person could "believe thoroughly in the absolute infallibility of the Bible and still be an evolutionist of a certain type." Historian Ronald L. Numbers notes that while the various authors of *The Fundamentals* "may not have liked evolution, . . . few, if any, saw the necessity or desirability of launching a crusade to eradicate it from the schools and churches of America."[7] The fundamentalist response to modernism was initially characterized by an aggressive attack on German biblical criticism and an almost benign tolerance of biological evolution.
- Following World War I, William Jennings Bryan helped turn the fundamentalist movement into a crusade against evolution. In 1921, Bryan warned about the dangers of evolutionary thinking in a stock speech titled "The Menace of Darwinism." "To destroy the faith of Christians and lay the

foundations for the bloodiest war in history," Bryan concluded, "would seem enough to condemn Darwinism."[8] Bryan took this message to Dayton, Tennessee, in 1925, where it became immortalized in the "Scopes Monkey Trial." The saga of the Scopes trial awakened all of America to the dangers lurking in "Darwin's dangerous idea" and, despite Bryan's "victory" at Dayton, evolution moved even closer to the center of America's cultural conversation.

- A decade later, Columbia University Press published *Genetics and the Origin of Species* by Russian-born geneticist Theodosius Dobzhansky, who went on to become one of the great biologists of the twentieth century. Dobzhansky's book played a major role in uniting two research traditions within biology: genetics and field biology. The resulting activity, including his own work on the genetics of natural populations, continued throughout the 1940s and has come to be known as the neo-Darwinian "synthesis." According to a leading historian of evolutionary thought, this synthesis "allowed Darwinism to re-emerge as a driving force in biology."[9] Whatever may have been the perception of evolution in the culture at large, within biology, evolution had become the central organizing principle. It would no longer be possible for biologists to work outside its broad outline.

- In 1953, Francis Crick and James Watson, in an act of great imaginative power, worked out the structure of deoxyribose nucleic acid (DNA), the famous double helix. Scientists were given a window into the chemistry of life. For the first time, biologists could conceptualize in detail how information flowed in reproduction from generation to generation and how variation was driven in nature. The general features of DNA were exactly what had been intuited by the neo-Darwinian synthesis, and this vindication further secured the place of evolution within biology.[10]

- Four years later, the successful launching of the Russian satellite *Sputnik* thoroughly shocked America. The resulting space race demanded a reform of the science curricula of American secondary schools. With National Science Foundation funding, a group of biologists established the Biological Sciences Curriculum Study (BSCS) center at the University of Colorado and created a new set of biology texts. Buoyed by the success of the neo-Darwinian synthesis and its role within biology, the BSCS authors made evolution a central feature of the high school biology curriculum. Nearly half the public high schools in America adopted BSCS texts and, for the first time, millions of schoolchildren were confronted with a full explication of Darwin's dangerous idea. Conservative Christians saw their faith under attack in public schools. The resulting backlash fueled the emergence of the modern creation science movement as an organized "scientific" alternative to evolution.[11]

- In 1970, Henry M. Morris turned down an offer of an endowed chair in civil engineering at Auburn University and moved to San Diego to establish a fundamentalist Christian college and a center for creation science research. Throughout the 1970s and 1980s, Morris and a number of like-minded associates developed the Institute for Creation Research into the world's leading antievolutionary organization.[12]

- In 1979, several presidents from small, unaccredited parochial colleges, including Morris of the decade-old Christian Heritage College, met and formed the Transnational Association of Christian Colleges and Schools (TRACS). These college presidents were finding it impossible to get their institutions accredited by recognized regional accrediting organizations, so they decided to create their own accrediting agency. In 1992, after a long process, the U.S. Department of Education recognized TRACS as a national accrediting body for Christian schools and colleges. TRACS-accredited schools are Bible-centered and creationist, since they must demonstrate compliance with a list of foundational biblical standards including the "[s]pecial creation of the existing space-time universe and all its basic systems and kinds of organisms in the six literal days of the creation week."[13]

- While Morris was busy at work building the infrastructure of the modern creation science movement, Dobzhansky was busy spreading the gospel of evolution. The title of a paper he gave at a gathering of the National Association of Biology Teachers has become an oft-quoted aphorism: "Nothing in Biology Makes Sense Except in the Light of Evolution."[14] Near the end of his address, Dobzhansky argued that "[e]volution as a process that has always gone on in the history of the earth can be doubted only by those who are ignorant of the evidence or are resistant to evidence, owing to emotional blocks or to plain bigotry."[15] American science and conservative American Christianity were running along increasingly diverging tracks that would periodically find the two constituencies pitted against each other in a variety of arenas, including courtrooms.

- On January 5, 1982, U.S. District Court judge William R. Overton issued a thirty-eight-page ruling in the so-called Arkansas creation science case. At question was a 1981 Arkansas statute mandating that the state's public schools give "balanced treatment to creation-science and to evolution-science." Judge Overton ruled that creation science was not a scientific theory, but a religious doctrine. "Creation science," he concluded, "not only fails to follow the canons defining scientific theory, it also fails to fit the more general descriptions of 'what scientists think' and 'what scientists do.'"[16] Scientific creationism would suffer a similar fate in other celebrated court battles as the scientific community banished it to the outer reaches of American academia.

- In 1989, veteran science writer Forrest Mims entered into negotiations with the editors of *Scientific American* to take over the long-standing "The Amateur Scientist" column. Mims had written some sample submissions and appeared to have the job clinched when questions emerged about his views on evolution. Upon discovering that he did not accept the theory of evolution, the editors grew deeply concerned lest the reputation of their leading popular science journal be compromised should Mims's "heretical" views become public. They attempted damage control by having Mims agree to keep his personal views on evolution out of the column and requiring that he get approval from *Scientific American* prior to publishing anything in other venues. But the risk of embarrassment was apparently too great, and Mims was dropped as a writer after three noncontroversial columns. Apparently to avoid a lawsuit, "The Amateur Scientist" column, begun in 1952, was dropped as well. The wire services picked up the story, and the Mims affair received attention in the mainstream press and on television outlets like CNN.[17]

- About the time that the editors of *Scientific American* were debating what to do about Mims, a group of scholars and lawyers met for a private conference, "Science and Creationism in Public Schools," at a Jesuit retreat center in Weston, Massachusetts, run by Boston College geologist and Jesuit priest James Skehan. Participants included University of Chicago paleontologist David Raup, University of Chicago theologian Langdon Gilkey, Harvard astronomer Owen Gingerich, Cornell geologist E-an Zen, biochemist author Charles Thaxton, first amendment lawyer Michael Woodruff, Harvard paleontologist Stephen Jay Gould (deceased), and Berkeley law professor Phillip E. Johnson. Johnson, who had been circulating manuscripts highly critical of evolutionary theory but devoid of biblical apologetics,[18] got into a spirited exchange with Gould, the most prominent American evolutionist. According to Johnson, the two of them squared off at the urging of the assembled group. The exchange apparently ended in a draw, but in the estimation of some antievolutionists, Johnson had demonstrated that he could hold his own in debate with a leading evolutionary scientist and spokesperson, something that nobody in the scientific creationism movement had been able to do.[19] A reinvigorated antievolutionism, which was soon known as the "intelligent design movement," was on the verge of acquiring a champion whose eloquence would reverse the declining fortunes of the antievolutionary camp.

- In 1995, the board of directors of the National Association of Biology Teachers (NABT), responding to the growing controversy, approved a statement on the teaching of evolution designed to assist biology teachers in their response to the antievolutionary arguments they were getting from some parents and students imbued with creationist notions. The NABT statement made an aggressive claim: "The diversity of life on earth is the result of evolution: an unsupervised, impersonal, unpredictable and natural process of temporal descent with genetic modification that is affected by natural selection, historical contingencies and changing environments." Soon letters to the editor and opinion-editorial pieces appeared, criticizing the NABT for adopting antireligious wording; by using the words "unsupervised" and "impersonal," the NABT had created an unanticipated public relations problem for itself. The situation came to a head in September 1997 when University of Notre Dame philosopher Alvin Plantinga and retired Syracuse University religion scholar Huston Smith urged the NABT board to drop the offending words from its official definition of evolution. The NABT had gone well beyond the boundaries of empirical science. "How could an empirical inquiry," Plantinga and Smith asked, "possibly show that God was not guiding and directing evolution?" Initially, the board did not budge, but eventually it dropped the "unsupervised" and "impersonal" references as unnecessary and beyond the realm of science qua science.[20]

- Two years later, newspapers across the country announced that the Kansas Board of Education had "removed evolution" from the state's science curriculum. The board's action technically eliminated evolution from statewide standardized testing and therefore made it possible for local school boards to drop evolution from their curricula. Critics, nevertheless, saw it as yet another attempt to ban evolution from public school classrooms altogether. An organized effort got underway to oust the old board members, and in February 2001 a new board voted to reinstate the theory of evolution into statewide science standards.[21]

- In the fall of 2000, Baylor University president Robert B. Sloan removed William A. Dembski, the leading academic authority in the established but still youthful intelligent design movement, from his position as the director of the Michael Polanyi Center for Complexity, Information, and Design. An angry Dembski promptly issued a scathing press release, which included the bitter assertion that "[i]ntellectual McCarthyism has, for the moment, prevailed at Baylor."[22]

- In the fall of 2001, WGBH in Boston, one of the nation's premier public television stations, produced a massive eight-hour series called simply *Evolution*.[23] The lavishly produced series, narrated by popular actor Liam Neeson, presented evolution as firmly established and all encompassing in its power to explain everything about human beings, from limbs to love to language. The tone of the series, however, was nonpolemical and finished with an installment titled "What about God?" that took a careful look at America's enduring "creation versus evolution" debate. The *Evolution* series came with a Web site, instructional aids, and other supplementary materials to facilitate its widespread use in classrooms.

- As the *Evolution* series was about ready to air, a number of unprecedented "advertisements" appeared in a number of leading journals and newspapers, including the *New York Times* and the conservative political magazine *Weekly Standard*. Underwritten by a conservative West Coast foundation called the Discovery Institute, the advertisement featured a list of signatures of prominent Americans who had doubts about Darwinism.[24]

- In another part of the cultural landscape and parallel to these developments relating primarily to Darwin's theory of evolution a rather different spring was starting to bubble. In 1955, G. J. Whitrow published a paper in the *British Journal of the Philosophy of Science* in which he argued that "a variety of astronomical conditions must be met if a universe is to be habitable." Other physicists and cosmologists extended this line of thinking for several decades, so that by 1986 British astronomer John D. Barrow and American mathematical physicist Frank J. Tipler published a dense book of extraordinary scholarship titled *The Anthropic Cosmological Principle*. This massive work, drawing on well over one thousand references, suggests that a strong teleological thread runs through cosmic history as evidenced in a surprising number of physical features of the universe. These features, which superficially appear to be nothing more than unrelated contingent facts, cooperate to make life possible. While many scientists reject the argument that the finely tuned structure of the universe can be taken as evidence that the universe has some "purpose" or even a direction to it, others see a compatibility between the anthropic coincidences and the view that the universe was in fact designed.[25] Contra evolution, discussion of the anthropic principle took up residence among conservative Christians, where it continues to generate discussion.[26]

As these vignettes illustrate, the topic of origins has become a permanent part of modern America's cultural conversation, a never-ending argument erupting constantly into battles of various sorts. That it shows no signs of going away is a significant matter. We hasten to point out that this "warfare" is not "science versus religion" in any simple sense. When creation and evolution have squared off in courtrooms, from Dayton, Tennessee, to Little Rock, Arkansas, there have been credentialed members of both the religious and scientific communities on both sides. At Little Rock, for example, theologian Langdon Gilkey was a witness against creationism. Gilkey rejected the Genesis account of creation (as a scientific account) on both scientific and theological grounds.[27] Analogously, astronomer Chandra Wickramasinghe, a Buddhist, testified against evolution.[28] But these are exceptions to the generally accurate perception that creationism draws its support primarily from religion while evolution rests on science. So, while it would be a misleading oversimplification to describe this as a "war between science and religion," there is a sense in which "warfare" can serve as a helpful metaphor for understanding the twentieth century's unfolding hostilities between creationism and evolution.

The warfare metaphor for the relationship between creation and evolution, or science and religion, has a long history. The warfare image was given widespread credence in Andrew Dickson White's seminal 1896 work *A History of the Warfare of Science with Theology in Christendom*.[29] White's was an eloquent polemic that presented the many historical encounters between "science" and "religion" as "battles" in which religion was generally defeated by science. The conclusion was that science and religion have been perpetually at war, that the open-minded search for scientific truth comes into inevitable conflict with traditional religion, and that religion generally loses credibility in such encounters. In this and numerous subsequent analyses using the same paradigm, "science" and "religion" are treated as monolithic entities, which have come into strident and uncompromising conflict in celebrated historical episodes like the Galileo affair, the Huxley–Wilberforce debate, the Scopes trial, and so on. In White's treatment, the extrapolation of the historical trajectory would eventually lead to the complete surrender of religion. Each historical defeat of religion by science would dismantle a little bit more of the traditional view. Eventually, White projected, it will all be gone, save for some wholesome moral residue.

Secularization theories like those of White predicted confidently that religious belief would wither away with the onward march of science. This, however, has conspicuously failed to happen, especially in the United States, where evolution has been remarkably unsuccessful in unseating creation. To borrow from A. N. Wilson, "[t]he God-question does not go away."[30] Every time a local schoolteacher deals with a student objecting to evolution, the God question is there in the background.

How are we to explain this apparent arresting of secularization and the failure of White's prediction? If an overpowering "science" is constantly winning battles against an obsolete "religion," then how does the religious challenge to science retain its vigor? Is it possible that the metaphor of ongoing "warfare" is no longer appropriate? Or perhaps it never was appropriate? Is the relationship between science and religion, incarnated in contemporary America as "creation versus evolution," better described in some other way as scholars are starting to suggest?[31] Perhaps science and religion are less opposed than we have been accustomed to think—and that such a metaphor, with the stark choices it seems to imply, is simply not adequate to describe present-day America. Maybe "creation versus evolution" is not the same as "religion versus science." Such is the emerging postmodern view among many scholars of the history of science and religion, such as John Hedley Brooke,[32] Numbers,[33] and David N. Livingstone,[34] who argue that science and religion have always had a complex and symbiotic relationship, even if scholars have failed, until recently, to acknowledge it. This scholarly turn offers hope that America's cultural division over origins can be healed, and that the paradox of its plural worldviews can be explained. But is that a false hope? Does such a paradigm-busting view serve to obscure the ways in which warfare, and specifically a "war over origins," continues to be a helpful metaphor for the "argument about origins" taking place in American culture?

In this book, we offer a map of this fascinating and important cultural conversation by surveying the views of leading Anglo-American intellectuals who are read broadly in America and who have addressed both their peers and the public on the topic of origins. We also take soundings of the views and attitudes of American culture as a whole as we measure how the various positions of the "elites" translate at the grassroots level. Where possible, these soundings are based on empirical polling data, but there are times when in the absence of such we necessarily resort to impressionistic assessments. Throughout, we use the term "origins" somewhat loosely to refer to matters related to both cosmology and biology. It is important, however, to distinguish between the origins of the universe and the origins of life. The former deals with the often arcane aspects of cosmology and particle physics that surface most obviously in intriguing and complicated notions like the Big Bang Theory and the Anthropic Principle. The latter deals with questions of evolution and common descent, which constitute the bulk, but not the entirety, of this book.

We shine a spotlight on the extraordinary and potentially dangerous cultural divide[35] that separates the almost completely secularized conventional academy from grassroots America and its "alternative academy" that retains a primarily religious foundation. The sweep of our spotlight identifies a number of alternative "creation myths" resident in American culture, all with large followings and considerable influence, but none with the tools to achieve concordance.

At the outset, a few qualifications are in order. Our overriding purpose is to give the general reader a sense of the "lay of the land" with regard to the ongoing origins debates in American culture. In this study, we have tried to keep our own views in the background but alert readers will no doubt be able to determine where our loyalties reside. Nevertheless, championing any one species of origins is simply not our goal in this book, either explicitly or implicitly. While we do have our own opinions (which are not identical, by the way), we have sought to portray the various positions in the origins debate critically, but fairly. Prominent historian of science Ronald L. Numbers has in many ways been our model for this "methodological agnosticism." In the introduction to his landmark history of scientific creationism, Numbers writes that while his own views are very different from that of the creationists, he intends to treat the creationists with as much respect as he would accord to evolutionists, a task he accomplishes. His further comments are well worth citing:

> For too long now students of science and religion have tended to grant the former a privileged position, often writing more as partisans than historians and grading religious "beliefs" by how much they encouraged or retarded the growth of scientific "knowledge." Recently, we have heard persuasive calls for a more even-handed treatment. But even academics who would have no trouble emphatically studying fifteenth-century astrology, or nineteenth-century phrenology seem to lose their nerve when they approach twentieth-century creationism and its fundamentalist proponents. The prevailing attitude, colorfully expressed at one professional meeting I attended, is that "we've got to stop the bastards." In other words, although many scholars seem to have no trouble respecting the unconventional beliefs and behaviors of peoples chronologically or geographically removed from us, they substitute condemnation for comprehension when scrutinizing their own neighbors.[36]

We are under no illusion that our effort to map out the contours of the contemporary origins debate can eliminate the sources of cultural discord; indeed, we are convinced that some differences cannot be bridged, and that the metaphor of "warfare" therefore has enduring descriptive value when applied to the contemporary American conflict over creation and evolution. But we also believe that there is enormous heuristic value in understanding these warring parties as contenders along a continuum and seekers after the same elusive goal: the power to define the generally accepted "origins story" for America. Our goal is not to crown a prospective winner, but to describe the combatants and the battle in such a way that all participants may understand and sympathize with their opponents, find common ground where appropriate, and resist oversimplifying the complex constituency that they perceive as their opposition.

It hardly needs to be pointed out that the relationship between science and religion has become a hot topic for writers and publishers alike in recent years. The numbers of books under the "Science and Religion" heading of the Library of Congress, most of which deal with origins, have increased several hundred percent over the past thirty years. Hundreds of articles and books now appear each year, numerous conferences are held, and new journals appear regularly. The development that perhaps most strongly indicates the emerging significance of this dialogue is the appearance within the past few years of hundreds of "science and religion" courses as well as doctoral programs at places like Oxford, Princeton, and Berkeley. Oxford University now has a chaired professorship in science and religion (held by John Hedley Brooke), and Cambridge University a chaired lectureship (held by Fraser Watts).

As our documentation will make clear, there are scores of books that explore the origins question. The great majority of these discuss only a facet of the topic and generally assume a familiarity with the ongoing conversation. We will not. We hope to provide general readers with a much needed nonpolemical *tour de horizon*. The book should prove especially useful to secular readers who seek guidance in distinguishing between and among various religious positions, and to religious readers who have encountered the major scientific popularizers primarily through the writing of their critics.

It is our hope that we can begin to dispel the notion that the only participants in this cultural conversation are the scientific creationists and their debunkers. We would like to challenge the near-universal impression that "creation versus evolution" is neatly dichotomized into the dualism that its label implies. Such dichotomizing lies behind the current controversies over the treatment of evolution in high school textbooks, which remain unable to present the ideas of evolution without creating inordinate difficulties for many students, teachers, and local school boards. Fundamentalist crusaders like Morris and Duane T. Gish have written scores of scientifically controversial but influential books targeted at popular audiences arguing for a biblically literal, six-day creation of the universe, a "young" earth, and a supernatural origin for life. At the same time, a number of gifted writers have emerged out of the scientific community to popularize mainstream science and, in some cases, challenge scientific creationism. Writers such as Richard Dawkins, Gould and Carl Sagan (both deceased), Peter W. Atkins, Steven Weinberg, and Edward O. Wilson represent the primary conduits through which the latest understandings of the scientific community flow to the popular culture. While almost all of their writings are simply popular science at its best, occasionally these authors direct their fire at traditional religious beliefs, sometimes even ridiculing the religious motivations of their critics. Such criticisms are then used by conservative evangelicals as evidence that *science* (as opposed to individual scientists) is hostile to traditional religion. And so the cycles of warfare continue.

In such a climate, nuances are missed. To take one example, many evangelical Christians view Harvard's Gould, who was the most influential of the current popularizers of science, as a villain. Their negative views of Gould have come not from reading Gould himself, but from reading his evangelical critics, such as Berkeley lawyer Phillip E. Johnson, the leader of the intelligent design movement. In his recent *Rocks of Ages: Science and Religion in the Fullness of Life,*[37] Gould is actually quite critical of his colleagues who create "worldviews" out of scientific theories. He presents a model of "nonoverlapping magisteria" (NOMA) that attempts to accord autonomy and integrity to both science and religion. Gould also wrote a number of essays defending the Judeo-Christian tradition against what he thought were unfairly negative charges. But all this nuance is lost when critics oversimplify the more "complex" Gould and place him squarely within the proevolution/anticreation camp. Yet Gould's NOMA model comes under fire for removing religious truth from the realm of the factual and thus effectively ruling out any understanding of origins that might incorporate both a scientific and religious perspective. In fact, Gould was strongly critical of Oxford University biochemist Arthur R. Peacocke who tries to create such an integrated view, based on "overlapping magisteria." Ironically, many conservative Christians seem to be as uncomfortable with Peacocke, who won the 2001 Templeton Prize for Progress in Religion, as they were with Gould.[38]

Errors and misunderstandings like these are all too common and result from the failure to acknowledge the stance of additional constituencies in the conversation about origins, particularly the intelligent design movement and the theistic evolutionists. Both of these seek a middle ground between the scientific creationists and the major science popularizers. Do such nuanced positions represent a breakthrough in the warfare between creation and evolution? Or do they merely attempt to evade the terms of the conflict while introducing yet other problematical issues? *Species of Origins* will not resolve these complex issues; in fact, we will argue that the disagreements that separate creationists from evolutionists are basically unresolvable. We will, however, give readers a clearer picture of a landscape that for many must seem to be shrouded in an impenetrable fog.

NOTES

1. Lawrence Sullivan, *Inchu's Drum: An Orientation to Meaning in South American Religions* (New York: Macmillan, 1988), 33.
2. Thomas Berry quoted in Paul Brockelman, *Cosmology and Creation: The Spiritual Significance of Contemporary Cosmology* (New York: Oxford University Press, 1999), 41, emphasis added.
3. Brockelman, *Cosmology and Creation*, 18.
4. See, for example, Brian Swimme and Thomas Berry, *The Universe Story: From the Primordial Flaring Forth to the Ecozoic Era—A Celebration of the Unfolding of the Cosmos* (New York: HarperCollins, 1992), 1–2.
5. Actually, the term was coined by Wilfred McClay, one of our editors, to whom we express our appreciation.
6. The term "fundamentalist" was coined in 1920. For an excellent treatment of *The Fundamentals*, see George M. Marsden, *Fundamentalism and American Culture: The Shaping of Twentieth-Century Evangelicalism, 1870–1925* (New York: Oxford University Press, 1980), 118–123.
7. Ronald L. Numbers, *The Creationists: The Evolution of Scientific Creationism* (Berkeley: University of California Press, 1993), 38–39.
8. William Jennings Bryan quoted in Edward J. Larson, *Summer for the Gods: The Scopes Trial and America's Continuing Debate over Science and Religion* (Cambridge, Mass.: Harvard University Press, 1998), 41–42.
9. Peter J. Bowler, *Evolution: History of an Idea*, rev. ed. (Berkeley: University of California Press, 1989), 307–319; Ernst Mayr, "Some Thoughts on the History of the Evolutionary Synthesis," in *The Evolutionary Synthesis: Perspectives on the Unification of Biology*, ed. Ernst Mayr and William B. Provine (Cambridge, Mass.: Harvard University Press, 1998), 29–30.
10. Bowler, *Evolution*, 340–341.
11. Numbers, *Creationists*, 238–240.
12. Numbers, *Creationists*, 283–290.
13. Transnational Association of Christian Colleges and Schools, "Foundational Standards: Biblical Foundations," at www.tracs.org/foundstandards.pdf (5 April 2001); Henry M. Morris, "The Battle for True Education," *Institute for Creation Research: Vital Articles on Science/Creation* (1995), at www.icr.org/pubs/btg-a/btg-081a.htm (10 April 2001).
14. Theodosius Dobzhansky, "Nothing in Biology Makes Sense Except in the Light of Evolution," *The American Biology Teacher* 35 (March 1973): 125–129.
15. Dobzhansky, "Nothing in Biology Makes Sense," 129.
16. Judge William R. Overton's Memorandum Opinion, *Rev. Bill McLean vs. the Arkansas Board of Education*, January 5, 1982, quoted in Langdon Gilkey, *Creationism on Trial: Evolution and God at Little Rock* (Charlottesville: University of Virginia Press, 1985, 1998), 268–295.
17. Jerry Bergman, "Censorship in Secular Science: The Mims Case," *Perspectives on Science and Christian Faith* 45 (March 1993): 37–45; Jerry Bergman, "Forrest Mims Responds," *Origins Research* 14 (spring–summer 1991): 12. "The Amateur Scientist" column has reappeared in recent years, but it has not recovered its original schedule of regular monthly publication.

18. Phillip E. Johnson, "Science and Scientific Naturalism in the Evolution Controversy," August 1988; Phillip E. Johnson, "Darwinism: The Faith and the Facts," September 1989.

19. This paragraph is based on Phillip E. Johnson, interview by the authors, 24 March 1999, and the following personal correspondence: James Skehan to Donald A. Yerxa, 7 October 1999; David Raup to Donald A. Yerxa, 4 October 1999; Owen Gingerich to Donald A. Yerxa, 19 October 1999; Michael Woodruff to Donald A. Yerxa, 29 October 1999.

20. Eugenie C. Scott, "Reply to an Open Letter of February 1998 Addressed to the National Association of Biology Teachers, the National Center for Science Education, and the American Association for the Advancement of Science," 1998, at fp.bio.utk.edu/darwin/Open%20letter/scott%20reply.htm (5 April 2001).

21. John W. Fountain, "Kansas Puts Evolution Back into Public Schools," *New York Times*, 15 February 2001; Kate Beem, "Kansas Board of Education's Science Standards Continue to Draw Controversy," *Kansas City Star*, 14 March 2000; Jerry White, "Kansas Board of Education Removes Evolution from Science Curriculum," 1999, at www.wsws.org/articles/1999/aug1999/kan-a13_prn.shtml (6 April 2001).

22. William A. Dembski, "Polanyi Center Press Release," 2000, at www.meta-list.org (5 March 2001).

23. *Evolution*, produced by WGBH/Nova Science Unit and Clear Blue Sky Productions, seven shows, 2001, videocassette.

24. One of the more prestigious venues in which the Discovery Institute placed a full-page ad listing academics who have problems with evolution was the *New York Review of Books*. The names surrounded a prominent callout: "We are skeptical of claims for the ability of random mutation and natural selection to account for the complexity of life. Careful examination of the evidence for Darwinian Theory should be encouraged." The first name on the list was Henry F. Schafer, described as a Nobel nominee. Other names on the list included Paul A. Nelson, Michael J. Behe, William A. Dembski, and Charles B. Thaxton. Discovery Institute, "A Scientific Dissent from Darwinism," *New York Review of Books* 48 (November 2001): 23.

25. John D. Barrow and Frank J. Tipler, *The Anthropic Cosmological Principle* (New York: Oxford University Press, 1986), especially 1–23; Karl W. Giberson, "The Anthropic Principle: A Postmodern Creation Myth?" *Journal of Interdisciplinary Studies* 9 (1997): 63–90.

26. Conservative evangelical astronomer Hugh Ross, who holds a Ph.D. from the University of Toronto, runs the organization Reasons to Believe, whose primary purpose is the exploration of cosmic design as evidence for existence of God. Reasons to Believe publishes the glossy magazine *Facts for Faith*, which promotes itself as "Proving God Exists — Quarterly." Ross has written a number of books on this topic. A helpful summary of his thoughts can be found in his essay "Big Bang Model Refined by Fire," in *Mere Creation: Science Faith and Intelligent Design*, ed. William A. Dembski (Downers Grove, Ill.: InterVarsity, 1998), 363–384.

27. See Gilkey, *Creationism on Trial*.

28. Norman L. Geisler, *The Creator in the Courtroom: Scopes II* (Milford, N.J.: Mott Media, 1982), 148–153.

29. Andrew Dickson White, *A History of the Warfare of Science with Theology in Christendom*, 2 vols. (New York: Appleton, 1896).

30. A. N. Wilson, *God's Funeral* (New York: Norton, 1999), ix.

31. The emerging paradigm for understanding the relationship of science and religion goes by the name of "complexity." By far the best book correcting the caricatured and "un-complex" history of White is John Hedley Brooke's *Science and Religion: Some Historical Perspectives* (Cambridge, U.K.: Cambridge University Press, 1991).

32. See Brooke, *Science and Religion*.

33. David C. Lindberg and Ronald L. Numbers, eds., *God and Nature: Historical Essays on the Encounter between Christianity and Science* (Berkeley: University of California Press, 1986), 1–18.

34. David N. Livingstone, *Darwin's Forgotten Defenders: The Encounter between Evangelical Theology and Evolutionary Thought* (Grand Rapids, Mich.: Eerdmans, 1987).

35. The PBS *Evolution* series refers to the creation evolution controversy as something that could "tear America apart."

36. Numbers, *Creationists*, xvi–xvii.

37. Stephen Jay Gould, *Rocks of Ages: Science and Religion in the Fullness of Life* (New York: Ballantine, 1999).

38. Phillip E. Johnson, *The Wedge of Truth: Splitting the Foundations of Naturalism* (Downers Grove, Ill.: InterVarsity, 2000), 89–90.

1

◆

The Modern Creation Story

For most of its history, the Western world has taken its creation story from the book of Genesis. "In the beginning," we are told, "God created the heavens and the Earth." This initial act of creation was followed by an amazing, busy week in which God created everything else, including the first man and woman—Adam and Eve—after which he rested. As fanciful as this story now sounds to some modern ears, it was accepted, universally and seemingly without question, by the thinkers that shaped Western intellectual history, from St. Augustine and St. Thomas Aquinas to William Shakespeare and Leonardo da Vinci, from Galileo Galilei and Isaac Newton to John Milton and Alexander Pope.[1] There were minor variations—St. Augustine thought the "days" of Genesis were just poetic license; Newton thought that the first three days were of uncertain duration because the Sun was not created until the fourth day. The Reverend Thomas Burnet, Newton's contemporary, understood the "days" of Genesis to be epochs, not unlike those Christians of today who seek to reconcile the Genesis account of creation with modern geology. But these were just variations on a common theme.

We should not be surprised that all of these early thinkers—it would be anachronistic to call any of them "scientists"—were committed to the biblical creation story, for it provided explanation for phenomena that were thought to be inaccessible to human understanding. From whence did everything in this gigantic, perhaps infinite, universe come? Who established the mathematical harmonies that ruled the heavens? What was the origin of the glorious diversity in nature? What was the wellspring of human creativity? Surely the answers to such questions transcended frail human intellect and could be found only in supernatural revelation.

Shortly before the dawn of the nineteenth century all this began to change. More than a century had passed since Newton had shone the penetrating light of his powerful mind into some of nature's darkest corners; a successful scientific tradition had been born, and confidence was building that human capabilities were indeed adequate for the task of solving the mysteries of nature.

The first attempts to do this borrowed heavily on the prevailing religious tradition and departed from it only in ways that seemed insignificant at the time. Johannes Kepler, even while maintaining a mystical spirituality that alienated many of his contemporaries, including Galileo, dared speculate that the Sun, rather than some supernatural agency, was responsible for the motion of the planets. The Reverend Burnet developed a sophisticated "Sacred History" of the earth that began to introduce naturalistic elements into the traditional biblical history of the creation, flood, and eschatological regeneration of the earth. Three of the greatest thinkers in seventeenth-century Britain—Newton, Robert Hooke, and Edmund Halley—made similar speculations.[2] The great French naturalist Georges-Louis Leclerc de Buffon was the first to attempt the measurement of the age of the earth using a natural process. Under the assumption that the earth was once molten and had cooled to its present temperature, he determined the age of the earth to be around seventy thousand years. This was followed by the more sophisticated measurements of the practitioners of the emerging science of geology—Charles Lyell, Georges Cuvier, John Playfair, and James Hutton.

All through the nineteenth century the traditional biblical chronology was in retreat. No longer was it considered scientifically plausible to date the earth by creating a history that started with Adam, ran through the patriarchs of the Old Testament, and eventually joined secular history at some later date. The measured age of the earth was continually increasing from its original thousands of years, to tens of thousands, then millions, and finally billions, where it remains today.[3]

At the same time that geologists and physicists were revealing the history of the earth, naturalists were secularizing the story of the organic world. The discovery of multiple mass extinctions in the fossil record suggested that life had gone through some rather dramatic episodes since its origin on planet Earth. The astonishing diversity of life catalogued by a new breed of globe-trotting naturalists strained the dimensions of Noah's ark until it became clear that this venerable biblical story must also be abandoned, at least in its literal form. There were simply too many animals to fit into an ark of the stated dimensions.[4] But life was not merely a collection of diversities, it was organized into groupings that cried out for explanation. That was provided by Charles Darwin in 1859 with the publication of his extraordinary volume *The Origin of Species by Means of Natural Selection.* One of the last sacred precincts of the supernatural had been invaded by an encroaching naturalism. Even the origin of species, including humans, could be accounted for, apparently, without recourse to the supernatural.[5]

All that remained to be explained, seemingly, was the origin of the universe. For a time, many thinkers entertained the notion that the physical universe was eternal. Developments in the infant science of cosmology during the first half of the twentieth century, however, indicated that the universe may have had a beginning in which it "erupted" or "exploded"—nobody knew how to describe the process—from something much smaller. George Gamow, a colorful Russian physicist who had fled Stalinism, made the decisive suggestion—if the universe had emerged in this way, it should be bathed in a certain type of radiation. In 1965, two researchers at Bell Laboratories discovered this cosmic background radiation, confirming what is now known as the "Big Bang Theory" of the origin and development of the physical universe.[6]

A few "details" remain to be filled in: the first few "moments" in the history of the universe seem to lie beyond current theories and experiments; the process of galaxy formation is not understood; a theory to explain the origin of the first life-form(s) has yet to be discovered; and the exact relationship of humans to their recent ancestors remains controversial in its details. But these are just details.[7]

There now exists a "secular" creation story.[8] The story starts with a universe exploding into existence about fifteen billion years ago and ends with the emergence of human beings in the recent geological past. The story is not one of supernatural acts, although it does inspire awe. Nor can the story be reconciled easily with any of the creation accounts in the religious literature of the Judeo-Christian tradition or, for that matter, any other religious tradition. But the story is an important one, which we will tell in the pages that follow without the obligatory qualifications that scientists make to cover themselves. Interested readers may consult the references to gain a more nuanced picture of some parts of the story. In the final section of this chapter we will look briefly at the empirical evidence for the various claims central to this modern scientific creation story.

THE SCIENTIFIC CREATION STORY

The contemporary scientific account of the creation mirrors many a great tale, beginning with a vague "once upon a time" and gradually unfolding into a remarkable story, full of surprise, excitement, and meaning. Fifteen billion years ago an event occurred that lies tantalizingly beyond the long reach of science. Something erupted, banged, exhaled, flared forth, exploded, and gave birth to our universe. The event remains scientifically opaque for two reasons: (1) there does not yet exist a viable theory that combines the relevant ingredients in a satisfactory way,[9] and (2) the experiments that would model the birth of the universe require energies that exceed any equipment that could be built on the earth.[10]

Despite these not-insignificant limitations, we do have a surprisingly complete picture of the events as they unfold from a time very (and we do mean very!)

shortly after the big bang—10^{-43} seconds after, to be exact in the way that only science can be. Prior to this so-called Planck Time, all the possible physical interactions in nature were part of a unified whole that contained within it the electromagnetic, strong and weak nuclear interactions, and gravity. The electromagnetic interaction is the source of the familiar attraction between particles with opposite charges; the strong nuclear interaction holds the particles in a nucleus together, despite the fact that many of them—the protons—repel each other electrically. The weak nuclear interaction is responsible for radioactivity, gently prodding certain unstable nuclei to disintegrate spontaneously. The familiar gravity is the fourth interaction. All of the changes in the universe, from the shining of a star to the recollection of a childhood memory take place under the "guidance" of the four fundamental interactions.[11]

When these different interactions are examined in regions of very high energy, they are found to merge together—to "melt" if you will. The incredibly high energies of the early Big Bang "melted" the various interactions into one homogeneous mix. Then, as the Big Bang proceeded and the universe expanded, the fundamental laws of physical interactions crystallized and acquired their present form, which we recognize today as gravity, electromagnetism, strong and weak nuclear forces.

Because the early universe was so incredibly hot, there was no matter of any form—only "pure" energy (if energy can be said to be pure). In far less than a second, however, matter began to precipitate out of the "energy bath" as things started to cool down. Electrons with charges of -1 and quarks with charges of $+\frac{2}{3}$ and $-\frac{1}{3}$ appeared. Newly minted laws[12] of nuclear physics received their first application as they "gathered" the isolated quarks into protons and neutrons. The curious rules for this process required that quarks unite in combinations with either no charge or a charge of $+1$; isolated particles with fractional charges disappeared from the universe, never to reappear.[13] One second had passed.

The universe was expanding and cooling; the chaotic jumble of electrically charged particles dissipated as negatively charged electrons dropped into tidy "orbits" around protons—orbits "prepared" for them by the laws of quantum mechanics. A proton with an electron in its orbit is a hydrogen atom. About 94 percent of the atoms in the universe are hydrogen. Three hundred thousand years had passed.

The hydrogen atoms were randomly arranged. Some locations in the new universe held concentrations that grew as other atoms, attracted by the increased gravity, began to move toward them. There were many centers of attraction, of varying size, randomly distributed throughout a universe still expanding and cooling. As the centers of attraction grew, they formed great clouds of hydrogen gas. A universe once packed almost solid with particles evolved slowly into one that was largely empty, save for a few billion vast clouds of hydrogen gas, separated by distances of unimaginable size. These clouds of hydrogen gas were enormous—trillions of miles in diameter. Under the relentless prodding of gravity the clouds began to shrink, growing steadily more dense, occasionally fracturing into multiple smaller clouds. The larger clouds shrank the fastest, compressing the hydrogen atoms into smaller and smaller volumes; this caused the temperature to increase as the atoms moved about with increasing speed, even while being pulled ever closer together. Eventually, the electrons, unable to continue orbiting in the developing thermal maelstrom, were ripped off the atoms. A certain critical temperature was reached and the furiously moving atoms—now just bare nuclei—began to collide with each other and *fuse*, their great speed overcoming their mutual electrical repulsion. Stars and galaxies were born. The universe was two billion years old.

The next major transformation in the universe was driven by the process of fusion as nuclei were bound together by the strong nuclear force. The fusion reaction converts a bit of mass into energy via $E = mc^2$, while steadily making larger atoms from smaller ones. Two hydrogens combine to make a helium. Add another hydrogen and you have lithium. As the temperature in the newborn stars increased still further, even the heavier combinations began to move about rapidly enough to collide with each other. The fusion of two heliums makes beryllium. A beryllium and a helium make a carbon. A carbon and a hydrogen make a nitrogen. And so on down the periodic table of elements until we get to iron, where the fusion reactions run out of steam, to use a metaphor strangely unsuited for a universe as yet without water. Iron is heavy and hard to move. It also has a large positive charge that strongly repels other protons, resisting any increase in its size.

Billions of years are needed for a star to make heavier elements from hydrogen. During this time, the star grows steadily denser as light elements disappear, replaced by heavier ones. Eventually, for many stars, the density becomes so great that the star collapses under its own weight. The result is a supernova explosion that spreads the chemically rich material from the star into a vast cloud, to once again be converted by gravity into a collection of smaller pieces. Our solar system is one such piece. Its rich chemical resources testify to its origin in a supernova. Planet Earth, thanks to a remarkable origin in a supernova cloud, is a "chemical Fort Knox." Our planetary home was born five billion years ago. The universe was ten billion years old.

The planets in our solar system were made from star dust, in the ultimate recycling project. What had once been but a huge cloud of hydrogen had been transformed through stellar fusion into a pantheon of chemical elements. These elements, many of them now comfortably incorporated into planets, quivered on the edge of a new voyage of discovery, waiting to explore new possibilities. One of the planets newly formed from the debris of the former star happened to be at a location where its temperature allowed water in the liquid form. As this new planet—the earth—cooled, its unusually rich and diverse chemical inhabitants began to combine in new ways. Simple molecules like water, nitrogen, and carbon dioxide combined to form larger molecules with complex structures and new capabilities. Facilitated by this unusually rich chemistry and liquid environment, complex molecules, like amino acids, formed. The environment was dynamic; the same processes that led to the formation of large molecules dismantled these newly formed molecules as fast as they could form. An equilibrium was established, in the midst of the active chemical explorations. Molecules were coming and going.

As the chemical environment of the early earth explored[14] the possibilities open to it, a very special molecular structure appeared, a structure with the amazing ability to replicate itself: ribonucleic acid (RNA). Now, instead of simply assembling and disassembling, these molecules started to make copies of themselves. These structures took over the environment of the early earth and transformed it into an "RNA world." They were at a clear advantage over other molecules, which simply assembled and disassembled at random.

Among the many possibilities open to the chemically rich RNA world was the spontaneous formation of tiny spheres encapsulated within thin membranes. Such spheres created tiny "worlds within the world," separating the interior of the sphere from the external world, while allowing the passage of some chemical ingredients through the membrane. It was perhaps inevitable that at some point some RNA would get trapped inside such tiny spheres and would flourish while protected from the rigors of the external RNA world. With the emergence of "replicating molecules protected within a membrane," the earth had what can only be called its first "life-form." A single cell capable of reproducing itself appeared on planet Earth about four billion years ago. It may very well have been the first life-form to appear anywhere in the universe. The universe was just over ten billion years old. The long process of conception was just about complete. Life, it should be noted, could not exist in a universe any younger.[15]

The reproduction of the first cell was made possible by the extraordinary ability of RNA to copy itself. But this first cell was able to do more than simply copy itself. The RNA-driven reproductive process is both stable and flexible—stable enough that basic structures, once established, would persist, but flexible enough to explore nearby options[16] and thus "evolve" into more optimum configurations. The options that proved to be most effective in making copies of themselves dominated at the expense of the less effective. Nature had begun the process of selection thanks to RNA—"the miracle molecule."[17]

The single-cell option remained viable, and countless variations of that basic concept developed over the next three billion years. But then, just over a half billion years ago, a more interesting option emerged—multicellularity. The structure of the cells was such that joining together created new possibilities. A cluster of such cells has an "inside" and an "outside," for example, that creates the possibility of specialization—exterior cells to deal with the environmental interface, interior cells to manage the affairs of the organism. Specialization creates the possibility of additional complexity, and soon the earth was populated with a variety of complex organisms that, over the course of a few hundred million years, discovered ways to see, smell, taste, hear, and feel the astonishing universe from which they had arisen. Almost every time an organism reproduced, the offspring were a bit different; this difference opened the door to the exploration of new ecological niches.

Species came and went; new species tried new ways of being in the world. Some were successful, some were not. Many became extinct and, with their exodus, opened territories for other species. About five million years ago,[18] on the rich terrain of Africa, one species of mammal—an ape-like primate—learned to walk upright and Mother Nature smiled on the innovation. Other successful species employing the new bipedalism appeared; about two and half million years ago some of these "bipeds" began to use their newly available "hands" to make tools. A million years later, in what remains a very mysterious part of natural history, their brains began to increase in size. Something akin to language arose. At some point our ancestors gave way to Homo sapiens. Perhaps one hundred thousand years ago,[19] a brief moment on the cosmic clock, human beings emerged with all of their rich complexity, to contemplate and ponder their fragile presence in this vast universe.

That, in a nutshell, is the contemporary creation story[20] told by our modern scientific culture. The story is remarkable, with episodes of great tension, suspense, and mystery. There are, of course, other creation stories. Every culture has at least one; indeed they form the stuff out of which cultures are made. But the scientific creation story is the only one that claims to be firmly based on strong empirical evidence.

WHAT IS THE EVIDENCE?

The scientific creation story is an unbroken tale of a universe evolving from a primordial simplicity to the richly textured present cosmos. This long journey can be, and often is, divided into sequential epochs that can be studied in isolation from each other. This periodization is all but demanded by the complexity inherent in the story of the universe—a complexity so great that one would need to master all the varied disciplines of the natural sciences to understand it fully. While there is no "standard" way to periodize the story of the universe, most discussions recognize a sequence[21] something like this:

1. The Big Bang "event" in which the universe, including matter, energy, time, and the laws of physics come into existence.
2. The period of stellar evolution in which stars are born, live, die, and occasionally explode to create clouds of chemically rich raw material. This process is responsible for the formation of the heavier elements on the periodic table, necessary for the development of complicated organic molecules.

3. The origin of life, in which complex organic molecules combine to form a simple living organism that is capable of replicating itself.
4. The development of natural diversity, in which a simple life-form branches onto numerous evolutionary trajectories that "explore" countless different possibilities.
5. The origin of human beings, including their intelligence.
6. The development of the human personality, including its psychological, social, moral, and religious propensities.

A full presentation of the evidence that underpins the developments associated with each of these periods goes far beyond the scope of the present work (or any work of reasonable size, for that matter). So we will confine our discussion to a few brief evidentiary remarks about each of these six steps in the scientific creation story. Interested readers may pursue this in more detail by consulting the references.

The Big Bang

The evidence for the Big Bang Theory comes from the field of cosmology, a relatively new science that has only "come of age" in the past few decades in the sense that there now exists a substantial scholarly community working with viable theoretical and observational material.[22] In the early twentieth century, cosmology was a highly speculative endeavor, as its practitioners tended to be physicists and mathematicians who contributed bits and pieces to a sketchy patchwork of ideas. One of the greatest physicists of this time was the Russian Lev Landau who liked to quip that "[c]osmologists are often in error, but never in doubt!"[23]

The situation has changed dramatically in the past half-century. The evidence for the Big Bang is now considered by most cosmologists so compelling that the theory is without serious challenge.[24] There are three primary lines of evidence for the Big Bang, all of them secure, all of them straightforward: (a) the expansion of the universe, (b) the universal background radiation, and (c) the distribution of the elements.

The Expanding Universe

The expansion of the universe was discovered by Edwin Hubble in the 1920s through the observation of galactic redshifts. Hubble was systematically cataloguing galaxies using the world's largest telescope—a technological wonder with a one-hundred-inch mirror atop Mount Wilson in California. He observed that light emitted from atoms in all but the very closest galaxies was "redder" than the light emitted from those same atoms here on the earth.[25] The only possible explanation for this "redshift," as it is known, was a recessional motion of those galaxies *away* from the earth. Further examination revealed that the more distant the galaxy, the greater the redshift. The universe appeared to be filled with galaxies that were all moving away from each other,[26] an observation that suggested that the universe was expanding—a controversial idea in the 1920s. Subsequent measurements with ever more sophisticated telescopes have extended and improved on Hubble's initial work, always to the same end—the demonstration that the galaxies are moving away from each other.[27]

The empirical observation that the universe was expanding gathered theoretical support from Albert Einstein's Theory of General Relativity, a highly successful explanation of gravity that had, in the early decades of the twentieth century, replaced Newton's more approximate theory. According to general relativity, the universe should be either expanding or contracting, in much the same way that a baseball would always be rising or falling. The universe could no more be static[28] than a baseball could hover in midair. The combination of strong observational evidence for the expansion of the universe and a robust theoretical explanation of that phenomenon makes the notion of the expanding universe compelling.

A universe that is presently observed to be expanding must have been much smaller in the past. This motivated theoretical speculation about a primordial "explosion" to account for the present expansion. Running the universe backwards in time increases the density, raises the temperature, and creates epochs of unimaginably high energies. An analysis of this process by Gamow and some coworkers in the 1940s and 1950s, at a time when the Big Bang Theory was not yet taken very seriously, resulted in a pair of predictions, both of which subsequent discoveries have confirmed. These discoveries form the second and third empirical legs for the Big Bang Theory.

Universal Background Radiation

The present universe should be filled with a "background radiation" left over from the "explosion" of the early universe. Certain events near the beginning of the universe[29] created radiation that must still be in the universe, since there is no way for it to get out. Gamow predicted the existence of this radiation years before anyone had any idea whether or not this radiation could be empirically observed. The discovery of this radiation by Arno Penzias and Robert Wilson at Bell Labs in 1965 confirmed the Big Bang Theory and won them a Nobel Prize.[30]

Distribution of Elements

The second prediction concerns the relative abundance of helium. If all the elements had formed in the "explosion" of the Big Bang, then hydrogen, being the simplest and by far the easiest to manufacture, should be most common, with element number two—helium—running second, and lithium (element number three) a very distant third. The calculation of the relative abundances of these elements is actually not particularly complex, and subsequent measurement of their cosmic abundance has been in striking accord with the original prediction. Recent measurements, for example, indicate that there is about one hundred million times as much helium in the universe as lithium-7.[31] (Lithium-7 is an isotope of the third simplest element with seven particles in the nucleus: three protons, and four neutrons.) This could be a mysterious feature of the universe, an arbitrary and inexplicable "brute fact." But, according to the Big Bang Theory, this is exactly what we would expect. The observed ratio can be *calculated* from the theory itself and then checked against observations.

The confirmation of exotic predictions is probably the single most important mechanism by which a scientific theory becomes established,[32] and the predictions of the universal background radiation and the cosmic element abundances are about as exotic as they come. This remarkable agreement between theory and experiment in Big Bang cosmology is responsible for its near universal acceptance.[33]

The first episode of the cosmic story is the Big Bang, which lays the foundations for subsequent epochs and explains the expansion of the universe and the preponderance of hydrogen and helium. But there is more to the universe, thankfully, than hydrogen and helium.

Origin of the Elements

Evidence that the elements are "cooked" in stars and supernova explosions comes directly from the observation that stars near the beginning of their lives have fewer heavy elements than their senior "colleagues." The subtle process of stellar aging, however, must be understood in order to make sense of this. Low-mass stars age very slowly; their gravity is weaker, which makes them less dense. Reduced density leads to a lower temperature, reduced brightness, and a slower rate of fusion. So a light star (simply defined as one with less mass) burns its hydrogen fuel at a much slower rate, which often means that its estimated lifetime, much of which is still in the future, can be significantly longer than the present age of the universe. Many such hydrogen-dominated "first generation" stars are observed. In contrast, heavier stars run hotter, fuse faster, and have greatly reduced lifetimes. Many supernova explosions have been observed as such stars have exploded at the ends of their lifetimes, creating chemically enriched clouds of raw material, out of which another star and even planets may form. A star like our Sun, which is five billion years old, is just such a "second generation" star, as evidenced by the greater presence of heavier elements in its spectrum and the chemically rich network of planets in orbit around it.

The observation of stars at different stages is also facilitated by the sheer size of the universe. As one looks out into space at faraway stars, one is also looking back in time at younger stars. When we examine a star that is five billion light years away, we are seeing it as it appeared five billion years ago. Looking out is looking back. Such observations have yielded clear indications that, as one looks further back in time, the universe is more and more dominated by hydrogen. Clouds of material that appear to be "primordial" tend to have a hydrogen/helium ratio that theory indicates was characteristic of the early universe. Clouds of material that appear to be supernova residue[34] have a much different chemical makeup and even physical appearance,[35] completely consistent with the general theory of stellar nucleosynthesis. The heavy element technetium-99, which does not even exist naturally on Earth since it decays radioactively in a relatively brief time, is observed in the spectrum of certain stars. The only explanation for its appearance in stars is its ongoing production via stellar nucleosynthesis.[36]

To understand stellar nucleosynthesis fully, one must be a proverbial "rocket scientist," but the basic theory is actually quite simple, the observations quite clear, and most astronomers consider stars to be "among the best-understood structures in the universe."[37]

The Origin of Life

"Anyone who tells you that he or she knows how life started on the Earth some 3.45 billion years ago is a fool or a knave," announces Stuart Kauffman in his influential book *At Home in the Universe*.[38] There can be no doubt that the origin of life from simple chemicals on the primordial earth is the weakest chapter in the scientific creation story. However, no significant body of evidence has been amassed that shows that life could *not* have originated this way. This is important to note in light of the claims of critics who interpret the weakness of this part of the scientific creation story as an evolutionary Achilles' heel, effectively undermining the entire theory.[39] The issue is rather different for several reasons, relating to the nature and practice of scientific research.

Virtually all research, from exotic experiments in particle physics to the search for a cure for cancer, requires vast amounts of funding, which typically comes from the government, private industry, or foundations. All of these sources have particular agendas and support research efforts that advance those agendas. Much basic research in biology and biochemistry is driven by the benefits that accrue to the medical profession from the basic research. The genome project, for example, has been well funded for several years largely because there are obvious medical benefits that flow from it. "Origin of life" research has no such benefits. There is great value in understanding how cells *work*, but knowledge of the mechanism by which a cell might *originate* on the primordial earth has no obvious near-term practical value. In the second place, this particular research problem is incredibly difficult. One observer has commented that it is "harder to evolve a cell than a human, given a cell."[40] Furthermore, since "life" is a holistic phenomenon, the problem does not naturally break down into a series of neatly compartmentalized smaller problems. Far from being a single "episode" in the long creation story, the origin of life may very well be the *major* part of the story, with the origin of the universe and the elements relegated to a preamble and the evolution of humans from this cell a concluding afterword. Finally, and perhaps most significantly, there exists no generally accepted paradigm under which this problem should be approached. Some of the earliest experiments mixed chemicals and electrical "storms" together in an attempted simulation of the atmosphere of the early earth;[41] subsequent approaches proposed that life arose on "clay templates;"[42] that it came from outer space;[43] or that it arose near thermal vents in the bottom of the ocean.[44] Some recent approaches are based on the emerging sciences of "complexity" and approach the problem of the origin of life from the perspective of complex systems such as computer programs. These researchers believe that the actual chemistry of life is secondary—the key is *organization*, not *composition*.[45] Despite these limitations, however, most scientists are confident that the problem can be solved. What is the basis for such confidence?

Answering this question is complicated by the absence of any clear definition of the "simplest life form." However, scientists who have thought carefully about this, like Nobel laureate Thomas Cech, look for "some kind of a cell with a defining envelope."[46] Inside the defining envelope, or cell membrane, the organism "can take in nutrients and energy from the environment and sequester them for its own uses, including its own reproduction."[47] A simple living cell must have metabolic machinery, reproductive apparatus, and a protective membrane to keep it all together. The coalescing of these three elements into a unified, functioning, replicating whole is enormously complicated, and nobody, as Kauffman has already reminded us, has a clear picture how this might have occurred. But there are hints.

For example, when certain oily liquids are mixed with water, they form into small spheres called coacervates that act like cell membranes in that nearby enzymes tend to diffuse into them and then remain inside.[48] Nucleic acids, like those that make up RNA and DNA, form naturally under conditions that some researchers argue are like those on the early earth.[49] Organic compounds similar to proteins also form naturally under certain conditions. And so on. Components resembling the pieces necessary to construct a simple living cell have been observed to appear in environments like those thought to be present on the early earth. So, even though the problem is far from being solved experimentally, researchers with the most experience in the field are optimistic that progress is being made and that the mysterious process by which life forms may soon be understood.

The Development of Natural Diversity

With this step we are back on solid ground once again. The number of species on Earth is enormous. Harvard biologist Edward O. Wilson puts the number at somewhere between 10 and 100 million, of which maybe 1.4 million have been catalogued.[50] There is nearly overwhelming evidence that these species are re-lated to each other in a way that makes sense only if they are descended from a common ancestor. The evidence comes from a number of lines.

A Common Genetic Code

All species share a common genetic code. There is nothing particularly unique about the chemicals or the coding on which DNA is based; most researchers are convinced that comparable codes could easily have been constructed in other ways. But we find no examples of alternate codes; the absence of these alterna-tives is what we would expect if all organisms are the descendants of a common ancestor from which they inherited their chemical coding. A stunning confir-mation of the universality of common descent was provided when it was discov-ered that prokaryotes, which were the only life-form on Earth for two billion years, have the same genetic code as that found in more sophisticated cells called eukaryotes, which came much later. Prokaryotic cells are dramatically different from eukaryotes in that they have no nuclei. But genetic researchers have estab-lished that they, too, like every other life-form of which we know anything, share the common genetic language.[51]

The Genetic Code

If the genetic code can be called a language, then the individual genes com-prising it are the sentences. Occasionally, a "random sentence" (called a "pseudogene") appears in an organism. The pseudogene has no function; it is just a bit of surplus grammar wedged in between more meaningful linguistic el-ements. But pseudogenes are "passed down" to offspring and, since they are harmless, can persist in the genetic sequence for millions of generations. A species can split into two, and both of the "daughter species" will carry the pseudogene. A daughter species can split into two "granddaughters," and so on. In time, identical pseudogenes will be found in many different species, which is clear testimony to a common ancestor, despite the considerable external differ-ences that developed since the original branching took place.

That all species share a common ancestor is considered by virtually all biolo-gists to be the only possible interpretation of the data from genetics. These data, perhaps more than any other, convince biologists that evolution has the status of fact rather than theory.[52]

Common ancestry by itself, of course, does not explain the diversity of the world. It would be entirely possible for the world today to consist of ten different species rather than ten million. The process by which species repeatedly split to generate the astonishing diversity that characterizes the natural world was exactly what Darwin was trying to explain in the *Origin of Species*. Some difficulties in defining a species exist, but biologists generally define a species in terms of its "reproductive isolation," which refers to the fact that species do not interbreed with each other but only with themselves. One of the primary mechanisms for the production of new species is *geographical* isolation, which leads to *reproductive* isolation. In a typical case, a barrier of some sort appears that splits the natural habitat of a species. Examples would include the emergence of a river running through a region, an island splitting off from a mainland, a chasm opening up, a mountain rising, or an intermediate region being occupied by a dangerous predator. The result is a geographical partition of a population that formerly shared a common habitat. This partition creates a separate genetic pool that, through routine processes like mutation, will change independently of the sibling population from which it is now isolated. Over time, the cumulative genetic changes will lead to a gene pool sufficiently distinct that interbreeding with the original population is no longer possible, even if the barrier that created the isolation disappears.

The observational data to support this central part of the evolutionary creation story are spread all over the globe and form the basis for the science of biogeography. Knowledge of biogeography is growing rapidly, driven partially by the recognition that obscure species occasionally possess extraordinarily valuable assets. (Merck, for example, produces Mevacor—a popular drug with overall sales in the billions of dollars—that is derived from a humble fungus.[53]) While speciation is a slow process and cannot be "observed" in the usual sense of the word, the end result of speciation is simple to observe—one simply catalogues as many species as possible, notes their habitat, barriers (both present and historical) that separate them from other species, and similarities between them and nearby species. The results provide clear evidence for the existence of countless natural mechanisms by which new species form, chief among them the geographical isolation discussed earlier.

The Origin of Human Beings

Conceptually, human evolution is not very different from any other kind of evolution, with the important exception that we are much more interested in it. Just as scientists point to a clear series of fossils that record the changing roster of species that preceded humankind, so there exists a roster of fossils that records the emergence and evolution of the human species. Like other aspects of evolution, there is broad agreement on the outlines of the story, with more work needing to be done in resolving details. The scientific consensus is that "our branch" of the family tree broke off from the larger primate trunk about eight million years ago. In a development that entailed an increasing brain size, an enhanced upright posture, and a number of less significant changes like a gradual loss of body hair, modern humans emerged from a sequence of ancestors referred to as hominids.

Fossils of our oldest ancestor go by the unmemorable name Australopithecus ramidus, which means, literally, "southern ape, root of humans." This species lived about 4.5 million years ago. Next in line is the familiar "Lucy,"[54] known from one of the most complete hominid skeletons that has been discovered to date. Lucy was discovered in 1974 and has been dated radiometrically to be 3.5 million years old. From the mechanical structure of the fossils it can be determined that Lucy and her fellow hominids weighed about sixty to eighty pounds as adults, walked erect, and had brains about the size of modern chimpanzees. It appears that upright walking preceded the dramatic enlargement of the hominid brain. While there is no way to say for sure exactly what happened, many evolutionary biologists believe that upright walking may have created the conditions that led to a steady increase in the size of the brain. Under this scenario, the upright posture freed the hands for other uses, which established a vast arena of new activities that required mechanical dexterity and a sophisticated hand–eye coordination. Under these conditions, larger brains may have conferred a significant competitive advantage, with the result that parents with larger brains had more children, thus spreading the genes for larger brains throughout the population.

In the middle of the twentieth century, fossils were discovered in East Africa that provide a direct link to modern humans. Named Homo habilis ("man the toolmaker"), this species lived two million years ago, had a large brain, and used tools. Homo habilis was followed by Homo erectus ("man with upright stature") whose fossils are found not only in East Africa, where the others were located, but also in Asia and the Middle East. Homo erectus was the first in the human ancestral line to use fire and survived until about five hundred thousand years ago.

Fossils belonging to a species anatomically resembling modern humans begin to appear in rocks dated to be about two hundred thousand years old and, while the fossil record generally does not allow scientists to determine things like the disappearance of body hair, there is every reason to believe that this was Homo sapiens ("man the knower").[55]

Additional support for the evolution of Homo sapiens comes from an interesting variety of other sources. The evidence from genetics provides a "family tree" that corresponds nicely with the history established by the examination of the fossil record. Genetic studies indicate that human DNA is about 98 percent identical to that of chimpanzees, our closest relative in the natural world.[56]

Studies of what are known as vestigial organs provide further evidentiary support for human evolution. Vestigial organs are organs found in humans that are "left over" from an earlier stage in our evolution when such organs played a meaningful role. A familiar example is the muscles that we use to wiggle our ears. There is no present significance to this ability, beyond the occasional humorous application, but during earlier stages of our evolution when our ears were different it probably was advantageous to be able to move them a bit, to "aim" them at sounds whose identification was important to survival. There are many such organs, and a discussion of them is standard fare in any survey text in biology.[57]

The fossil record provides a reasonably detailed physical picture of human origins. But one of the reasons why human evolution remains controversial and under endless discussion, even among professional biologists who are comfortable with the evolutionary paradigm, is the collection of questions that we would like answered. The fossil record cannot record the specific environmental stimulus that initiated the enlargement of the brain or the disappearance of body hair. Even less accessible are the circumstances that gave birth to attributes like our moral and religious sensibilities, our enthusiasm for music and art, even our love of spectator sports.

The Development of the Human Personality

With this final "chapter" in the scientific creation story, we enter once again into speculative territory. Unlike the speculations that attend origin of life scenarios which are driven by a paucity of data, these speculations are overwhelmed by a mass of ambiguous data. This part of the contemporary scientific creation story belongs to a relatively new field generally considered to have been started in the 1970s by Harvard biologist and world-class ant specialist Edward O. Wilson.[58] The goal of this new field, originally known as "sociobiology" and now more frequently called "evolutionary psychology," was to bring human behavior, both individual and social, under the explanatory paradigm of evolution. Wilson believed that, just as considerable light had been shed on the behavior of ant colonies by looking at them from the perspective of evolution, so too it ought to be possible to shed some light on the behavior of human societies by hypothesizing that certain widespread human behaviors—from maternalism to philandering to altruism—might be explicable in terms of the standard evolutionary model.

The basic argument is fairly simple: There are certain behaviors that confer competitive reproductive advantages on humans. When these behaviors appear, they are "selected" by nature, in the same way that superior eyesight or higher intelligence is selected. Much of the so-called evidence used in evolutionary psychology consists of "just-so" stories that show how certain behaviors *could* have conferred a selective advantage on those who practiced them.

Evolutionary philosopher Michael Ruse provides an example: "[I]f I battle with another of my species until one is totally vanquished, no one really gains, for even the winner, beaten and exhausted, is left in poor shape for future tasks. By contrast, if we co-operate, although we must share the contested resource, there will be no big losers and both will benefit."[59]

Even though accounts such as these have been widely criticized,[60] this style of reasoning appears to be able to explain a number of curious human behaviors. Why is monogamy so common? Because two parents raising "their" child together provide the best chance for "their" genes—including those for monogamy, if they exist—to make it into the next generation. Predispositions toward monogamy in our ancestors conferred reproductive advantage on those that possessed them. If monogamy is "natural," however, why do men philander? Because spreading their genes around can't hurt; men can father large numbers of children "on the side" and still help raise the child at home. Why are women much more tolerant of promiscuity than their mates? Because a woman has much less to lose; if her mate has an affair but returns to her to help raise the children, her "reproductive fitness" has not been compromised. However, if a woman has an affair and gets pregnant, then her reproductive capacity has been shut down for a year while she brings another man's offspring into the world. Why do stepfathers abuse their stepchildren? Because they "know" their stepchildren are not carrying their genes and resent the attention that must be "wasted" on them. And so on. Many widespread human behaviors are illuminated, and often even explained, by hypothesizing that such behaviors conferred a reproductive advantage on those organisms in which they first appeared.[61]

Empirical support for these conclusions is hard to come by. In worst-case scenarios, the explanations are accepted simply because they follow so clearly from standard evolutionary assumptions that have demonstrated their veracity in a number of other, less ambiguous contexts. In other cases, the evidence derives from similarities between different cultures, or between human and primate cultures. In *The Third Chimpanzee*, Pulitzer Prize–winning biologist Jared Diamond presents an extraordinary roster of similarities between human and chimp culture.[62] Accounting for these similarities in any other way presents considerable challenges.

Not all of the "data" in the field of evolutionary psychology, however, are as "soft" as this. Much of it is on firm ground, tested in rigorous field studies and further refined in response to initial insights. Space precludes a full discussion, so we will confine ourselves to a single example, the problem of explaining the apparently universal rejection of sibling marriages, not only by societies (in that there exists various prohibitions against sibling marriages) but, more significantly for our purposes here, in the innate revulsion most people have at the prospects of mating with their siblings. This powerful sentiment is deeply rooted in the human psyche, and presents us with a profound mystery.

Social taboos against the marriage of close blood relations are not difficult to explain. Such unions are known to result in a disproportionate number of defective offspring and, whether one explains the unfortunate consequence in terms of genetics or the wrath of offended deities, there can be no doubt that societies are well advised to discourage such matings. And, since such matings can be "counterreproductive," natural selection should favor those whose "natural" predispositions steer them away from such ill-advised matings, even in the absence of social taboos. And this is exactly what we find. Virtually nobody wants to marry his or her sibling; this apparently moral injunction does indeed appear to have some sort of biological basis in that human beings seemed to be "programmed" in such a way that the question of mating with one's sibling simply does not come up. What is the origin of this "programming"?

The research that has been done on this particular version of incest avoidance is fascinating and highly suggestive. Incest avoidance is common in our closest nonhuman relatives, the chimps, where it certainly does not derive from any purely social taboos. Like us, they have an inbuilt aversion to incest. A key insight into the mechanism of incest avoidance comes from unusual social customs practiced in China and Israel. The Chinese custom involves the practice of families "adopting" unrelated baby girls to be raised alongside their sons with the intent that the biological son would later, at the appropriate age, marry the adopted daughter. In a fascinating study of fourteen thousand cases, researchers examined the fate of adopted Chinese girls who had spent a significant fraction of the first thirty months of their life in close familial proximity to their stepbrothers. What they discovered was remarkable: the girls strongly resisted later attempts to have them marry their "brothers." In many cases, the marriages were coerced with unfortunate results; divorce was three times more likely than in conventional marriages, and the marriages produced 40 percent fewer children. More or less identical results were found in another study of unrelated children raised as closely as siblings in Israeli kibbutzim. Of almost three thousand marriages of young adults that had been raised in the communal kibbutz setting, not one was "between members of the same kibbutz peer group who had lived together since birth." These results led Wilson to conclude that "it is evident that the human brain is programmed to follow a simple rule of thumb: *Have no sexual interest in those whom you knew intimately during the earliest years of your life.*"[63] The incest avoidance mechanism, while it works indirectly (and incorrectly, in the case of the stepbrothers), clearly serves to enhance the biological fitness of species that have it.

Because of the complexity of the phenomena under investigation, the results of such research are not expected to yield rigorous theories and compelling observational data. The human personality is not an atomic nucleus. It must be considered significant, however, that mysterious human personality traits, like incest avoidance, can be studied at all. Of course, the results are incomplete and much is left unexplained. But they certainly encourage the belief that evolutionary explanations are, in principle, available to explicate even esoteric human behaviors. Fruitful research along these lines is being conducted on the nature and origins of humanity's religious, aesthetic, musical, and linguistic predispositions.

CONCLUSION

From the origin of the universe to the origin of our preference for unrelated mates, the modern creation story provides a coherent and, in the main, empirically viable evolutionary explanation. Most of the story is quite well understood and is supported by a wealth of scientific data. Even the more speculative parts are not without empirical support. Adherents anticipate that the speculative character of some portions of the modern creation story will diminish as they slowly yield up their secrets to careful and painstaking research. The scientific creation story crackles with drama and surprise, evoking wonder, and captivating many of those who take the time to learn it. There are some who tell the story with a missionary zeal, convinced that it can heal our fragmented culture;[64] there are even those who would have us worship it.[65] The zealotry of the missionaries is rarely shared by the rank-and-file scientists who toil patiently in the fields of cosmology, physics, chemistry, biology, and psychology. But these same ordinary scientists find the evolutionary paradigm a solid and reliable guide.

Textbooks in our public schools present the scientific creation story to our children. From elementary school through college and university, they learn of the Big Bang, the origin of the earth, and the development of life on this planet. And yet, when pollsters ask Americans if they *believe* the scientific creation story, they answer, in overwhelming numbers, with a resounding "NO!"

How can this be?

NOTES

1. Paul K. Conkin, *When All the Gods Trembled: Darwinism, Scopes, and American Intellectuals* (Lanham, Md.: Rowman & Littlefield, 1998), 17.

2. Colin A. Russell, *Cross Currents: Interaction between Science and Faith* (Leicester, U.K.: InterVarsity, 1985), 129.

3. An excellent discussion of the various sciences that have contributed to our modern understanding of the age of the earth can be found in Timothy Ferris's acclaimed *Coming of Age in the Milky Way* (New York: Anchor, 1989), 215–282.

4. Christian Europe had a difficult time accepting that the biblical story of Noah's Flood was not historical, so deeply ingrained had this idea become in its explanations of the surface features of the globe, not to mention the related theological and biblical issues. Christian geologist Davis A. Young has written an excellent account of this: *The Biblical Flood: A Case Study of the Church's Response to Extrabiblical Evidence* (Grand Rapids, Mich.: Eerdmans, 1995).

5. We hasten to add that both historically and logically there is no necessary antagonism between evolutionary thought and supernatural explanations. Ever since Darwin, theists have found ways to accommodate evolution as a mechanism of God's creative activity. See, for example, David N. Livingstone, *Darwin's Forgotten Defenders: The Encounter between Evangelical Theology and Evolutionary Thought* (Grand Rapids, Mich.: Eerdmans, 1987); James R. Moore, *The Post-Darwinian Controversies: A Study of the Protestant Struggle to Come to Terms with Darwin in Great Britain and America, 1870–1900* (Cambridge, U.K.: Cambridge University Press, 1979); Mark A. Noll and David N. Livingstone, eds., *B. B. Warfield: Evolution, Scripture, and Science: Selected Writings* (Grand Rapids, Mich.: Baker, 2000).

6. There are a number of excellent accounts of how cosmologists came to a general consensus on the Big Bang Theory as the best explanation for the origin of the universe. Perhaps the best is Timothy Ferris, *The Whole Shebang: A State of the Universe Report* (New York: Simon and Schuster, 1997). A briefer and somewhat less technical account can be found in his earlier work *Coming of Age in the Milky Way*, 211–214, 273–274.

7. For an accessible account of these remaining details and the likelihood of arriving at a "final theory," see Steven Weinberg, "The Future of Science, and the Universe," *New York Review of Books* 48 (November 2001): 58–63.

8. Cosmologist Brian Swimme and historian Thomas Berry contend that the modern world does not have "a comprehensive story of the universe," one that combines a secular scientific creation story with an account of world history. But, they maintain, a new universe story is taking shape. Their version of it is a "cosmic liturgy," a celebration of the emergent universe that exhibits a "pressing toward modes of being and ever more intimate presence of things to each other." See Brian Swimme and Thomas Berry, *The Universe Story: From the Primordial Flaring Forth to the Ecozoic Era—A Celebration of the Unfolding of the Cosmos* (New York: HarperCollins, 1992), especially 1–5, 263–268. For a more sober attempt at advancing a "Grand Unified Theory of the Past," an overview of all known history from the beginning of the universe to the present, see the amazingly slim volume by Fred Spier, *The Structure of Big History: From the Big Bang until Today* (Amsterdam: Amsterdam University Press, 1996).

9. The problem relates to the difficulty of combining general relativity with quantum mechanics. Quantum mechanics describes the world of the very small—atoms and molecules—and general relativity describes the world of large objects that are gravitationally attracted to each other—planets and stars, baseballs and moons. On the scales where general relativity is most often applied, quantum mechanics is not relevant. There are no measurable quantum effects associated with baseballs. However, there are also no measurable gravitational effects associated with atoms. But there was a time in the early stages of the Big Bang when the entire universe was the size of an atom. During this early phase, both gravitational effects requiring general relativity for their explication and small-scale quantum effects were occurring. The search for a theory of "quantum gravity" is the central quest of theoretical physics, which has as its goal a comprehensive mathematical structure in which all of the known interactions in nature are contained. There are many excellent texts that describe the search for this comprehensive "theory of everything." One of the best is Ferris's *Coming of Age in the Milky Way*, although now slightly dated. John D. Barrow's *Theories of Everything: The Quest for Ultimate Explanation* (Oxford: Clarendon, 1991) explains just what is and is not contained within a theory of everything. The most promising recent work in this field lies in the area of what is known as "string theory," a complex extradimensional mathematical theory that attempts to treat particles like electrons as if they were strings rather than points. See Brian Greene, *The Elegant Universe: Superstrings, Hidden Dimensions, and the Quest for the Ultimate Theory* (New York: Norton, 1999); see also Weinberg, "The Future of Science, and the Universe."

10. Experiments that model the early universe are done in large colliders that accelerate particles like electrons and protons to speeds near that of light and then smash them into each other. The energies released in these collisions are so high that they approach the energies that unleashed the Big Bang and gave birth to our present universe. But as experiments try to model increasingly earlier, and thus more energetic, regimes of the early universe, the accelerators have to be larger and larger. To model an energy regime

arbitrarily close to the moment of the Big Bang would require an accelerator larger than the Earth. Because of the impossibility of actually doing such an experiment, physicists generally believe that any understanding of the actual moment of the Big Bang will have to come from theory. This is something of a scientific quicksand—it has been compared to putting up a tent in the wind without pegs—and most theorists are uncomfortable searching for theories in the total absence of experimental constraint. Empirical data are the "pegs" that secure the tent of theory. Experiments generally provide a series of anchor points that "tie down" theories and prevent them from getting totally decoupled from the reality they purport to describe. Physicist David Lindley has written an eloquent warning about what he sees as the dangerous epistemological state of current theoretical physics. See his *The End of Physics? The Myth of a Unified Theory* (New York: Basic, 1993).

11. These interactions are sometimes referred to as "forces," which, while the term is more familiar, can be misleading. The "interactions" inside the nucleus—strong and weak—do not exactly "force" the particles. The term "interaction" is achieving more common currency now to reflect this understanding.

12. The origin of the fundamental laws of physics is profoundly mysterious. "Metarules" appear to specify, at least partially, what kind of laws of physics are even permissible. It also appears that fundamental physical laws exhibit a hierarchical structure, with some laws being more basic than others (e.g., all laws seemingly must have a quantum dimension to them). See John D. Barrow, *The Universe That Discovered Itself* [New York: Oxford University Press, 2000]).

13. This is known as "quark confinement." When quarks were first postulated, experimental physicists searched for them everywhere, hoping to find them in isolation—that is, a particle with a charge of ⅓. Some investigators even went poring through the data that had been used to determine the charge on the electron to see if there were any stray ⅓ charges that had showed up, only to be discarded as too anomalous. This turned out to be a fruitless search. Quarks, while on secure ground both theoretically and experimentally, simply do not exist as isolated particles. An excellent account of the development of quark theory is in Michael Riordan, *The Hunting of the Quark* (New York: Simon and Schuster, 1987).

14. This, of course, is very anthropomorphic language. There is no "exploring" going on in the sense of "searching for something suspected to exist." The "exploring" is simply the process by which natural processes try out different possibilities. Describing these processes without invoking teleological metaphors is almost impossible.

15. Given that the universe expands through time as it slowly produces the complex chemicals necessary for life, it follows that life cannot exist in a universe much younger or smaller than this one. What appears to be the inordinate size of our universe is really seen as just the incidental by-product of a universe that gets larger as it evolves the chemical ingredients for life. The incredible size of the universe has been used in arguments that diminish the significance of life. But our modern understanding of the relationship between life and the physical conditions necessary for life undermines this claim. Life can no more evolve in a tiny universe than a baseball slugger can hit a home run in a batting cage.

16. This "exploration" is sometimes described as taking place in a "design space" that consists of all possible characteristics that an organism and its offspring can possess. See Daniel C. Dennett, *Darwin's Dangerous Idea: Evolution and the Meanings of Life* (New York: Touchstone, 1995), 85ff.

17. Of course, life is now more intimately associated with DNA, which is different from RNA in some superficial and minor ways that have significant implications. Through processes not well understood at present, the RNA gave way to our modern DNA world, with RNA now serving as a "reproductive assistant." See Christian de Duve, *Vital Dust: Life As a Cosmic Imperative* (New York: Basic, 1995), 75–82.

18. The time frames used in this chapter are meant to be within the range suggested by the historical placement of fossils—the so-called fossil clock. The "molecular clock" gives different numbers. The overall point of this account is not materially affected by the particular time frames suggested, all of which are constantly being updated in minor ways.

19. There is no universal agreement on these dates. It is all but impossible to determine precisely when the various unambiguously human features and behaviors appeared. See, for example, Jared Diamond, *The Third Chimpanzee: The Evolution and Future of the Human Animal* (New York: HarperCollins, 1993), 41–54; Ian Tattersall, "Human Evolution: An Overview," in *An Evolving Dialogue: Theological and Scientific Perspectives on Evolution*, ed. James B. Miller (Harrisburg, Pa.: Trinity Press International, 2001), 197–209.

20. There have not been many attempts to explicate this scientific creation story, probably because of its strongly interdisciplinary character. The way that academics tend to specialize mitigates against any of them having the requisite background knowledge—or any knowledge, for that matter—in cosmology, nuclear physics, astronomy, geology, biochemistry, evolutionary biology, anthropology, and so on. Cosmologist Brian Swimme is attempting to create a "modern creation story" in his role as the director of the Center for the Story of the Universe at the California Institute of Integral Studies in San Francisco. See, in particular, Swimme and Berry, *The Universe Story*, which aims at "transcending the science–humanities division in the educational process" (5). At a much more technical level, Harvard astronomer David Layzer attempts to create a purely scientific creation story in *Cosmogenesis: The Growth of Order in the Universe* (New York: Oxford University Press, 1990). Layzer's creation story starts with the Big Bang and ends with the appearance of the human brain.

21. There are superficial, although suggestive, parallels between scientific sequences like this and the creation sequence described in the first chapter of Genesis—the six "days" of creation. Over the years, many religious scientists have tried to bring these two sequences into some sort of concordance, suggesting that perhaps the creation story in Genesis was indeed a supernatural revelation from God containing an outline of the actual evolutionary history of the universe, appropriately simplified to make sense to the early Hebrew community. One of the first attempts to accomplish this "concordance" was that of the great French naturalist Georges-Louis Leclerc de Buffon (1707–1788), best known for his forty-four-volume *Histoire naturelle*, one of the most impressive achievements of the French Enlightenment. In his *Epochs of Nature* (1778), Buffon proposed a scenario in which the "days" of creation in Genesis were expanded into epochs. He justified this departure from the traditional interpretation, in part, by consideration of the particular structure of the verbs used in Genesis. This kind of concordism has been popular ever since, as Christians (and even some Jews) look for ways to reconcile their religion and their science. A recent attempt—both creative and sophisticated—is that of Gerald Schroeder who has a Ph.D. in physics from Massachusetts Institute of Technology. In *The Science of God: The Convergence of Scientific and Biblical Wisdom* (New York: Free Press, 1997), Schroeder,

who is Jewish, divides the scientific creation story into six epochs chosen to parallel the six days of creation in Genesis: the Big Bang, formation of the Milky Way and the Sun, formation of Earth and first life-forms, formation of Earth's oxygen-rich atmosphere, origin of multicellular animals, and the massive extinction and subsequent appearance of humans (67). Schroeder employs some complex interpretative strategies, involving relativity-induced ambiguities surrounding time to argue that the "six days" of Genesis are really analogous to the fifteen billion years of the Big Bang. All such efforts, however, are highly speculative, scientifically dubious, enterprises.

22. The relative youth of cosmology can be seen by going back to 1965, the year that the Big Bang is considered to have been confirmed by a measurement of the universal background radiation made by Penzias and Wilson at Bell Labs. Prior to 1965, Fred Hoyle's steady-state theory was also considered as a serious contender. Most cosmologists today were born before the Big Bang Theory became the reigning paradigm in cosmology. The field is young, but expanding. In 1977, there were fewer than one hundred cosmologists in the world, but today there are more than one thousand. See Ferris, *Whole Shebang*, 18.

23. Landau quoted in John C. Polkinghorne, "Creation and the Structure of the Physical World," *Theology Today* 44 (April 1987): 61.

24. Three eminent cosmologists, Hoyle, Geoffrey Burbidge, and Javant Vishnu, have proposed a steady-state theory as an alternate interpretation of the basic Big Bang evidence. They claim that their model of the universe, which is neither expanding or contracting, explains questions of what existed prior to the Big Bang better than other current theories. See Sir Fred Hoyle et al., *A Different Approach to Cosmology: From a Static Universe through the Big Bang towards Reality* (Cambridge, U.K.: Cambridge University Press, 2000). Their view is not shared by many of their colleagues.

25. Every atom, under the right circumstances, emits a set of characteristic wavelengths or colors, although many of the wavelengths are in invisible regions of the spectrum and thus do not really have a "color." A wavelength longer than that which would be emitted by a stationary atom, is said to be "reddened," or to have a "redshift," since red is the color at the long wavelength end of the visible spectrum (the rainbow). If the wavelength is shorter, the light is said to have a "blueshift."

26. The observation that the galaxies are all rushing away from the earth should not be taken to mean that the earth is somehow stationary at the center of the universe. The Milky Way is rushing away from the other galaxies just as they are rushing away from it. An oft-invoked analogy is that of raisins in a loaf of rising bread dough. Each raisin is moving away from every other raisin, with the most distant raisins moving the fastest and the adjacent raisins moving the slowest. Yet any individual raisin is not actually moving "through" the dough. The dough carries the raisins with it. This is only a partial analogy and should not be taken too literally as it presumes a standard three-dimensional structure for space, which is not the same as the structure of the universe on a large scale.

27. The value of the Hubble constant (H_0), which is the ratio of recessional velocity to distance or the rate of expansion of the universe, is a matter of considerable debate. Depending on the galaxies used to determine the constant, the values usually range anywhere from 50–80 kilometers per second per megaparsec (km/s/Mpc). A recent introductory astronomy text uses 65 km/s/Mpc. See Eric Chaisson and Steve McMillan, *Astronomy: A Beginner's Guide to the Universe*, 3d ed. (Upper Saddle River, N.J.: Prentice-Hall, 2001), 397–398. An article in *Astronomy* produced a figure of 71 km/s/Mpc

plus or minus 7. See Robert Naye, "An Inconstant Constant," *Astronomy* 28 (March 2000): 54.

28. The relatively primitive telescopic observations available at the time Einstein developed his theory indicated that the universe was static—neither expanding nor contracting. In an attempt to account for this empirical evidence, Einstein modified his theory by introducing an unnatural "fudge factor," the cosmological constant, that he was only too happy to remove when better observations ruled out a static universe. This is a very fascinating story that forms a standard part of any account of the Big Bang Theory. One of the best is Ferris, *Whole Shebang*, especially 41.

29. The event that gave rise to the background radiation is known as "decoupling." This refers to the transition that occurred when the universe was cool enough for electrons to drop into stable orbits about nuclei-forming atoms. The formation of these electrically neutral atoms from formerly separated charged particles dramatically alters the relationship between matter and radiation. When the basic elements of matter became neutral, radiation, in the form of photons, became "decoupled" from matter and the universe became transparent, as radiation could travel effectively through the electrically neutral clouds of atoms.

30. It also crushed the dreams of Robert Dicke at nearby Princeton University who was concurrently working to build a telescope to look for this radiation. There is irony in the fact that Penzias and Wilson won a Nobel Prize for "accidentally" discovering phenomena that Dicke was looking for deliberately.

31. See John Fix, *Astronomy: Journey to the Cosmic Frontier*, 2d ed. (Boston: McGraw Hill, 2001), 612.

32. See also Larry Laudan, *Beyond Positivism and Relativism: Theory, Method, and Evidence* (Boulder, Colo.: Westview, 1996), 131; Irving Copi and Carl Cohen, *Introduction to Logic*, 10th ed. (Upper Saddle River, N.J.: Prentice-Hall, 1998), 566.

33. Widespread acceptance of the Big Bang Theory should not be taken to imply that the Big Bang has no ambiguities, or that it answers all cosmological questions. There are still details to be worked out, and some very basic questions like "Why is there a universe at all?" are simply left unanswered.

34. Often, such clouds have a clear physical shape that testifies to their origin in a supernova explosion.

35. Most astronomy textbooks contain pictures of the Crab Nebula, the remnant of a supernova that exploded in 1054 and was recorded by Chinese astronomers. The explosion was brilliant, with some observers claiming the "new" star was as bright as the Moon! See, for example, Chaisson and McMillan, *Astronomy*, 486–487. A curious anomaly associated with this extraordinary celestial event is its complete absence from extant historical records of Western astronomers. A new star, visible for months, so bright you could read by it at night, was somehow missed, probably because the prevalent Greek-influenced paradigm for understanding the heavens precluded the possibility of actual change. All too often our theoretical preconceptions determine what is seen or not seen. See Thomas T. Arny, *Explorations: An Introduction to Astronomy*, 2d ed. (Boston: McGraw-Hill, 2000), 167–168.

36. Chaisson and McMillan, *Astronomy*, 487–488.

37. John F. Hawley and Katherine A. Holcomb, *Foundations of Modern Cosmology* (New York: Oxford University Press, 1998), 125.

38. Stuart Kauffman, *At Home in the Universe: The Search for the Laws of Self-Organization and Complexity* (New York: Oxford University Press, 1995), 31.

39. See, for example, Michael J. Behe, *Darwin's Black Box: The Biochemical Challenge to Evolution* (New York: Free Press, 1996), especially 172–173.

40. H. Allan Orr, "Darwin v. Intelligent Design (Again)," *Boston Review* 21 (1996–1997), bostonreview.mit.edu/BR21.6/orr.html (12 April 2001).

41. This is the famous "Stanley Miller Experiment" now generally discredited because scientists believe Miller's simulated early Earth was nothing like the actual thing. See de Duve, *Vital Dust*, 19.

42. A. G. Cairns-Smith, "The First Organisms," *Scientific American* 252 (June 1985): 90–100.

43. Sir Fred Hoyle and Chandra Wickramasinghe, *Evolution from Space: A Theory of Cosmic Creationism* (New York: Simon and Schuster, 1981).

44. See John Horgan, "In the Beginning . . . ," *Scientific American* 254 (February 1991): 2, 121–122.

45. See, for example, Kauffman, *At Home in the Universe*. Kauffman and his colleagues at the Santa Fe Institute are investigating the emerging science of "complexity," which studies the way that complex systems emerge from simple ones. Their work suggests that there may be common underlying mathematical laws that describe the process by which complex and diverse things like life, ecosystems, global economies, and the Internet arise. These "laws of organization" exist independently of any particular raw material through which they might be expressed. Life may have originated in a natural, even common way, when the chemistry of the primordial oceans reached a certain level of complexity—not because laws of chemistry took over and produced the right reactions, but because laws of organization expressed themselves through the molecules. In another setting, these same laws could express themselves through free markets or Internet grids. "General laws may govern the evolution of complex entities, whether they are works of nature or works of man" (206). A more technical presentation of these ideas can be found in Stuart Kauffman, *The Origins of Order: Self-Organization and Selection in Evolution* (Oxford: Oxford University Press, 1993). An accessible and very brief introduction to Kauffman's work can be found in John Brockman, *The Third Culture* (New York: Simon and Schuster, 1995).

46. Thomas Cech, "The Origin of Life and the Value of Life," in *Biology, Ethics, and the Origins of Life*, ed. Holmes Rolston III (Boston: Jones and Bartlett, 1995), 23.

47. Cech, "Origin of Life," 23.

48. John Casti, *Paradigms Lost: Images of Man in the Mirror of Science* (New York: William Morrow, 1989), 97.

49. Douglas Futuyma, *Science on Trial: The Case for Evolution* (New York: Pantheon, 1983), 223.

50. Edward O. Wilson, *The Diversity of Life* (Cambridge, Mass.: Belknap, 1992), 132–133.

51. Ernst Mayr, *One Long Argument: Charles Darwin and the Genesis of Modern Evolutionary Thought* (Cambridge, Mass.: Harvard University Press, 1991), 163.

52. It is of great significance that Behe, the Lehigh University biochemist whose book attacking evolutionary explanations for the origin of life has made him a leading figure of the intelligent design movement, accepts the standard evolutionary thesis of common ancestry. See Robert T. Pennock, *Tower of Babel: The Evidence against the New Creationism* (Cambridge, Mass.: MIT Press, 1999), 264. Another major design theorist, Paul A. Nelson, a philosopher, is not convinced, according to advance notices of a forthcoming book on common descent.

53. Wilson, *Diversity of Life*, 325.

54. Lucy got her name from the Beatles' song "Lucy in the Sky with Diamonds," which the paleontologists who discovered her sang around the campfire.

55. James Trefil and Robert Hazen, *The Sciences: An Integrated Approach* (New York: Wiley, 1999), 580–582.

56. Care should be taken not to overstate the significance of this finding. The DNA sequences have identical molecules in 98 percent of the locations. But not all portions of the DNA sequence are of equal relevance, and some portions do nothing at all. However, some sections of the DNA exert significant control over other sections and influence the development of the organism in ways that go far beyond what might be expected. An analogy can be helpful. On the one hand, the sequences 1000.0 and 0100.0 differ only slightly, but the placement of the differences tends to "amplify" the significance of the differences. On the other hand, the numbers 201 and 102 are markedly different. The real significance of differences at the genetic level—the genotype—is the influence such differences create at the level of the organism itself—the phenotype. This is not sufficiently well understood to establish the "real" significance of the genetic differences between chimpanzees and humans.

57. See, for example, Peter H. Raven and George B. Johnson, *Biology*, 5th ed. (Boston: McGraw-Hill, 1999).

58. In the final chapter of his seminal *The Insect Societies* (Cambridge, Mass.: Harvard University Press, 1971), Edward O. Wilson suggests that "the same principles of population biology and comparative zoology that have worked so well in explaining the rigid systems of the social insects could be applied point by point to vertebrate animals." He quotes himself in Edward O. Wilson, *On Human Nature* (Cambridge, Mass.: Harvard University Press, 1978), ix.

59. Michael Ruse, "Evolutionary Ethics: A Defense," in *Biology, Ethics and the Origins of Life*, ed. Holmes Rolston III (Boston: Jones and Bartlett, 1995), 95.

60. Phillip E. Johnson states that "[b]asically, evolutionary psychology proceeds by erecting a mountain of speculation on the basis of fragmentary evidence about primitive cultures." See Phillip E. Johnson, *The Wedge of Truth: Splitting the Foundations of Naturalism* (Downers Grove, Ill.: InterVarsity, 2000), 113.

61. This discussion, of course, is dealing with human behaviors from an exclusively biological point of view. Evolutionary psychology is based on the idea that human beings, solely on the basis of their humanity, have tendencies to behave in certain ways. These tendencies developed in more or less the same Darwinian way as fingers, toes, and orgasms—the enhancement of reproduction. Traditional understandings of "morality" play no role in the discussion other than as behaviors to be explained. Strong proponents of this viewpoint even go so far as to argue that "ethics as we understand it is an illusion fobbed off on us by our genes to get us to cooperate." See Edward O. Wilson and Michael Ruse, "The Evolution of Ethics," *New Scientist* 108 (October 17, 1985): 52. There is, of course, some very articulate criticism of this highly reductionist interpretation of human behavior. For a critique of evolutionary psychology from the perspective of biology, see Steven Rose, *Lifelines: Biology beyond Determinism* (Oxford: Oxford University Press, 1997). For a broader perspective encompassing biological, philosophical, and theological perspectives, see Holmes Rolston III in his Gifford Lectures published as *Genes, Genesis and God: Values and Their Origins in Natural and Human History* (Cambridge, U.K.: Cambridge University Press, 1999).

62. Diamond, *Third Chimpanzee*. The title derives from the evolutionary family tree on which there are three "chimps"—the common chimpanzee (Homo troglodytes), the pygmy chimpanzee (Homo paniscus), and the human chimpanzee (Homo sapiens). The three chimps diverged from the gorilla lineage roughly ten million years ago and would thus be expected to share a rather large number of attributes.

63. Edward O. Wilson, *Consilience: The Unity of Knowledge* (New York: Knopf, 1998), 176, emphasis in the original.

64. Theologian Loyal Rue concludes his poetic account of the importance of evolution and its ability to unite the fragmented human species with these words: "We are, at the moment, in many different places, with many histories and hopes. But we are now called together to one place, to a shared history and to a common vision of enduring promise. If there are saints enough among us we shall survive." See Loyal Rue, *Everybody's Story: Wising up to the Epic of Evolution* (Albany: SUNY Press, 2000), 138. Swimme and Berry tell a similar story in *Universe Story*.

65. See Dennett, *Darwin's Dangerous Idea*.

2

❖

The Triumph of Evolution?

For virtually all scientists and even nonscientists engaged in the enterprise of science popularization,[1] the "species of origins" presented in the preceding chapter—the modern scientific creation story—is utterly convincing. Exceptions are rare. The eminent particle physicist Murray Gell-Mann, for example, speaks fairly for the scientific community when he states that evolution is simply "the scientific account of how life developed on earth."[2] Period. It is just that simple. The earth is round, not flat. The earth orbits the Sun, not vice versa. Life developed via evolution, not supernatural creation. There may indeed be some mysteries as yet unresolved, but the broad contours of development of life on this planet are scientifically understood.

Consequently, most scientists cannot fathom how anyone with intelligence could accept any alternative species of origins, especially creationism, with its explicit invocation of the supernatural and wholesale rejection of much of contemporary science.[3] Again, Gell-Mann quite fairly represents the scientific community when he claims that belief in creationism is explicable only if one starts "from some form of fundamentalist religious dogma."[4]

This chapter will survey the rhetoric of scientists and science popularizers on the triumph of evolution as America's definitive creation story, establishing that Gell-Mann's confident assertion is indeed typical and represents the consensus of the scientific academy. We will then ask whether the rhetoric matches the reality revealed from numerous opinion polls. Has evolution carried the day, not just in the academy, but also in the culture at large? How significant and widespread is the dissent? And are those who do not accept the modern scientific creation story merely uneducated bumpkins or religious fanatics?

THE SCIENTIFIC TRIUMPH OF EVOLUTION

Biologists consider evolution to be central to their field and often refer to it as the "main unifying idea in biology."[5] Most college biology textbooks make extensive use of the evolutionary framework to explicate their material, whether it be ecology,[6] comparative anatomy,[7] developmental biology,[8] or botany.[9] To reject evolution is to reject biology. Evolution, in a more general sense, extends far beyond the borders of biology, however, as we have seen in the previous chapter, organizing and explicating much of the data of cosmology, astronomy, geology, physics, and so on. In this larger sense, evolution has become one of the conceptual anchors of modern science, securing virtually all the data of biology, much of the data of other fields, and correlating otherwise disparate fields with each other. The rejection of evolution becomes tantamount to a wholesale rejection of, not just biology, but all of science.[10] This, of course, is unthinkable. So strong is the conviction that evolution is the appropriate framework for thinking about science that Sir Peter Medawar, a Nobel laureate biologist,[11] boasts that "[t]he alternative to thinking in evolutionary terms is not to think at all."[12] Of course, the rhetoric of evolution is not uniform in its eloquence or its stridency, and there are many areas of science that are beyond its long reach. So to convey a sense of how scientists and especially science popularizers speak to the culture about evolution, we will provide examples and citations.

We start with the National Academy of Sciences (NAS). A committee commissioned by the NAS to address the teaching of evolution reported in 1998 that evolution is "the most important concept in modern biology." The report stated that "[c]ompelling lines of evidence demonstrate beyond any reasonable doubt that evolution occurred as a historical process and continues today." Evolution, the NAS report continued, is the only plausible scientific explanation for an extensive array of observations ranging from the fossil record, genetic information, the distribution of plants and animals, and the similarities across species of anatomy and development. Without evolution, biologists would be left with "a huge body of unconnected observations." The committee asserted that "[i]t is no longer possible to sustain scientifically the view that living things did not evolve from earlier forms or that the human species was not produced by the same evolutionary mechanisms that apply to the rest of the living world."[13]

NAS president Bruce Alberts notes in the preface to a 1999 NAS publication *Science and Creationism* that the concept of biological evolution "is one of the most important ideas ever generated by the application of scientific methods to the natural world." Alberts indicates that evolution is at the core of genetics, biochemistry, neurobiology, physiology, ecology, and other biological disciplines. Evolutionary theory helps explain such things as "the emergence of new infectious diseases, the development of antibiotic resistance in bacteria, the agricultural relationships among wild and domestic plants and animals, the composition of the earth's atmosphere, the molecular machinery of the cell, the similarities between human beings and other primates, and countless other features of the biological and physical world."[14]

Harvard zoologist Ernst Mayr is one of the most influential evolutionary scientists of the twentieth century. He was prominent in the efforts to forge a synthesis of Charles Darwin's ideas with genetics, the so-called evolutionary synthesis that defines the modern meaning of the term. Not surprisingly, Mayr considers the evidence so overwhelming that evolution should be considered as much a fact as the earth's motion around the sun. Because it is beyond dispute, no evolutionary biologist "wastes time looking for further evidence." Only the burdensome task of refuting creationists forces the scientific community to assemble "the powerful evidence that has accumulated in the last 130 years proving evolution."[15] We will return to Mayr shortly, but at this point we enlist the corroborating comment of Massachusetts Institute of Technology (MIT) evolutionary psychologist Steven Pinker, who agrees with Mayr that the evidence in favor of evolution is overwhelming. In his highly readable and award-winning book *How the Mind Works*, Pinker states simply and categorically that there are "no alternatives" to evolution.[16]

A basic premise of Daniel C. Dennett's important book *Darwin's Dangerous Idea* is that evolution is "about as secure as any [idea] in science."[17] Dennett, a Tufts University philosopher, cautions that the sometimes intense intramural debates among evolutionary thinkers[18] should not obscure the fact that the fundamental core of Darwinism (DNA-based reproduction and evolution) is "beyond dispute among scientists." Its explanatory power manifests itself in a number of sciences, including geology, meteorology, ecology, agronomy, and genetics. Dennett's admiration for evolution is so strong that he enthusiastically nominates it as his candidate "for the single best idea anyone has ever had." It "unifies all biology and the history of our planet into a single grand story."[19]

Steve Jones and Mayr agree. Jones, a prominent geneticist, trumpets that evolution has become "more than a science, as its ideas are used, wittingly or otherwise, in economics, politics, history, art and more."[20] And in a recent article in *Scientific American*, Mayr describes the way Darwin's ideas have so thoroughly permeated modern thought that "almost every component in modern man's belief system is somehow affected by Darwinian principles." He calls attention to the "Darwinian *Zeitgeist*" that has allowed humankind the freedom to abandon the supernatural as an explanation for the unexplainable. By the way, in this article Mayr repeats the common claim in popular science that "[n]o educated person any longer questions the validity of the so-called theory of evolution, which we now know to be a simple fact."[21]

Oxford evolutionary biologist Richard Dawkins is probably the most influential and controversial science popularizer of our time.[22] Currently, he holds the Charles Simonyi Chair for the Public Understanding of Science at Oxford University. His *The Selfish Gene*, *The Blind Watchmaker*, and *River out of Eden* have all been best-sellers and are remarkable in the clarity of their assertion of the truth of evolution.[23] He has shaped our understanding of evolution by coining such widely used terms as the "selfish gene" (the notion that organisms can be understood as survival machines for their genes) and the "meme" (a metaphor for a unit of cultural inheritance, like a poem, song, or pattern of behavior that "catches on" and is passed down from one generation to the next).[24] And Dawkins is the author of one of the most oft-quoted comments about evolution: "Darwin made it possible to be an intellectually fulfilled atheist."[25] This pithy line is used by both supporters and critics to emphasize the very real tension between evolution and belief in God as Creator. Dawkins, not surprisingly, pulls no punches in his confident assertion of the truth of Darwinism, as the following quotes amply demonstrate:

> It is absolutely safe to say that if you meet somebody who claims not to believe in evolution, that person is ignorant, stupid or insane (or wicked, but I'd rather not consider that).[26]

> Today the theory of evolution is about as much open to doubt as the theory that the earth goes around the sun.[27]

> No serious biologist doubts the fact that evolution has happened, nor that all living creatures are cousins of one another.[28]

> There's only one general principle in biology, and that, of course, is Darwinism. Nobody doubts the importance of evolutionary theory; nobody doubts that Darwinian evolution is the central theory of biology.[29]

Evolution is absolutely beyond doubt for Dawkins because of its "superabundant power to explain." Dawkins argues that, other than Darwinism, there are only two other rival explanations: Lamarckianism[30] and God. He takes great pains in the *Blind Watchmaker* to dismiss both views by refuting their assumptions. So convinced is he of the validity of evolution that he asserts "even if there were no actual evidence in favour of the Darwinian theory (there is, of course) we should still be justified in preferring it over all rival theories."[31] This is an extraordinary assertion and one that has not endeared Dawkins to all of his fellow scientists, most of whom have a much higher appreciation for the importance of evidentiary support.[32] The explanatory power of Darwinian theory has, in Dawkins's eloquent prose, "a sinewy elegance, a poetic beauty that outclasses even the most haunting of the world's origin myths."[33] There can be no doubt that this last broadside is aimed squarely at the Judeo-Christian creation account in Genesis, as indicated by the name he chose for his contribution to the Science Masters' series of popular books: *River out of Eden.*

Dawkins is keenly aware that in the United States Darwinism is still a hotly contested matter. He concludes that attacks on Darwinism stem from ignorance, although he acknowledges that his "resolutely materialistic, non-mystical view of life"[34] is certainly not congenial to the deep-rooted religious sensibilities of American culture. In Dawkins's view, science and religion (belief in some kind of supernatural intervening consciousness) are in conflict and cannot peacefully coexist. They "are trespassing on the same territory, because both of them are about the nature of reality, the nature of existence." The belief in a supernatural creator is for Dawkins a scientific claim, "which is either wrong or not."[35] In Dawkins's ultrareductionist worldview, "all purpose comes ultimately from natural selection."[36]

Together with Peter W. Atkins, Dennett, Edward O. Wilson, and a few others, Dawkins holds to the view that there is an unavoidable theological conflict between a worldview in which evolution is taken to be true and one in which it is not. In their view, belief in God can only be sustained if evolution is inadequate and thus God is required in order to "explain" the origin and development of life. This strong view, which gets considerable media attention because of its aggressive simplicity, is, nevertheless, not shared by all of Dawkins's colleagues and fellow evolutionary enthusiasts, among them Niles Eldredge and the late Stephen Jay Gould.

Eldredge is a prominent paleontologist and a prolific writer. He believes that evolution is "one of the most fruitful ideas ever introduced in Western civilization," as well established as "any other complex theoretical position in science." The basic notion of evolution (i.e., common ancestral descent of all living creatures) is so thoroughly corroborated that it is in the same category as gravity or the sphericity of the earth.[37] That life evolves is beyond dispute; the questions that occupy evolutionary scientists revolve around *how* life evolved, not *whether* it evolved. Consequently, Eldredge considers the debate over evolution sterile: "Intellectually, the debate has been dead since 1859!" While evolution is "triumphant in the intellectual realm," it is certainly under siege in the political arena because the real battleground is the public school classroom. Eldredge decries the antievolutionary linkage of evolution to ethics (i.e., evolution erodes the basis for traditional morality)[38] and the attempt to insert creationist views into science classrooms. Unfortunately, the science culture wars pit a creationism that "lost its last vestiges of intellectual content not long after 1859" against arrogant scientists who claim that evolution demonstrates that there is no God. This is for Eldredge a "stupid, hurtful little political battle" that has deflected attention away from serious issues like the great loss of biodiversity.[39]

Gould, a Harvard paleontologist and colleague of Eldredge, was an eloquent science essayist and America's best-known champion of evolution. Within the field of evolutionary biology, however, he was a controversial figure. In 1972, he and Eldredge first advanced their notion of "punctuated equilibrium," suggesting that evolution was not uniformly gradual but proceeded in fits and starts. On the basis of the fossil record, Gould and Eldredge proposed that new species were only rarely the product of gradual, linear evolution. Stability or stasis is the norm until a major event in the physical environment triggers rapid speciation, at which

time a new species "suddenly" appears.[40] Over the years, Gould's ideas led him
to advocate positions that have drawn considerable fire from within the guild of
evolutionary biology. He believed that the "gene-centered" view of natural selection championed by Dawkins and Dennett is inadequate to account for evolution at the level of populations and species. This has led to a spirited debate
over "evolutionary mechanics" that some critics of evolution have exploited in
an attempt to demonstrate that evolutionary thought is hopelessly confused.
Gould was quite clear, however, that though this intramural debate continues,
"everyone knows that evolution is true; the issue is [only] how it occurs."[41] While
Gould was highly critical of Dawkins and could appear to be irenic in his attempt to find a truce between science and religion in general,[42] he could also
employ some very tough rhetoric against those who object to evolution. Witness
the following examples:

> Within a decade [of the publication of the *Origin of Species*], he [Darwin] con-
> vinced the *thinking world* that evolution had occurred.[43]

> The battle shifted long ago from a simple debate about evolution: *educated people*
> now accept the evolutionary continuity between humans and apes.[44]

> Although *no thinking person* doubted the fact of evolution by 1909.[45]

We could provide many more examples of how science writers speak to the
culture about evolution, but we will supply just two more. Kenneth R. Miller is
a cellular biologist at Brown University, a science popularizer, and a practicing
Catholic whose work we will revisit. Committed to both a strong Christian faith
and evolution, he obviously believes that these two supposed antagonists can be
reconciled, perhaps even harmonized. And he certainly does not believe that
evolution has undermined the Christian belief in creation. For our present purposes, though, we will focus on how he communicates the triumph of evolution
in his recent book *Finding Darwin's God*.[46] On the very first page, Miller states
without equivocation that "[e]volution remains the focal point, the organizing
principle, the logical center of every discipline in biology today." Midbook, he
adds that in the "real world of science, in the hard-bitten realities of lab bench
and field station, the intellectual triumph of Darwin's great idea is total." From
the perspective of the working scientist, evolution provides a "seamless explanatory integration of past and present," one that can accommodate new data and
ideas from many different fields. In short, evolution is so successful because it
works![47]

   Miller is not alone among prominent evolutionists in his belief that Darwin's
theory need not be at war with the Christian faith. Another Christian scientist anticipated Miller by almost thirty years. Theodosius Dobzhansky was one of the
twentieth century's leading geneticists. In 1972, he gave at a gathering of the National Association of Biology Teachers a paper, the title of which has become an

oft-quoted aphorism: "Nothing in Biology Makes Sense Except in the Light of Evolution."[48] After surveying the state of biological science, Dobzhansky asserted that evolution makes biology arguably "the most [intellectually] satisfying and inspiring science." Without evolution, it becomes "a pile of sundry facts—some of them interesting or curious but making no meaningful picture as a whole." Near the end of his address, Dobzhansky minced no words: "Evolution as a process that has always gone on in the history of the earth can be doubted only by those who are ignorant of the evidence or are resistant to evidence, owing to emotional blocks or to plain bigotry." Although conceding that the mechanisms of evolution still needed further study and clarification, he stated, nevertheless, that "[t]here are no alternatives to evolution as history that can withstand critical examination."[49]

The picture developed earlier indicates that those who speak for the scientific community are quite confident in their belief that evolution is supported by vast amounts of scientific evidence and is on solid theoretical ground. We should thus not be surprised that this confidence is reflected in introductory-level biology textbooks,[50] where it is likely to be encountered by undergraduate students. Three examples will suffice. McGraw-Hill's college-level text *Biology* notes that the theory of evolution "is the only scientifically defensible explanation for the origin of life and development of species." The authors dismiss the creationist challenge to evolution as "a fruitless debate" and relegate discussion of it to a sidebar.[51] Another McGraw-Hill text suggests that no serious student of biology questions evolution in the light of overwhelming evidence.[52] Addison Wesley Longman's introductory college biology text devotes an entire unit to the mechanisms of evolution, contending quite simply that scientists would have discarded the concept of evolution long ago if it were not consistent with observations. To the contrary, new discoveries, including those in molecular biology, "continue to validate the Darwinian view of life." Critics of evolution should take no comfort in the intramural debates about how life has evolved. "Debates about evolutionary theory," the authors assert, "are like arguments over competing theories about gravity; we know that objects keep right on falling while we debate the cause."[53]

Clearly, the overwhelming consensus of the professional scientific community is that evolution is beyond question. Only some of the details are subject to debate. There really are no leading scientists on record who dispute the truth of evolution, and among the handful of reputable scientists who have expressed significant doubts about aspects of it, few appear to be arguing from a purely scientific perspective. There is simply very little voice with recognized professional standing opposing evolution from within the scientific community. But what about outside the scientific community?

Jacques Barzun is one of the most respected cultural historians of our time and was for decades one of the guiding lights of liberal education in this country. Barzun noted recently that while there is great diversity about its character and mechanism, "[n]obody questions evolution—there seems no reason to."[54] The great British philosopher Father Frederick Copleston, famous for debating Bertrand Russell on the existence of God and writing a classic nine-volume history of Western philosophy, stated almost a half century ago that "the idea of evolution is now common coin and is taken for granted by very many people who would be quite unable either to mention or to weigh the evidence adduced in its favour." Understanding why it was ever controversial, argues Copleston, is impossible "[u]nless we happen to live in one of the few surviving pockets of fundamentalism."[55]

The views expressed by Copleston and Barzun are near universal among Western intellectuals, whether their field is science, history, philosophy, or whatever. While many open questions remain in the details of evolutionary theory, there is very little scholarly debate within the academy about evolution per se.[56] It is Western Civilization's new creation story and can even serve as a bridge to the other great cultures once they accept the truth of evolution, as theologian Loyal Rue has suggested in *Everybody's Story*.[57]

EVOLUTION ON MAIN STREET

While intellectuals and cultural historians take their cue from the scientific community and pronounce the matter settled,[58] in American culture as a whole the situation differs dramatically. On Main Street America, acceptance of evolution is far from universal, and there are a great many communities where the opposition is dominant.[59] Numerous polls taken over the past twenty years indicate that the scientific community has been astonishingly unsuccessful in getting its point across to the American public. Furthermore, evidence is mounting that the debate over evolution may well be a symptom of a clash of widely held but incompatible worldviews. The "debate over evolution" is much more than a debate over the scientific theory of evolution, with answers to be determined by reference to scientific data. Rather, belief in evolution is often connected to fundamental worldview assumptions about the nature of truth, the existence of God, and the authority of the Bible. Untangling this cultural and philosophical mess is our task in this book.

We now turn to an examination of various polls, particularly those conducted by the George Gallup Organization, to see just what ordinary Americans think about evolution. Our goal will be to ascertain the relative strength of belief in evolutionary theory versus belief in that other species of origins, creationism. We will see that not only is there widespread cultural dissent about evolution, but that the opposition also tends to be coalesced around a particular alternative model that is rooted in Genesis. In subsequent chapters, we will address the extraordinary resiliency of American creationism, a surprisingly popular cultural alternative to the modern scientific creation story.

In 1978, Gallup researchers conducted over fifteen hundred interviews with American adults in a survey sponsored by *Christianity Today* magazine. Fifty percent agreed with the statement that "God created Adam and Eve, which was the start of human life." This, of course, comes straight from the first chapters of Genesis. Another 20 percent accepted that God initiated an evolutionary cycle of all living things, including man, "but personally intervened at a point in time and transformed man into a human being in His own image." Thus, in 1978, almost three-quarters of the American populace understood origins to be an explicitly supernatural process driven by miraculous intervention, contrary to the consensus of the scientific community. Eleven percent indicated that God began an evolutionary cycle for all living things, including man, but "did not personally intervene at a point in time and transform man into a human being in His own image." Twelve percent agreed to the statement that "[t]he origin of man is unknown." And 8 percent simply "didn't know."[60] Of the half that believed that God began human life with the creation of Adam and Eve, one-third were college graduates.[61]

Four years later, the Gallup Organization conducted two additional polls related to evolution. In April 1982, researchers asked a representative sample of American adults whether they agreed "more with the theory of evolution or more with the theory of creationism." By over three to one, the respondents agreed to creationism (54 percent) over evolution (only 15 percent).[62] In July 1982, another Gallup poll refined this question and revealed that creationism and evolution were much more evenly matched in American public opinion, though creationism still held the edge. This same poll also indicated strong opposition to teaching in public schools that God had no part in the evolutionary process (see table 2.1).[63]

The Gallup Organization asked the same basic questions regarding evolution and creationism several times in the 1990s. The picture that emerged is a fairly consistent one of over 40 percent believing in creationism and another 35 to 40 percent believing in a God-guided evolutionary process. In America, evolutionary theory without reference to God is decidedly and consistently unpopular (see table 2.2).[64]

Table 2.1.   Gallup Poll and Results (July 1982)

God created man pretty much in his present form at one time within the last ten thousand years.	44%
Man has developed over millions of years from less advanced forms of life. God had no part in this process.	9%
Man has developed over millions of years from less advanced forms of life, but God guided this process, including man's creation.	38%
Other; don't know	9%

Table 2.2   Changes over Time to Gallup Poll Creationism/Evolution Questions

	Humans Developed with God Guiding	Humans Developed; God Not Part	God Created	Other; No Opinion
1999	40%	9%	47%	4%
1997	39%	10%	44%	7%
1993	35%	11%	47%	7%
1991	47%	9%	40%	4%
1982	38%	9%	44%	9%

The message of these polls is crystal clear. Despite the near universal acceptance of evolution within the academy, despite the confident proclamation that evolution is "fact, not theory," despite claims that evolution is "as well established as the sphericity of the earth," despite the complete absence of mainstream textbooks that teach alternatives, the majority of Americans are getting their ideas on origins from conservative, even fundamentalist, religious sources rather than from the scientific community. This is an amazing result. If only 10 percent of Americans were sympathetic to creationism, that could be attributed to a variety of factors like illiteracy, religious home and private schooling, and so on. But when almost three-fourths of Americans reject evolution as articulated by the scientific community, one is forced to recognize that millions of Americans complete their public high school education where they study evolution, attend college where evolution is taught in introductory biology courses, and yet they simply do not accept what they have been taught.

Predictably, there is a positive correlation between Americans' level of education and their acceptance of evolution. Only 41 percent of Americans polled who had not attended college favored evolution in the 1999 Gallup poll. The favorability rating increased to 50 percent among those who attended some college, to 58 percent among college graduates, and to 66 percent among those with some postgraduate education.[65] It remains the case, however, that more than one-third of Americans with postgraduate educational experience reject evolution.

Interestingly, Americans' views about teaching evolution and creationism in public schools is slightly more complicated. In 1996, the Gallup Organization asked a representative sample of American adults whether they would favor a law requiring that the "biblical doctrine of creationism" be taught along with evolution in public schools. Fifty-eight percent said "yes." In 1999, a Gallop poll refined this to a series of three questions: (1) Should creationism be taught along with evolution in public schools? (2) Should creationism be taught instead of evolution in public schools? and (3) Should evolution be required in public school instruction? While 68 percent favored teaching both evolution and creationism, 55 percent opposed substituting creationism for evolution, and only 21 percent believed that evolution should not be offered at all.[66]

This ambivalence on evolution and creationism in public school education was mirrored by results of an ambitious national survey released in March 2000 by the anticreationist organization People for the American Way (PFAW). In the wake of a controversial decision by the Kansas Board of Education to drop evolution from its statewide science standards, the PFAW commissioned DYG, Inc., a polling firm headed by Daniel Yankelovich, to undertake extensive interviews on evolution and creationism in public education. PFAW's press release announced triumphantly that the "Public Wants Evolution, Not Creationism, in Science Class," and reported that "83% of Americans say Darwin's theory of evolution belongs in the nation's science classes." The DYG poll, however, also indicated that 79 percent of Americans believe that creationism has a place in public school curricula, though only 29 percent want creationism taught as science.[67] Consistent with the Gallup polling data, but in total opposition to the confident claims of the scientific community, the DYG poll found that almost half the respondents agreed that evolution "is far from being proven scientifically." And 68 percent indicated that it is possible to believe in evolution while also believing that God created humans and guided their development. "To put it simply," PFAW Foundation president Ralph G. Neas admitted, "this poll shows that most Americans believe that God created evolution."[68]

We will examine one last poll. In 1996, *Free Inquiry* magazine commissioned a survey by Goldhaber Research Associates to assess religious belief and disbelief in America. In sum, and not surprisingly, the poll revealed a strong commitment to religious belief in America. Several of the questions in the poll related to evolution. The Goldhaber poll assessed public opinion as to whether evolution is the *best possible explanation of human existence*. Only 39 percent agreed and 46.4 percent disagreed. As might be expected, there was a high correlation between respondents' level of education and their level of agreement with this assertion. But for our purposes, and consistent with the Gallop poll discussed earlier, it is very significant to note that over 35 percent of the respondents with graduate or professional degrees did *not* believe that evolution is the best possible explanation of human existence. Another significant correlation is between religious attitude and agreement with the statement that evolution is the best possible explanation of human existence. Here, 59 percent of respondents who characterized themselves as religious liberals agreed with the statement; whereas only 23 percent of those who considered themselves as religiously conservative agreed.[69] In this data, for the first time we begin to see clearly the larger context of the controversy that extends beyond science into more fundamental world-view assumptions.

The Goldhaber poll also asked for further responses to refine American public opinion. To the statement "God started evolution, then let it continue by itself," respondents split almost evenly: 42 percent agreed and 43 percent disagreed. Here again education and religious attitudes were major correlating factors. People with graduate or professional degrees were found to be most likely to agree (50 percent) and least likely to disagree (35 percent), and people who described themselves as religiously conservative were least likely to agree

(30 percent) and most likely to disagree (60 percent). Goldhaber Research associates tabulated similar results in response to the statement "God created the cosmos, but let it run on its own."[70]

To determine the level of support for what might be called conservative creationism, the Goldhaber poll asked for responses to the statement "God created the cosmos about five thousand to ten thousand years ago." In one of its most interesting findings, Goldhaber associates found that only 19 percent of those surveyed agreed to this creationist statement. Here again, people who described themselves as very nonreligious were least likely to agree (9 percent), and those who viewed themselves as very religious were most likely to agree (22 percent), but the level of agreement was decidedly small. And one has to wonder about the almost 9 percent of Americans who described themselves as "very nonreligious" and yet accept the "young-earth" creationist position. One might realistically suppose that "very nonreligious" implies "not significantly influenced by religious teachings on origins." But this would be a mistake.

In the same way we saw with the earlier Gallop poll, education is another correlating factor: 26 percent of those surveyed with high school education or less agreed to the young-earth statement, whereas only 13 percent with a graduate or professional degree agreed.[71] So the Goldhaber poll, like the others, indicates that Americans are genuinely in disagreement about evolution. A great many Americans, even well-educated ones, reject the scientific community's fundamental theory of origins.

HOW CAN THIS BE?

The picture that emerges, then, is of a scientific community at odds with Main Street America. The scientific community considers evolution to be as safe and reliable a theory as gravity, conceding little more than that it cannot explain all of the mechanisms of either with much precision. In contrast, Main Street America is genuinely divided over evolution.

One clue to this curious state of affairs can be found in yet another set of surveys conducted in recent years by Pulitzer Prize–winning historian Edward J. Larson and journalist Larry Witham. They revisited James Leuba's pioneering surveys of 1914 and 1933 on the attitudes of American scientists toward God. In his 1914 survey, Leuba found that about 58 percent of the one thousand scientists contacted expressed either disbelief or doubt about the existence of a personal God. Leuba also polled the scientific elite and found that the disbelief–doubt level increased to 74 percent. In 1933, Leuba found that this level had increased to 85 percent. Larson and Witham repeated Leuba's survey of rank-and-file scientists in 1996 and arrived at very similar results: about 40 percent of American scientists still believe in a personal God. But the response to these two widely separated polls is interesting.

In 1914, the 40 percent response was generally interpreted as a sign of an alarming loss of faith within the scientific community. Many Americans were dismayed to discover that only 40 percent of scientists believed in God. In 1996, however, more or less identical survey results received the opposite reaction. Americans were surprised at the resilience of scientists' belief in God. A different picture emerges, however, when the focus is narrowed to the scientific elite. In 1998, Larson and Witham surveyed the members of the NAS and reported that the rate of belief in a personal God among the American scientific elite had declined to a mere 7 percent. NAS biologists were the most skeptical, with 95 percent of them adopting atheistic or agnostic stances. Larson and Witham drew the obvious conclusion: There is "acute disbelief" at the top of the American scientific establishment.[72]

Obviously, there is a significant gap in American culture between the views of the average American and the top scientists on matters of faith. Compare the 7 percent belief in God response of NAS scientists and the 5 percent response of NAS biologists, with the 89 percent affirmative response in the Goldhaber poll to the statement "there is a personal God who can answer prayer."[73] Main Street Americans are more than ten times as likely to believe in God than are the members of the NAS. This is an extraordinary gap.

Data gathered by pollsters, however, will hardly convince scientists to reject their central theories, especially scientists who think they can explain the origins of popular beliefs and thus undermine the polls themselves! MIT evolutionary psychologist and leading science popularizer Steven Pinker notes that, while religion may be revealed as a live option in opinion polls, religious concepts are merely "human concepts with a few emendations that make them wondrous and a longer list of standard traits that make them sensible to our ordinary ways of knowing." So that his readers will make no mistake, Pinker asserts that "[c]ompared to the mind-bending ideas of modern science, religious beliefs are notable for their lack of imagination."[74] Pinker's line of reasoning clearly will not persuade most Americans and, in fact, illustrates in a rather precise way one of the reasons for the failure of evolutionary theory to win over the majority of Americans: the condescending proclamations of elite science popularizers who would explain away cherished beliefs as bogus intellectual baggage accumulated along the evolutionary path.

The triumph of evolution in the sciences has not translated to a triumph in American culture because the bedrock issue is not a matter of scientific evidence. As Miller notes, "[p]ublic acceptance of evolution . . . does not turn on the logical weight of carefully considered scientific issues." Rather, it is because the science of evolution is seen to be entwined with a worldview hostile to their own. Miller concludes that evolution is resisted because "of a well-founded belief" that it is used "to justify and advance a philosophical worldview that . . . [a significant percentage of Americans] regard as hostile and even alien to their lives and values."[75] British geneticist R. J. Berry shares Miller's concern. Evolution as a science must be distinguished from what he calls "evolutionism," which is an "attitude or philosophy which uses science as its base."[76]

On Main Street America, evolution is often interpreted as a creation story for atheists. Already in this chapter we have seen how the work of Pinker, Dawkins, and Dennett can be used to support this view. A further example of this is Dawkins's Oxford colleague Peter W. Atkins, who claims boldly that religion has contributed "nothing" to our understanding of the origin of the universe. Science, in Atkins's thinking, is a "glorious achievement of the human intellect," growing out of religion, but surpassing and replacing it as a means of understanding the world. Atkins asserts that people must choose "between the feather bed of religion, which appeases the fears of the weak and encourages false hopes, and the rack of science, which exposes the true heart of the world, despite the discomfort of what we find when we look at truth without the soft cushions of sentiment." Atkins goes further: "Gone is purpose, gone is the afterlife, gone is the soul, gone is protection through prayer, gone is design, gone is false comfort. All that is left is an *exhilarating loneliness* and the recognition that through science we can come to an understanding of ourselves and this glorious cosmos."[77] And no less a figure than Nobel laureate Steven Weinberg, holder of the Josey Regental Chair in Science at the University of Texas at Austin, has stated in a *New York Review of Books* essay that " [t]hough aware there is nothing in the universe that suggests a purpose for humanity, one way that we can find a purpose is to study the universe by the methods of science, without consoling ourselves with fairy tales about its future, or about our own."[78]

No better examples of science as worldview can be offered, and no better reason why so many Americans remain suspicious of evolutionary theory. Its scientific explanatory power is purchased at far too dear a price for such a stubbornly religious society as contemporary America. Atkins's "exhilarating loneliness" or Weinberg's "science as purpose" is meager reward for banishing God from both the cosmos and the American heart.

A profound tension exists within American culture between two worldviews that are implacably hostile to each other. On the one hand, Americans are a deeply religious people that by and large believes in a personal God who answers prayer. On the other hand, America is also a scientifically sophisticated culture that confers great authority on its elite scientists and often uses scientific rhetoric to enhance the credibility of truth claims.[79] (The reader has no doubt heard advertisers upgrading their studies by stating that something is a "scientific" fact, as if that is a better kind of fact than the usual sort.) This scientific elite, for the most part, holds to a secular worldview that has no room for supernatural explanations, especially of natural phenomena. The resulting tension between these competing worldviews that coexist and intertwine within American culture is precisely why the origins debate in America will not go away. And it explains why so many Americans, even well-educated ones with a degree of scientific literacy, remain open to alternatives to evolutionary theory that do not appear so threatening to their religious commitments. Most evolutionary theorists and science writers fail to appreciate this basic tension and unwittingly alienate a large fraction of their audience with their casual dismissal of and outright attacks on the religious concerns of their readers. The result is a constant cultural unrest about evolution that often requires that the champions of evolution engage in time-consuming and distracting defenses of evolutionary theory.

Unfortunately, this responsibility is often interpreted as a tiresome burden imposed by scientifically unsophisticated, religiously motivated zealots. Geneticist Steve Jones, for example, notes that there is "a kind of invincible ignorance among anti-evolutionists that bores—when it does not exasperate—those seriously interested in the subject."[80] That perception is most certainly shared by many of Jones's colleagues. We argue in this book that this charge is unfair and derives from a certain parochialism on the part of the scientific community.

If we are to make any headway in understanding the contemporary origins debate in America, we must examine the ideas and literature of the "creationists," those people most vocal in their opposition to evolution, and those who have articulated the species of origins that a great many Americans affirm when they see it on a public opinion poll. We contend that, while creationism has drawn considerable scientific and theological criticism, it is not without its unique sophistication and persuasiveness, especially considering the assumptions on which it is based. Just as many in the science community are tired of fending off antievolutionary attacks, creationists have grown weary of seeing their views portrayed so consistently with sneering ridicule.[81] Creationists welcome with open arms those champions who arise from among them to do battle with a secular, atheistic science that does not respect their religious commitments and indoctrinates their children with a hostile worldview that celebrates the exhilaration of "cosmic loneliness," as they learn that they are nothing but a particularly interesting arrangement of molecules.

While there is much in creationism that is problematic, detractors who dismiss it as little more than fundamentalist ranting, and there are certainly plenty of those, almost always miss the reasons why creationism remains such a powerful influence in contemporary American culture. Unless we understand the inner logic and appeal of creationism, America's search for a creation story will continue to be utterly incomprehensible, inexplicably polarized, and alarmingly confrontational. This latter aspect must not be minimized. In the 2001 *Evolution* series, the creation–evolution controversy is said to be at "the heart of a struggle that threatens to tear this nation apart."[82] Consequently, we devote the next three chapters to a detailed examination of creationism. Our goal is to give it a sufficiently sympathetic and nondismissive treatment so that skeptical readers can begin to understand its internal coherence and enduring attraction.

NOTES

1. Throughout this book, we will make repeated references to "science popularizers." This important group of influential intellectuals does not have well-defined boundaries.

On the one hand, professional writers like Robert Wright, Gregg Easterbrook, Dennis Overbye, and Timothy Ferris are very effective at bringing science to popular audiences without themselves having a lot of training in science and never having done much real science themselves. At the other end of the spectrum are Nobel laureates like Christian de Duve, Francis Crick, Murray Gell-Mann, and Steven Weinberg, who are themselves leading scientists but who write so well that their books are widely read and appreciated by a vast readership. Books by such leading scientists, however, almost always range far beyond the particular expertise and training of their authors. Crick, for example, became scientifically prominent for his discovery (with James Watson) of DNA. His primary work of science popularization was *The Astonishing Hypothesis: The Scientific Search for the Soul* (New York: Scribner, 1994), which had virtually nothing to do with DNA. In between these two ends of the spectrum lie some of the most effective and prolific science popularizers like Richard Dawkins, Paul Davies, the late Stephen Jay Gould, the late Carl Sagan, and the late Isaac Asimov. Members of this group are scientifically credentialed and have participated in significant scientific activities, though their peers tend to consider writing books for popular audiences to be less important than scientific research.

2. Murray Gell-Mann quoted in John Brockman, *The Third Culture* (New York: Simon and Schuster, 1995), 66. Because he is a physicist and not a biologist, Gell-Mann is a useful yardstick for the consensus of the scientific community. Biologists, who feel their work is actually threatened by creationism, often resort to "warfare" rhetoric and may overstate their case.

3. The movement known as "scientific creationism" is the primary challenger of the scientific creation story for millions of Americans. In the next three chapters we will be looking at this movement.

4. Gell-Mann quoted in Brockman, *Third Culture*, 66.

5. John Maynard Smith, preface to the first edition of *The Theory of Evolution* (Cambridge: Cambridge University Press, 1958, 1997), xvii.

6. Robert L. Smith and Thomas M. Smith, *Elements of Ecology*, 4th ed. (Reading, Mass.: Benjamin Cummings, an Imprint of Addison Wesley Longman, 2000).

7. Kenneth V. Kardong, *Vertebrates: Comparative Anatomy, Function, and Evolution*, 2d ed. (Boston: WCB McGraw-Hill, 1998).

8. Scott F. Gilbert, *Developmental Biology*, 5th ed. (Sunderland, Mass.: Sinauer Associates, 1997).

9. Peter H. Raven, Ray F. Evert, and Susan E. Eichhorn, *Biology of Plants*, 6th ed. (New York: Freeman, 1999).

10. We will see in the next chapter that the creationist critique of evolution goes far beyond biology into areas of geology, astronomy, and nuclear physics.

11. Medawar's Nobel Prize was in medicine. Alfred Nobel did not endow a prize specifically for biology.

12. Medawar quoted in Chet Raymo, *Skeptics and True Believers: The Exhilarating Connection between Science and Religion* (New York: Walker, 1998), 137. It should be noted that Medawar also argued that science was decidedly unfit to provide answers to questions regarding the purpose of life or the existence of God. See also R. J. Berry, "Science and Religion: Friends or Foes?" *Science Progress* 83 (2000): 13–14.

13. National Academy of Sciences, *Teaching about Evolution and the Nature of Science* (Washington, D.C.: National Academy Press, 1998), preface, 16, 56. Since evolution is "the central organizing principle that biologists use to understand the world," the NAS

committee concluded that it is untenable to teach biology without explaining evolution. For a book-length creationist response, see Jonathan Sarfati, *Refuting Evolution: A Response to the National Academy of Sciences' Teaching about Evolution and the Nature of Science* (Green Forest, Ark.: Master, 1999).

14. Bruce Alberts, preface to *Science and Creationism: A View from the National Academy of Sciences*, 2d ed. (Washington, D.C.: National Academy Press, 1999), viii–ix.

15. Ernst Mayr, *This Is Biology: The Science of the Living World* (Cambridge, Mass.: Belknap, 1997), 178.

16. Steven Pinker, *How the Mind Works* (New York: Norton, 1997), 162.

17. Daniel C. Dennett, *Darwin's Dangerous Idea: Evolution and the Meanings of Life* (New York: Touchstone, 1995), 19.

18. For decades now there has been an intense intramural debate within the community of evolutionary scholars about the nature of evolution. Put simply, one group favors a gene-centered view. This group (which includes Dawkins, Edward O. Wilson, , and Pinker) contends that evolution proceeded slowly and gradually, "driven by competition among organisms to transmit their genes from generation to generation." The other group (led by Gould [now deceased] and Niles Eldredge) looks at evolution from a paleontological perspective. The fossil record does not suggest gradualism; rather, it is marked by long periods of stasis punctuated by episodes of rapid evolutionary activity. The paleontologists understand evolution to be driven by environmental factors, not gene competition. The debate over sociobiology ("the scientific study of the biological basis of social behavior" in all kinds of organisms, including humans) or evolutionary psychology, as it is now more often called, feeds into these so-called Darwin wars. See Niles Eldredge, *Reinventing Darwin: The Great Debate at the High Table of Evolutionary Theory* (New York: Wiley, 1995); Andrew Brown, *The Darwin Wars: The Scientific Battle for the Soul of Man* (London: Simon and Schuster, 1999); Ullica Segerstrale, *Defenders of the Truth: The Battle for Science in the Sociobiology Debate and Beyond* (New York: Oxford University Press, 2000).

19. Dennett, *Darwin's Dangerous Idea*, 20–21. Dennett's book, which was a finalist in the 1995 National Book Awards, is an exploration of how evolutionary thinking is "a universal solvent capable of cutting right to the heart of everything in sight," especially our most fundamental beliefs about the meaning of life.

20. Steve Jones, *Darwin's Ghost: The Origin of Species Updated* (New York: Random House, 1999), xx.

21. Ernst Mayr, "Darwin's Influence on Modern Thought," *Scientific American* 282 (July 2000): 79–83.

22. Despite the claims of people like Jones that Dawkins is "the most successful popularizer of all," Dawkins does not like the label. He believes the term "science popularizer" is used dismissively and does not adequately capture the creativity in his work. He argues that he does not simply translate technical scientific literature to the general public; rather, he changes how people—especially scientists—think. See Brockman, *Third Culture*, 84–85, 95. While one could make a distinction between "science popularizers" and "scientists writing for the general public," we have opted to use the former in a non-derogatory manner.

23. Richard Dawkins, *The Selfish Gene*, 2d ed. (Oxford, U.K.: Oxford University Press, 1989); Richard Dawkins, *The Blind Watchmaker: Why the Evidence of Evolution Reveals a Universe without Design* (New York: Norton, 1986, 1996); Richard Dawkins, *River out of Eden: A Darwinian View of Life* (New York: Basic, 1995).

24. The name of this book reflects the meme-like character of the name of Darwin's original text on evolution.

25. Dawkins, *Blind Watchmaker*, 6. Dawkins contends that without Darwin's *Origin of Species*, he could not imagine being an atheist, but that following its publication there was no longer a need for supernatural explanations.

26. This originally appeared in a 1989 *New York Times Book Review*. Dawkins has since revisited this remark and stands by it with one modification. He would now add a fifth category: "tormented, bullied, or brainwashed." See Richard Dawkins, "Ignorance Is No Crime," *Free Inquiry* (2001), at www.secularhumanism.org/fi/index.htm (15 November 2000).

27. Dawkins, *Selfish Gene*, 1.

28. Dawkins, *Blind Watchmaker*, 287. Dawkins recognizes that, of course, biologists may debate the particulars of how evolution happened.

29. Dawkins quoted in Brockman, *Third Culture*, 86.

30. Lamarckianism is named for Jean-Baptiste de Lamarck, the great French naturalist of the nineteenth century who taught a view of evolutionary change driven by the "inheritance of acquired characteristics." This view held that organisms could pass on to their offspring traits that they acquired or developed during their lifetime. If a person developed great strength or speed through cultivating those skills, then his or her offspring would also possess great strength or speed. This view is completely at odds with the now-accepted view that organisms pass on nothing but genes to their offspring. No matter how much one develops one's innate potential, such efforts do not show up in the next generation. Dawkins's use of Lamarckianism in this context is a clever rhetorical ploy, since it has been thoroughly discredited scientifically, and by juxtaposing it with belief in God, he makes it appear as if belief in God can be refuted in more or less the same way.

31. Dawkins, *Blind Watchmaker*, 287. Dawkins also contends that only Darwinism can account for adaptive complexity.

32. John C. Polkinghorne, *The Faith of a Physicist: Reflections of a Bottom up Thinker* (Princeton, N.J.: Princeton University Press, 1994), 16.

33. Dawkins, *River out of Eden*, xi.

34. The phrase is from science writer and former *Scientific American* senior editor John Horgan's *The End of Science: Facing the Limits of Knowledge in the Twilight of the Scientific Age* (New York: Broadway, 1997), 116.

35. Dawkins quoted in Chris Floyd, "A Trick of the Light: Richard Dawkins on Science and Religion," *Science and Spirit* 10 (July–August 1999): 24–25; see also Dawkins, *River out of Eden*, 98; Brockman, *Third Culture*, 86. Perhaps the most strident proponent for the power of reductionism and science is Oxford physical chemist Peter W. Atkins. See his "The Limitless Power of Science," in *Nature's Imagination: The Frontiers of Scientific Vision*, ed. John Cornwell (Oxford, U.K.: Oxford University Press, 1995), 122–132.

36. Dawkins quoted in Horgan, *End of Science*, 117; see also Dawkins, *River out of Eden*, 96–99.

37. Niles Eldredge, *The Triumph of Evolution and the Failure of Creationism* (New York: Freeman, 2000), 12, 31, 188.

38. Eldredge, who calls himself a lapsed Baptist, categorically rejects the notion that there is a "set of ethical implications implicit in the very idea of evolution—or emanating from any subset of evolutionary theory." Eldredge is, of course, aware that Dawkins's strident "selfish gene" views underlying sociobiology do conjure up for many the noxious

odors of a social Darwinist worldview. But he also suggests that the great Christian geneticist Theodosius Dobzhansky constructed a harmonious worldview whereby "Christianity and evolution went hand in hand." Eldredge believes that both the Dawkins and the Dobzhansky approaches introduce extraneous matters into the science of evolution. See Eldredge, *Triumph of Evolution*, 18, 153–154.

39. Eldredge, *Triumph of Evolution*, 168–169.

40. The geological abruptness of the appearance of new species (speciation) is "sudden" compared to the vast chunks of time that species last in the fossil record. Eldredge offers as a rough estimate that "speciation events" occur in periods ranging from five to fifty thousand years as compared to periods of stasis for species duration lasting between five to ten million years. Geologically speaking, this one-thousand-times-shorter rate "looks instantaneous in the fossil record." See Eldredge, *Reinventing Darwin*, 99.

41. Brockman, *Third Culture*, 59–64; Horgan, *End of Science*, 120–121; Eldredge, *Triumph of Evolution*, 85–86; Stephen Jay Gould, *Bully for Brontosaurus: Reflections in Natural History* (New York: Norton, 1991), 458.

42. Stephen Jay Gould, *Rocks of Ages: Science and Religion in the Fullness of Life* (New York: Ballantine, 1999).

43. Stephen Jay Gould, *Ever since Darwin: Reflections in Natural History* (New York: Norton, 1979, 1992), 11, emphasis added.

44. Gould, *Ever since Darwin*, 50–51, emphasis added.

45. Stephen Jay Gould, *Hen's Teeth and Horse's Toes: Further Reflections in Natural History* (New York: Norton, 1983), 11–12, emphasis added; Stephen Jay Gould, "Darwinism Defined: The Difference between Fact and Theory," *Discover* 8 (January 1987): 64–70.

46. Kenneth R. Miller, *Finding Darwin's God: A Scientist's Search for Common Ground between God and Evolution* (New York: Cliff Street/HarperCollins, 1999).

47. Miller, *Finding Darwin's God*, xi, 165–166.

48. Theodosius Dobzhansky, "Nothing in Biology Makes Sense Except in the Light of Evolution," *The American Biology Teacher* 35 (March 1973): 125–129.

49. Dobzhansky, "Nothing in Biology Makes Sense," 129.

50. This description was taken from Doug McElroy, "Evolutionary Biology," in *Encyclopedia of Genetics*, vol. 1, ed. Jeffrey A. Knight (Pasadena, Calif.: Salem, 1999), 200.

51. Burton S. Guttman and Johns W. Hopkins III, *Biology* (Boston, McGraw-Hill, 1999), 9, 767.

52. Peter H. Raven and George B. Johnson, *Biology*, 5th ed. (Boston: McGraw-Hill, 1999), 419–421.

53. Neil A. Campbell, Jane B. Reece, and Lawrence G. Mitchell, *Biology*, 5th ed. (Menlo Park, Calif.: Benjamin Cummings, an Imprint of Addison Wesley Longman, 1999), 422–426.

54. Jacques Barzun, *From Dawn to Decadence: 500 Years of Western Cultural Life, 1500 to the Present* (New York: HarperCollins, 2000), 571.

55. Frederick Copleston, *History of Western Philosophy*, vol. 8, *Bentham to Russell* (New York: Doubleday, 1966), 103.

56. There is nothing like total agreement on all aspects of evolutionary theory. In many areas, such as the relationship between developmental and evolutionary biology, the question of genetic information, the relationship between ecology and evolution, and especially the whole matter of evolutionary psychology, there is much ongoing debate. See

Kim Sterelny and Paul E. Griffiths, *Sex and Death: An Introduction to Philosophy of Biology* (Chicago: University of Chicago Press, 1999), 324–336, 380–381; Anthony O'Hear, *Beyond Evolution: Human Nature and the Limits of Evolutionary Explanation* (New York: Oxford University Press, 1997), 50–83, 213–214.

57. Loyal Rue, *Everybody's Story: Wising up to the Epic of Evolution* (Albany: SUNY Press, 2000), 129–138. Rue states that the "epic of evolution is the biggest of all pictures, the narrative context for all our thinking about who we are, where we have come from, and how we should live" (xii).

58. A. N. Wilson, *God's Funeral* (New York: Norton, 1999), *passim.*

59. In Great Britain, for example, studies suggest that only 7 percent of adults reject evolution. See Ian G. Barbour, *When Science Meets Religion: Enemies, Strangers, or Partners* (New York: Harper San Francisco, 2000), 1.

60. Polling data on evolution and creationism supplied to the authors by the Gallup Library.

61. Jerry Bergman, "The Attitude of Various Populations toward Teaching Creation and Evolution in Public Schools," *CEN Technical Journal* 13 (1999): 118.

62. Four percent agreed with evolution and creationism the same, and 27 percent had no opinion. Polling data on evolution and creationism supplied to the authors by the Gallup Library.

63. Polling data on evolution and creationism supplied to the authors by the Gallup Library; Richard Milner, *The Encyclopedia of Evolution: Humanity's Search for Its Origins* (New York: Facts on File, 1990), 100.

64. Polling data on evolution and creationism supplied to the authors by the Gallup Library; David W. Moore, "Americans Support Teaching Creationism As Well As Evolution in Public Schools," *Gallop Poll Releases* (1999), at www.gallup.com/poll/releases/pr990830.asp (12 November 2000).

65. Moore, "Americans Support Teaching Creationism As Well As Evolution."

66. Polling data on evolution and creationism supplied to the authors by the Gallup Library.

67. In February 2000, John Zogby's American values poll indicated that 64 percent of American adults believe creationism should be part of the public school curriculum, but as the DYG poll suggests, the issue is whether creationism is taught as belief or science. See Nancy Pearcey, "We're Not in Kansas Anymore," *Christianity Today* 44 (May 2000): 49.

68. People for the American Way, "Press Release," 2000, at www.pfaw.org/news/press//show.cgi?article=952702330 (7 November 2000); James Glanz, "Poll Finds That Support Is Strong for Teaching 2 Origin Theories," *New York Times*, 11 March 2000, A1; David Neff, "You Talk about an Evolution," *Christianity Today* 44 (May 2000): 7.

69. Council for Secular Humanism, "Religious Belief in America: A New Poll," *Free Inquiry* 16 (summer 1996): 36–37.

70. Council for Secular Humanism, "Religious Belief in America," 37.

71. Council for Secular Humanism, "Religious Belief in America," 37.

72. Edward J. Larson and Larry Witham, "Scientists Are Still Keeping the Faith," *Nature* 386 (April 1997): 435–436; Edward J. Larson and Larry Witham, "Leading Scientists Still Reject God," *Nature* 394 (July 1998): 313; Edward J. Larson and Larry Witham, "Scientists and Religion in America," *Scientific American* 281 (September 1999): 88–93; Karl

W. Giberson and Donald A. Yerxa, "Inherit the Monkey Trial: An Interview with Edward Larson," *Christianity Today* 44 (May 22, 2000): 50–51.

73. Council for Secular Humanism, "Religious Belief in America," 34.

74. Pinker, *How the Mind Works*, 554–557.

75. Miller, *Finding Darwin's God*, 167.

76. Berry, "Science and Religion," 11.

77. Peter W. Atkins, "Science and Religion: Rack or Featherbed: The Uncomfortable Supremacy of Science," *Science Progress* 83 (2000): 28–31, emphasis added.

78. Steven Weinberg, "The Future of Science, and the Universe," *New York Review of Books* 48 (November 2001): 63.

79. This almost Tocquevillian observation about American culture is elaborated in some detail in theologian Langdon Gilkey's fascinating account of his participation in the Arkansas creation–evolution trial: *Creationism on Trial: Evolution and God at Little Rock* (Charlottesville: University Press of Virginia, 1985, 1998), 161–208.

80. Steve Jones, "Evolution, Creation, and Controversy," in *The Cambridge Encyclopedia of Human Evolution*, ed. Steve Jones, Robert Martin, and David Pilbeam (Cambridge, U.K.: Cambridge University Press, 1992), 15.

81. A notable exception is Ronald L. Numbers, *The Creationists: The Evolution of Scientific Creationism* (Berkeley: University of California Press, 1993).

82. "Show 7: What about God?" *Evolution*, prod. WGBH/Nova Science Unit and Clear Blue Sky Productions, seven shows, 2001, videocassette.

3

Scientific Creationism:
The Biblical Dimension

Based on the polling data of the previous chapter, millions of Americans apparently believe that the world is about ten thousand years old. This "young-earth" position is obviously far removed from the findings of science, which put the age of the earth at about five billion years. *All* the data considered solid by the scientific community—astronomical measurements on stars, geological measurements of rock strata, radioactive dating of rocks, and evolutionary reconstructions of the history of life on the planet—converge on this calculation. Nevertheless, much to the chagrin of the academy and the established institutions of American intellectual culture, one of the most popular and aggressively promoted species of origins in America today claims that the universe is ten thousand years old. It is known as scientific creationism.

Contrary to popular opinion, young-earth creationism in its details is not based on a self-evident reading of the Bible, in the sense that the general conclusions of scientific creationism are themselves stated in the Bible. The Bible, for example, contains neither a date for creation nor any explicit suggestions for calculating one precisely. Nevertheless it can be done roughly without too much effort. One starts by creating a genealogical table starting with Adam, who is assumed to be the first man and created within days of the earth itself. Then one must carefully work through Adam's descendants up to the birth of Christ, assuming, of course, that the Bible provides the exhaustive genealogical information needed for such a calculation. Furthermore, there are a number of additional assumptions that must be made to determine the age of the earth from the Bible. The most obvious, and often challenged, of these regards the length of a day in the first chapter of Genesis, which states clearly that God's creative work was spread out over six days. Options range from viewing days as long

67

periods of time (the "day-age" view), to seeing them as literal days separated by long periods of time (the "intermittent-day" view), to understanding days to be a literary device and not a chronological sequence (the "framework hypothesis"). And there are subvarieties within each of these positions depending on how correlations are made between various features in the Bible and phenomena in nature, such as the antiquity of the human race.[1]

The widespread belief that the world is roughly ten thousand years old comes in large part, or even entirely, from the success of the scientific creationists in convincing people—mostly conservative Protestants—that their literal reading of the biblical creation accounts is the most legitimate and, curiously, the only valid one based on the scientific evidence. Prior to the 1961 publication of *The Genesis Flood*,[2] written by an Old Testament scholar and a hydraulic engineer, conservative Christians tended to favor the day-age and gap theories,[3] which allowed for a very old earth as determined by science. But, according to Ronald L. Numbers, over the course of a few decades, proselytizers for scientific creationism essentially "co-opted the generic creationist label for their hyperliteralist views, which only a half-century earlier had languished on the margins of American Fundamentalism."[4] The unquestioned leader of this scientific creationist movement is its founder, Henry M. Morris, a former engineering professor turned antievolutionist, who may well be one of the most effective grassroots communicators in America. Morris has written over fifty books[5] and founded the Institute for Creation Research, a journal (*Creation Research Society Quarterly*), and a college (Christian Heritage College). All of Morris's various enterprises are dedicated to the proposition that evolution is hopelessly flawed and scientific creationism provides a far better explanation of the evidence, both scientific and scriptural, that bears on the origins of the cosmos, earth, life, and humanity. His success has been so great that according to the polling data presented in the previous chapter approximately 40 percent of the American populace conceive of "creation" essentially on his terms.[6]

CREATION ACCORDING TO HENRY M. MORRIS

Critics make a serious, albeit common, mistake when they dismiss Morris's work as mindless drivel based on simple-minded acceptance of a fundamentalist reading of the Bible.[7] Morris's scientific creationism is an intricate and elaborate tapestry of interwoven arguments from the Bible, science, common sense, sociology, logic, philosophy, and theology. Another set of critics makes a different error by viewing creationism as the result of "bad science."[8] These critics miss the fact that the creationist understanding of origins is an integral part of a full-blown worldview that provides a paradigm for understanding, or at least addressing, virtually all aspects of human experience. This worldview nurtures and sustains millions of American fundamentalist Christians, and

Morris's work provides the essential elements of a foundational creation story. We will argue later that it is the comprehensive character of this worldview that accounts for the astonishing popularity and durability of some of its components—like the belief that the earth is ten thousand years old.

The intricacy of creationism makes a brief summary somewhat problematic.[9] We will pursue our investigation of creationism along three separate lines: biblical, scientific, and social—an approach in keeping with the creationists' own standard presentation recently made explicit with the publication of a three-volume boxed set *The Modern Creation Trilogy*.[10] We will examine each of these interlinked arguments in the next three chapters. Our guide will be Morris.

At its heart, scientific creationism is a conservative Christian movement. There are no secular thinkers in its ranks. And with very few exceptions,[11] all of the literature of the movement contains an explicitly religious dimension. The biblical dimension of the creationist argument is predicated on the assumption that the Bible is the "Word of God." It contains the account of God's actions in history through the creation of the world and humanity in the image of God, the establishment of a special relationship with the people of Israel, and the redemption of humanity through the birth, life, and death of God's son Jesus Christ. The Bible also points toward a final resolution of the tensions inherent in creation as God brings everything to a glorious close, destroying evil and establishing a new heaven and earth. Virtually every Christian denomination and sect maintains a belief that the Bible is a sacred text and in some sense represents the "Word of God." What makes the creationist interpretation distinctive is the insistence that the complex theological concept of "Word" should be understood, roughly, as "words." The Bible contains the "words" of God as if God dictated them to the writers. Creationists assume then that the story of creation in Genesis was given to human authors by God and cannot, therefore, contain any errors. The creation chapters of Genesis (Gen. 1:1–2:3, 2:3–5:1) provide "marvelous and accurate accounts of the actual events of the primal history of the universe." Moreover, Genesis gives data and information "far beyond those that science can determine," while offering "an intellectually satisfying framework within which to interpret the facts that science *can* determine."[12]

To understand the power and appeal of the biblical dimension of scientific creationism, it is necessary to appreciate how significant the Bible is in the life of millions of conservative Christians.[13] For these people, the Bible is *the* central text, and issues of biblical interpretation loom large. Individuals raised in this religious subculture literally "grow up" with the Bible in their homes and in their churches.[14] Their first picture books are likely to be illustrated biblical stories, and they will likely own a "child's Bible" by the time they have learned to read. Children in this tradition are encouraged to read the Bible daily with the goal of reading it cover to cover as many times as they can, memorizing key verses along the way. This emphasis on the centrality of the Bible in the believers' life will be reinforced by weekly Sunday school and church attendance, where they will receive biblical instruction based on a straightforward hermeneutic of literalism. This may well be supplemented by small group Bible studies that meet during the week, summer Bible schools and camps, and competitive Bible quizzing emphasizing fast recall of biblical details. By the time they finish high school, many conservative evangelical Christian youth possess a narrative and devotional familiarity with the Bible. They will know many of the stories and main characters of the Bible, but will likely focus on those passages that relate most closely to the temptations and struggles of their daily life. As a result, the Bible is revered as a timeless supernatural guide to help navigate the waters of an increasingly unfriendly modern world. The extraordinary importance of the Bible for this subculture is perhaps best symbolized by the discomfort that many conservative Christians feel when another book is physically placed on top of the Bible. The 1960 film classic *Inherit the Wind* captures this nicely in the closing scene, when agnostic lawyer Henry Drummond (based on Clarence Darrow and played by Spencer Tracy) balanced a Bible and Charles Darwin's *The Origin of Species by Means of Natural Selection* and then placed the Bible on top as he prepared to leave the courtroom.

In contemporary America, millions of conservative Christians still consider the Bible to be an utterly reliable sacred text. While written by humans, its actual author was God. Morris reflects this understanding when he contends that "[t]he only proper and true view of the inspiration of the Bible is that it is completely and literally inspired, altogether free of error and conveying exactly what God wished to say to man."[15] This view, known doctrinally as the "plenary verbal inspiration of Scriptures," suggests that a human author of a given biblical text may have produced a text that contained information he did not understand. Such information could be in the form of scientific insights that would have been incomprehensible to the writer, prophecies to be fulfilled later, or, more controversially, even secret mathematically encoded information.[16] According to Morris, all of the ancient biblical writings are "actual *firsthand accounts written by eyewitnesses.*" Consequently, Adam was the author of Genesis 2:3-5:1, and God himself, "either with His own 'finger'" (as in the Ten Commandments) or by "direct supernatural revelation" wrote Genesis 1:1–2:3.[17] It is to this thoroughly biblical culture that creationism speaks so loudly. For Morris to contend that his notions of creationism are explicitly taught in the Bible is the most compelling argument he can make to many conservative Christians.

The cardinal doctrine of scientific creationism is that this world and everything in it did not originate by evolutionary processes, but by a supernatural special creation. The sovereign God of the Bible created everything out of nothing by his "Word."[18] Morris makes his case for creationism using the "two models" approach: either everything has originated through "strictly naturalistic processes" or through "supernatural processes" associated with the creative activity of God. Since these supernatural processes are no longer operating, they are outside the explanatory purview of science.[19] The only way to learn about such processes would be via direct communication from God. Fortunately, this communication is exactly what God has provided in the Bible, primarily in Genesis—the "Book of Beginnings."

Starting with these assumptions and guided by the conviction that the Bible is the verbally inspired word of God that should be allowed to speak for itself, Morris builds an elaborate biblical model of creation revolving around "three great worldwide events." First is the six-day period of special creation and formation of all things, the completion and permanence of which are now manifest in the Law of the Conservation of Energy. Then comes "the Fall," which depicts the rebellion of the first man and woman and the resultant curse of God on all of humanity's dominion, formalized now in the Law of Increasing Entropy. Last is the world-destroying flood in the days of Noah, leaving the postdiluvian world largely under the "domain of natural uniformity."[20] Morris's biblical model of creation is constructed by placing a scientific interpretation on each of these creative acts of God. Before we look at these in more detail, it should be noted that while critics often react sharply to creationist claims that modern scientific laws are actually outlined in the Bible,[21] they fail to account for the nature of the creationists' assumptions about the Bible. If, in fact, the Bible had in some fashion been dictated by God, and if it were God's intention to explain how he created the world, then no modern reader should be surprised to find that the Bible makes reference to scientific developments that came much later. Such references would not, of course, be recorded in the technical mathematical language characteristic of contemporary science; they would be recorded in a manner consonant with the limited scientific understanding and vocabulary of the ancient reader.

THE SIX DAYS OF CREATION (GEN. 1:1–2:4)

To understand the creationist argument, there is no substitute for reading the relevant sections of the Bible directly:

> In the beginning God created the heaven and the earth. And the earth was without form, and void; and darkness was upon the face of the deep. And the Spirit of God moved upon the face of the waters. And God said, Let there be light: and there was light. And God saw the light, that it was good: and God divided the light from the darkness. And God called the light Day, and the darkness he called Night. And the evening and the morning were the first day.
>
> And God said, Let there be a firmament in the midst of the waters, and let it divide the waters from the waters. And God made the firmament, and divided the waters which were under the firmament from the waters which were above the firmament: and it was so. And God called the firmament Heaven. And the evening and the morning were the second day.
>
> And God said, Let the waters under the heaven be gathered together unto one place, and let the dry land appear: and it was so. And God called the dry land Earth; and the gathering together of the waters called he Seas: and God saw that it was

good. And God said, Let the earth bring forth grass, the herb yielding seed, and the fruit tree yielding fruit after his kind, whose seed is in itself, upon the earth: and it was so. And the earth brought forth grass, and herb yielding seed after his kind, and the tree yielding fruit, whose seed was in itself, after his kind: and God saw that it was good. And the evening and the morning were the third day.

And God said, Let there be lights in the firmament of the heaven to divide the day from the night; and let them be for signs, and for seasons, and for days, and years: And let them be for lights in the firmament of the heaven to give light upon the earth: and it was so. And God made two great lights; the greater light to rule the day, and the lesser light to rule the night: he made the stars also. And God set them in the firmament of the heaven to give light upon the earth, And to rule over the day and over the night, and to divide the light from the darkness: and God saw that it was good. And the evening and the morning were the fourth day.

And God said, Let the waters bring forth abundantly the moving creature that hath life, and fowl that may fly above the earth in the open firmament of heaven.

And God created great whales, and every living creature that moveth, which the waters brought forth abundantly, after their kind, and every winged fowl after his kind: and God saw that it was good. And God blessed them, saying, Be fruitful, and multiply, and fill the waters in the seas, and let fowl multiply in the earth. And the evening and the morning were the fifth day.

And God said, Let the earth bring forth the living creature after his kind, cattle, and creeping thing, and beast of the earth after his kind: and it was so. And God made the beast of the earth after his kind, and cattle after their kind, and every thing that creepeth upon the earth after his kind: and God saw that it was good.

And God said, Let us make man in our image, after our likeness: and let them have dominion over the fish of the sea, and over the fowl of the air, and over the cattle, and over all the earth, and over every creeping thing that creepeth upon the earth. So God created man in his own image, in the image of God created he him; male and female created he them. And God blessed them, and God said unto them, Be fruitful, and multiply, and replenish the earth, and subdue it: and have dominion over the fish of the sea, and over the fowl of the air, and over every living thing that moveth upon the earth. And God said, Behold, I have given you every herb bearing seed, which is upon the face of all the earth, and every tree, in the which is the fruit of a tree yielding seed; to you it shall be for meat. And to every beast of the earth, and to every fowl of the air, and to every thing that creepeth upon the earth, wherein there is life, I have given every green herb for meat: and it was so. And God saw every thing that he had made, and, behold, it was very good. And the evening and the morning were the sixth day.

Thus the heavens and the earth were finished, and all the host of them. And on the seventh day God ended his work which he had made; and he rested on the seventh day from all his work which he had made. And God blessed the seventh day, and sanctified it: because that in it he had rested from all his work which God created and made. These are the generations of the heavens and of the earth when they were created.

Many translations exist, but those most frequently used by creationists include the classic King James Version and the more recent New International Version.

Genesis 1:1–2:4 forms the textual support for the creationists' "first great world-wide event." Morris walks his readers through the six days of creation, explicating the modern scientific meaning of the ancient Hebrew text as follows:

Day One: Energizing of the physical elements of the cosmos
Day Two: Formation of the atmosphere and hydrosphere of the earth
Day Three: Formation of the lithosphere and biosphere of the earth
Day Four: Formation of the astrosphere and its heavenly bodies
Day Five: Formation of life in the atmosphere and hydrosphere
Day Six: Formation of life for the lithosphere and biosphere
Day Seven: Rest from the completed work of creating and making all things[22]

The creation work done by God during this first week of seven twenty-four-hour days completes the initial great worldwide event on which the creationist model is based. The universe is made fully functional, perfect, and prepared for the first humans, Adam and Eve, to commence their mandate from God to populate the earth. The new universe, according to Morris, is also created with "an appearance of history." And in this world, there was no carnivorous activity, no bloodshed, no death. All creatures were herbivores, living on plants which Morris does not consider to be "alive" in the same sense that animals are alive. God could not possibly have employed "such a sadistic process as survival of the fittest, struggle for existence, and natural selection to create and maintain His 'very good' masterpiece."[23]

The perfection and integral harmony of this newly created world is reflected in the First Law of Thermodynamics, the law of conservation of energy, as well as other physical laws that both conserve initial quantities and guarantee orderly activity.[24] This world, which God had pronounced in Genesis 1:31 as "very good" was, however, "different from the present world in many significant ways."[25] Morris develops this more fully in the second volume of the *Creation Trilogy*. At this early stage of his argument, it is enough to say that he considers the conservation principle to be "clearly set forth by the fact of a *completed* creation which is now being *sustained* by its Creator." Morris goes on further to contend that, according to both Scripture and the First Law of Thermodynamics, nothing is now being created. Consequently, scientific study of present processes cannot reveal anything about God's creative processes, which are now no longer operative.[26] We will return to this controversial claim in the next chapter.

THE FALL OF MAN AND THE CURSE OF GOD (GEN. 3:3–24)

Now the serpent was more subtil than any beast of the field which the LORD God had made. And he said unto the woman, Yea, hath God said, Ye shall not eat of every tree of the garden? And the woman said unto the serpent, We may eat of the fruit of the trees of the garden: But of the fruit of the tree which is in the midst of the garden, God hath said, Ye shall not eat of it, neither shall ye touch it, lest ye die. And the serpent said unto the woman, Ye shall not surely die: For God doth know that in the day ye eat thereof, then your eyes shall be opened, and ye shall be as gods, knowing good and evil. And when the woman saw that the tree was good for food, and that it was pleasant to the eyes, and a tree to be desired to make one wise, she took of the fruit thereof, and did eat, and gave also unto her husband with her; and he did eat. And the eyes of them both were opened, and they knew that they were naked; and they sewed fig leaves together, and made themselves aprons.

And they heard the voice of the LORD God walking in the garden in the cool of the day: and Adam and his wife hid themselves from the presence of the LORD God amongst the trees of the garden. And the LORD God called unto Adam, and said unto him, Where art thou? And he said, I heard thy voice in the garden, and I was afraid, because I was naked; and I hid myself. And he said, Who told thee that thou wast naked? Hast thou eaten of the tree, whereof I commanded thee that thou shouldest not eat? And the man said, The woman whom thou gavest to be with me, she gave me of the tree, and I did eat. And the LORD God said unto the woman, What is this that thou hast done? And the woman said, The serpent beguiled me, and I did eat. And the LORD God said unto the serpent, Because thou hast done this, thou art cursed above all cattle, and above every beast of the field; upon thy belly shalt thou go, and dust shalt thou eat all the days of thy life:

And I will put enmity between thee and the woman, and between thy seed and her seed; it shall bruise thy head, and thou shalt bruise his heel. Unto the woman he said, I will greatly multiply thy sorrow and thy conception; in sorrow thou shalt bring forth children; and thy desire shall be to thy husband, and he shall rule over thee. And unto Adam he said, Because thou hast hearkened unto the voice of thy wife, and hast eaten of the tree, of which I commanded thee, saying, Thou shalt not eat of it: cursed is the ground for thy sake; in sorrow shalt thou eat of it all the days of thy life; Thorns also and thistles shall it bring forth to thee; and thou shalt eat the herb of the field; In the sweat of thy face shalt thou eat bread, till thou return unto the ground; for out of it wast thou taken: for dust thou art, and unto dust shalt thou return.

And Adam called his wife's name Eve; because she was the mother of all living. Unto Adam also and to his wife did the LORD God make coats of skins, and clothed them.

And the LORD God said, Behold, the man is become as one of us, to know good and evil: and now, lest he put forth his hand, and take also of the tree of life, and eat, and live for ever: Therefore the LORD God sent him forth from the garden of Eden, to till the ground from whence he was taken. So he drove out the man; and he placed at the east of the garden of Eden Cherubims, and a flaming sword which turned every way, to keep the way of the tree of life.

Morris, of course, must account for the profound differences between the newly created world and our own. Many of the most significant features of the present world were not part of God's original creative intent and, therefore, were not present at the creation. They were introduced into the creation by the decision of Adam and Eve to disobey God's command to abstain from eating the fruit from "the tree of the knowledge of good and evil." Thus, the Edenic Fall is central to the creationist model.

When the first human couple sinned, they destroyed the perfection of the creation and introduced death into it. Such a claim, so familiar to conservative Christians, entails some rather agile verbal gymnastics, to explain how human beings—even if they were vegetarians—could escape the food chain prior to "that unfortunate afternoon in the Garden."[27]

Death came into the world only when sin came into the world (Rom. 5:12, 8:22). Man would have lived forever had he not sinned, and so, apparently, would have the animals (at least all those possessing the *nephesh*, the "soul"). Plant life, of course, is not conscious life, but only very complex replicating chemicals. The eating of fruits and herbs was not to be considered "death" of the plant materials since they had not created "life" (in the sense of consciousness) anyhow.[28]

Because of Adam's sin, a creation intended to function without death had to be modified dramatically to accommodate this new reality. Some formerly vegetarian animals had to develop new teeth to enable them to kill and chew other animals, new bodies to enable them to catch prey, new enzymes to digest flesh, and so on.[29]

In the creationist model, sin has such catastrophic physical consequences for the human and nonhuman world that the laws of nature are changed in spectacular fashion. After the Fall, the Second Law of Thermodynamics is superimposed on the first law—conservation of energy—installed by God at the creation. The second law states that while energy is never destroyed, it becomes less available for further work. All processes manifest a tendency to deterioration and disintegration with a net increase in entropy or disorder. "Things fall apart"; they wear out, get old, and deteriorate. Morris depicts the second law as an "intruder into the divine economy, not a part of either the original creation or God's plan for His eternal kingdom." The second law is today one of the most general laws in all of science.[30] It is the law that facilitates almost all of the chemical reactions that occur, so the creationist understanding is that when Adam sinned, even basic chemistry was dramatically changed.

Sin has always played an important role in Christian theology. Adam's free choice to sin is widely used to explain how an initially "good" creation presents so much that is "bad" to us. A central Christian belief across the centuries has been that Christ died to save humans from their sins. A popular interpretation of this core Christian belief—one that can be traced to St. Paul in the fifth chapter of his Letter to the Romans—is that Jesus Christ is the "second Adam," who corrects the damage done by the first Adam and redeems the fallen creation. Theologians make highly nuanced connections between creation and redemption, and in some theological schemes these two notions are inextricably linked. To be sure, not all of these theological models demand that the story of the Fall in

Genesis be interpreted literally, but a literal interpretation, based on a straight-forward reading of the texts, continues to be very convincing to millions of conservative Christians.[31] So the literal Fall of Adam not only plays a crucial role in the theological system of conservative evangelicals, but its importance is also essential to the creationist understanding of origins. God responded to Adam's sin with "the curse." In the King James Version, Genesis 3:17, 19 reads: "Cursed is the ground for thy sake . . . for dust thou art and unto dust shalt thou return." In the New Testament, this curse is called the "bondage of corruption" (or "bondage of decay"), and St. Paul describes the whole creation as "groaning" and "travailing in pain" (Rom. 8:20–22). Creationists, like Morris, conclude therefore that "[t]his universal 'bondage of decay' can be nothing less than the universal principle that scientists have finally formalized as the Second Law of Thermodynamics."[32]

THE GREAT FLOOD (GEN. 6:11–8:19)

The earth also was corrupt before God, and the earth was filled with violence. And God looked upon the earth, and, behold, it was corrupt; for all flesh had corrupted his way upon the earth. And God said unto Noah, The end of all flesh is come before me; for the earth is filled with violence through them; and, behold, I will destroy them with the earth. Make thee an ark of gopher wood; rooms shalt thou make in the ark, and shalt pitch it within and without with pitch. And this is the fashion which thou shalt make it of: The length of the ark shall be three hundred cubits, the breadth of it fifty cubits, and the height of it thirty cubits. A window shalt thou make to the ark, and in a cubit shalt thou finish it above; and the door of the ark shalt thou set in the side thereof; with lower, second, and third stories shalt thou make it. And, behold, I, even I, do bring a flood of waters upon the earth, to destroy all flesh, wherein is the breath of life, from under heaven; and every thing that is in the earth shall die. But with thee will I establish my covenant; and thou shalt come into the ark, thou, and thy sons, and thy wife, and thy sons' wives with thee. And of every living thing of all flesh, two of every sort shalt thou bring into the ark, to keep them alive with thee; they shall be male and female. Of fowls after their kind, and of cattle after their kind, of every creeping thing of the earth after his kind, two of every sort shall come unto thee, to keep them alive. And take thou unto thee of all food that is eaten, and thou shalt gather it to thee; and it shall be for food for thee, and for them. Thus did Noah; according to all that God commanded him, so did he.

And the LORD said unto Noah, Come thou and all thy house into the ark; for thee have I seen righteous before me in this generation. Of every clean beast thou shalt take to thee by sevens, the male and his female: and of beasts that are not clean by two, the male and his female. Of fowls also of the air by sevens, the male and the female; to keep seed alive upon the face of all the earth. For yet seven days, and I will cause it to rain upon the earth forty days and forty nights; and every living substance that I have made will I destroy from off the face of the earth. And Noah did according unto all that the LORD commanded him.

And Noah was six hundred years old when the flood of waters was upon the earth. And Noah went in, and his sons, and his wife, and his sons' wives with him, into the ark, because of the waters of the flood. Of clean beasts, and of beasts that are not clean, and of fowls, and of every thing that creepeth upon the earth, There went in two and two unto Noah into the ark, the male and the female, as God had commanded Noah. And it came to pass after seven days, that the waters of the flood were upon the earth. In the six hundredth year of Noah's life, in the second month, the seventeenth day of the month, the same day were all the fountains of the great deep broken up, and the windows of heaven were opened. And the rain was upon the earth forty days and forty nights. In the selfsame day entered Noah, and Shem, and Ham, and Japheth, the sons of Noah, and Noah's wife, and the three wives of his sons with them, into the ark; They, and every beast after his kind, and all the cattle after their kind, and every creeping thing that creepeth upon the earth after his kind, and every fowl after his kind, every bird of every sort. And they went in unto Noah into the ark, two and two of all flesh, wherein is the breath of life. And they that went in, went in male and female of all flesh, as God had commanded him: and the LORD shut him in.

And the flood was forty days upon the earth; and the waters increased, and bare up the ark, and it was lift up above the earth. And the waters prevailed, and were increased greatly upon the earth; and the ark went upon the face of the waters. And the waters prevailed exceedingly upon the earth; and all the high hills, that were under the whole heaven, were covered. Fifteen cubits upward did the waters prevail; and the mountains were covered. And all flesh died that moved upon the earth, both of fowl, and of cattle, and of beast, and of every creeping thing that creepeth upon the earth, and every man: All in whose nostrils was the breath of life, of all that was in the dry land, died. And every living substance was destroyed which was upon the face of the ground, both man, and cattle, and the creeping things, and the fowl of the heaven; and they were destroyed from the earth: and Noah only remained alive, and they that were with him in the ark. And the waters prevailed upon the earth an hundred and fifty days.

And God remembered Noah, and every living thing, and all the cattle that was with him in the ark: and God made a wind to pass over the earth, and the waters asswaged; The fountains also of the deep and the windows of heaven were stopped, and the rain from heaven was restrained; And the waters returned from off the earth continually: and after the end of the hundred and fifty days the waters were abated. And the ark rested in the seventh month, on the seventeenth day of the month, upon the mountains of Ararat. And the waters decreased continually until the tenth month: in the tenth month, on the first day of the month, were the tops of the mountains seen.

And it came to pass at the end of forty days, that Noah opened the window of the ark which he had made: And he sent forth a raven, which went forth to and fro, until the waters were dried up from off the earth. Also he sent forth a dove from him, to see if the waters were abated from off the face of the ground; But the dove found no rest for the sole of her foot, and she returned unto him into the ark, for the waters were on the face of the whole earth: then he put forth his hand, and took her, and pulled her in unto him into the ark. And he stayed yet other seven days; and again he sent forth the dove out of the ark; And the dove came in to him in the evening; and, lo, in her mouth was an olive leaf pluckt off: so Noah knew that the waters were abated from off the earth. And he stayed yet other seven days; and sent forth the dove; which returned not again unto him any more.

And it came to pass in the six hundredth and first year, in the first month, the first day of the month, the waters were dried up from off the earth: and Noah removed the covering of the ark, and looked, and, behold, the face of the ground was dry. And in the second month, on the seven and twentieth day of the month, was the earth dried. And God spake unto Noah, saying, Go forth of the ark, thou, and thy wife, and thy sons, and thy sons' wives with thee. Bring forth with thee every living thing that is with thee, of all flesh, both of fowl, and of cattle, and of every creeping thing that creepeth upon the earth; that they may breed abundantly in the earth, and be fruitful, and multiply upon the earth. And Noah went forth, and his sons, and his wife, and his sons' wives with him: Every beast, every creeping thing, and every fowl, and whatsoever creepeth upon the earth, after their kinds, went forth out of the ark.

The third pillar of scientific creationism is the devastating worldwide flood at the time of Noah. Consistent with his interpretation of the Creation and the Fall, Morris draws scientific implications from a literal reading of the account of the Flood provided in Genesis 6:11–8:19 . God, accordingly, sent the flood waters to destroy a human race that had become wicked. The Flood was not localized, but was a worldwide cataclysm of such magnitude and intensity that it killed all living creatures save those Noah rescued in his ark. Genesis mentions torrents of water falling from the skies and vast reservoirs of water—"the fountains of the deep"—opening up. Morris extrapolates that all this was accompanied by violent tidal actions and great gusting winds that would have generated massive geological disruptions, reshaping the entire topography of the earth.[33] A more detailed examination of the Flood will appear in the next chapter when we explore the scientific dimensions of creationism. For now, we need only suggest how Morris's approach honors a literalist reading of the Bible, despite the challenges posed by science.

The Flood, of course, has been the source of considerable discussion ever since the early nineteenth century, when its historicity was challenged by the fledgling science of geology. It constitutes an excellent case study in how biblical interpretation can be adjusted to accommodate extrabiblical discoveries.[34] The basic problem with the biblical account was that it seemingly could not be reconciled with investigations of certain portions of the earth's surface that appeared to have lain undisturbed since long before the Flood. There were two ways to deal with this difficulty while adhering to the historicity of the biblical account. Either the Flood was a localized event[35] that did not cover the entire earth, or the Flood was worldwide but "tranquil" in such a way as to come and go without leaving any traces.[36]

Morris, however, is unpersuaded by such accommodationist solutions, which compromise the strict literal meaning of the Bible to adjust to the discoveries of science. To those who would argue that the Flood was local, Morris points out that

Genesis 7:19–20 says that the "Flood covered the tops of the highest mountains" for at least nine months—hardly a localized event! Moreover, why construct an ark? If the Flood were a limited, regional affair, then why spend a century preparing a huge vessel to carry animals from the whole world?[37] Furthermore, Morris argues, if Jesus Christ, the Son of God, referred to a flood that destroyed "them all," then it must have happened.[38] And to those who suggest that the Flood was tranquil, he responds that floods are anything but tranquil events. *"The idea of a worldwide, year-long 'tranquil' flood is hydrologically and geophysically absurd,"* Morris notes, *"about like a tranquil worldwide explosion!"*[39]

While the biblical framework for scientific creationism is based on a literalist interpretation of three great events—the six-day period of special creation, the Fall, and the Great Flood—Morris develops a variety of other creationist arguments both directly and indirectly from scripture. He assigns the Tower of Babel account from Genesis 11 importance only slightly less than that of the Flood. Babel, according to Morris, was the "primeval source of all spiritual adultery and idolatry in the world's false religions." And God dealt with this postdiluvian rebellion decisively by confusing the languages and dispersing the peoples throughout the world. Morris offers the Tower of Babel narrative as the explanation for the origin of languages and the emergence of distinctive human physiological characteristics.[40]

A theme running through Morris's work is that creationism best accounts for what we know from a straightforward reading of scripture. Consequently, he is as much concerned with developing arguments against evolution and those species of origins that accommodate to evolutionary theory as he is in favor of creationism. There can be no compromise for Morris. Bible-believing Christians who flirt with notions of progressive creation and theistic evolution are courting hermeneutical disaster. If the early chapters of Genesis are interpreted in allegorical or poetic fashion in order to avoid "scientific embarrassment," the entire biblical system of truth is undermined, according to Morris. Such exegetical strategies not only "invalidate" the accounts of the Creation, Fall, Flood, and Tower of Babel, they also make vulnerable core Christian doctrines like the virgin birth and resurrection of Christ.[41] Based on this line of reasoning, Morris admonishes Christians "either to believe God's Word all the way, or not at all."[42]

The Bible cannot be reconciled with evolutionary thinking on many grounds. For instance, the Bible teaches that God created "all things as He wanted them to be, each 'kind' with its own particular structure." And while the Hebrew word *min* that is translated as *kind* does not have precise meaning, Morris contends that the Bible is clear that God created distinct categories of life that cannot evolve from other kinds. Moreover, the biblical account is of a finished creation, not one that continues into the present. And a good, loving, powerful, and purposive God would not use evolutionary processes that take millions of years, unfold randomly, and utilize violently cruel methods.[43] "Surely an omniscient God could devise a better process of creation than the random, wasteful, inefficient trial-and-error charade of the so-called geological ages," Morris argues forcefully, "and certainly a loving, merciful God would never be guilty of a creative process that would involve the suffering and death of multitudes of innocent animals in the process of arriving at man millions of years later."[44] (The widespread destruction of life in the Flood was due to sin, which was not a part of God's original plan of creation.)

This brief survey of the scriptural dimension of scientific creationism—with its emphasis on Creation, Fall, and Flood—suggests that at its core creationism is a biblical movement. The Bible, interpreted literally, is its primary source and authority. For millions of people steeped in a thoroughly biblical religious tradition, creationism is attractive because it takes the Bible at face value and places its authority above that of science or other secular authority. Creationism, especially in the hands of a skillful communicator like Morris, can be made to appear integral to the larger theological structure of Christianity. Without its precepts, other, more central doctrines, like original sin and redemption may seem somewhat incoherent.[45] Indeed, scientific creationists like Morris consider biblical creation as the most important of all of the Bible's teaching. Because it is foundational, the "whole structure of God's revelation" is built on it.[46] But scientific creationism is not just a biblical movement. Scientific creationism is a highly technical species of origins that weaves hermeneutical and theological assumptions with scientific notions into a conceptual fabric that is very durable in conservative Protestant circles. We will turn our attention to the highly controversial scientific arguments of the creationists in the next chapter.

NOTES

1. See Robert C. Newman, "Progressive Creation," in *Three Views on Creation and Evolution*, ed. J. P. Moreland and John Mark Reynolds (Grand Rapids, Mich.: Zondervan, 1999), 106.

2. John C. Whitcomb Jr. and Henry M. Morris, *The Genesis Flood: The Biblical Record and Its Scientific Implications* (Philadelphia: Presbyterian and Reformed Publishing, 1961).

3. The gap theory posits a major gap between the first two verses of Genesis, wherein a series of catastrophes, possibly resulting from Satan's rebellion, are inserted.

4. Ronald L. Numbers, *Darwinism Comes to America* (Cambridge, Mass.: Harvard University Press, 1998), 5–6. Numbers's research suggests that at the end of the nineteenth century, most biblical literalists accepted the antiquity of life on Earth. Moreover, the so-called young-earth position, which attributed the fossil record to effects of Noah's Flood, was largely a Seventh-Day Adventist position not in the mainstream of conservative Christianity.

5. Including Whitcomb and Morris, *Genesis Flood*; Henry M. Morris, *The Twilight of Evolution* (Grand Rapids, Mich.: Baker, 1964); and Henry M. Morris, ed., *Scientific Creationism*, 3d ed. (Grand Rapids, Mich.: Baker, 1998).

6. We concur with Numbers's conclusion that an explanation for the dramatic rise in the popularity of scientific creationism is difficult to document. He is skeptical of claims that scientific creationism's appeal is to the uneducated (25 percent of those who profess belief in a recent special creation have college degrees) or culturally alienated (Pentecostals show less enthusiasm for scientific creationism than fundamentalists). In the light of the conservative Christian view that contemporary America was adrift morally and needed to return to a more Bible-centered faith, Numbers's suggestion seems reasonable that the creationists' insistence that the Bible be given a higher warrant of authority than science resonated with conservative Christians who took the Bible as literally as possible. See Numbers, *Darwinism Comes to America*, 6–7.

7. Dismissive comments about creationism abound. For example, see Steve Jones, *Darwin's Ghost: The Origin of Species Updated* (New York: Random House, 1999), 2; George Johnson, *Fire in the Mind: Science, Faith, and the Search for Order* (New York: Vintage, 1995), 313; John Brockman, *The Third Culture* (New York: Simon and Schuster, 1995), 66; Richard Dawkins, *The Blind Watchmaker: Why the Evidence of Evolution Reveals a Universe without Design* (New York: Norton, 1986, 1996), 251; Stephen Jay Gould, *Rocks of Ages: Science and Religion in the Fullness of Life* (New York: Ballantine, 1999), 149.

8. A good example of this approach is Philip Kitcher, *Abusing Science: The Case against Creationism* (Cambridge: MIT Press, 1982), 4–5, 48–50, and *passim*.

9. By far the best history of scientific creationism is Ronald L. Numbers, *The Creationists: The Evolution of Scientific Creationism* (Berkeley: University of California Press, 1993).

10. Henry M. Morris and John D. Morris, *The Modern Creation Trilogy*, 3 vols. (Green Forest, Ark.: Master, 1996). Since Henry Morris is the recognized leader of contemporary creation science and almost all of the arguments offered in the *Modern Creation Trilogy* have appeared in his earlier works, we will refer to Henry Morris as the author of this series, though the books' coauthor is Morris's son John. John Morris holds a doctorate in geological engineering from the University of Oklahoma and since the mid-1980s has assumed increasing administrative authority in the Institute for Creation Research. See Numbers, *Creationists*, 290.

11. Not all critics of Darwinism are creation scientists. British science journalist Richard Milton, for instance, has written a scientific critique of evolutionary theory that does not rely at all on the Bible or belief in God. Milton insists that he is definitely not a creationist, since he does not have "any religious beliefs of any kind." Moreover, he suggests that anyone, like himself, daring to register skepticism about Darwinism is likely to be "subjected to a campaign of vilification." See Richard Milton, *Shattering the Myths of Darwinism* (Rochester, Vt.: Park Street, 1997), 265–272.

12. Morris and Morris, *Modern Creation Trilogy*, 1:13–14.

13. Contemporary conservative Protestantism is generally divided into two somewhat overlapping groups: evangelicals and fundamentalists. Evangelical Christians, according to historian George M. Marsden, profess "complete confidence in the Bible and [are] preoccupied with the message of God's salvation of sinners through the death of Jesus Christ." Fundamentalism is a type of "militantly anti-modernist Protestant evangelicalism" that emerged in the early twentieth century and is marked today by a strict biblical literalism. See George M. Marsden, *Fundamentalism and American Culture: The Shaping of Twentieth-Century Evangelicalism, 1870–1925* (New York: Oxford University Press, 1980), 3–8.

14. The conservative Christian devotion to the Bible resembles that of Orthodox Jews to the Torah, although the latter devote much more time to its serious study—both textual and the rabbinical tradition of interpretation.

15. Henry M. Morris, *Many Infallible Proofs: Practical and Useful Evidences of Christianity* (San Diego: Creation-Life Publishers, 1974, 1996), 164.

16. Regarding modern scientific insights, Morris understands certain biblical passages to contain allusions to planetary orbits, radio waves, atomic disintegration, the equivalence of mass and energy ($E = mc^2$), and a number of other modern scientific ideas from the fields of hydrology, geology, astronomy, meteorology, biology, and physics. For example, he sees anticipatory evidence for mass–energy equivalence in Hebrews 1:3 and Colossians 1:17. See Morris, *Many Infallible Proofs*, 235–243. Discerning how modern scientific notions might be anticipated in the Bible is not unique to fundamentalist Christians. For example, Hugh Ross, an old-earth creationist who accepts the scientific claim the earth is billions of years old, speculates that the biblical passages that refer to God "stretching out the heavens" (e.g., Job 9:8, Psalm 104:2, Isaiah 49:22) anticipate the Big Bang Theory. See Hugh Ross, "Facing up to Big Bang Challenges," *Facts for Faith* (2001): 5, 44.

17. Morris and Morris, *Modern Creation Trilogy*, 1:15–16.

18. Morris and Morris, *Modern Creation Trilogy*, 1:12.

19. Morris and Morris, *Modern Creation Trilogy*, 1:9.

20. Morris and Morris, *Modern Creation Trilogy*, 1:33.

21. For example, see Laurie R. Godfrey, ed., *Scientists Confront Creationism* (New York: Norton, 1983); xxiv–xxv; Karl W. Giberson, *Worlds Apart: The Unholy War between Religion and Science* (Kansas City: Beacon Hill, 1993), 138–154.

22. Morris and Morris, *Modern Creation Trilogy*, 1:18. For a more detailed analysis of the biblical model of creation, see Henry M. Morris, *The Genesis Record* (Green Forest, Ark.: Master, 1976), a tour de force of fundamentalist exegesis. The publication of this volume in 1976 demonstrated the stature that Morris had achieved among conservative evangelicals. A limited number of leather-bound, autographed editions were sold at $100 apiece.

23. Morris and Morris, *Modern Creation Trilogy*, 1:20.

24. There are a great many conservation laws in physics. Some conserve familiar quantities like momentum, angular momentum, and charge, while others conserve more exotic quantities like "baryon number" or "strangeness."

25. Morris and Morris, *Modern Creation Trilogy*, 1:20.

26. Morris and Morris, *Modern Creation Trilogy*, 1:24–25.

27. The phrase is Father Richard John Neuhaus's made in conversation with Peggy Noonan in the PBS series: Peggy Noonan, *On Values: Talking with Peggy Noonan: Faith*, prod. and dir. Michael Epstein, sixty min., Films for the Humanities and Sciences, 1995, videocassette.

28. Morris and Morris, *Modern Creation Trilogy*, 1:21.

29. Morris makes this argument implicitly in Morris and Morris, *Modern Creation Trilogy*, 1:103–108. For a more developed treatment, see Morris, *Genesis Record*, 125–126.

30. Morris and Morris, *Modern Creation Trilogy*, 1:24–28.

31. Some liberal theologians who reject the notion of a historic fall retain the symbol of fallenness to account for the understanding that something is amiss in the human condition. See, for example, Langdon Gilkey, *Nature, Reality, and the Sacred: The Nexus of*

Science and Religion (Minneapolis: Fortress, 1993), 22–24; see also Emil Brunner, *Man in Revolt: A Christian Anthropology* (Philadelphia: Westminster, 1947), 129–133; Holmes Rolston III, *Genes, Genesis and God: Values and Their Origins in Natural and Human History* (Cambridge: Cambridge University Press, 1999), 214.

32. Morris and Morris, *Modern Creation Trilogy*, 1:27.

33. Morris and Morris, *Modern Creation Trilogy*, 1:28–29, 65–72.

34. See Davis A. Young, *The Biblical Flood: A Case Study of the Church's Response to Extrabiblical Evidence* (Grand Rapids, Mich.: Eerdmans, 1995).

35. Recently, underwater archeologists announced the discovery of a man-made structure three hundred feet below the surface of the Black Sea, "providing dramatic new evidence of an apocalyptic flood . . . that may have inspired the biblical story of Noah." The Flood, as understood by some contemporary geologists, was certainly cataclysmic, but it was a regional, not a global, affair. Columbia University geologists William Ryan and Walter Pitman posit that the Black Sea was formed seventy-five hundred years ago when water from melting glaciers raised the level of the Mediterranean to the point where it spilled over "the natural dam at the Bosporus" and into an existing fresh water lake in a torrent two hundred times the volume of Niagara Falls. The rising waters of what would become the Black Sea submerged thousands of square miles. See Guy Gugliotta, "Black Sea May Hold Mystery of Flood," *Boston Globe*, 13 September 2000, A21.

36. There are, of course, other possibilities, such as the view that the story of the Flood in Genesis does not describe a historical event and should be interpreted only as an "object lesson" that warns of the consequences of sin. Such interpretations, however, cannot be reconciled with a literalist reading of the Bible.

37. Morris and Morris, *Modern Creation Trilogy*, 1:67. An appendix to Morris's *Genesis Record* lists one hundred reasons why the Flood should be considered a "true global cataclysm." The first sixty-four are arguments from the Bible. See Morris, *Genesis Record*, 683–686.

38. Not surprisingly, Morris uses ten Gospel passages to argue that Jesus was a creationist. See Morris and Morris, *Modern Creation Trilogy*, 1:139–141.

39. Morris and Morris, *Modern Creation Trilogy*, 1:69, emphasis in the original.

40. Morris and Morris, *Modern Creation Trilogy*, 1:31.

41. Morris and Morris, *Modern Creation Trilogy*, 1:61–64.

42. Morris and Morris, *Modern Creation Trilogy*, 1:95.

43. Morris and Morris, *Modern Creation Trilogy*, 1:29–40.

44. Morris and Morris, *Modern Creation Trilogy*, 1:76.

45. Many Christians' beliefs are informed by "systematic theologies." These structures of interlocking theological notions attempt to achieve coherence by relating different ideas to each other. The demands of coherence often lead theologians to reject certain plausible interpretations of biblical passages because these interpretations do not fit with other ideas. For example, many conservative theologians demand that there must be some historical basis for the Fall of Adam so that God's original creation can be deemed perfect and without sin. Even though Adam himself may be considered a mythological figure, the event of the Fall is not. This type of systematization promotes a certain robustness in the overall framework of ideas. Weaknesses of specific notions are mitigated by the important role they play in a system, which taken as a whole, is less susceptible to criticism. Creationism is an excellent example of this.

46. Morris and Morris, *Modern Creation Trilogy*, 1:113.

4

❖

Scientific Creationism:
The Scientific Dimension

While scientific creationism is first and foremost a movement grounded in the authority of the Bible, creationists expend most of their efforts supporting the scientific pillar of their model. Creationists are essentially "preaching to the conservative Christian choir" when they make the case that their reading of the Bible is the most faithful. A common-sense reading of Genesis, while problematic for many theologians, is certainly consistent with the general features of the creationist model. In contrast, the challenges of establishing the scientific dimensions of creationism are more formidable. It is no small matter to refute the established scientific paradigm for understanding the history of life on this planet.

In brief, the creationists' scientific argument is based on the assumption that "true science" cannot be in disagreement with the account set out in the Bible, since God is clearly the author of both. (This is the same argument that Galileo Galilei made as he attempted to reconcile the new astronomy of his day with the Bible.) Creationists then proceed to lay out a straightforward dichotomy, arguing that the world is either the product of divine creation as described in the Bible or it is the product of naturalistic evolutionary processes as described by contemporary mainstream science. Having reduced the range of choices in this way, they create a logical framework in which weaknesses in evolutionary theory become evidentiary support for creationism or at the least warrant for claiming that creationism is a defensible scientific alternative to evolution. Consequently, most of their "scientific" argument is focused on refuting the theory of evolution, a task they believe they have accomplished.

Once again, Henry M. Morris will be our primary guide through this aspect of scientific creationism. He states his case in volume two of *The Modern Creation*

Trilogy early on with astounding boldness: "It is not too much to say that there is literally no scientific evidence whatever—past, present, or future—for any real evolution. Belief in evolution is strictly a matter of faith." Morris continues: "[E]volution and creation are on the same ground. Both must be seen with the eye of faith, because neither can be seen taking place with our physical eyes. But this very fact is a strong argument *for* creation and *against* evolution. One could very legitimately *predict*, from the creation model, that we cannot now see creation taking place, since it is postulated as a supernatural event completed in the past."[1]

Since this paragraph summarizes much of the creationists' scientific approach, we need to examine it carefully. Morris has been stating that creation and evolution are on the "same ground" for over a half-century now, and it has become a staple of creationist argumentation.[2] Scientific creationism, like evolution, is a model for understanding origins, so the argument goes, and both should be "on the table" in science discussions and especially in classrooms. When both models are held up to the same standards of evaluation, fair-minded people (high school students, in this case) will conclude that evolution is fatally flawed and creationism is superior.[3] Creationists are fond of quoting a fictitious statement attributed to Clarence Darrow, who in response to Tennessee's decision to outlaw the teaching of evolution, was said to have quipped that "[i]t is bigotry for public schools to teach only one theory of origins."[4] The bigotry to which Darrow allegedly referred was, of course, a bigotry that excluded evolution. From the creationist perspective, bigotry has done an about-face and now excludes creationism.

One other aspect of the "two models approach" should be noted. The basic creationist philosophy of science is reflected in the statement: "Both [creation and evolution] must be seen with the eye of faith, because neither can be seen taking place with our physical eyes."[5] Science, according to Morris, is "[t]he systematic observation and correlation of present physical relationships and natural processes involving the properties of matter, the forces of nature and the phenomena of life." From this definition, the study of origins—whether by creation or evolution—is outside of the scope of science.[6] This notion of science has its roots in the writings of Francis Bacon (1561–1626) and the common-sense realism of Scottish philosopher Thomas Reid (1710–1796). In this tradition, science is understood to be primarily an *inductive* enterprise in which facts are gathered with dispassionate objectivity, and conclusions are drawn that should not go beyond those facts. A careful scientist should refrain from speculation about processes that are not observable in the present.[7]

While it is one of our goals to critique this "two models" approach as an oversimplification and show that there are actually a number of different models or "species" of origins at play in America, we need to note at this point that the creationists are not the only ones who are attracted to a two-model framework. For example, Morris enlists prominent evolutionary biologist Douglas Futuyma, expert witness at the Arkansas trial in 1981 and author of a major college textbook, to support the two-models notion: "Creation and evolution, between them, exhaust the possible explanations for the origins of living things. Organisms either appeared on the Earth fully developed or they did not. If they did not, they must have developed from preexisting species by some process of modification. If they did appear in a fully developed state, they must indeed have been created by some omnipotent intelligence."[8]

Morris's two-models framework is the basis for a line of argumentation in which problems with evolution become automatically evidence for creation. Consequently, throughout his work he adopts a two-fold strategy to reach the conclusion that "the creation model of origins correlates far better with scientific data than the evolution model."[9] Morris looks for any observational data that either disagree with evolutionary theory or support creationism. He also scours the scientific literature for signs of internal debate and disagreement among evolutionary thinkers, and then presents their dissenting comments in such a way as to cast doubt on the viability of evolution itself. Quotes from leading evolutionists appear on nearly every page, creating the impression not only that Morris has really done his homework, but more importantly that the creationists' objections to evolution are based on serious scientific grounds. We remind the reader, however, that Morris's scientific argumentation should be seen in the light of his prior commitment to a literalist reading of scripture.[10]

Morris's scientific arguments for creationism fill eleven chapters in his second volume of *The Modern Creation Trilogy*. We will summarize his scientific evidence in eleven brief corresponding sections.

EVOLUTION DOES NOT OCCUR IN THE HERE AND NOW

Morris's first scientific argument in support of creationism is that evolution is not in evidence right now. "[N]o natural processes of evolutionary development from a simpler kind of organism to a more complex kind of organism can be observed operating today," he contends. Consequently, "the facts clearly favor the creation model. All biologists know that biological processes today are not producing more highly developed kinds."[11] He develops this by a series of five arguments that has become fairly standard in antievolutionary literature. First, evolution should yield a continuum of organisms that should render any classification system impossible; therefore, the very existence of the science of taxonomy based on discrete gaps between various kinds of organisms favors creationism over evolution.[12] Second, evolutionary theory should identify an observable biological process that "impels simple organisms to advance to complex organisms." Morris concludes that since no such process can be "observed in the present" and "species remain the same species," evolution must surrender its scientific status.[13] Third, evolution's supposed mechanism, natural selection, is tautologous: natural selection "was supposed to insure 'the survival of the fittest,' but the only pragmatic way to define 'the fittest' is 'those who survive.'" Put another way, "[n]atural selection is a force that somehow causes the survivors to survive."[14] Fourth, mutations, which are the source of all generic variation, are extremely rare, and there have been no documented instances of mutations beneficial to the creature experiencing it.[15] Fifth, the argument that imperfect adaptations point to natural selection rather than divine creation is challenged on the two-fold basis that there are very few instances of so-called bad design or suboptimal improvisation, and those that can be isolated reveal deterioration from their originally created forms.[16]

Morris frequently substantiates these claims with comments from leading evolutionary theorists who are themselves exploring exactly how it is that evolutionary processes produce new kinds of organisms. For example, he quotes leading British evolutionist Colin Patterson: "No one has ever produced a species by mechanisms of natural selection;"[17] world-renowned geneticist Francisco J. Ayala: "Although mutation is the ultimate source of all genetic variation, it is a relatively rare event;"[18] and Oxford University biologist Richard Dawkins: "In real life, the probability that a gene will mutate (that is, in one generation) is often less than one in a million."[19]

EVOLUTION NEVER OCCURRED IN THE LONG AGO

If evolution is not occurring in the present, then perhaps it can be shown to have occurred in the past. After all, does not the fossil record bear witness to a natural history in which increasingly more complex organisms are steadily evolving from simpler ones? No. Scientific creationists contend that a careful examination of the fossil record reveals that transitional forms documenting the evolution of one species into another simply do not exist. Morris claims that, despite the existence of many billions of fossils preserved in the sedimentary rocks of the Earth's crust, *"no true transitional fossil forms* have yet been discovered!"[20] Once again, he enlists authorities—this time no fewer than eight—to support this aggressive critique of evolution. The most noteworthy of these are the two very prominent paleontologists introduced in chapter 2, Harvard's Stephen Jay Gould and Niles Eldredge of the American Museum of Natural History. They point out that gradual transitions in basic morphology are problematic because smooth intermediates are "are almost impossible to construct, even in thought experiments."[21] Morris also makes use of Gould's interpretation of the so-called Cambrian explosion, the rather sudden and spectacular appearance in the fossil record (especially in the Burgess Shale in the Canadian Rockies on the eastern order of British Columbia) of virtually all major groups of modern animals within a brief geological time span of a few million years.[22] "[T]he problem of the Cambrian explosion has not receded," Morris quotes Gould as stating, "since our more extensive labor has still failed to identify any creature that might serve as a plausible immediate ancestor for the Cambrian fauna."[23] Morris provides similar comments to support the claim that there is a general absence of transitional forms between other major groups. For example, he enlists Gould and Eldredge again to challenge the validity of proffered transitional forms like the famous *Archaeopteryx*, said to be intermediate between reptiles and birds. Rather than a key transitional form, *Archaeopteryx* is viewed as a "curious mosaic" of useful and functioning structures found also in other creatures.[24]

NEITHER DID IT HAPPEN IN THE RECENT PAST

Continuing in the same vein, Morris challenges the evidentiary value of some celebrated and more recent mammalian evolutionary sequences. He enlists another prominent paleontologist, David Raup of the University of Chicago, to question the fossil sequence used to support the evolution of horses, which has historically been one of the best examples of a documented and easily visualizable evolutionary lineage: "The record of evolution is still surprisingly jerky and, ironically, we have even fewer examples of evolutionary transition than we had in Darwin's time. By this I mean that some of the classic cases of Darwinian change in the fossil record, such as the evolution of the horse in North America, have had to be discarded or modified as a result of more detailed information."[25]

Whales with feet (*Basilosaurus*), various "ape-men," and other alleged transitional forms meet the same fate. Morris contends that these examples of fossil evidence for transitional forms are better understood as specially created with specific structures suited for their particular environments. He also notes that in celebrated cases such as the Piltdown man, Java man, and Nebraska man extravagant claims were made based on hoaxes or the mistaken identification of animal bones as being those of ape-men.[26]

EVOLUTION NEVER HAPPENED AT ALL

One of the creationists' favorite targets is the debate within the evolutionary community over the rate at which evolution occurs. The controversy revolves around Gould's aforementioned notion of *punctuated equilibrium*, the view that according to the fossil record species do not evolve at a slow steady rate, but rather remain in stasis for long periods of time and then rapidly evolve, perhaps in response to an environmental change. Gould claimed that his "model of 'punctuated equilibria' holds that evolution is concentrated in events of speciation and that successful speciation is an infrequent event punctuating the stasis of large populations that do not alter in fundamental ways during the millions of years that they endure."[27]

Predictably, Morris pounces on this issue and uses it to impress on his readers that "[e]volution is nothing but a naive and credulous religious faith in the omnipotence of matter—a faith exercised blindly, in spite of the universal evidence against it."[28] To him it is clear that Gould, a leading evolutionist, thought there was something wrong with the standard Darwinian model of evolution, and this becomes, in the rhetorical arsenal of a creationist like Morris, a powerful weapon against evolution itself. His assessment of Gould's model reveals Morris at his rhetorical best: "This is certainly fascinating. Evolution, which means 'change' is characterized mainly by stasis, which means 'no change!' The 'punctuations' that produce new species occur so rapidly and so rarely that they can never be observed. Since we can never observe evolution in action, it is presumed to happen very rapidly when we are not looking. No wonder it has been so hard to learn how evolution works!"[29]

Morris further ridicules evolution on the basis of the punctuated equilibrium model. Evolution as presented by Gould is "the product not of any evidence—but rather lack of evidence." Moreover, Gould was forced to propose this flawed model because conventional evolutionary theory "had proved impotent." According to Morris, the Harvard paleontologist made "an amazing excursus into the logic of wonderland" motivated by an "innate rebellion against the concept of creation."[30] Morris concludes that since the testimony of the fossil record is that organisms from the distant past are basically the same as organisms today, the "equilibrium" is never punctuated and there is no real "history" in the fossil record of new species emerging. Nor does the fossil record testify to great extinctions as is so commonly believed. Even the dinosaurs are still with us in the form of lizards. The really large dinosaurs, he suggests, existed side by side with humans, hence accounts of legendary dragons. Morris goes so far as to suggest that there is "considerable reason to suppose that many dinosaurs were animals well known to earlier nations by the name of dragons."[31]

We should note here that one of the unstated premises of the punctuationist model is that Darwinian selection is such an efficient agent of change that some explanation was needed for the persistence of species like amoebas and horseshoe crabs that have maintained their present form for about two hundred million years.[32] Furthermore, while other evolutionists, especially Dawkins, have aggressively challenged Gould's understanding, both Gould and Eldredge vigorously objected to what they considered to be a gross creationist misreading of their stance.[33] Nevertheless, because of the use that Morris and other antievolutionists make of his dissenting notions within the community of evolutionary theorists, Gould has been labeled "the accidental creationist."[34]

EVOLUTION IS NOT EVEN POSSIBLE

Having argued that evolution does not and has not happened, Morris attempts to explain why evolution is not even possible. Evolution, it turns out, is "precluded by the very laws of science." There are two very general laws that evolution disobeys: (1) the principle of cause and effect, which states that no effect can be greater than its cause, and (2) the law of increasing entropy, which forms "an impenetrable barrier that no evolutionary mechanism yet suggested has ever been able to overcome." The first of these arguments is based on the observation that, whatever caused the universe, it produced the space-mass-time continuum and all that we find with that continuum: "force, motion, and energy, as well as life, intelligence, volition, morality, beauty, and emotion." It follows, then, that "the First Cause must be an eternal, omniscient, omnipotent, living, volitional, moral, aesthetic, emotional being!"[35] The second argument is based on the Second Law of Thermodynamics, which we encountered in the previous chapter in our discussion of the Fall. This law is one of the most fundamental principles in all of science and contains a precise mathematical statement that a certain measure of the *disorder* of a system (entropy) must increase any time the system undergoes a change. While the technical content of the second law is highly abstract and mathematical, the law has a popular connotation in the sense that it describes the way that things, left to themselves, tend to deteriorate. Creationists like Morris believe that the second law points inexorably to decreasing complexity, whereas evolution posits a universal law of increasing complexity. Not only are evolution and entropy depicted as "opposing and mutually exclusive concepts," but Morris contends that the second law utterly refutes the very possibility of evolution while it confirms the basic creation model.[36] According to Morris:

> Not only does the creation model predict the entropy principle, but the entropy principle directly points to creation. That is, if all things are now running down to disorder, they must originally have been in a state of high order. Since there is no naturalistic process that could produce such an initial condition, its cause must have been supernatural. The only adequate cause of the initial order and complexity of the universe must have been an omniscient programmer, and the cause of its boundless power an omnipotent energizer. The Second Law of Thermodynamics, with its principle of increasing entropy, both repudiates the evolution model, and strongly confirms the creation model.[37]

THE PROBABILITY OF LIFE IS ZERO

A living cell, even a hypothetical primordial cell simpler than any that currently exist, is enormously complex, requiring a network of tightly interlinked processes to carry out the business of life. At the present time there is no viable model for how such a cell might originate via natural processes. Morris builds on the comments of leading biochemist Leslie Orgel, which appeared in *Scientific American*: "It is extremely improbable that proteins and nucleic acids, both of which are structurally complex, arose spontaneously in the same place at the same time. Yet it also seems impossible to have one without the other. And so, at first glance, one might have to conclude that life could never, in fact, have originated by chemical means."[38]

If indeed the complex sequence of DNA that exists in even the simplest cell was assembled through an entirely random process, then the formation of the first cell was an event of great improbability. The calculation of this improbability has long been a staple of the creationists' case against evolution and is a variation on the venerable "argument from design," which holds that an intelligent designer is a more plausible explanation than random physical forces for the fact that organisms are both intricate and well adapted. Morris thinks that the notion that a complex structure or system can be formed by chance is "a persistent [evolutionist] delusion."[39]

To substantiate this claim, Morris uses a familiar analogy. The evolutionary argument is akin to saying that, given enough time, a monkey could eventually arrive at a sequence of letters recognizable as William Shakespeare's *Hamlet*. He performs a rough calculation and shows that the odds are so great that, even if the universe is billions of years old, there is no chance that the molecules that make up even a simple cell could ever have come together by chance. "Life, at the very simplest level conceivable," Morris concludes, "has absolutely no possibility of having been generated by any other means than special creation by a living Creator."

Morris laments that so many scientists doggedly hold to the evolutionary model, and he attributes their allegiance to a variety of motivating factors. Orgel apparently holds his ideas out of a sense of "desperation." He casts Nobel laureate Ilya Prigogine as a dreamer who "wistfully expresses the hope that his speculations may someday lead to an understanding of how life may have evolved from non-life." Morris compares Prigogine's efforts to an attempt to build a "perpetual-motion machine," the most unambiguously quixotic project in all of science and one undertaken only by fools with no understanding of science whatsoever. The leading German biochemist Manfred Eigen is "arrogant" in his glossing over evolution's problems. And noted biochemists Stanley Miller and Jeffrey Bada have simply joined forces to engage in "rampant speculation."[40] Morris infers that at some level "spiritual blindness" is operative in the failure of scientists to give credence to the "scientific" position of the creationists. Of course, this only strengthens the argument that scientific creationism is fueled primarily by religious concerns:

Despite the intense prejudice against creationism (possibly, in many cases an unrecognized but intense emotional desire to escape any possibility of human responsibility to one's Creator) and against creationist scientists, regardless of their qualifications, the fact still remains that the creation model is the only model of origins that explains and correlates the scientific data relative to the origins of life. If this entails any personal responsibility to the Creator, so be it. The honest and true scientist should accept the testimony of clear and evidential factuality even if it makes him emotionally—or spiritually—uncomfortable.[41]

THE HEAVENS DON'T EVOLVE EITHER

Morris's next target is cosmology. In his view, evolutionists are so driven to exclude God from any meaningful relation to the universe that they devise complex speculative models of cosmic, stellar, galactic, and planetary evolution. Their task is to construct "explanations for everything without God."[42] Morris's critique of what might be called "cosmic evolution" follows his standard rhetorical structure. He identifies weaknesses in the theory, piles up quotes from authorities, and then presents an array of observations that fit the creation model better than the evolution model.

Consistent with his Baconian philosophy of science, Morris is strongly critical of the highly theoretical character of cosmology, with its reliance on mathematics and creativity, rather than observation and experiment.[43] He refers, for example, to Stephen W. Hawking's theorizing as a collection of "mind games." After describing the Big Bang Theory and pointing out its many seemingly bizarre elements, such as the "inflationary universe" and "cold dark matter," Morris suggests that all the cosmological speculation is "enchantingly preposterous" and so clearly impossible that it could well appear to be a "creationist plot to make evolutionists look ridiculous!" He concludes with the hope that "when all else fails, perhaps the evolutionists will try creation."[44]

THE CIRCUMSTANTIAL EVIDENCE SAYS NO TO EVOLUTION

Morris's discussion of circumstantial evidence is centered on two long-standing arguments for evolution: vestigial organs and embryonic recapitulation. Both have an ambiguous history and can be effectively challenged by the creationists. Consider the case of vestigial organs. Most, perhaps all, organisms have body parts that they do not use or need to use. Familiar examples in humans include the appendix, the tail bone, and the muscles to wiggle our ears. Why do we have such things? Where did they come from? One answer was provided by Darwin's theory of evolution: such "vestigial" organs are left over from our animal ancestors, for whom they were once useful. Examples of vestigial organs were often used as "bad design" arguments against creation (since God would not deliberately create an organism with dysfunctional parts) as well as evidence for our animal ancestry.[45] But Morris responds that, just because we cannot find the function for a vestigial organ, this does not mean that one does not exist. He contends that the list of vestigial organs in human beings has steadily shrunk from over a hundred to zero.[46] Second, Morris suggests that the "ontogeny recapitulates phylogeny" argument, which asserts that "the development of the embryo from conception to birth recapitulates the evolutionary history of the species," is also disintegrating. Once again, he utilizes a quotation of "accidental creationist" Gould to the effect that the recapitulation theory "should be defunct today."[47]

THE ROCKS AND FOSSILS TELL OF SUDDEN DEATH

As Morris sees it, he has piled up argument after argument to refute evolution and support creationism. He concludes that based on the evidence alone "creation is a far better model than evolution by which to explain and correlate the known facts of science." By this point in his argument, he is confident he has established that evolution, via mutation and natural selection, "could never in a trillion years generate higher, more complex organisms."[48] But what of the evidentiary support for evolutionary theory found in the fossil record? Examination of progressively older geological strata reveals increasingly simpler life-forms—very simple life in Precambrian strata, more complex body plan in Cambrian strata, complex mammalian life appearing in more recent Jurassic strata, and human fossils found only in the most recent strata. If this sequence does not suggest that life has evolved into more complex forms through time, what is its message?

Morris argues that the extensive record of past life—actually, past death—recorded in the fossil record points toward some sort of sudden global catastrophe that killed virtually all of the animals on the earth at the same time.[49] The existence of "great fossil 'graveyards'" and huge salt deposits suggests "massive catastrophism." Morris's argument for this has two parts: (1) the process by which a dead animal turns into a fossil is exceptional. Under normal circumstances dead animals do not fossilize.[50] (2) There are no real "breaks" or divisions in the geological column[51] that truly allow successive geologic epochs to be distinguished, "even at the Cambrian–Precambrian boundary." If animals rarely fossilize, and there are no real markers to distinguish geological epochs, then is it not more likely the geological strata record but a single catastrophic event in which all the fossils formed at one time? The entire geological column must represent "one continuous intense depositional episode, a one-of-a-kind 'rare event.'" Rather than depicting the evolution of life over many ages, the sedimentary geological column in the earth's crust actually "represents the vast destruction and burial of life in one age."[52] This vast act of destruction was, of course, the worldwide Flood that killed everything on the earth except for Noah, his family, and the animals that survived in the ark.

THE GEOLOGIC AGES ARE VANISHING

Morris identifies another problem from historical geology in the *sequence* of the fossils in the geological record, which are observed to progress from simpler to more complex as one proceeds from old to young rocks. This systematic increase in the complexity of fossils in the geological strata is often used as a "marker" to help identify the various geological epochs, with fossils of a particular complexity corresponding to strata of a certain age. Precambrian rock strata, for instance, can be identified by the simple Precambrian fossils that they contain; Cambrian strata can be identified by more complex Cambrian fossils, and so on. Morris demonstrates that this strategy for identifying rock strata is common with a quote from the *Bulletin of the Geological Society of America*, a reputable trade publication: "Fossils have furnished, through their record of the evolution of life on this planet, an amazingly effective key to the relative positioning of strata in widely-separated regions, and from continent to continent."[53] This quote, illustrating a kind of "short hand" for the identification of geological strata, only works if one *assumes* that the fossil sequence is the result of evolution. If, however, the fossil sequence is not a record of evolution (change through vast eras of time), then a geologist should not be using "index fossils" to identify strata. Morris accuses evolutionists of circular reasoning when they claim that fossils provide "the only historical, documentary evidence that life has evolved from simpler to more and more complex forms." He charges that "[t]he system of evolution arranges the fossils, the fossils date the rocks, and the resulting system of fossil-dated rocks proves evolution! Around and around we go."[54]

In place of what he considers to be the complex, circular, largely imaginary construction of historical geology, Morris suggests that it is "much more simple and direct . . . to explain the fossil bearing rocks as the record in stone of the destruction of the ancient world by one great flood." But if the sequence, from simple to complex, is not the result of evolutionary change through time, then how did it originate? The sequence is not a testimony to evolutionary change but rather to differential mobility and intelligence. More complex animals were able to run from the approaching deluge and escaped initially to higher elevations. The simpler marine invertebrates are "found at the lower elevations in each geological column, for the simple reason that they live at the lowest elevations and would be first affected and buried in a global cataclysm."[55] The sequence, then, is the result of "ecological zonation and is exactly what a great flood would cause."[56]

Morris also addresses a number of other geological topics, including the critical creationist claim that the earth was created with a thick layer of water vapor high in the atmosphere, a "thermal vapor canopy"[57] that provided a worldwide greenhouse before it was precipitated to facilitate the flood of Noah. The significance of this vapor canopy idea is that the 4.6 billion years that evolutionists posit as necessary for the history of the earth and its inhabitants is entirely false. There was really "only one primeval age, characterized by a year-round pleasantly warm climate everywhere, lush vegetation, and a great variety of animal life." That age, Morris contends, "came to a dramatic and traumatic end in a global hydraulic/tectonic/volcanic cataclysm that produced the Earth's great fossil-bearing sedimentary crust."[58]

REALLY, HOW OLD IS THE EARTH?

Ever since the science of historical geology emerged at the end of the eighteenth century, the biblical chronology has been under relentless critique. Initially, the age of the earth was pushed back from the six-thousand-year value obtained by analysis of the "history" in the Old Testament to numbers roughly ten times as large. But as new ways to measure the age of the earth were developed, the number grew into the millions, then hundreds of millions, and finally into the billions. A number of scientific disciplines, from nuclear physics to paleontology to geology, all claim to have reliable data that point to an age for the Earth of just under five billion years.

Morris is not convinced. In the final section of *Science and Creation*, he presents the classic creationist arguments against the antiquity of the earth. The unanimity of the sciences on the age of the earth derives, he claims, not from the data, but from "intellectual peer pressure."[59] The five-billion-year age of the earth was conveniently provided by a number of scientific disciplines to ensure that there would be enough time for evolution to occur. But if it can be established that the age of the earth should be measured in thousands of years, rather than billions, evolution is ruled out immediately simply for lack of time.[60]

The creationists have developed a standard set of arguments against the conventional dating of the Earth, all of which are based on the belief that attempts to estimate the age of *anything* that preceded human history are highly speculative and demand assent to an unreasonable set of assumptions, the most important of which is that "the system" (in this case, a reference to the earth) has been closed to external influences throughout its history. And there is simply "no way of *knowing* that assumptions such as these are valid."[61] Furthermore, since God created a world that was complete, in the sense of being fully functional as soon as it appeared, there would have been a number of brand new things that had the appearance of age. The trees in the Garden of Eden, for example, would have had rings that pointed to a history they did not possess. Stones in the stream would be smooth as if weathered. Adam and Eve would have had navels, testimony of births that never took place. Starlight from distant stars would be falling on the Earth, even though the stars were hundreds, even thousands, of light years away. "If anything at all has been truly created, it must have been created with an appearance of at least some prior history. It would only 'look' old to one who rejects the very possibility of special creation."[62]

Having made this very general claim, Morris then presents a number of specific arguments that support his contention that the earth is thousands, not billions, of years old. By estimating the rate at which the human population grows through time and working backwards, Morris argues that humans beings cannot have been on the Earth for more than a few thousand years.[63] An analysis of radiocarbon dating leads him to the conclusion that the earth's atmosphere is much younger than fifty thousand years.[64] Measurement of the "decay" of the earth's magnetic field shows that "the Earth must be only a few thousand years old!"[65] Morris makes a similar argument based on the disintegration of comets. The well-known and spectacular cometary "tail" represents material that is being "burned off" the comet and, since comets erode a bit with each passage near the Sun, they will eventually shrivel away to nothing. Thus, there is no way that a comet could have been orbiting with a typical trajectory that gets close the Sun for billions of years; its material would have burned up long ago. Consequently, most comets, like Halley's, are believed to be much younger than the solar system, and have not been executing typical cometary orbits for billions of years. Instead, astronomers believe they come from a gigantic collection of "comet wanna–bes" far beyond the orbit of Pluto called the "Oort Cloud" (after the astronomer Jan Oort). These "potential comets" in the Oort Cloud orbit lazily at great distances from the Sun until some gravitational disturbance sends them hurtling into the inner solar system where they can be seen from Earth and, in essence, *become* comets. Morris, however, challenges this traditional explanation, which appears in every introductory astronomy text. The Oort Cloud, he argues, is "imaginary," a conveniently "invented" notion. "The only evidence for its existence is the evolutionary need for it, to keep from admitting that the solar system is young."[66]

Most of Morris's conclusions about the very young age for the Earth are emphasized with exclamation marks. This suggests the critical role that these arguments play in the entire creation model. If the Earth is only a few thousand years old, then the entire structure of the historical sciences is hopelessly confused. Evolution cannot have occurred in a few thousand years, so things must have been created in much their present form. The geological column cannot have been created by conventional processes in a few thousand years, so it must have originated in the great flood of Noah. If well-established human history goes back only a few thousand years, then human history is coextensive with the history of the universe and there is no argument that human beings are simply the end product of a long mindless process. "[T]he most logical thing for the Creator to do," Morris asserts, "would be to create the entire cosmos—including the Earth and all its living creatures—complete and functioning right from the start. He surely would have some high purpose in creation—after all, an omnipotent Creator would not be uncertain or capricious in His actions—so He would definitely not wait eons of time in trial and error evolutionary meandering, involving incredible waste and cruelty, before beginning, to accomplish that purpose!"[67]

CONCLUSION

As a result of this reasoning, Morris believes that he is justified in concluding that "the solar system is young, and the Earth is even younger!"[68] Moreover, as a result of the collection of arguments made in *Science and Creation*, Morris considers the scientific case for evolution weak and that for creationism compelling. The biblical argument developed in the first volume of the *Modern Creation Trilogy* is buttressed by the weight of the scientific evidence offered in the second in support of creationism. There is yet another category of considerations that scientific creationists employ, and that will occupy the next chapter.

Before we close this discussion of the scientific arguments of creationism, it is important that the reader appreciate that, while Morris's views are not shared by every creation scientist, they certainly represent the mainstream of contemporary creationism.[69] The basic stance presented in this chapter is shared by a collection of creationists, including but by no means limited to Gary E. Parker, Larry Vardiman, Duane Gish, John Ankerberg, John Weldon, Jeremy Walter, Jerry Bergman, Jonathan Sarfati, James Perloff, Kurt Wise,[70] and Kenneth Ham.[71] That does not mean that each one of these creationists is in total agreement with Morris on every single argument. But certainly most creationists are in broad agreement with him.[72]

In the previous chapter, we concluded that the engine that drives creationism is fidelity to a literalist reading of the Bible. In this chapter, we have seen that creationists also firmly believe that they have advanced serious scientific reasons to question evolution and to support creation science. Geologist Kurt Wise, who studied under Gould at Harvard, is quite candid at this very point: "Although there are scientific reasons for accepting a young earth, I am a young-age creationist because that is my understanding of the Scripture. As I shared with my professors years ago when I was in college, if all the evidence in the universe turns against creationism, I would be the first to admit it, but I would still be a creationist because that is what the Word of God seems to indicate. Here I must stand."[73]

Wise's candor is also reflected in the views of two other creationists who put forth a brand of creationism that is similar to that of Morris in its essentials, but very different in its tone. Paul A. Nelson and John Mark Reynolds are philosophers by training. They represent what could be called a subspecies of origins: provisional young-earth creationism.[74] Nelson and Reynolds are creationists essentially out of religious and philosophical conviction. They find it very difficult to jettison a plausible biblical account that favors a recent creation as well as the clear teaching of the Christian Church down through the ages. But they recognize that most of the scientific data *as currently interpreted* are against their young-earth creationist stance. In fact, they confess that at the moment recent creationism is "implausible on purely scientific grounds." So why do they align themselves with creationism? They see creationism as having the potential of providing "a great boon to religious belief" while simultaneously offering a satisfying reinterpretation of the scientific data. Nelson and Reynolds suggest that creationism as a scientific research program is still in its infancy and remains underdeveloped. In order to produce a truly satisfying reinterpretation of the scientific data, they argue, young-earth creationists must pursue serious empirical research in areas like plate tectonics and information theory. But if their research program is to have any chance of success, it must, according to them, be given the opportunity to progress, which involves funding and a measure of patience for the research to mature. This will never occur if creationism is summarily and routinely ruled out of the court of science. By virtue of their less triumphalist tone and admission that creationism has by no means cinched the scientific case,

Nelson and Reynolds are at the taxonomical boundaries of two species of origins: creationism and a newer species called intelligent design that we will explore in a future chapter.

NOTES

1. Henry M. Morris and John D. Morris, *The Modern Creation Trilogy*, vol. 2, *Science and Creation* (Green Forest, Ark.: Master, 1996), 13, emphasis in the original.

2. See Henry M. Morris, *The Genesis Flood* (Green Forest, Ark.: Master, 1976), 440–441; Henry M. Morris, *Scientific Creationism*, 3d ed. (Green Forest, Ark.: Master, 1974), 1–16.

3. Richard Bliss, a leading creationist and long-time collaborator of Morris, earned his doctorate in education by investigating the pedagogical consequences of the "two models approach." The results showed that "students using a two-model [creation–evolution] approach to origins showed more improvement in inquiry skills than those using the traditional evolution-only approach. And the two-model students learned evolutionary concepts better than those taught evolution only." See Henry M. Morris and Gary E. Parker, *What Is Creation Science?* rev. ed. (Green Forest, Ark.: Master, 1987), 73.

4. Edward J. Larson, *Summer for the Gods: The Scopes Trial and America's Continuing Debate over Science and Religion* (Cambridge, Mass.: Harvard University Press, 1997), 258.

5. A variation on this theme is the call from some young-earth creationists for an "open philosophy of science," one that is "open to a God who works in scientifically detectable ways" and that gives creation scientists permission to pursue their research program within the academy. See Paul A. Nelson and John Mark Reynolds, "Young Earth Creationism," in *Three Views on Creation and Evolution*, ed. J. P. Moreland and John Mark Reynolds (Grand Rapids, Mich.: Zondervan, 1999), 98–99.

6. Henry M. Morris, *Many Infallible Proofs: Practical and Useful Evidences of Christianity* (San Diego: Creation-Life Publishers, 1974, 1996), 249.

7. See Ronald L. Numbers, *The Creationists: The Evolution of Scientific Creationism* (Berkeley: University of California Press, 1993), 32, 90, 246. Another aspect of the creationist philosophy of science evident in the Morris quotation is the role of prediction. Prediction plays a very important role in science. A proper scientific theory should be able to make predictions about phenomena that have yet to be studied. One of the crowning successes of Newton's theory of universal gravitation was that it was used in 1781 to predict the existence of the planet Uranus. The Big Bang Theory was not taken very seriously until its prediction of the universal background radiation was confirmed in 1965. While predictions can be derived from both the creationist and the evolutionary models, Morris maintains that creationism manifests superior predictive capability. For a critical discussion of prediction in scientific creationism and evolution, see Philip Kitcher, *Abusing Science: The Case against Creationism* (Cambridge, Mass.: MIT Press, 1982), 35–50.

8. Futuyma quoted in Morris and Morris, *Modern Creation Trilogy*, 2:18.

9. Morris and Morris, *Modern Creation Trilogy*, 2:25.

10. We concur with Kitcher's assessment that creationists are "not down on Darwin because the methodology of evolutionary biology offends their scientific sensibilities"; rather

"[t]he root of the trouble is that the theory of evolution contradicts a literal reading of the first eleven chapters of Genesis." Kitcher, *Abusing Science*, 186.

11. Morris and Morris, *Modern Creation Trilogy*, 2:30. Note the relationship between this statement and the definition of science Morris provides earlier.

12. Morris and Morris, *Modern Creation Trilogy*, 2:26–27.

13. Morris and Morris, *Modern Creation Trilogy*, 2:29–33.

14. Morris and Morris, *Modern Creation Trilogy*, 2:33–37. For a good analysis of "tautology objection," see Kitcher, *Abusing Science*, 55–60.

15. Morris and Morris, *Modern Creation Trilogy*, 2:38–39. For a very different view of the role of mutations in variation, see Niles Eldredge, *The Triumph of Evolution and the Failure of Creationism* (New York: Freeman, 2000), 119.

16. Morris and Morris, *Modern Creation Trilogy*, 2:46–48. See Kurt Wise, "The Origin of Life's Major Groups," in *The Creation Hypothesis: Scientific Evidence for an Intelligent Designer*, ed. J.P. Moreland (Downers Grove, Ill.: InterVarsity, 1994), 221–223.

17. Patterson quoted in Morris and Morris, *Modern Creation Trilogy*, 2:35.

18. Ayala quoted in Morris and Morris, *Modern Creation Trilogy*, 2:38.

19. Dawkins quoted in Morris and Morris, *Modern Creation Trilogy*, 2:38.

20. Morris and Morris, *Modern Creation Trilogy*, 2:56, emphasis in the original. This point is elaborated in considerable detail in the work of fellow creationist Duane T. Gish. See his *Evolution: The Challenge of the Fossil Record* (El Cajon, Calif.: Creation-Life Publishers, 1985).

21. Gould and Eldredge quoted in Morris and Morris, *Modern Creation Trilogy*, 2:70.

22. For differing views of the meaning of the Cambrian explosion, see Stephen Jay Gould, *Wonderful Life: The Burgess Shale and the Nature of History* (New York: Norton, 1989); Simon Conway Morris, *The Crucible of Creation: The Burgess Shale and the Rise of Animals* (New York: Oxford, 1998), especially 138–168; and Eldredge, *Triumph of Evolution*, 32–60.

23. Gould quoted in Morris and Morris, *Modern Creation Trilogy*, 2:59. Simon Conway Morris's work cited earlier would challenge Gould on this point. See Morris, *Crucible of Creation*, 142–147.

24. Morris and Morris, *Modern Creation Trilogy*, 2:70. See Eldredge, *Triumph of Evolution*, 125–126.

25. Raup quoted in Morris and Morris, *Modern Creation Trilogy*, 2:74–75. For a detailed creationist critique of the use of *Archaeopteryx* as a transitional form between reptiles and birds, see Jonathan Wells, *Icons of Evolution: Science or Myth?* (Washington, D.C.: Regnery, 2000), 111–135.

26. Morris and Morris, *Modern Creation Trilogy*, 2:79–91. For further documentation and discussion of the whale evolutionary series, see Denis O. Lamoureux, "Evangelicals Inheriting the Wind: The Phillip E. Johnson Phenomenon," in *Darwinism Defeated? The Johnson–Lamoureux Debate on Biological Origins*, ed. Phillip E. Johnson and Denis O. Lamoureux (Vancouver: Regent College Publishing, 1999), 24. Morris concludes this section with a discussion of the evolutionary challenge to the notion that human language is unique. He recruits celebrated MIT linguist Noam Chomsky to help argue that human language cannot possibly be the result of evolution. Morris suggests that Chomsky's "universal grammar" may be the "key to man's original language," presumably the language spoken in the Garden of Eden (91–99).

27. Gould quoted in Morris and Morris, *Modern Creation Trilogy*, 2:102.

28. Morris and Morris, *Modern Creation Trilogy*, 2:107.

29. Morris and Morris, *Modern Creation Trilogy*, 2:101–102.

30. Morris and Morris, *Modern Creation Trilogy*, 2:102–103.

31. Morris and Morris, *Modern Creation Trilogy*, 2:120.

32. Andrew Brown, *The Darwin Wars: The Scientific Battle for the Soul of Man* (London: Simon and Schuster, 1999), 62.

33. See Richard Dawkins, *The Blind Watchmaker: Why the Evidence of Evolution Reveals a Universe without Design*, rev. ed. (New York: Norton, 1986, 1996), 229–252; Niles Eldredge, *Reinventing Darwin: The Great Debate at the High Table of Evolutionary Theory* (New York: Wiley, 1995), 103–104; Eldredge, *Triumph of Evolution*, 89.

34. Robert Wright, "The Accidental Creationist: Why Stephen Jay Gould Is Bad for Evolution," *New Yorker* 75 (December 1999): 56–65.

35. Morris and Morris, *Modern Creation Trilogy*, 2:125–127.

36. Morris and Morris, *Modern Creation Trilogy*, 2:125–127. Opponents of this creationist line of reasoning object that the Second Law of Thermodynamics applies to closed systems, that is, those that neither give energy to their environment nor receive energy from it. Evolutionary theory presupposes an open system in which the earth receives large amounts of energy from the Sun. If the Sun and the earth and those parts of the universe that exchange energy with them are considered as a closed system, then entropy will indeed increase overall, but pockets of that system can exist in which entropy actually decreases. Nevertheless, the creationists counter effectively that most open systems "run down" thermodynamically just like closed systems. For an expanded discussion of this, see Kitcher, *Abusing Science*, 89–96; Eldredge, *Triumph of Evolution*, 96–98; and Morris and Morris, *Modern Creation Trilogy*, 2:156–158.

37. Morris and Morris, *Modern Creation Trilogy*, 2:149–150.

38. Orgel quoted in Morris and Morris, *Modern Creation Trilogy*, 2:162.

39. Morris and Morris, *Modern Creation Trilogy*, 2:163. We will develop the design argument more fully in chapter 9.

40. Morris and Morris, *Modern Creation Trilogy*, 2:162–198

41. Morris and Morris, *Modern Creation Trilogy*, 2:201.

42. Morris and Morris, *Modern Creation Trilogy*, 2:203.

43. Cosmology, the science of the universe, including its origin, development, present large-scale properties and future course, is an unusual science, to say the least. Cosmology is a new science having "come of age" in the 1970s as particle physicists and astronomers studying the Big Bang began to interact and discovered that their two areas of study had much in common. (The elementary particles and the laws that govern their mutual interactions originated in the first few moments of the Big Bang, according to the theory.) Cosmology is a highly counterintuitive science with many elements that simply cannot be visualized, such as the "curved space" of general relativity, the "false vacuum" of the inflationary epoch, or the "virtual particles" that come and go in an endless dance of interaction. Cosmology also deals with physical quantities that challenge and even overwhelm our imaginations. A number of important events in the history of the universe happened prior to the time that the universe was 10^{-35} seconds old. The nearest star is several trillion miles away. There are 10^{80} baryons in the universe. And so on. The combination of counterintuitive notions, speculations that of necessity cannot be grounded in observation or experiment (like the moment of the Big Bang), serious gaps in basic knowledge (like the character of the dark matter that makes

up 90 percent of the universe), legitimate controversies, and occasional unwarranted forays into metaphysics can easily create the impression that cosmology is motivated by wishful thinking carried out in the imagination. It may even produce fantasies whose primary claim to fame comes from their ability to avoid lapsing into theology. For an informed criticism of the extravagant claims of cosmology, see the work of Stanley L. Jaki, particularly his "Cosmology: An Empirical Science?" in *The Limits of a Limitless Science and Other Essays* (Wilmington, Del.: ISI Books, 2000), 127–148; *God and the Cosmologists*, 2d ed. (Fraser, Mich.: Real View, 1998). For a good assessment of the creationist philosophy of science, see Del Ratzsch, *The Battle of Beginnings: Why Neither Side Is Winning the Creation–Evolution Debate* (Downers Grove, Ill.: InterVarsity, 1996), 136–157.

44. Morris and Morris, *Modern Creation Trilogy*, 2:210–232.

45. See, for example, Stephen Jay Gould, *The Panda's Thumb* (New York: Norton, 1980); Kitcher, *Abusing Science*, 138–139.

46. Morris and Morris, *Modern Creation Trilogy*, 2:254.

47. Morris and Morris, *Modern Creation Trilogy*, 2:234–236.

48. Morris and Morris, *Modern Creation Trilogy*, 2:255–257.

49. See Richard Milton, *Shattering the Myths of Darwinism* (Rochester, Vt.: Park Street, 1997), especially 92–95.

50. If it were normal for a dead animal's bones to lie around in anticipation of fossilization, then America's national forests would be knee-deep in bones. Literally billions of animals have died in these forests in the recent past, yet it is very unusual to come upon the remains a dead animal. The natural activities of predators, wind, erosion, etc. generally result in the complete disintegration of animal remains.

51. The geological column is the construct used to indicate the sequence of sedimentary rock strata that contains "the outline of events in Earth history." It is generally depicted in graphic form as an imaginary cross-section through the earth's crust and is correlated with the sequence of divisions of geological time (Paleozoic, Mesozoic, and Cenozoic). See Morris and Morris, *Modern Creation Trilogy*, 2:258; Eldredge, *Triumph of Evolution*, 104–105.

52. Morris and Morris, *Modern Creation Trilogy*, 2:283.

53. H. D. Hedberg quoted in Morris and Morris, *Modern Creation Trilogy*, 2:289.

54. Morris and Morris, *Modern Creation Trilogy*, 2:289. For critical examination of this circular reasoning argument, see Kitcher, *Abusing Science*, 63–66; Eldredge, *Triumph of Evolution*, 103–108; and Ratzsch, *Battle of Beginnings*, 148–152.

55. Morris and Morris, *Modern Creation Trilogy*, 2:289.

56. Morris and Morris, *Modern Creation Trilogy*, 2:299.

57. Morris and Morris, *Modern Creation Trilogy*, 2:310.

58. Morris and Morris, *Modern Creation Trilogy*, 2:312.

59. Morris and Morris, *Modern Creation Trilogy*, 2:313. Compare this claim with Eldredge's claim that "the notion that the Earth has had an extremely long history is one of the great intellectual achievements of human thought." See Eldredge, *Triumph of Evolution*, 98.

60. It is universally agreed that the processes thought to drive evolution—random mutation and natural selection—work so slowly that, even for those who consider these processes adequate, there is no way that the evolutionary history of life on this planet can be compressed into a few thousand years.

61. Morris and Morris, *Modern Creation Trilogy*, 2:315.

62. Morris and Morris, *Modern Creation Trilogy*, 2:316.

63. Morris and Morris, *Modern Creation Trilogy*, 2:317–320.

64. Morris and Morris, *Modern Creation Trilogy*, 2:320–322.

65. Morris and Morris, *Modern Creation Trilogy*, 2:322–326.

66. Morris and Morris, *Modern Creation Trilogy*, 2:327.

67. Morris and Morris, *Modern Creation Trilogy*, 2:335.

68. Morris and Morris, *Modern Creation Trilogy*, 2:328.

69. Nor are they shared by every antievolutionist. A noteworthy example is British science journalist Richard Milton who accepts many of the creationists' scientific objections to evolution while distancing himself from creationism per se by retaining a personal stance of religious agnosticism. See Milton, *Shattering the Myths of Darwinism*, 269.

70. Professor Kurt Wise has gained a reputation both as scientific creationism's leading paleontologist and someone who is "often brutally critical of recent creationist ideas." See Nelson and Reynolds, "Young Earth Creationism," 50.

71. See John F. Ashton, ed., *In Six Days: Why Fifty Scientists Choose to Believe in Creation* (Sydney: New Holland, 1999); James Perloff, *Tornado in a Junkyard: The Relentless Myth of Darwinism* (Arlington, Mass.: Refuge, 1999); Jonathan Sarfati, *Refuting Evolution: A Response to the National Academy of Sciences' Teaching about Evolution and the Nature of Science* (Green Forest, Ark.: Master, 1999); John Ankerberg and John Weldon, *Darwin's Leap of Faith: Exposing the False Religion of Evolution* (Eugene, Ore.: Harvest House, 1998); Kenneth A. Ham, *The Lie: Evolution* (El Cajon, Calif.: Master, 1987).

72. Biologist Wayne Frair and physical chemist Gary D. Patterson provide an example of broad agreement with some variation. They defend the traditional creationist stance on many points while entertaining the notion that an entirely consistent literalist reading of the Bible may not be warranted. See Wayne Frair and Gary D. Patterson, "Creationism: An Inerrant Bible and Effective Science," in *Science and Christianity: Four Views*, ed. Richard F. Carlson (Downers Grove, Ill.: InterVarsity, 2000), 19–51.

73. Wise quoted in Ashton, *In Six Days*, 332.

74. See Nelson and Reynolds, "Young Earth Creationism," 98.

5

◆

Scientific Creationism:
The Social Dimension

In the preceding chapters, we have argued that scientific creationism is a species of origins that combines a literalist biblical perspective with a wide-ranging critique of evolution. However, anyone familiar with actual creationists will attest to the fact that they are not drawn to their viewpoints on origins out of a deep and abiding interest in science. The passion for creationism is fueled by something else, namely, the sense that contemporary America is "slouching toward Gomorrah," literally going to hell.[1] Evidence that society is rapidly heading toward moral anarchy is seen at every turn. For tens of millions of Americans, the increasing acceptance of homosexuality, the rise of divorce and abortion rates, widespread acceptance of pornography, rampant sexual promiscuity and perversion, degrading entertainment, coarse language, abuse of alcohol and drugs, school shootings, and road rage—all testify to the erosion of the traditional morality on which American society must be based in order to receive God's blessing. For creationists, the relationship of all this to evolution is abundantly clear. The spread of these numerous social "cancers" is a function of a wholesale abandonment of belief in God as the creator and of recognition that the Bible contains absolute moral guidelines for human behavior. To the extent that the theory of evolution undercuts the traditional belief in God as creator, it is manifestly not just a matter of scientific disagreement. Creationists link acceptance of evolution with moral decay.

Henry M. Morris devotes the final volume of the *Modern Creation Trilogy* to an exploration of the social argument on behalf of scientific creationism. There is nothing subtle or soothing in Morris's approach to this aspect of his topic; in fact, the third volume makes everything he wrote in the first two volumes appear rather tame. From the beginning of *Society and Creation*, he fires one rhetorical salvo after another in a sustained effort to link evolution with the various satanic forces

105

he sees unleashed in the world. "The evolutionary deception and its evil influences," Morris asserts, "have, indeed, corrupted every area of human life on this planet, and this fact in itself should be enough to demonstrate its ultimate satanic source." "Evolutionism," according to this view, does not testify to the power of human understanding; rather, it is a "false religion, designed to turn men and women away from belief in the true God of creation." As such, it will poison not only a believer's views about the meaning and purpose of life, it will also inevitably infect society and *all* human relationships.[2]

Society and Creation is the most aggressive critique imaginable of evolution and "evolutionism." The stridency of this concluding volume is such that a great many unsympathetic readers are likely to dismiss the book, its author, and any subculture where these ideas are taken seriously. This would be a serious mistake. Such disregard would mean missing the powerful inspiration that lies at the very heart of creationism, the power that rallied the audiences of William Jennings Bryan and the power that continues to inspire parents across America to join the antievolutionary movement.

Morris argues that evolutionary theory is the primary strategy that Satan has used throughout history to accomplish his untoward goals. "[E]volutionism," he charges, has provided "the pseudo-scientific justification for almost every deadly philosophy and every evil practice known to man!"[3] Indeed, the "long tragic history of the outworking of human belief" has centered on "the grand satanic delusion of evolution."[4] To substantiate this, he equates any view that does not hold to the ex nihilo (out of nothing) special creation of the universe by God with evolution. Consequently, wherever and whenever materialism, pantheism, polytheism, or even occult supernaturalism are found in history, there is evidence of the operation of a fundamentally evolutionary worldview.[5] Furthermore, the basic notions of evolution actually *originated* with Satan, who, Morris speculates, presented it to an evil Babylonian potentate from whence it began its long invidious diffusion throughout the world, relentlessly destroying all that was good, leaving suffering and misery in its wake.[6] Evolution, having "infected every area of human thought," now stands virtually unchallenged, dominating the physical sciences—biology, physics, geology, and astronomy—and profoundly influencing the life sciences—psychology, sociology, and anthropology—as well as history, ethics, and religion. Evolutionary assumptions are at the foundation of the philosophy and methodology of our public educational system, resisted only by a small minority of true believers holding to the creationist cosmology.[7]

Morris believes that Charles Darwin gets far too much credit for the triumph of evolution. His scientific accomplishments were "relatively insignificant" by modern standards and were largely derivative. Morris quotes leading evolutionary scholars Ernst Mayr and Loren Eiseley to support the view that Darwin most certainly was not "the inventor of the theory of evolution." Darwin borrowed from a number of predecessors: his grandfather Erasmus Darwin, Jean-Baptiste de Lamarck, Robert Chambers, Charles Lyell, and Herbert Spencer, to name a few. And the publication in 1859 of his *The Origin of Species by Means of Natural Selection* was followed by a "relentless evolutionary propaganda campaign" by Julian Huxley, Ernst Haeckel, Herbert Spencer, and others that soon converted most of the world to "evolutionism."

What is so significant about all this for Morris is that science heretofore had been dominated by men who believed in a Creator God whose design was evident in the complexities and orderly relationships found in nature. Morris contends that anti-Christian thinkers and movements needed to undermine these notions of biblical creation, which are so foundational to Christian theology. By explaining away the argument from design and replacing it with a naturalistic explanation, Darwin and his fellow evolutionists essentially presided over "God's funeral."[8] So Darwin, according to Morris, is not really that significant as a scientist but rather as a symbol of nineteenth-century man's "eagerness to discover a justifiable excuse for rejecting God as his Creator." He came along at just the right time, with just the right persuasion, to transform in a single generation "a society that was already seething with inner rebellion against the predominant theological and biblical view of the world, into a humanity in open and often violent rebellion against its Creator."[9] The timing of all this, Morris suggests, was not coincidental and was the product of centuries of antecedent developments.

Morris supplies his readers with a genealogy of the "deadly anti-Christian philosophy and world view"[10] of evolution, which lies like a serpent across history. In the centuries immediately before Darwin, Morris isolates various voices in the scientific wilderness preparing the way for Darwin: Immanuel Kant and Pierre-Simon de Laplace with their nebular hypotheses,[11] Baruch Spinoza with his pantheism, and René Descartes with his mechanistic philosophy. Back further in time, during the formative centuries of the Christian tradition, several of the most significant figures in Christian history promoted interpretive schemes that encouraged nonliteral readings of the creation story in Genesis, thus opening the door for Christians eventually to embrace evolution. With their allegorical and symbolic understandings of the biblical accounts of creation, Origen in the third century, St. Basil and St. Gregory of Nyssa in the fourth century, St. Augustine in the fifth century, and St. Thomas Aquinas in the thirteenth century, all unwittingly laid the foundations for future deadly compromise.[12]

In the pre-Christian world, Aristotle "believed in spontaneous generation," which Morris considers to be a form of evolution."[13] But to criticize Aristotle is also to indict his illustrious teacher Plato, who was influenced by Socrates, who in turn was influenced by Thales and the pre-Socratics, who were also "evolutionists and materialists."[14] Pushing even further back in time, Morris notes that Thales was influenced by the Egyptians and Phoenicians, who subscribed to evolutionary cosmogonies[15] and worldviews, as did the ancient Chinese and Indians. What an extraordinary confusion it is, claims Morris, to make Charles Darwin in the nineteenth century the father of evolution when it was universal in the ancient world! "Not only do evolutionary systems appear among all the ancient philosophies and religions, however. In spite of many differences in detail, it is well-known that the very religions themselves are all essentially the same. Whether in Greece, Rome, Egypt, Canaan, India, or anywhere else, the basic systems prove to be equivalent to each other."[16]

These similarities revolve around a commitment to pantheistic polytheism and astrology. All this suggests a "common origin"[17] to all the world religions and provides Morris with the clue from which he believes he can trace the ultimate source of "the great global age-long deception of evolution." The origin of all this evolutionary paganism was "undoubtable at Babel," and the culprit in all of this, Morris speculates, was probably Nimrod, the "founder and first ruler of Babylon" and the man most likely responsible for the "introduction of this entire religious system into the life of mankind."[18] However, like Darwin some three millennia later, Nimrod was just a link in the great chain. An evil deception capable of ensnaring the entire world can hardly be the work of one man, even if he was the ruler of a powerful empire. Nimrod, as the primary architect of the Tower of Babel, knew he was building a monument to Satan and the powers of darkness. In fact, he may have actually encountered these evil forces on the top of the tower. "These evil spirits [Morris speculates] perhaps met with Nimrod and his priests there, to plan their long-range strategy against God and His redemptive purposes for the post-deluge world. This included especially the development of a non-theistic cosmology, one which could explain the origin and meaning of the universe and man without acknowledging the true God of creation."[19]

All this suggests to Morris that "Satan himself" could be "the originator of the concept of evolution," and that the linkage of Satan to evolutionary cosmology offers insight into biblical passages about how Satan has "deceived the whole world" (Rev. 12:9) and "blinded the minds of them which believe not" (2 Cor. 4:4).[20]

Evolution, almost every responsible scholar agrees, has indeed been used inappropriately to justify some very nasty practices and rhetoric, including some of the worst excesses of laissez-faire capitalism and Social Darwinism.[21] More so than any other theory, evolution has been pressed into service in a wide variety of social causes. Aggressive American capitalists like John D. Rockefeller, for instance, looked to evolution for the validation of a business world where the strong companies grew stronger by trampling the weak; Nazis found in evolution a rationalization for their genocidal racial policies. The catch phrases of evolutionary thinking were shibboleths like "survival of the fittest," "natural selection," "struggle for existence," and so on. These notions were profoundly malleable and readily transformed into scientific clubs to be wielded in a variety of causes. But Morris goes much, much further. By defining "evolutionism" so loosely as to include almost anything other than biblically literalist Christianity, Morris has created a rhetorical device for linking evolution with virtually anything wrong or objectionable both in human history and the contemporary world.

Ever since it was first preached by Nimrod and his followers at Babel, the "grand satanic delusion of evolution" has produced a remarkable variety of "corrupt fruits."

According to Morris, "practically all the harmful practices and deadly philosophies that plague mankind have their roots and pseudo-rationale in evolutionism."[22] And he devotes about one-half of *Society and Creation* to a breathtakingly aggressive survey of the "corrupt fruits" of evolution and the "deadly social philosophies" it has spawned. Rather than explore Morris's argument regarding each of these philosophies and cultural developments, we will simply list them here and develop his treatment of only one by way of illustration. Morris's list includes several problems facing humanity today: the "plague of abortionism,"[23] the sexual revolution, chauvinism and feminism, the "promotion of homosexuality," the "explosive increase of drug use," the deterioration of family life, the ecological crisis, the population problem, exobiology (life on other planets), and a distortive science education. All are either the result of or exacerbated by evolution. Furthermore, we should anticipate that infanticide and euthanasia will soon be justified by appeals to arguments informed by evolution. After all, so the reasoning goes, if man is merely an evolved animal, then on what basis would we argue against such practices? In terms of more expanded philosophical positions, Morris lists the "Great Chain of Being" argument, Sigmund Freud's "atheistic psychological system," Social Darwinism, Nazism, modern racism (which did not reach its "most intense and virulent level until it received pseudo-scientific sanction from Darwinism"), communism, and the New Age movement (a revival of ancient pantheistic evolutionism).[24]

Morris's treatment of the close relationship of evolution to Marxism is typical of his line of argument throughout the middle portions of *Society and Creation*. Morris never really establishes a causal linkage, but relies instead on a series of quotes to illustrate the common affinity of both evolutionary thought and communism for atheism. Both denigrate religion and view humans as essentially animals in no way created in God's image. Morris notes that while both Karl Marx and later communists were uncomfortable with some of the uniformitarian aspects of Darwinism,[25] they "honored Darwin because of the scientific respectability that he had given to naturalism and atheism."[26] But Morris goes much further. He proclaims without any substantive documentation that all socialism, communism, and anarchism is founded on evolutionism and atheism. Then he concludes, it is "time—high time, late time—for Christians to become alert to the fact that creationism is the only real antidote to this left-wing ideology that in one form enslaved more than half the world."[27]

Much of Morris's treatment of Marxism is devoted to a discussion of the degree to which Marxist thinking influenced Stephen Jay Gould and Niles Eldredge in their theory of punctuated equilibrium.[28] This flows into a brief discussion of the so-called Darwin wars between the punctuationist paleontologists (like Gould and Eldredge) who have emphasized evolutionary discontinuities and the so-called Darwinian fundamentalists (like John Maynard Smith, Daniel C. Dennett, Richard Dawkins, and Edward O. Wilson) who adopt a gene-centered, continuity view of evolution as the result of the competition for reproductive success. Morris uses this lively and complex debate to make a few basic creationist points:

Darwinists of either stripe "hold their views for non-scientific reasons."[29] "[E]vo-lution," Morris asserts, "is not science; it is always religion in one form or another." As such, all the sects of evolutionism form a united front against their common enemy: scientific creationism.[30]

Morris concludes the third volume of his trilogy with a scathing criticism of "compromising Christians" who have bought into evolutionary theory. He is deeply concerned about this on two counts. Alas, those Christians who think they can incorporate evolutionary theory into their Christian theologies and worldview are being seduced by Satan to sell their religious birthright. Moreover, these liberal Christians, in their attempt to curry favor with the ruling intellec-tual elites, are often more hostile toward creationism than the humanists and nat-uralists. Quoting St. John's Gospel, Morris laments "they loved the praise of men more than the praise of God" (John 12:43). Morris likens Christian evolutionists to Christian thieves, liars, and adulterers: they are all inconsistent and in deep moral error. He bolsters this argument with a challenge that those who attempt to accommodate Christianity and evolutionary theory must certainly confront that if evolution is God's creative method, God would be a monster, since evo-lution is a very bloody mechanism. How could a good God use such a "brutal and inefficient" process to accomplish his creative ends?[31] For Morris, the an-swer is clear. Satan has used "the deceptive lure of evolution" to entice Chris-tians into believing a lie.

SOME FINAL REFLECTIONS ABOUT CREATION SCIENCE

As we did at the end of the previous chapter, we need to comment on the repre-sentativeness of Morris's views on society and creation. We would be remiss to suggest that the aggressive argument Morris makes in Society and Creation is fully shared by all creationist authorities. Many, like Kurt Wise and a number of other scientists who contributed to a recent creationist anthology, do not explore the social dimensions of creationism examined in this chapter. They carefully confine their creationist argumentation to the biblical and scientific realms, al-though they may very well embrace Morris's strong "evolution is the root of all evil" belief privately.[32] But others, like Duane T. Gish, James Perloff, and Ken-neth A. Ham, applaud Morris's linkage of evolution with many of the social evils of our day.[33] At the popular level, however, this linkage is abundantly clear and frequently made. One need only casually peruse popular creationist periodicals like Creation ex Nihilo or Answers Update to see that issues like abortion, the de-cline of the family, and the overall moral decay of America and the West are as-sociated with the satanic delusion of evolutionism.

We have examined creationism in some detail through the writings of its founder, leading spokesperson, and primary inspiration, Henry M. Morris. In fo-cusing on his views, we have not selected the most outrageous example of creation science rhetoric that we could find. While certainly not every creationist would agree with him on all points, Morris is as mainstream creation science as you can get. Ronald L. Numbers, the leading authority on creationism, has noted that no one has done more in the late twentieth century to popularize scientific creationism than Morris. Numbers, in turn, cites a grassroots anthropological study of creationism in North Carolina that concludes that Morris is by far its leading authority.[34]

Morris's *Modern Creation Trilogy* gathers and summarizes a vast literature of the past half-century (only a fraction of which we have cited in our notes). We contend that these three compact volumes accurately reflect the overall state of scientific creationism in America. Like it or not, the contemporary debate on origins cannot be adequately comprehended if one ignores Morris, the scientific creationism he champions, and the audience he influences. Moreover, we contend that detractors fundamentally misunderstand scientific creationism when they dismiss it as simply a mindless, ignorant, intolerant, or superstitious position,[35] rather than viewing it in the context of a complex and, to its adherents, satisfying worldview, one that provides considerable comfort and some explanatory power in a rather hostile world.

The first volume, *Scripture and Creation*, resonates powerfully with the substantial Christian fundamentalist subculture within America. There are tens of millions of Americans for whom the Bible is the final authority on all matters on which it speaks. For them, science cannot undermine their literalist understanding of events like the Creation, the Fall, and the Flood of Noah. They look at much of science as a speculative enterprise, constantly in need of revision, while for them the simple biblical message persists, a "shelter in the time of storm"—a comfortable constant in a disturbing world of change. This deeply religious subculture remains "pre-Enlightenment" in the sense of being relatively unaffected by the scientific and religious upheavals of the last few centuries.[36] In these circles, the critical German biblical scholarship of the nineteenth century is still anathematized, Darwin's insights have never been appreciated,[37] and science itself has all but lost its way.

This subculture's relationship to science is rather complex. A case can and has been made that the "centerpiece of [contemporary] conservative Christianity," biblical literalism, was introduced in the sixteenth century by the Protestant Reformers and was vital to the rise of science in the seventeenth century. The literal approach to biblical texts, particularly the first chapters of Genesis, informed and motivated natural philosophers in their quest to master nature.[38] From this vantage point, creation science is "good, cutting-edge science—of four hundred years ago."[39] And the conservative Christian subculture is not entirely "antiscience" today. Far from it. This subculture is by no means Luddite in its approach to modern communications, transportation, and medical technologies. But, more significantly, science and scientists within its ranks are accorded celebrity status, and there are a number of organizations that unite scientists of similar religious belief (most notably Morris's Institute for Creation Research, the Creation Research Society, and the Geo-Science Research Institute).[40] Science, in the reckonings of this deeply religious subculture, has detached itself from its roots in the simple observation of the world. Recall Morris's definition of science: "The systematic observation and correlation of present physical relationships and natural processes involving the properties of matter, the forces of nature and the phenomena of life."[41]

Note the terms of this definition and how, once this definition is adopted, certain developments end up outside the purview of science. If all science requires "systematic observation," then processes that are invisible, or only marginally detectable, are ruled out. Darwin may have made many "observations" while he was on the HMS *Beagle*, but he certainly never observed evolution. The Big Bang Theory may claim to have some observational support, but this is, at best, exceedingly indirect. If science can only be done on "present physical relationships," then scientific theorizing about past events and the multitudinous historical contingencies that make up the theory of biological evolution is ruled out a priori. "The study of origins—whether by creation or evolution—is," according to Morris, "necessarily outside the scope of science in its real sense." If a proper definition of science rules out speculation and theorizing about past events, then what is the status of such speculations? "[T]he theory of evolution is not science but is rather a belief, a religious philosophy of origins."[42] And, if one is looking for what now amounts to essentially religious insight, then the Bible is a much better place to look than secular scientific journals.[43]

Of course, the previous definition of science can be criticized.[44] It is, perhaps, an adequate description of the majority of what goes on under the umbrella of science,[45] but much of what it rules out is certainly considered to be science by the overwhelming majority of practicing scientists. In the context of the 1981 Arkansas creation science trial, philosopher Michael Ruse notes that the creationists' naive empiricism ignores the basic presupposition that makes any scientific inquiry possible: there is a "pervasive and stable *order* of natural laws, extending throughout the entire spatio-temporal scope of the universe." Geneticist Francisco J. Ayala goes even further when he notes that "[n]othing important in science is observable; you can't observe the intellectual construct—and *that* is science."[46] The real point here is that engaging creationism on this matter quickly leads one into realms of the philosophy of science, biblical exegesis, and theology—places unfamiliar to all but a few Americans. For most laypeople, the negotiation of these esoteric fields requires a proper guide—one who can be trusted—one who shares their fundamental orientation. And, for fundamentalist Christians, one could not find a better guide than Henry M. Morris, Ph.D., college professor, prolific author, and Bible believer.

Morris's second volume, *Science and Creation*, is sufficiently technical that a full grasp of the arguments is beyond the reach of all but the most scientifically sophisticated readers. The scientific arguments in that volume, outlined in the previous chapter, invoke concepts from such a wide range of disciplines that even a scientifically educated reader is likely to encounter unfamiliar material. Morris cites hundreds of authorities from a cross-section of the scientific community to support his arguments. Furthermore, he often cites the work of well-known scholars published in reputable journals—Gould in *Paleobiology*,[47] Dawkins in *New Scientist*,[48] Richard E. Leakey in *American Scientist*,[49] George Gaylord Simpson in *Science*.[50]

Most of the conclusions in *Science and Creation* are far outside the mainstream of contemporary science and have been for over a century. It is virtually impossible to find a geology course in an accredited institution of higher education that teaches that the earth is ten thousand years old or that the surface geological features of the earth are the result of Noah's Flood. Similarly, college-level biology courses are based, to a large degree, on evolution. There are no nuclear physics courses that suggest that radioactive dating be viewed with suspicion. There are no astronomy courses that are tentative on the reality of stellar evolution, or the five-billion-year age of our sun. And so on. The only exceptions are found at religiously fundamentalist colleges. The "science" in *Science and Creation* simply does not exist within the mainstream scientific community. It is a science long ago banished to a grassroots ghetto—its books are produced by religious publishing houses for popular, largely sympathetic audiences, and its research is presented at specialized conferences emphasizing creationism and is published in similarly parochial journals. Scientific creationism is simply not a part of what we might call the "culture" of science today. Its alternate theories and explanations are not in dialogue with their mainstream counterparts. But how is the average conservative Christian in America, without significant scientific literacy, to assess all this? How is he or she to distinguish between the relative scientific credibility of the *Creation Science Quarterly* and the *Scientific American*?

Despite its hyperbolic argumentation, the final volume, *Society and Creation*, could raise concerns about the implications and influence of evolutionary theory even among those who are not inclined for religious reasons to reject it. There is an oft-quoted story in the evolutionary literature about how the wife of the bishop of Worcester, on being informed in 1860 that Darwin's new theory explained how humans had descended from apes, exclaimed, "Let us hope that it is not true, but if it is, let us pray that it will not become generally known."[51] Those who find Morris's science utterly unconvincing[52] need to recognize that there are a number of very chilling notions that are implied, even if weakly, by evolutionary theory. Rutgers University mathematician Norman Levitt puts it eloquently when he writes that "[despite] a litany of denial from liberal religionists and conciliatory biologists alike, evolutionary theory, presented soberly and honestly, subverts the foundational view of morality."[53] For example, if we consider humans to be valuable (by whatever criteria), it follows—again, perhaps only weakly—that the process that produced them is a process to be appreciated, respected, even valued. But how can we respect a process that improves a species by ruthlessly, mindlessly, callously weeding out the unfit, without passing de facto tacit approval on eugenics? Is the human species somehow compromised by allowing mentally disabled humans to reproduce? And, if so, then are we not led to at least *consider* forced sterilization of such individuals? Of course, these aggressive conclusions certainly do not follow with any kind of airtight logical entailment from the fact of evolution, but they do find support there. And such arguments have been made in a number of historical settings, as Morris points out with clarity and passion.

Though some academics and animal rights activists might object,[54] most people believe that human beings are more "valuable" than animals. One of the ways of quantifying this "value added" dimension is to note that human beings are more highly "evolved" than the animals. In a vague, general sense, we tend to value species on a scale that is roughly proportional to their state of evolution. That is why we spend hundreds of millions of dollars assuring the comfort of dogs and cats in our homes and similar amounts assuring the discomfort of cockroaches. If the "evolutionary level" of a species is proportional to its value, how do we avoid "devaluing" those that we see as less "evolved"? This issue has such dire social and political implications that scientists put their careers in jeopardy simply by proposing to investigate the "relative evolutionary level" of different groups of humans.[55] If it could be ascertained scientifically that one branch of the human race is less evolved than another, there would be horrifying social ramifications. The fruit of this particular tree of knowledge is best left uneaten.

None of this gloomy speculation is *necessarily* tied to evolution. There are certainly many more considerations that come into play in such discussions than those associated with evolution. But the history of political appeals to the social implications of evolution sends a clear and chilling warning that we must maintain a constant vigilance against those who would derive social policies from the theory of evolution. A great deal of mischief has been justified in its name.

Is it any wonder, then, that tens of millions of religious people in America today are so ready to recoil in horror from evolution, reject the findings of mainstream science, and embrace the comfort of an alternative species of origins, namely scientific creationism?

NOTES

1. For a similar argument with slightly different emphasis, see Philip Kitcher, *Abusing Science: The Case against Creationism* (Cambridge, Mass.: MIT Press, 1982), 186–187; Niles Eldredge, *The Triumph of Evolution and the Failure of Creationism* (New York: Freeman, 2000), 10, 156.

2. Henry W. Morris and John D. Morris, *The Modern Creation Trilogy*, vol. 3, *Society and Creation* (Green Forest, Ark.: Master, 1996), 9–12.

3. Morris and Morris, *Modern Creation Trilogy*, 3:129.

4. Morris and Morris, *Modern Creation Trilogy*, 3:56.

5. Morris and Morris, *Modern Creation Trilogy*, 3:45.

6. Morris and Morris, *Modern Creation Trilogy*, 3:53–56. Curiously, while evolutionists will utterly reject Morris's argument as hyperbolic and nonsensical ranting, in their more candid moments, some do, in fact, recognize that evolution can be very corrosive to traditional religious understandings of life. For example, see Daniel C. Dennett, *Darwin's Dangerous Idea: Evolution and the Meanings of Life* (New York: Touchstone, 1995), 18, 521, and *passim*.

7. Morris and Morris, *Modern Creation Trilogy*, 3:12–24. Readers should recall the discussion relating to the second volume of Morris and Morris's *Modern Creation Trilogy*. Strictly speaking, evolution is exclusively a biological theory that deals only with the origin and development of life. But, since evolution often appeals to other sciences for support—to nuclear physics for radioactive dating of strata, for example, or astrophysics for the age of the solar system—Morris lumps these sciences together as a part of "evolution."

8. The phrase is from the title of a Thomas Hardy poem that also serves as the title of a recent book by A. N. Wilson on the loss of faith in the Victorian era: *God's Funeral* (New York: Norton, 1999).

9. Morris and Morris, *Modern Creation Trilogy*, 3:32–40.

10. Morris and Morris, *Modern Creation Trilogy*, 3:42.

11. The nebular hypothesis was the belief that the solar system, including the Sun and all the planets, formed from a gigantic rotating cloud of interstellar material. Under the influence of gravity, material in the cloud clumped into a large ball that we call the Sun and a number of smaller balls we call planets. Because the original cloud was rotating, the resultant system of planets all ended up revolving about the central sun in the same direction. Prior to the nebular hypothesis, there was no explanation for the observation that the planets all revolved about the sun in the same direction. This apparent "coincidence was, in fact, often used in arguments that the solar system had been designed and created by God."

12. Morris and Morris, *Modern Creation Trilogy*, 3:42–43.

13. Morris and Morris, *Modern Creation Trilogy*, 3:45. It should be noted here that spontaneous generation was a near universal belief in Western culture until Louis Pasteur's famous 1859 experiment disproving it. A piece of decaying meat, for example, was thought to spontaneously generate the maggots that were inevitably found on it.

14. Morris and Morris, *Modern Creation Trilogy*, 3:46.

15. Cosmogony is the branch of cosmology that focuses on origins.

16. Morris and Morris, *Modern Creation Trilogy*, 3:48.

17. It is ironic that Morris, who rejects out of hand the argument of common descent of species, seems surprising comfortable with a conceptually similar argument with regard to world religions.

18. Morris and Morris, *Modern Creation Trilogy*, 3:53–54.

19. Morris and Morris, *Modern Creation Trilogy*, 3:55.

20. Morris and Morris, *Modern Creation Trilogy*, 3:55.

21. Morris, of course, is not alone in pointing out the tremendously pernicious influence of Darwinist ideas misappropriated to social ethics. No less an evolutionist than Gould made similar charges in a number of places, some of which Morris quotes. See also the cogent comments of John C. Greene, *Darwin and the Modern World View* (Baton Rouge: Louisiana State University Press, 1961), 126–128. Contemporary philosophers of evolution like Michael Ruse go to considerable lengths to decouple social ethics

and Darwinian evolution. See Michael Ruse, *Taking Darwin Seriously: A Naturalistic Approach to Philosophy* (Amherst, N.Y.: Prometheus, 1998), 80–93; correspondence of Ernst Mayr to John Greene, April 19, 1990, quoted in John C. Greene, *Debating Darwin: Adventures of a Scholar* (Claremont, Calif.: Regina, 1999), 240–241.

22. Morris and Morris, *Modern Creation Trilogy*, 3:57.

23. Morris has a penchant for "isms."

24. These lists are compiled from chapters 3 through 5 of Morris and Morris, *Modern Creation Trilogy*, 3:57–179.

25. We note that while Marxists have certainly found Darwinian materialism congenial, Marxist theories of history have not meshed well with a biological view of human nature. A cherished leftist notion is that human nature is malleable. This has been the basis for the left's hope in the creation of a different kind of human society in the future. Darwinism, however, has preached that human nature is highly constrained by competitive evolutionary forces. See Peter Singer, *A Darwinian Left: Politics, Evolution and Cooperation* (New Haven, Conn.: Yale University Press, 1999), 20–30.

26. Morris and Morris, *Modern Creation Trilogy*, 3:107.

27. Morris and Morris, *Modern Creation Trilogy*, 3:113.

28. Whether or not Gould was and/or Eldredge is a Marxist has been a matter of much comment. Gould admitted that he had been brought up by a Marxist father and that may have predisposed him "toward being friendly to the kind of ideas that culminated in punctuated equilibrium." But, Gould noted, this Marxist influence "has absolutely nothing to do with whether punctuated equilibrium is true or not, which is an independent notion that has to be validated by nature." For his part, Eldredge has stated: "I am no Marxist, and neither for that matter is Steve [Gould]. . . . Punctuated Equilibrium is no Marxist fantasy." See John Brockman, *The Third Culture* (New York: Simon and Schuster, 1995), 60; Niles Eldredge, *Reinventing Darwin: The Great Debate at the High Table of Evolutionary Theory* (New York: Wiley, 1995), 102; Dennett, *Darwin's Dangerous Idea*, 309; Ruse, *Taking Darwin Seriously*, 65.

29. There is a growing body of literature, some of it unavailable to Morris when he wrote his *Creation Trilogy*, dealing with the intramural debates among evolutionists. Dawkins, one of the chief protagonists in these intense debates, makes it clear that punctuationists and gradualists all are opposed to "redneck creationism." See Richard Dawkins, *The Blind Watchmaker: Why the Evidence of Evolution Reveals a Universe without Design* (New York: Norton, 1986, 1996), 251. More recent volumes include Eldredge, *Reinventing Darwin*; Andrew Brown, *The Darwin Wars: The Scientific Battle for the Soul of Man* (London: Simon and Schuster, 1999); Ullica Segerstrale, *Defenders of the Truth: The Battle for Science in the Sociobiology Debate and Beyond* (New York: Oxford University Press, 2000).

30. Morris and Morris, *Modern Creation Trilogy*, 3:108–113.

31. Morris and Morris, *Modern Creation Trilogy*, 3:181–186. We will explore theistic evolution in chapter 8. Given the date of the publication of the *Modern Creation Trilogy*, Morris can hardly be faulted for not commenting on Pope John Paul II's support for theistic evolution given in his address to the Pontifical Academy of Sciences in October 1996. See John Paul II, "Theories of Evolution: An Address to the Pontifical Academy of Sciences, October 22, 1996," *First Things* 71 (March 1997): 28–29. But it is clear that his harsh words are leveled not so much at Roman Catholicism, but at evangelical Protestants and the colleges and universities they sponsor. What is far less excusable, however, is his

use (*Modern Creation Trilogy*, 3:187) of a 1974 source to criticize Christian colleges for ignoring the creation–evolution debate. The discussion and debate surrounding both cosmological and biological origins serve to make science and religion issues among the hottest topics of discussion at many, if not most, of the more than one hundred institutions of the Council for Christian Colleges and Universities over the past couple of decades.

32. John F. Ashton, ed., *In Six Days: Why Fifty Scientists Choose to Believe in Creation* (Sydney: New Holland, 1999).

33. See, for example, Kenneth A. Ham, *The Lie: Evolution* (El Cajon, Calif.: Master, 1987), 83–95; James Perloff, *Tornado in a Junkyard: The Relentless Myth of Darwinism* (Arlington, Mass.: Refuge, 1999), 219–234.

34. Ronald L. Numbers, *The Creationists: The Evolution of Scientific Creationism* (Berkeley: University of California Press, 1993), 283.

35. See, for example, Steve Jones, *Darwin's Ghost: The Origin of Species Updated* (New York: Random House, 1999), 2; George Johnson, *Fire in the Mind: Science, Faith, and the Search for Order* (New York: Vintage, 1995), 313; Brockman, *Third Culture*, 66; Dawkins, *Blind Watchmaker*, 251; Stephen Jay Gould, *Rocks of Ages: Science and Religion in the Fullness of Life* (New York: Ballantine, 1999), 149.

36. Theologian Langdon Gilkey's perspective is certainly worth noting at this point. He understands creation science to be "a form of popular science allied with popular religion." In his estimation, creation science could only be born "in a scientific culture where religious understanding takes on the lineaments of scientific truth and where much of science in turn aspires to have the global ultimacy of religion." See Langdon Gilkey, *Creationism on Trial: Evolution and God at Little Rock* (Charlottesville: University Press of Virginia, 1985, 1998), xii, 40.

37. David N. Livingstone and Mark A. Noll have pointed out that no less prominent a figure than Princeton Theological Seminary theologian B. B. Warfield (1851–1921) was open to the possibility of evolution. This is very telling since more than any other theologian Warfield helped to define the doctrine of biblical inerrancy, which, as we suggested in chapter 3, forms the intellectual basis for contemporary creation science. See David N. Livingstone and Mark A. Noll, "B. B. Warfield: A Biblical Inerrantist As Evolutionist," *Isis* 91 (June 2000): 283–304; Mark A. Noll and David N. Livingstone, eds., *B. B. Warfield: Evolution, Science, and Scripture: Selected Writings* (Grand Rapids, Mich.: Baker, 2000).

38. Peter Harrison, *The Bible, Protestantism, and the Rise of Natural Science* (Cambridge: Cambridge University Press, 1998), 8–10, 269–270.

39. Paul Jerome Croce, "Beyond the Warfare of Science and Religion in American Culture—and Back Again," *Religious Studies Review* 26 (January 2000): 30.

40. See, for example, Ashton, *In Six Days*. Approximately half of the contributions are from American scientists.

41. Henry M. Morris, *Many Infallible Proofs: Practical and Useful Evidences of Christianity* (San Diego: Creation-Life Publishers, 1974, 1996), 249.

42. Morris, *Many Infallible Proofs*, 249.

43. Ashton concludes his introduction to *In Six Days*: "I am convinced that a literal understanding of the Genesis account of creation is the most reasonable explanation out of all the current theories of how we came to be here" (vi).

44. Building consensus on a proper definition of science has been a notoriously challenging task and has generated a substantial literature. Philosopher of science Larry Laudan

has even made a strong argument that there can never be a satisfactory definition of science. Laudan's point is somewhat technical, however, and really only addresses the challenge of establishing the precise boundary to separate science from "nonscience." At a less esoteric level, there are a number of broadly accepted functional definitions that work well in the laboratory and the field. Components of these include Karl Popper's falsification principle and the notion of inference to best explanation. See Larry Laudan, *Beyond Positivism and Relativism: Theory, Method, and Evidence* (Boulder, Colo.: Westview, 1996), 85–86, 210–230.

45. Media portrayals give an extremely misleading impression of science. The overwhelming majority of professional science journals often go for years without publishing a single article that would, when appropriately recast, be of general interest. Scientific discoveries covered by the media, like finding possible organic material on a meteorite from Mars, or cloning a sheep, or making a carbon molecule in the shape of a soccer ball, all have some special feature—a controversy, a religious implication, a beautiful picture—that makes them "newsworthy."

46. Ruse and Ayala cited in Gilkey, *Creationism on Trial*, 131–132.

47. Morris and Morris, *Modern Creation Trilogy*, 3:37.

48. Morris and Morris, *Modern Creation Trilogy*, 3:38.

49. Morris and Morris, *Modern Creation Trilogy*, 3:87.

50. Morris and Morris, *Modern Creation Trilogy*, 3:93.

51. Quoted in Richard E. Leakey and Roger Lewin, *Origins: What New Discoveries Reveal about the Emergence of Our Species and Its Possible Future* (New York: Dutton, 1977), 21.

52. At the end of his sustained critique of scientific creationism, Kitcher cannot fathom that anyone would take Morris seriously when he presents his fantastic history of ideas linking evolution with a satanic conspiracy of delusion. "If the issues were not so serious," he notes, "laughter would be the appropriate response." See Kitcher, *Abusing Science*, 193–201.

53. Norman Levitt, *Prometheus Bedeviled: Science and the Contradictions of Contemporary Culture* (New Brunswick, N.J.: Rutgers University Press, 1999), 71, 327. Levitt notes that claims like those given by Steven Pinker in "Why They Kill Their Newborns," which argue that under certain circumstances there is a good deal of evolutionary logic to infanticide, only reinforce the view that evolutionary theory gives rise to ethical nihilism. Eldredge emphatically denies that there is a "necessary set of ethical implications [good or evil] implicit in the very idea of evolution." See Eldredge, *Triumph of Evolution*, 154.

54. Peter Singer's work challenging the moral division between humans and animals and exploring the extension of equality to animals comes to mind. See Peter Singer, *Rethinking Life and Death: The Collapse of Our Traditional Ethics* (New York: St. Martin's, 1995); Paolo Cavalieri and Peter Singer, eds., *The Great Ape Project: Equality beyond Humanity* (New York: St. Martin's, 1994).

55. The "Bell Curve" controversy of the mid-1990s, which explored the very taboo subject of the relationship of intelligence to ethnicity, provides the most obvious recent example of this. See Richard J. Herrnstein and Charles Murray (contributor), *The Bell Curve: Intelligence and Class Structure in American Life* (New York: Free Press, 1994); Bernie Devlin et al., eds., *Intelligence, Genes, and Success: Scientists Respond to The Bell Curve* (New York: Copernicus, 1997); Steve Fraser, ed., *The Bell Curve Wars: Race, Intelligence, and the Future of America* (New York: Basic, 1995).

6

‹—◆—›

The "Council of Despair": Popular Science versus Traditional Religion

In our first chapter, we looked briefly at the modern creation story that science has developed and continues to refine. This story rests on a number of basic scientific ideas, some quite secure and well understood by the scientific community and some not. But, whether the science behind the story is solid or shaky, there can be no doubt that an overwhelming challenge faces anyone attempting to understand more than a small piece of the vast scientific foundation on which the modern creation story rests. Even scientists highly trained in one field have few advantages over nonscientists when trying to understand a field other than their own.[1] The distinguished particle physicist John C. Polkinghorne, for example, accepts the theory of biological evolution.[2] But he has observed that, speaking as a physical scientist, he would be more comfortable with evolution if an evolutionary biologist would explain to him "how many small steps take us from a slightly light-sensitive cell to a fully formed insect eye, and of approximately the number of generations required for the necessary mutations to occur."[3] A physicist might well conclude that, compared to something like quantum theory, evolutionary theory is vague and underdetermined. Moreover, the physicist might naively expect that an explanation for a remarkable evolutionary achievement like the eye should actually be similar in clarity and quantitative rigor to the explanation provided by the physicists for how carbon atoms arise from hydrogen—an explanation that certainly could be provided to the satisfaction of a biologist. Oxford evolutionary biologist Richard Dawkins, the world's leading "explainer" of evolution, has ridiculed Polkinghorne's query as an "Argument from Personal Incredulity." But Dawkins does not respond directly to Polkinghorne's request for a "physics-style" explanation, other than to repeat the evolutionary shibboleth about the "shattering enormity of geological time" and then give some entertaining analogies about how "[t]rudging from coast to coast dramatizes the time *available* for the evolution of the eye" as if Polkinghorne's problem—his "incredulity"—would disappear if he only could understand big numbers.[4]

The challenge faced by physicists who would like to understand how an optically sophisticated eye evolves from a light-sensitive cell is partially mitigated by the background knowledge they bring to the investigation. Physicists understand light sensitivity and the general optical principles of functional eyes; the molecular maneuverings of DNA as it replicates and mutates present no challenges; and the mathematics of "differential reproduction" that describe the spread of advantageous mutations through the gene pool of a species is trivial compared to that required to master quantum theory. But these are just helpful pieces of a much more complicated whole. In the final analysis, physicists will have to work very hard to rise to the level of the biologists in understanding the eye and its origins and will most likely just assume that the conclusions of their bright colleagues in biology are probably reliable.

The challenges faced by the physicist, however, are dwarfed by those that confront a nonscientist, say, a historian,[5] for whom almost every piece of such explanations poses substantial challenges. So how does one go about trying to understand the science on which the modern creation story is based?

Scientific understanding flows from the scientific community to the culture at large in a number of different ways: textbooks, whose primary readers are schoolchildren and college students majoring in science, newspapers and magazines, the Internet, television, and books that "popularize" science. These various media also create the general cultural impressions of the scientific community, impressions that are especially and profoundly influenced by those practicing scientists who make the considerable effort to write for the general public.[6] A certain authoritative credibility animates books in which leading scientists present the latest findings from their own fields—fields to which the authors have, in many cases, made important contributions. Scientists like Dawkins, Stephen Jay Gould, Freeman Dyson, and Edward O. Wilson wield powerful pens. And when Nobel laureates with potent literary powers, like Steven Weinberg, write about particle physics,[7] or Christian de Duve about the origin of life,[8] or James Watson about DNA,[9] the texts can be elevated into something resembling "scientific scripture." The overwhelming majority of scientists, however, publish technical findings primarily in obscure, esoteric journals read only by their peers. They do not write for the general public and rarely make any effort to bring their ideas to a wider audience.[10]

Public perceptions of science are thus shaped in important ways by that very small subset of the scientific community who write about science for the literate reading public. Whether or not their portrayal of science is accurate depends on the degree to which this small subset—the "popularizers" of science—is truly representative of the scientific community as a whole and to which the science they present is itself representative of the whole. The last few decades have seen the emergence of a group of extraordinary science writers, many of whom are also active and contributing members of the scientific community. This chapter will look at this group of influential science popularizers and the portrayal of science that comes through in their writings.[11]

THE THIRD CULTURE

In his celebrated book *The Two Cultures and the Scientific Revolution*,[12] C. P. Snow lamented the divide between two different types of intellectual—the practicing scientist and the traditional humanist. The former, so the argument goes, knows calculus, thermodynamics, and genetics, but next to nothing about literature; the latter knows Latin, William Shakespeare, and literary criticism, but is ignorant of science. Neither can talk to the other. Viewed across Snow's divide, the caricatured scientist is parochial, narrow, and overly pragmatic; the caricatured humanist is obscure, pompous, and irrelevant. Snow lamented this divide but expressed some hope in the second edition of the *Two Cultures* that a few brave humanists will emerge who will make the effort to learn science and then write about it in a way that will bring the "two cultures" together. He called these anticipated literary pioneers the "third culture."

An argument has recently been advanced that Snow's third culture is here, but incarnated somewhat differently than he predicted. The scientifically literate humanist has not appeared, but the literate scientist has stepped into the breach and has emerged as the new public intellectual.[13] These third-culture intellectuals have flawless academic pedigrees. They do good science. Some of them are at the forefront of their disciplines, advancing the state of knowledge in their fields. Some of them worked with Albert Einstein; some even have scientific exotica named after them. And yet they write exceedingly well. One would have to be profoundly disinterested in science not to enjoy their books. The third culture is represented by people like the late Carl Sagan and Gould, Dawkins, Wilson, Daniel C. Dennett (the only nonscientist in the group, but exceptionally well informed), Peter W. Atkins, Weinberg, Dyson, and Francis Crick. As a group, these public intellectuals sport Nobel, Pulitzer, and Templeton Prizes.

Through their voluminous, often literary, and surprisingly popular writings and their regular appearances on public television, these third-culture intellectuals communicate the nature and content of science, as they understand it, to the larger culture. For millions of readers and viewers, their pronouncements constitute science. In this chapter, we highlight six of the more prominent members of this elite group. Our purpose is not so much to spotlight their ideas about origins and evolution, but rather to argue that, despite their scientific and literary sophistication, in some ways they are the mirror image of prominent creationists like Henry M. Morris. At the very least, in the context of American culture—which remains both scientifically advanced and persistently religious[14]—third-culture intellectuals often fuel the creationist movement with occasional disregard for the limitations of scientific knowledge and their dismissal of the concerns of traditionally religious people. No doubt, they will be insulted by or at least take issue with this claim, but it goes a long way toward explaining why almost half of all Americans believe in the young-earth creationism of Morris.

The popularizers of science—the writers that make up the third culture—speak for a rather large community of scientists, 40 percent of which, according to a recent survey, hold fairly traditional views of religion that include such things as praying to a God expected to care and respond.[15] Surprisingly, there is not a single leading popularizer of science who openly holds traditional religious views, and there are very few who hold any views that could be described as religious, even in some generous New Age sense. There are, however, several who are positively hostile to traditional religion and committed to demonstrating that science not only fails to corroborate any religious perspectives, but can also actually dismantle and refute any religious perspective on the world.[16] The majority of the leading science popularizers writing today are committed to the proposition that there is no transcendent meaning to the universe or human experience. This commitment expresses itself in a variety of ways, ranging from a strong conviction that human beings are better off without the obfuscating delusion that some things may actually have a purpose, to a sadness that science has failed to find such a purpose, to a fiendish delight in attacking and ridiculing religious beliefs.

The prevalence of this widespread agnosticism among the writers of the third culture is troubling for people who hold traditional religious beliefs. Of even greater concern, of course, is the occasional foray into outright nihilism. But, paradoxically, this is also a legitimate cause for concern for the scientific community, given the declining importance attached to basic research and even general science literacy in the culture at large. As interesting as science is, and as important as it is to understand the science behind current controversies like nuclear power, the environment, cloning, genetic engineering, and so on, many ordinary citizens recoil in horror from the bleak worldview that sometimes comes through in the writings of the third culture. If this is what science concludes about the world, then many Americans assume that there must be something wrong somewhere. Maybe the problem is with the science that supposedly underlies this stark view of reality.

THE "COUNCIL OF DESPAIR"

The popularizers of science certainly exert significant influence over the public discourse on science; in fact, their public presentations and conversations in some ways *are* the public discourse on science. Their high-quality literary works contribute greatly to the public's understanding and appreciation of science. And no doubt there are countless young scientists who were inspired in their careers through the writings of people like Gould, Wilson, and Weinberg.

From the perspective of traditional religious believers, however, the science popularizers unfortunately resemble what we are going to call, somewhat whimsically, a "Council of Despair." The world that some of the most prominent popularizers of science would have us understand, and the worldviews they would have us embrace are, in many ways, barren in the most literal sense of that word. The Council of Despair provides us with little reason to believe that the world might have a purpose and no reason to cling to the old-fashioned idea of hope.[17] The council includes such luminaries as Wilson, Weinberg, Stephen W. Hawking, Gould (deceased), Dawkins, and Atkins. All of them reject traditional understandings of purpose in the world. Wilson and Weinberg express a certain sadness at the apparent inability of contemporary science to supply such a purpose. Dawkins and Atkins, at the other end of the spectrum, celebrate their liberation from the asphyxiating confines of traditional religion and eagerly preach the new gospel of scientific nihilism. What follows is an attenuated bibliographical profile of these writers, focusing on their views of "purpose."

Richard Dawkins

Richard Dawkins is the first holder of the endowed Charles Simonyi Professorship of Public Understanding of Science at Oxford University.[18] He is renowned for his articulate defense of classical Darwinian evolution, which he has championed in a number of popular books, some of which have become classics in the genre of science writing.[19] In some ways, he functions as a sort of "chair" of the Council of Despair. He appears to be on a tireless quest to find the most reductionistic, nihilistic, and meaningless species of origins imaginable, which he describes in the most reductionistic language possible. Together with Harvard's Gould (recently deceased), he has become the most well-known target of critics who charge that science has been taken over by atheistic materialism.[20] Dawkins moved to center stage with the 1976 publication of *The Selfish Gene*, the pithy title of which became a standard phrase in subsequent discourse on origins. In *The Selfish Gene*, Dawkins argues that the organic world is actually ruled by DNA, and our bodies, with their complicated brains, sophisticated mechanics, powerful instincts, and complex motivations, are simply the apparatus that the DNA uses to propagate itself.

Dawkins's argument about the selfishness of the gene is certainly not without foundation; in some ways, it is classical Darwinism, which argues that organisms will acquire, through mutation and natural selection, adaptations that enhance their fitness and enable them to leave more offspring. Better eyesight, stronger muscles, and higher intelligence are all examples of adaptations that, in obvious ways, increase the fitness of the organisms that acquire them. In less obvious, but equally legitimate ways, there are psychological adaptations that enhance evolutionary fitness. Various forms of sharing, for example, can, paradoxically, enhance one's fitness, if sharing leads to a communal structure that increases everybody's chances to pass genes to the next generation. A gene, or constellation of genes, that predisposes its owner to share can spread through a population for entirely "selfish" reasons, namely the survival of multiple copies of themselves. The natural human tendency to share, often applauded as a virtue, is transformed by Dawkins into a Machiavellian legacy of greedy molecules bent on taking over the gene pool. All natural human predispositions, to the extent that they derive from the genes,[21] are "selfish" in this particular sense of the word. In Dawkins's stark and startling prose, "[w]e are survival machines—robot vehicles blindly programmed to preserve the selfish molecules known as genes." (The blindness of which he speaks derives from the inability of the genes to *anticipate* what behaviors or outcomes will result from their competition.) While such a revelation might bring some to despair, Dawkins does not find this scenario at all a gloomy picture, for it is a truth that fills him "with astonishment."[22]

Six years after the *Selfish Gene*, Dawkins published a sequel in which he responded to criticisms and elaborated further on its thesis. The central argument of the sequel is that organisms, under the mindless direction of their genes, alter the world around them in ways that should be considered extensions of their physical "bodies" or phenotypes,[23] which are themselves largely determined by their genes. Beavers build dams, birds build nests, gophers dig tunnels, and people make cars and highways. The world we have created around us—the art, the music, the religion, and the technology—is best understood as an extension of the "will" of these selfish genes, hence, the title *The Extended Phenotype: The Long Reach of the Gene.*

Dawkins's perspective was further elaborated in his now classic *The Blind Watchmaker*. This bestseller was praised by people like Wilson, Francisco J. Ayala, and Michael Ruse. Even Isaac Asimov (now deceased), in a back cover blurb on the American edition, said: "A lovely book. Original and lively, it expounds the ins and outs of evolution with enthusiastic clarity, answering, at every point, the cavemen of creationism." A reviewer in *The Good Book Guide* praised it as "the most important book on evolution since Darwin."[24]

The phrase "blind watchmaker" refers to the God that William Paley invoked in his classic nineteenth-century argument about design that opened with the following oft-quoted classic passage:

> In crossing a heath, suppose I pitched my foot against a *stone*, and were asked how the stone came to be there, I might possibly answer, that, for any thing I knew to the contrary, it had lain there forever: nor would it perhaps be very easy to show the absurdity of this answer. But suppose I had found a *watch* upon the ground, and it should be inquired how the watch happened to be in that place, I should hardly think of the answer which I had before given, that for anything I knew, the watch might have always been there.[25]

Paley draws the obvious conclusion that, unlike stones, watches display clear evidence of having been designed and, since design implies a designer, the existence of watches implies the existence of some intelligent being that designed the watch. A small additional leap and the existence of an intelligent, creating God is inferred from complex "designed" structures in the natural world. The eye is the paradigmatic example.

Dawkins's subtitle *Why the Evidence of Evolution Reveals a Universe without Design*[26] suggests that he wants to "explain away" the designing God of Paley and to show that the genetic blueprints that give rise to the complex structures of nature can arise on their own through completely natural processes. This he does with style and flair, not retreating in the least from some of the more challenging marvels of the natural world. In fact, the book contains an extended discussion of the astonishing complexity of the bat's radar system, a technological marvel that greatly exceeds the sophistication of any radar systems designed by human engineers.[27]

The *Blind Watchmaker* is an effective counterargument against the natural theology of nineteenth-century thinkers like Paley. Throughout this and his other provocative books, Dawkins argues consistently and aggressively that *any* appeal to *any* form of transcendent intelligence in the universe is misguided, and he celebrates our modern liberation from such notions, especially "the small-mindedness of the medieval church."[28] Invoking God to explain the complexity of the DNA replication machinery is described as a "transparently feeble argument."[29] In *Climbing Mount Improbable*, Dawkins presents some of the objections that physicists—including Sir Fred Hoyle—have raised against evolution that suggest to them, with their physicist sensibilities, that perhaps there is some intelligence behind the evolutionary process. Ridicule is heaped on their muddled heads as Dawkins corrects their misunderstanding—evolution is not really about "chance" he scolds—and then speculates about why it is "so hard for even sophisticated scientists to grasp this simple point?"[30] Whatever we may think about Dawkins's hyperbolic rhetorical style, this point in particular illustrates the complexity that this topic presents to a lay person. If Dawkins is even partially correct, and he most certainly is, that some scientists have trouble making sense of certain evolutionary arguments, what chance is there for a nonscientist to wade through these conceptual swamps?

Dawkins's strident and literary presentations of scientific ideas are peppered with snide commentary about religion and the hapless confusion of religious believers who, overwhelmed by the complexity of the world, revert to nineteenth-century misunderstandings about the origins of apparent design in the world. While there is little reason for concern about the science described in Dawkins's books, the presentation is coupled to a polemical antireligious agenda that can easily give the impression that the scientific ideas themselves are somehow at odds with religion qua religion. The medieval universe to which Dawkins has bid good riddance may have been a tidy garden filled with wondrous beings and structures that had come straight from the mind of God, but there was far more to medieval Christianity than this now-discarded cosmology (which actually owed more to classical Greek than explicitly Christian influences). At an even deeper level, Dawkins's insistence on viewing evolution in such aggressively reductionistic terms and his choice of metaphors—*selfish* gene and *blind* watchmaker—can be alienating. Most people in America, and the rest of the world for that matter, believe in some kind of transcendent purpose—their existence has meaning and they are not simply the product of exclusively blind forces. Few Americans identify themselves as atheists. Dawkins's worldview, firmly grounded in science, does not provide an attractive alternative to despair about the meaning of human life for the overwhelming majority of ordinary Americans.

Peter W. Atkins

Dawkins's Oxford colleague Peter W. Atkins, a lecturer in physical chemistry, expresses similar sentiments. Like Dawkins, who established himself initially as a competent scientist before becoming a writer, Atkins has a solid reputation within the scientific community, having written a number of important books, including a well-respected textbook in physical chemistry, now in its sixth edition.[31] And again, like Dawkins, he has become an important voice in the cultural conversation on origins through his popular books and essays.[32] He has also appeared in televised debates on theism, one of which—an April 1998 debate moderated by William F. Buckley at the Carter Presidential Center in Atlanta that pitted Atkins against well-known theistic philosopher and Christian apologist William Lane Craig—has been widely circulated.[33]

Atkins's foray into the world of popular science began in 1981 with the publication of *The Creation*,[34] one of the most speculative books ever written by a practicing scientist[35] and one that illustrates with considerable clarity the complexities faced by ordinary readers who would like to understand the scientific view of the world. Atkins is a *physical chemist*, which means that his "official" field of knowledge extends from the behavior of small atoms to large molecules. Physical chemistry does not deal, on one end of the spectrum, with the origins of matter, for that is the province of the particle physicist. Nor does it deal, on the other end of the spectrum, with the complexities of life, for that is the province of the organic chemist and the biologist. Physical chemistry is primarily concerned with the various mechanisms by which atoms form into molecules and molecules form into other molecules. Nevertheless, the *Creation* is a work of cosmology that attempts to answer fundamental questions about the ultimate origins of everything. As Atkins puts it, his "aim is to argue that the universe can come into existence without intervention, and that there is no *need* [author's emphasis] to invoke the idea of a Supreme Being in one of its numerous manifestations."[36]

Atkins invites his readers to embark, in faith, on a journey "to the edge of space, time, and understanding." There is "nothing that cannot be understood . . . there is nothing that cannot be explained . . . everything is extraordinarily simple."[37] Atkins discusses a number of relatively noncontroversial ideas like the origin of elephants and electrons, but gradually he approaches the question of ultimate origins—why is there something rather than nothing? Using explicitly biblical language, he writes: "In the beginning there was nothing. Absolute void, not merely empty space. There was no space; nor was there time, for this was before time. The universe was without form and void. By chance there was a fluctuation, and a set of points, emerging from nothing and taking their existence from the pattern they formed, defined a time. . . . From absolutely nothing, absolutely without intervention, there came into being rudimentary existence."[38]

This, of course, implies that as human beings we have "no need to regard ourselves as anything other than the ramifications of chance." Atkins concludes, eloquently, poetically, and triumphantly: "This is really the end of our journey. We have been back to the time before time, and have tracked the infinitely lazy creator to his lair (he is, of course, not there)."[39]

Atkins's speculations in the *Creation* are misleading, and, inasmuch as those speculations are presented as science, the presentation borders on dishonesty. There exists no theory in cosmology that shows how "a set of points" emerged from "nothing" (whatever that is). Current theories of cosmological origins are plagued by the absence of a theory that reconciles quantum mechanics with general relativity in the realm of the very small. General relativity is the modern theory of gravitation, accepted more or less universally as the proper theory for understanding the universe on a large scale. Quantum mechanics is accepted universally as the proper theory for understanding the universe on the smallest scales such as the atom. Under normal circumstances these two theories are rarely applied to the same phenomena. Inside the atom, for example, gravity is so weak that it can be ignored and quantum mechanics provides a complete description. On the scale of the solar system, quantum effects become immeasurably small, and general relativity provides a complete description. When the universe began, however, the mass densities were so high that general relativity is necessary to explain the intense gravitational fields. The universe is so small at its beginning that quantum mechanics is necessary to explain the probability distribution of the matter. But these two theories do not "fit" together. They give different, contradictory results. Atkins's speculations presuppose an as yet undiscovered theory reconciling quantum mechanics and general relativity—a theory that somehow provides us with nonexistent "points" that can assemble themselves into something.

In language, tone, and content, the *Creation* is a sophisticated attempt by a reputable scientist to convince the general reader that science can resolve that classic philosophical question about why there is something rather than nothing. Atkins's motivation, partially submerged, is clearly an enthusiasm to do away with the idea that there might be a Creator.

Atkins's agenda is completely exposed in his essay "The Limitless Power of Science."[40] In this aggressive essay, he lays all of his cards on the table: "science liberates." "Scientists . . . are privileged to be at the summit of knowledge."[41] "Theologians," he argues, "have contributed nothing."[42] Atkins looks forward to a day when science will have explained everything and demonstrated to all that "[r]eligion has failed, and its failures should stand exposed."[43] He is unruffled by the absence of meaning in his worldview and celebrates science for doing away with purpose. "Science," he claims, "can perform its elucidation without appealing to the shroud of obscurity of man-made artifice, including that supreme artifice, the presumption of purpose."[44]

Atkins believes that the universe created itself out of nothing; life is a chance assemblage of atoms; human beings are one product of a meandering, blind evolutionary process; and everything will end in meaningless thermodynamic decay. But these notions should not scare off the intellectually honest. While he confesses that his scientific worldview is "bleak" and "bony," it forms "the sparse working hypothesis to account for our existence." Other "rosier" worldviews are seductive in their imposition of "the hypothetical extraneous" on our understanding. "Religion," he asserts, is simply "argument by sentiment." "Soft flabbiness" describes such nonscientific thinking, "which typically lacks any external criterion of success except popular acclaim or the resignation of unthinking acceptance." Atkins concludes that all "softenings" of his "absolutely barren view of the foundations of this wonderful, extraordinary and delightful world are sentimental wishful thinking." Whereas science explains in terms of "a purposeless, knowable, and understandable fully reduced simplicity," religion, according to Atkins, seeks to explain by resort to "purposeful, unknowable, and incomprehensible irreducible complexity." Such a contrast exposes religion as a failure. "Science," he announces, "with its currently successful pursuit of universal competence through the identification with the minimal, the supreme delight of the intellect, should be acknowledged king."[45]

For Dawkins and Atkins, science is like a powerful liberating army, overrunning territory occupied by religion and freeing the captives from the confines of their delusional, if comfortable, prisons. There are certainly others who share this austere and triumphalist view of science.[46] But perhaps more typical are the responses of leading scientists like Wilson and Weinberg, who sense that something has been lost along the way. The liberating army of science may have burned down the prisons and freed the captives, but it failed to notice that there was no place for the newly liberated populace to live or even to go.

Edward O. Wilson

Edward O. Wilson is the Pellegrino University Research Professor at Harvard University and one of the most respected and influential scientists in the world. A prolific author, he has written two Pulitzer Prize–winning books, *On Human Nature* (1978) and *The Ants* (1990, with Bert Holldobler), and an award-winning scientific memoir, *Naturalist* (1995).[47] Wilson is widely recognized as the founder of sociobiology, which has "evolved" in recent years into the field of evolutionary psychology.

The goal of evolutionary psychology, as we outlined in chapter 1, is to provide genetically based explanations for human behaviors. A great many human behaviors possess a universality that makes sense only if such behaviors derive, at least partially, from the genes that every human being shares, in contrast to human cultures, which are not universal. Adolescent male aggression, maternal love, sexual attraction, and friendship are obvious examples of universal human behaviors that transcend local cultures and most certainly have a genetic basis. Just as traditional evolutionary theory attempts to explain the physical features of organisms as by-products of a natural selection that favors *physical variations* that lead to the production of more offspring, so evolutionary psychology looks to natural selection to favor *behaviors* that lead to the production of more offspring. Genes that influence their hosts to behave in ways that increase the number of their offspring will be successful and spread throughout the gene pool. For example, why do men philander? To spread their genes about. Nonphilanderers don't leave genes for nonphilandery, simply because they do not spread their genes around as effectively as their philandering neighbors. Why are men interested in women's hips and breasts? Because those are the parts relevant to having children. Men who paid no attention to this and mated with women whose shapes were not optimized for childbearing did not leave as many offspring. Why do women naturally choose men who they believe will commit to long-term relationships? Because they want help with the task of raising that offspring to childbearing age, to ensure that their genes—the ones that influenced their selection of a faithful mate—make it into the next generation. And so on. Just as conventional evolution provides plausible explanations for why we have big brains and good eyesight, evolutionary psychology provides plausible, if somewhat more speculative, explanations for why we behave in certain ways.[48]

Wilson's central insight about the evolutionary origins of human behavior came from his study of ants and their complex social behavior, a subject for which his enthusiasm and expertise are unequaled. Ants, as is well known, possess an extraordinary social structure in which vast numbers of them coordinate highly specialized behaviors. This sophisticated "ant culture" clearly derives from genetic influences. Soldier ants, for example, do not go to "soldier ant school" to learn their trade. They are born knowing how to be soldiers.

The insights of evolutionary psychology, which are considerable and often quite illuminating, nevertheless transform human motivations, from the most lofty to the most vulgar and degraded, into the natural consequences of an entirely unsupervised materialistic evolutionary process. There is no room in this expansive new inn for the central religious idea that a purposeful Creator may have played even a tiny role in the origin of human beings or their moral codes and motivations. In fact, religion is itself a by-product of the evolutionary past, derived from a primordial "pack mentality" that, for reasons of social stability, motivates us to gather together to worship the leader of the pack.[49] (All of which, ultimately, helps us leave more offspring to carry our genes into the future.)

One of Wilson's most substantial works, playing a major role in contemporary intellectual discourse, is *Consilience* that, while attempting to be properly respectful of the universal human impulse toward religion, nevertheless "explains" religion by "explaining it away." The central idea of Wilson's consilience worldview is that "all tangible phenomena, from the birth of stars to the workings of social institutions, are based on material processes that are ultimately reducible, however long and tortuous the sequences, to the laws of physics."[50] This is an extraordinary claim. The laws of physics most relevant to life are those that govern the behavior of atoms, prescribing the way that the electrons behave as they orbit about the nucleus. If the "consilience proposal" is correct, we should be able, in principle, to start with atoms and work our way to, say, organized religion.

The story would go something like this: Atoms combine to make molecules. Very large molecules can be combined to make simple life-forms. Simple life-forms can become more complex by combining with other large assemblages of molecules. Assemblages with the ability to reproduce effectively will take over their chemical world. Modifications that enhance this process will be preferentially selected and become more common. Various molecular structures that enhance reproduction will be favored. Some of these structures will perform specialized functions like "seeing" or "smelling," but all they are "really" doing is enhancing reproduction. An assemblage of molecules that can think and plan emerges and is enhanced through the selective processes of nature. Any molecular patterns that promote behaviors in their host organism that enhance reproduction are selected. Some patterns give rise to complex interactive behaviors that we call "culture" providing those behaviors enhance reproduction. Marriage, religion, shopping malls, and major league baseball all originated in this way.

The consilience vision promises to explain human culture as physics writ large. Consequently, religion is but one of several complex social behaviors "invented" by DNA molecules to replicate themselves into the next generation. The skeptical reader may be tempted to dismiss Wilson's consilience as just so much scientific posturing, as a sort of takeover ploy in which one science claims all fields as its own. After all, as yet there has been absolutely no link discovered between genes and, say, organized religion. Nor does there exist a theory of how this might work to suggest effective ways to look for such a link. Evolutionary psychologists would respond that this reflects the relative youth of this area of science. After all, we still don't know how genes make eyes, but nobody seriously doubts that this is what occurs. Skeptics should also recognize that *Consilience* is a speculative work, charting a proposed course for future investigation. It is not a summary of work that has already been done, or even work in progress. And Wilson's speculations emerge from a half-century of sociobiology/evolutionary psychology during which time a number of fruitful discoveries have lent credibility to this general approach.[51]

Unlike Atkins and Dawkins, who look with unrestrained eagerness for religion to pass away as the cold light of scientific truth chases the darkness from its cathedrals of ignorance, Wilson expects that religion will be durable and persist long after its evolutionary origins have been fully identified and explicated. But scientific materialism will win slowly. According to Wilson, "the final decisive edge enjoyed by scientific naturalism will come from its capacity to explain traditional religion, its chief competitor, as a wholly material phenomenon."[52] So deeply embedded are human religious motivations that Wilson is convinced that they can never be expunged. They are part and parcel of human nature. But they can be rechanneled. Wilson admits that "[p]eople need a sacred narrative. They must have a sense of larger purpose, in one form or other, however intellectualized. They will refuse to yield to the despair of animal mortality. They will continue to plead in company with the psalmist, *Now, Lord, what is my comfort?* They will find a way to keep the ancestral spirits alive."[53]

In *Three Scientists and Their Gods*, science journalist Robert Wright pressed Wilson on what kind of "sacred narrative" might replace the traditional myths of religion. Wilson responded that people should "get their epiphanies the way he's gotten his"—by becoming engrossed in the "endless unfolding of new mysteries" and by investing their faith not in Genesis but in "the evolutionary epic."[54]

Wilson was raised in Alabama as a fundamentalist Southern Baptist, with all the traditional elements—a born-again conversion experience, baptism by immersion, twice reading the Bible cover to cover, and so on. He has abandoned all of his religious heritage except for a marginal belief that the universe might require a deistic sort of creator and a profound appreciation for the psychological depths of religious experience.[55] One looks in vain through his excellent books for snide remarks about religion,[56] or celebration at his liberation from it. But, in the powerful and reflective pages that close his discussions of religion, there is little room for anything resembling the traditional religions that, collectively, command the allegiance of virtually everyone on the planet.

Steven Weinberg

Steven Weinberg is the Josey Regental Professor of Science at the University of Texas at Austin and winner of the 1979 Nobel Prize in physics. His 1977 book *The First Three Minutes*—now a classic in a new edition—was hailed by Martin Gardner in the *New York Times Book Review* as "science writing as its best."[57] It was also Weinberg's inauguration into the third culture. Since that time, he has been an important public spokesperson for science, playing a major role as an advisor on the ill-fated Superconducting Supercollider Project.

The *First Three Minutes* is an account of the early stages of the origin of the universe—the Big Bang. Surprisingly, Big Bang Theory suggests that the universe actually "matured" significantly within those first three minutes, as several major cosmological epochs unfolded. Weinberg takes the reader through this trio of minutes in a series of "frames," outlining in accessible prose the origins of the basic particles of the universe—the quarks and leptons (the electron is the most familiar member of the lepton family), the formation of protons and neutrons from combinations of quarks, and the formation of helium nuclei from protons and neutrons. (The electrons do not drop into orbits about the nuclei for another three hundred thousand years.)

Weinberg won the Nobel Prize for his work in showing how two of the four interactions in nature[58] split apart from a less specific interaction during the first second of the Big Bang. This accomplishment is elegant, profound, and exposes some of the deepest mathematical beauty at the foundations of physical reality, an aesthetic dimension that comes through in Weinberg's often poetic writings.

Weinberg concludes the *First Three Minutes* with some reflections about how human beings place themselves in the extraordinary cosmos of the Big Bang: "It is almost irresistible for humans to believe that we have some special relation to the universe, that human life is not just a more-or-less farcical outcome of a chain of accidents reaching back to the first three minutes, but that we were somehow built in from the beginning."

Weinberg rejects this view: "It is very hard to realize that this all is just a tiny part of an overwhelmingly hostile universe. It is even harder to realize that this present universe has evolved from an unspeakably unfamiliar early condition, and faces a future extinction of endless cold or intolerable heat. The more the universe seems comprehensible, the more it also seems pointless."[59]

Weinberg's membership in the Council of Despair was secured with this concluding lament about the pointlessness of the universe. In fact, this lament, particularly the last sentence, has become a part of the folklore of physics, and has been the subject of considerable discussion in the years since it was first written.[60]

In 1992, Weinberg published *Dreams of a Final Theory*, one of best meditations on science and its implications ever written by a leading scientist. In a highly personal style, Weinberg defends reductionism, attacks philosophy, destroys the "science is a social construction" perspective, and explains a good bit of particle physics along the way. In the penultimate chapter "What about God?" he returns to the issue of purpose. In moving prose, he discusses his personal sense of loss that we no longer live in "a world in which the heavens declared the glory of God."[61] The passage warrants quoting in full:

> About a century and a half ago Matthew Arnold found the withdrawing ocean tide a metaphor for the retreat of religious faith, and heard in the water's sound "the note of sadness." It would be wonderful to find in the laws of nature a plan prepared by a concerned creator in which human beings played some special role. I find sadness in doubting that we will. There are some among my scientific colleagues who say that the contemplation of nature gives them all the spiritual satisfaction others have traditionally found in a belief in an interested God. Some of them may even really feel that way. I do not.[62]

Weinberg and Wilson are world-class scientists with poetic souls. They take no satisfaction in the success that their science has had in sterilizing a world once pregnant with meaning and purpose. A religious believer might draw some consolation from the exuberance with which Dawkins and Atkins proclaim the cold truth of science. Their evangelistic style makes them appear like polemicists, in love with the argument, but not with the truth. Not so for Weinberg and Wilson, whose backs appear bent under the full weight of the implications of their science.[63]

Stephen Jay Gould

Until his death in the spring of 2002, Stephen Jay Gould was the Alexander Agassiz Professor of Zoology and a professor of geology at Harvard University. He was unmatched as a scientific writer in his combination of breadth, depth, literary style, and sheer volume of output. After Carl Sagan, Gould was probably the best known member of the American scientific community. He wrote or contributed to more than twenty books, about half of which are collections of essays and reflections from his *Natural History* column.[64] The remainder are single-theme books on a variety of topics, some of which he approached with considerable passion.[65] His *Mismeasure of Man* is an outstanding exposure of the dangers of quantifying human intelligence and the sobering injustices that have resulted from this pseudoscience in the past. His more recent *Questioning the Millennium* is a charming and erudite romp through the significance and timing of millennial passages. An avid baseball fan, Gould endeared himself to many Americans who couldn't care less about paleontology and evolution with an occasional enthusiastic essay on baseball.[66]

When he touched on religion, Gould was generally respectful and rhetorically restrained. He often strongly criticized those who ridicule religion with false caricatures. For example, in "The Late Birth of a Flat Earth," he corrected the widespread impression that Christians up until the time of Christopher Columbus believed the earth was flat, heaping scorn on those who, because they have an antireligious agenda, are all too willing to believe the worst of religious believers.[67]

That said, Gould held two views that alienate and even antagonize many traditional religious people: (1) Evolution, properly understood, is completely without direction. There is no "tendency toward greater complexity," and humankind is not the "end-product" of evolution. (2) Religion and science are "non-overlapping magisteria." Science "owns" the realm of factual reality, while religion owns the realm of values.

The utter randomness and contingency of evolution is a topic that Gould visited on occasion in his essays, but his clearest exposition is in *Wonderful Life*, where he waxed eloquently about the "awesome improbability of human evolution."[68] *Wonderful Life* is an account of the classification of fossils from an important rock formation named the Burgess Shale (found in a British Columbia limestone quarry)— an esoteric topic that only a master like Gould could render interesting. The Burgess

Shale find was important because it is the "only extensive, well-documented window upon that most crucial event in the history of animal life, the first flowering of the Cambrian explosion."[69] When the fossils were first discovered by Charles Walcott in 1909, he classified them in accordance with his understanding of evolution, which tended to see it as a process steadily producing more advanced life-forms. This led him to "shoehorn" the Burgess fossils into existing groups, completely missing the fact that the majority of the Burgess animals, which appeared rather suddenly and in remarkable diversity, had become extinct and were not members of any modern group. Human beings trace their ancestry back to one of the few species that survived—a worm-like creature called Pikaia. If Pikaia had not won the evolutionary lottery, then you would not be here to read about it.

Gould observed further that "[t]he history of life is a story of massive removal followed by differentiation within a few surviving stocks, not the conventional tale of steadily increasing excellence, complexity, and diversity."[70] Walcott, alas, could not see this, because of his belief that evolution was the mechanism by which God created humans. Such a process is not going to be characterized by massive, meaningless extinctions, and lottery-winning survivors. Gould argued that Walcott missed this message of the Burgess Shale because of his religious presuppositions: "If the history of life shows God's direct benevolence in its ordered march to human consciousness, then decimation by lottery, with 100,000 possible outcomes (and so very few leading to any species with self-conscious intelligence), cannot be an option for the fossil record."[71]

Wonderful Life ends with reflections on the nature of history. History, as we know, is filled with at least two kinds of events—the inevitable and the contingent. Wars are inevitable, but the loss of any particular life in a war is contingent. Discoveries are inevitable, but individual discoverers are contingent. And so on. That human beings exist on this planet is a contingent event. Many random events happened along the way and the meandering course of a blind evolutionary process stumbled across Homo sapiens. Start the process over, different contingent events will occur, and there will be no Homo sapiens at the end of the process. "Replay the tape a million times from a Burgess beginning," Gould asserted, "and I doubt that anything like Homo sapiens would ever evolve again."[72]

Gould made a related, although more subtle, argument in *Full House*.[73] His argument goes like this. Life-forms, even the simplest ones, are very complex. There are significant challenges to the spontaneous formation of a living cell from inorganic molecules, and one must reasonably assume that the first life-forms were as simple as possible. It is very, very unlikely that life would get started in some highly complex mode if there were simpler modes available. Life probably began in the simplest possible form that was capable of doing the things that living things do—mainly replicating itself. Gould charted the complexity of life-forms along a graph running from simple to complex, from left to right, from primordial life-forms to Homo sapiens. Life begins at the far left on the graph, at what Gould called the "Left Wall of Minimal Complexity."

Now here is the interesting point. What can a species do once it gets started at the "Left Wall of Minimal Complexity"? It can't move to the left, because that would mean it was getting simpler, and it is already as simple as possible. A minimally complex species can either remain minimally complex or become more complex by moving away from the "Left Wall." Increasing complexity, therefore, is not something mysterious—it is, rather, the only possible change that can occur.

Some readers may recognize Gould's argument as the old "Drunkard's Walk" from elementary statistics. Put a drunk at the point (0, 0) on a gigantic piece of graph paper. Let him stagger (completely randomly[74]) for a while and see where he ends up. He can't get any closer to the origin for he is already there. He either does nothing or staggers away. And, as every student of statistics knows, the drunkard will stagger further and further from the origin almost as if he is moving away from the origin on purpose. So it is with life. Life-forms stagger through a "design space" of possibilities and randomly move away from the Left Wall of Minimal Complexity.

While Gould's argument in *Full House* is different from that of *Wonderful Life*, the conclusion is exactly the same: "We are glorious accidents of an unpredictable process with no drive to complexity, not the expected results of evolutionary principles that yearn to produce a creature capable of understanding the mode of its own necessary construction."[75] Gould might seem to be echoing Dawkins's selfish gene–blind watchmaker argument here, but there is an important difference. The blind watchmaker argument does not preclude the possibility that evolution might have a built-in tendency to increase the complexity of organisms.[76] If one believes, as Dawkins does, that evolution is easily capable of generating increasing complexity, then one can believe, as Dawkins does not, that there is some inherent "purpose" in the process—that the game has been "rigged" in such a way as to head in the general direction of Homo sapiens.

All this is critical for our discussion of the Council of Despair. Gould's insistence that any apparent direction to evolutionary change is but an artifact of life's origin at the Left Wall of Minimal Complexity effectively ruled out the possibility that there may have been any intelligence behind the evolutionary process. As long as the evolutionary process is understood to be one of "progress"—no matter how haphazard—it is possible to construe evolution as a possible mechanism by which God created animals, plants, and people. Indeed, as we will see in a later chapter on theistic evolution, this is precisely what thinkers in that camp have tried to conceptualize.

Gould's view of the proper relationship between science and religion was the second aspect of his thought that alienated traditional religious believers. As the world's best-known and most public evolutionist, he was very much at home on the battlefields of science and religion. He had long been a primary target of creationists and served as an expert witness at the 1981 Arkansas creation–evolution trial. Over the years, his essays occasionally treated issues that bore on the relationship of science and religion. And he got flak from fellow evolutionists for his criticism of colleagues who seemed to go out of their way to exaggerate conflict between the two.

One of Gould's most visible forays into these choppy waters came in 1992 when he reviewed Phillip E. Johnson's antievolutionary polemic *Darwin on Trial* for *Scientific American*.[77] In a hostile and ad hominem review,[78] Gould weighed in on, among other things, the relationship between science and religion, pointing out that a number of very famous evolutionists—Darwin's American contemporary Asa Gray, Burgess Shale discoverer Charles Walcott, and leading geneticist Theodosius Dobzhansky—were all religious believers. He concluded: "Either half my colleagues are enormously stupid or else the science of Darwinism is fully compatible with conventional religious beliefs—and equally compatible with atheism, thus proving that the two great realms of nature's factuality and the source of human morality do not strongly overlap."[79]

In a 1999 book-length essay, Gould elaborated the general notion that science and religion can be neatly compartmentalized into two realms—one of fact, the other of value. His *Rocks of Ages* defends the familiar model in which science and religion belong to separate spheres that do not interact. These separate spheres are described as "non-overlapping magisteria" or NOMA for short. Gould assigned science the task of documenting "the factual character of the natural world" and developing "theories that coordinate and explain these facts." Religion, however, "operates in the equally important, but utterly different realm of human purposes, meanings, and values—subjects that the factual domain of science might illuminate, but can never resolve."[80]

Rocks of Ages presents and defends NOMA from a variety of perspectives. The historical discussion is particularly helpful, arguing that science and religion generally get along provided everyone works under an implicit NOMA paradigm, which they do most of the time. Major disturbances of this arrangement of "respectful noninterference" occur when NOMA is temporarily and unnecessarily set aside.[81] The Galileo affair of the seventeenth century is a prime example. Gould was right that the overwhelming majority of what happens within the magisterium of science has no connection to what happens within the magisterium of religion. One has only to pick up a leading scientific journal and place it beside a leading religious journal to realize just how nonoverlapping these two magisteria are.

While Gould was clearly attempting to broker a truce, most traditionally religious people will not appreciate the terms. Being told that their religion—with its particular magisterium—contains nothing that is really factual borders on insulting, regardless of the intention. While most of religion can probably reside comfortably within the realm of values, virtually all religions have some "facts" that are of more than passing relevance. The existence of God, for most religious believers, is a "fact" not unlike the existence of other complex things that do not advertise themselves in journals of sensory perception. Of particular interest on this account is the belief that God created human beings. Gould permitted nothing on this score beyond the simple affirmation that, whatever the magisterium of science says about origins, religion may claim that God "superintended" the process. "Some personal versions of creation," Gould conceded, "fall entirely within the spirit of NOMA . . . —the belief, for example, that God works through laws of evolution over the long time scale determined by geology, and that this style of superintendence may be regarded as a mode of creation."[82]

There are a variety of interpretations of the "laws of evolution" and even some ambiguity about whether one can speak of such things. Many religious believers accept evolution in some form but understand that it is "directed" in some way by God[83]—that the process is not one in which an entirely "blind" chance offers up variations to an equally blind selection process. It is precisely at this point that the most vigorous disagreement appears between scientists like Gould and religious believers. Religious believers would like to be able to affirm that God exists and Gould, charitably following the guidelines of NOMA, would have extended them that courtesy, and even fought on their side against some of his colleagues who would hold that belief up to challenge and ridicule. However, the God that Gould was willing to tolerate was not allowed to *do* anything. Gould's God could watch evolution taking place, but could not interact with the process in any way. This highly constrained NOMA-motivated concession did little to convince the traditional religious believer that there is any room for belief in God within the scientific worldview.

Stephen W. Hawking

The final member of the Council of Despair that we will profile is the celebrated Cambridge cosmologist Stephen W. Hawking, well known for the extraordinary courage he has showed in continuing his research while an incurable disease has savaged his body. Hawking holds the Lucasian Chair of Mathematical Physics at Cambridge, once held by Isaac Newton and more recently by Paul Dirac. He has made major contributions to physics, particularly in the physics of black holes. He is widely respected and considered by many to be one of the greatest theoretical physicists since Einstein. Hawking became an international sensation in 1988 with the publication of A *Brief History of Time* which, despite its esoteric content, has sold millions of copies—considerably more than Madonna's book on sex, as its author has pointed out with relish.[84] The book was on the best-seller lists for more that one hundred weeks and has been translated into over thirty languages. In 1999, at a sold-out lecture at Boston's Wang Center, Hawking received a wildly enthusiastic reception akin to that accorded rock-star and movie celebrities.

The key idea that Hawking presents in A *Brief History of Time* is the "no boundary" universe concept, perhaps the most complex idea ever explicated in a popular book. In the standard Big Bang cosmology, which we outlined briefly in chapter 1, there emerges a troubling ambiguity in trying to understand the very earliest moments of the universe. The theory provides a solid description of the universe for virtually the entirety of its ten- to twenty-billion-year history. As the clock is rewound from the present to the distant past, straightforward application of well-understood theory illuminates the many epochs of the universe. We can get back before the time of stars, before the time of molecules, before the time of atoms, and so on. Nothing is encountered that we cannot, in principle, explain. Moving forward from these early times is equally straightforward, and the universe opens up with all the familiar wonder of a chrysalis.[85] But there is a mystery!

What happens when we get to the actual birth of the universe? How do we understand this "point" out of which the universe emerged? When we extrapolate back to this point, we get what is called a "singularity," where space and time become so distorted that, in the language of general relativity, we say that the "curvature of spacetime has become infinite." This is a rather mathematical notion, but it comes quite directly out of general relativity—the modern theory of how gravity works. General relativity is a well-established theory that shows how matter distorts space and time. Matter changes the space around it in such a way that a light beam curves as it passes through the space. Matter influences the passage of time in such a way that the rate at which time passes (as measured by any device capable of keeping time) changes depending on the strength of the gravitational field. Clocks at the top of tall buildings at Harvard University have been observed to run more slowly than those same clocks when they are in the basement.[86] As we journey back to the beginning of time, the universe gets smaller and smaller but the total amount of matter[87] in the universe remains constant. This causes the density of the universe to increase without limit. Consider that all the matter that currently comprises the planets, stars, and galaxies was once compressed into a space the size of a golf ball. Such densities are unimaginable, but general relativity provides equations that show just how time and space will be distorted in such an extraordinary regime. As we journey back to the very beginning, where the universe has no size at all, and the clock is rewound all the way back to zero, the distortion of space and time become infinite, and the equations suddenly become nonsensical. This point is called a "singularity." When cosmologists awaken at night in cold sweats, it is because they have dreamed of a singularity.

Physical theories fail completely at singularities; this is the regime where quantum mechanics and gravity must both apply, and nobody has figured out how to reconcile these two rather different theories. (Quantum theory, for example, states explicitly that a singularity of the form predicted by general relativity cannot exist.) If we extrapolate the present behavior of the universe backwards in time to the point where t = 0, we find the universe suddenly appearing, as if from nowhere, uncaused, with no antecedents. Uncaused events with no antecedents are disturbingly beyond the grasp of scientific explanation and many physicists simply throw up their hands at this point.[88] Introductory astronomy texts, for example, generally provide Big Bang time lines that include such relatively well-understood phenomena as the origin of the stars and galaxies, the formation of atoms, and even the first appearance of elementary particles. But such time lines, taking care not to mix speculation with science, don't run their time lines to t = 0; rather, they start at very early, but nevertheless "postabsolute-beginning times."[89]

There is "an event" here that seems forever beyond the reach of science, representing a fundamental boundary, not merely a spatiotemporal boundary to our universe, but an epistemological boundary to scientific knowledge. As Hawking notes, "even if there were events before the big bang, one could not use them to determine what would happen afterward, because predictability would break down at the big bang."[90] His goal in *A Brief History of Time* is to suggest a speculative mechanism to "explain away" this unsettling t = 0 beginning. Rather than speculate about what happens "before" the point t = 0, he suggests that there is no "before t = 0" point. To do this he introduces some very speculative physics, like "imaginary time,"[91] but the end result is a universe that does not have a beginning. It just is.

Hawking explains his model with the aid of a geometrical analogy. He suggests that traveling though time to the beginning of the universe is like traveling across the surface of the earth to the North Pole. The t = 0 point in time is like 0 degrees latitude on the earth. Just as the earth does not "begin" in any sense at the North Pole, and there is actually nothing peculiar about that point, so the universe does not "begin" at t = 0. He explains further that the distance from the North Pole represents imaginary time, while the size of the earth represents the spatial size of the universe. "The universe starts at the North Pole as a single point. As one moves south, Hawking continues, "the circles of latitude at constant distance from the North Pole get bigger, corresponding to the universe expanding with imaginary time."[92] We do not "experience" the universe behaving in this way because we are in "real-time." The history of the universe in real-time, however, would look very different. At about ten or twenty billion years ago, it would have a minimum size that was equal to the maximum radius of the history in imaginary time.[93]

To understand how this works requires years of training in physics and mathematics, and even those who understand it do not agree that this represents the actual state of affairs at the "beginning" of the universe. But, as Hawking correctly points out, it is a *possibility*.[94] He goes on to point out that there are currently insurmountable difficulties in conducting any observational tests. We cannot dismiss Hawking's proposal, however, simply because it is too speculative and not grounded firmly in observation. Nicolaus Copernicus's idea that the earth was not at the center of the universe once seemed too speculative for some of its critics, and it was a rather long time until it was conclusively established by observation. Hawking's proposal is *logically possible* and not in *disagreement* with anything that is known about the first moments of the universe. The problem is that we know so little. Scientific theories are sometimes compared to tents flapping in the wind, with observational pegs holding them down. A solid theory has many pegs and is held securely; a speculative theory has few or no pegs and flaps free. Hawking's theory that the universe had no beginning flaps quite freely in the wind.

Hawking believes his proposal has profound theological implications that constrain what God may or may not have done as creator of the universe. In straightforward language that makes reference to God as if God were just another particle in the universe, he says: "The idea that space and time may form a closed surface without boundary also has profound implications for the role of God in the affairs of the universe."[95] By removing the "event" that occurs at t = 0, there is no specific creative act for God to perform at that juncture as he reaches across the "boundary" of the physical world to perform the creative act described in Genesis 1:1—"In the beginning God created the heaven and the earth." Hawking pushes the implications of his views to their logical conclusion: "[I]f the universe is really completely self-contained, having no boundary or edge, it would have neither beginning nor end: it would simply be. What place, then, for a creator?"

Like Atkins's *Creation*, Hawking's *A Brief History of Time* is aimed directly at the idea that God created the universe. Hawking mentions God many times as the explanation for what happens at a boundary of the universe, as something that becomes irrelevant if there is no boundary. The late Carl Sagan wrote the preface. After introducing Hawking and the general topic, he concludes:

> This is also a book about God . . . or perhaps about the absence of God. The word God fills these pages. Hawking embarks on a quest to answer Einstein's famous question about whether God had any choice in creating the universe. Hawking is attempting, as he explicitly states, to understand the mind of God. And this makes all the more unexpected the conclusion of the effort, at least so far: a universe with no edge in space no beginning or end in time, and nothing for a Creator to do.[96]

Hardly sentiments with which to soothe the religious soul looking for solace and comfort amid the vagaries of life and the prospect, one day, of death.

THE COUNCIL OF DESPAIR

We have looked at six major science writers: Richard Dawkins, Peter W. Atkins, Edward O. Wilson, Steven Weinberg, Stephen Jay Gould, and Stephen W. Hawking. What can we conclude? Dawkins and Atkins are quite pleased to be able to fashion, from science, a club with which to bash religion and drive purpose from the universe. Weinberg and Wilson lament the failure of science to either maintain or discover purpose in the universe. Gould wants desperately to be charitable but seems unable to abide anything beyond an emasculated form of religion confined to the realm of values. Hawking thinks he has developed a mathematical proof that God did not create the universe. None of them participate in any traditional religion; all of them believe that science has basically ruled out anything resembling religion.

In their rejection of purpose in the universe, the science popularizers have become for many a Council of Despair.[97] We are but selfish genes in a purposeless world, matter became conscious, fighting a powerful delusion that we are here for a purpose. And the Council of Despair is in fact much larger. We have looked at only six of the most prominent popularizers of science. We could have chosen Daniel C. Dennett, a professor of philosophy at Tufts and author of *Darwin's Dangerous Idea*, a book that describes Darwinism as a "universal acid" eating away, among other things, traditional religious beliefs.[98] The now-deceased Carl Sagan and Isaac Asimov,[99] two of the most prolific writers on science in the century just past, were both aggressively hostile to the idea of religion. Sagan is famous for his opening line in the marvelous PBS *Cosmos* series: "The cosmos is all that is, ever was, or ever will be." Asimov was an outspoken atheist who was active in the American Humanist Association. He provided a cover blurb for the paperback editions of the *Blind Watchmaker*, which praised Dawkins, as we mentioned earlier, for the way he countered the "cavemen of creation." Nobel laureate Francis Crick, codiscoverer of DNA, wrote an entire book arguing that neurobiology has disproven the religious concept of the soul.[100] Cosmologists Lee Smolin and Martin Rees have both written books outlining alternative models for an uncreated universe,[101] and so on.

Of course, there are exceptions to this general pattern—prominent scientists like Paul Davies, Freeman Dyson, and Ursula Goodenough. Cosmologist Paul Davies argues in *The Mind of God* that the highly rational character of the physical laws of the universe points to a transcendent ordering Mind.[102] But Davies's "ordering Mind" is only "God" in a metaphorical sense, and certainly not the "God of Abraham, Isaac, and Jacob." Comparable sentiments are expressed by Dyson in his remarkable autobiography *Disturbing the Universe*, where he wrote, in a memorable and oft-quoted phrase: "The more I examine the universe and study the details of its architecture, the more evidence I find that the universe in some sense must have known that we were coming."[103] Dyson is not a hard-nosed materialist and, in fact, criticizes his colleagues who champion that viewpoint.[104] Officially, he calls himself an agnostic, but his writings make it clear that his agnosticism is tinged with something akin to deism. Cellular biologist Ursula Goodenough is keenly interested in combating the notion that a rigorously held scientific worldview must generate existential despair. Quite the opposite. For her the scientific account of how things are and came to be can stir something she calls "religious naturalism." This amounts to reverence and gratitude for the sacredness of life—its astonishing complexity and the vast eons of time it took to generate such diversity of life. This can combine with the mythos of traditional religions, and may or may not include notions of a God, though Goodenough's religious naturalism certainly entails "a covenant with Mystery."[105]

While Davies, Dyson, and Goodenough are definitely religious in their deep appreciation of the mystery of existence, they are not in the mainstream of any portion of American religious culture. Goodenough, it must be noted, joined a Presbyterian church, and even sang in the choir for a time. But one finds no affirmation of Christian orthodoxy in her *Sacred Depths of Nature*, for Goodenough, curiously, is an atheist. And while both Davies and Dyson have received the prestigious Templeton Prize for Progress in Religion,[106] neither of them is a part of any religious tradition.[107] Their awards were based, in part, on their willingness to accept the evidence for the finely tuned design of the universe at face value, rather than attempt to "explain it away" as the majority of their colleagues are wont to do. The presence of this perspective in their writings, a central feature of the Judeo-Christian tradition's concept of creation, constitutes scientific support for religion.

CONCLUSION

We have repeatedly made reference to polls showing that less than 10 percent of the population of America accepts that its origin is the result of random processes driven by purely materialistic forces. An even smaller fraction of Americans is prepared to claim the label "atheist." And yet, among the leading popularizers of science, we find commonplace the belief in purely materialistic causes for the origin of the universe and life. We also find an unbridled, often evangelical, enthusiasm for atheism.

What is extremely significant for our purposes of trying to explain why the origins question is so persistent in American culture is that brilliant scientists in their popular writings have launched what amounts to an assault on "purpose." Their alternative sentiments are unlikely to generate much enthusiasm in an American society with deep religious roots. In attacking the notion that the universe—indeed, life itself—has a purpose, they have also created a widespread impression that the scientific community as a whole is uncongenial, or even hostile, to the traditional religious beliefs that play such a large role in American culture.

The members of the Council of Despair have at times also gone far beyond the warrant of their respective disciplines to speak with amazing confidence about that which is at best highly speculative and certainly beyond that which they can say with much confidence *as scientists*. Not unlike the creationists they bash for speaking with unwarranted authority about that which they have not fully comprehended, the science popularizers may be guilty of using their platforms as respected public intellectuals to pontificate on matters that they cannot, as scientists, know. Some of them will, perhaps, be deeply irritated by this comparison, but in some respects they have become the mirror image of crusading creationists like Morris.

Is there a middle ground?

NOTES

1. Of course, there are *some* advantages, particularly since the sciences have so much overlap, and it is quite impossible to master one science without picking up quite a bit from others. There is also a general intuition about how to approach a complicated problem, a sense of how to find appropriate literature, ready access to relevant experts, and a reasonable chance that you took an introductory course in that field. But there is also the potential for a very serious type of misunderstanding as the experience obtained in one field may actually lead one into confusion about another. Physicists, for example, bring from their field an expectation of order, simplicity, and mathematical elegance that is virtually absent from biology. Francis Crick, who won a Nobel Prize for the discovery of the structure of DNA, was exceptional in that he moved successfully from physics to biology and was able to make good use of his physical intuitions. But, in his autobiography, Crick observed that "[p]hysicists are all too apt to look for the wrong sorts of generalizations, to concoct theoretical models that are too neat, too powerful, and too clean. Not surprisingly, these seldom fit well with the data." See Francis Crick, *What Mad Pursuit: A Personal View of Scientific Discovery* (New York: Basic, 1988), 139. British science writer Colin Tudge argues that all too often leading spokespersons of science convey the impression that science is far too difficult for the ignorant public to understand or even appreciate adequately. The danger of this position is that it leads to the impression that science is best left to the experts. Such an appeal to authority, Tudge claims, runs counter to the notion that "[s]cience's greatest quality is that it does *not* rely upon authority at least in principle." Tudge is not suggesting, of course, that laypeople should join scientists in the laboratory, verifying their conclusions for themselves. But he is suggesting that scientists owe the public more than smug assurances that they are correct. See Colin Tudge, "Why Science Should Warm Our Hearts," *The New Statesman* (2001), at www.consider.net/forum_new.php3?newTemplate=OpenObject&newTop=200102260015&newDisplayURN=200102260015 (3 March 2001).

2. Polkinghorne's position, which we will examine in the next chapter, is known as "theistic evolution," an umbrella term that covers a number of different understandings of evolution with the common feature that God is considered to be involved in the process in some way. In versions such as that articulated by Polkinghorne, there is no rejection of the possibility that the standard evolutionary mechanisms are sufficient to explain things like how a light-sensitive cell might evolve into an eye. There is, however, an explicit acknowledgment that one is not constrained to purely naturalistic explanations. If an explanation that contains reference to an ordering mind seems to be warranted, it should not be rejected a priori out of hand.

3. John C. Polkinghorne, *The Faith of a Physicist: Reflections of a Bottom up Thinker* (Princeton, N.J.: Princeton University Press, 1994), 16.

4. Richard Dawkins, *River out of Eden: A Darwinian View of Life* (New York: Basic, 1995), 77–78.

5. We remind the reader that the coauthors of this book are a physicist and a historian. This analysis emerges in part from their attempts to develop a mutual understanding of the various topics that are covered in this book.

6. We will not attempt here to establish a general conclusion about the relative significance of the various ways that scientific knowledge is disseminated. Sufficient for our purposes is the fact that a number of major books by leading popularizers have exerted a profound influence on America's cultural conversation on origins.

7. Steven Weinberg, *Dreams of a Final Theory: The Search for the Fundamental Laws of Nature* (New York: Pantheon, 1992).

8. Christian de Duve, *Vital Dust: Life As a Cosmic Imperative* (New York: Basic, 1995).

9. James Watson, *The Double Helix: A Personal Account of the Discovery of the Structure of DNA* (New York: Athenaeum, 1968).

10. One very practical reason for this is the simple fact that a great many scientists simply cannot write very well. One of the idiosyncrasies of science education is a remarkable lack of emphasis on writing. Science majors in college generally write less than just about every other major and rarely take any writing courses beyond an obligatory freshman rhetoric course.

11. The term "science popularizer" has a negative connotation in the scientific community, suggesting oversimplification and caricaturization. Some scientists may so orient their careers to communication with the broader public that they cease to do the kinds of empirical and lab work that earn them the professional respect of their peers. It was no doubt because the late Carl Sagan was hailed as the greatest science popularizer of the twentieth century that he was never elected to the prestigious National Academy of Sciences. Sociobiologist Edward O. Wilson and theoretical physicist Steven Weinberg, however, have written very successful, award-winning books of science popularization, without jeopardizing their standing within the elite of the scientific community. Wilson, it should be noted, prefers the term "science literature" to "science popularization." Nevertheless, for the sake of convenience, we use the term "science popularizers." It should be obvious that in a book of this nature, we do not intend to suggest anything dismissive about scientists, or any scholars for that matter, writing for a general audience. See Harvey Blume, "Edward O. Wilson: Aliens, An Interview," *Boston Book Review* (1995), at www.bookwire.com:80/bbr/interviews/edward-wilson.html (11 October 2000).

12. C. P. Snow, *The Two Cultures and the Scientific Revolution* (New York: Cambridge University Press, 1961), 1–22; C. P. Snow, *The Two Cultures: And a Second Look* (Cambridge, U.K.: Cambridge University Press, 1964), 97–100.

13. John Brockman, *The Third Culture* (New York: Simon and Schuster, 1995), 18–20.

14. Langdon Gilkey, *Creationism on Trial: Evolution and God at Little Rock* (Charlottesville: University Press of Virginia, 1985, 1998), 190. We are greatly indebted to Gilkey's insightful argument found in chapter 7 of *Creationism on Trial*.

15. Edward J. Larson and Larry Witham, "Scientists and Religion in America," *Scientific American* 281 (September 1999): 89.

16. See Tudge, "Why Science Should Warm Our Hearts."

17. Of course, this claim is challenged by some of the third culture, but the basis they give for hope is generally so foreign to the religious sensibilities of ordinary people that it seems incomprehensible. Edward O.Wilson, for example, at the end of *Consilience: The Unity of Knowledge* (New York: Knopf, 1998), his tour de force, suggests that "[t]he legacy of the Enlightenment is the belief that entirely on our own we can know, and knowing, understand, and in understanding, choose wisely" (297). He goes on to outline how this can become the basis for a sort of secular religion replete with "sacred oath" (298). In *The First Three Minutes*, rev. ed. (New York: Basic, 1988), Steven Weinberg suggests that the "effort to understand the universe" (155) can provide meaning. Francis Crick makes a similar proposal in the last chapter of *The Astonishing Hypothesis: The Scientific Search for the Soul* (New York: Scribner, 1994), which is entitled, suggestively, "Dr. Crick's Sunday Morning Service" (255–263).

18. The chair was endowed by Charles Simonyi who made a fortune as one of the founders of Microsoft. Simonyi was impressed with the quality of Dawkins's popular writing and endowed this chair so that Dawkins would have more time to write.

19. Among Richard Dawkins's most important works are: *The Selfish Gene*, 2d ed. (New York: Oxford University Press, 1989); *The Extended Phenotype: The Long Reach of the Gene*, rev. ed. (New York: Oxford University Press, 1999); *The Blind Watchmaker: Why the Evidence of Evolution Reveals a Universe without Design* (New York: Norton, 1986, 1996); *River out of Eden*; *Climbing Mount Improbable* (New York: Norton, 1996); *Unweaving the Rainbow: Science, Delusion and the Appetite for Wonder* (Boston: Mariner, 1998).

20. For example, the index to Berkeley lawyer Phillip E. Johnson's attack on naturalism contains ten entries for Dawkins, thirteen for Stephen Jay Gould, and eleven for Charles Darwin. See Phillip E. Johnson, *Reason in the Balance: The Case against Naturalism in Science, Law and Education* (Downers Grove, Ill.: InterVarsity, 1995), 242.

21. Wilson and others are convinced it is time to stand "biology on its head" and show how ethics derives from genetics. See Francisco J. Ayala, "The Difference of Being Human," in *Biology, Ethics, and the Origins of Life*, ed. Holmes Rolston III (Boston: Jones and Bartlett, 1995), 113–135.

22. Dawkins, *Selfish Gene*, ix.

23. The genotype is, roughly, the name for the genetic blueprint of the organism; the phenotype is the name for the organism itself as it develops under the influence of both the genes and the environment. The genotype establishes the parameters of the organism but the actual phenotype itself is also strongly influenced by the environment and behavior patterns of the organism. The reader's genes have established many of the physical details of that reader, but exercise, diet, prenatal care, and so on have strongly influenced the actual body within the parameters established by the genes.

24. Dawkins, *Blind Watchmaker*, back cover.

25. William Paley, *Natural Theology: Or Evidences of the Existence and Attributes of the Deity Collected from the Appearances of Nature* (Philadelphia: Johnson and Warner, 1814), 5.

26. Dawkins's subtitle—*Why the Evidence of Evolution Reveals a Universe without Design*—is strangely parochial and misleading. There are two primary scientific design arguments. One derives from the complex structures found in nature, like the eye. The other derives from the intricate balance of the physical laws of the universe, for example, the force of gravity is balanced with the speed of the earth so that it can orbit stably at the right distance from the Sun. Both of these different styles of design arguments, which are only tangentially related to each other, were presented by Paley in his classic *Natural Theology*. Most of Paley's critics, like Dawkins, argue that Darwinian evolution has done away with Paley's design argument, apparently oblivious to the fact that Darwinian evolution says absolutely nothing about any design that may be inherent in the laws of physics. The British edition of Dawkins's book, by the way, does not have the subtitle.

27. The reader can easily grasp the complexity of the bat's radar system by recalling that huge numbers of bats fly together in caves and each one of them has to be able to pick out and process its own signal from an astonishingly complex background that includes the signals from countless other bats. Dawkins's explication of this is marvelous.

28. Dawkins, *Blind Watchmaker*, 143.

29. Dawkins, *Blind Watchmaker*, 141.

30. Dawkins, *Climbing Mount Improbable*, 75.

31. Peter W. Atkins, *Physical Chemistry*, 6th ed. (Oxford: Freeman, 1997).

32. One interesting contrast between Dawkins and Atkins is the ratio of their "mainstream" scientific work to their "popular" books. Atkins has written a number of textbooks that deal exclusively with chemistry and make no metaphysical pronouncements about any "ultimate" implications that derive from chemistry. The majority of his published works are in this category. In contrast, almost all of Dawkins's books champion a particular philosophical view claimed to derive from the evolutionary biology that forms the basis of the presentations.

33. William Lane Craig and Peter W. Atkins, "Craig–Atkins Debate: What Is the Evidence for/against the Existence of God," 1998, at www.leaderu.com/offices/billcraig/docs/craig-atkins.html (15 November 2000).

34. Peter W. Atkins, *The Creation* (Oxford, U.K.: Freeman, 1981).

35. We would grant the award for the "most speculative" book written by a practicing scientist to Frank J. Tipler, *The Physics of Immortality: Modern Cosmology, God and the Resurrection of the Dead* (New York: Archer, 1995).

36. Atkins, *Creation*, vii, emphasis added.

37. Atkins, *Creation*, 3.

38. Atkins, *Creation*, 119.

39. Atkins, *Creation*, 115.

40. Peter W. Atkins, "The Limitless Power of Science," in *Nature's Imagination: The Frontiers of Scientific Vision*, ed. John Cornwell (Oxford, U.K.: Oxford University Press, 1995), 122–132.

41. Poetry, on the other hand, merely "titillates," and poets provide nothing more than "entertaining self-deception." This, however, is an improvement over theology, which merely "obfuscates."

42. Atkins, "Limitless Power of Science," 123.

43. Atkins, "Limitless Power of Science," 132.

44. Atkins, "Limitless Power of Science," 128.

45. Atkins, "Limitless Power of Science," 130–132.

46. A sustained and cogent critique of scientific triumphalism can be found in moral philosopher Mary Midgley's 1990 Gifford Lectures, published as *Science As Salvation: A Modern Myth and Its Meaning* (London: Routledge, 1994).

47. Edward O. Wilson, *On Human Nature* (Cambridge, Mass.: Harvard University Press, 1978); *The Ants* (Cambridge, Mass.: Belknap, 1990); *Naturalist* (New York: Warner, 1995). Among his other significant books are *Biophilia* (Cambridge, Mass.: Harvard University Press, 1984); *The Diversity of Life* (Cambridge, Mass.: Belknap, 1992); *Consilience*; *Sociobiology: The New Synthesis, Twenty-Fifth Anniversary Edition* (Cambridge, Mass.: Harvard University Press, 2000).

48. Evolutionary psychology has come of age and is now a standard, if relatively new, scientific field. An excellent undergraduate textbook covering this new field is John Cartwright's *Evolution and Human Behavior* (Cambridge, Mass.: MIT Press, 2000).

49. This is essentially a caricature. For a full and informed discussion of the evolutionary origins of religion, see Pascal Boyer, *Religion Explained* (New York: Basic, 2001).

50. Wilson, *Consilience*, 266.

51. One remarkable (and early) achievement of sociobiology has been its explication of the origins of the universal cultural taboos against incest and the related sexual aversion that siblings have for each other. Why do teenage boys find their older sisters com-

pletely uninteresting? That they do has evolutionary advantages, since the offspring of siblings are more likely to possess genetic defects. See Wilson, *On Human Nature*, 36–39.

52. Wilson, *On Human Nature*, 192.

53. Wilson, *Consilience*, 264–265.

54. Robert Wright, *Three Scientists and Their Gods: Looking for Meaning in an Age of Information* (New York: Times Books, 1988), 190.

55. Wilson, *Consilience*, 6, 241; Wilson, *Naturalist*, 33–38, 42–46.

56. Wilson is critical of the excesses of religion, such as the atrocities committed in its name. But most religious believers would share this view. He is also concerned about the Christian emphasis on the importance of the "afterlife"—an emphasis that he thinks leads Christians to disrespect the environment. See Wilson, *Consilience*, 245.

57. From the dust jacket of Steven Weinberg, *Dreams of a Final Theory: The Search for the Fundamental Laws of Nature* (New York: Pantheon, 1992).

58. The four interactions, or "forces" as they are often called, are electromagnetism, gravity, the strong nuclear force, and the weak nuclear force. All events in the physical universe are ruled by these four interactions. Nothing can occur outside their prescription. Weinberg won the Nobel Prize for showing how electromagnetism and the weak nuclear interaction can be combined into what is known as the "electroweak" interaction. This demonstration was a partial realization of Einstein's dream of a unified theory of everything into which all the forces of nature could be fit. It has to be considered one of the most significant breakthroughs in physics in the twentieth century.

59. Weinberg, *First Three Minutes*, 154.

60. Alan Lightman and Roberta Brawer interviewed twenty-seven cosmologists on a variety of topics related to the larger implications of their work. The concluding question asked of them was what they thought of Weinberg's lament. See Alan Lightman and Roberta Brawer, *Origins: The Lives and Worlds of Modern Cosmologists* (Cambridge, Mass.: Harvard University Press, 1990). Weinberg himself reflects at some length on the response to his lament in his *Dreams of a Final Theory*. The discussion forms part of an entire chapter devoted to the question of God's existence.

61. Weinberg, *Dreams of a Final Theory*, 256.

62. Weinberg, *Dreams of a Final Theory*, 256.

63. An extremely eloquent historical study of intellectuals who lost their faith in the nineteenth century can be found in A. N. Wilson, *God's Funeral* (New York: Norton, 1999). The authors interviewed Wilson shortly after his book appeared. For excerpts of the interview, see Karl W. Giberson and Donald A. Yerxa, "God's Funeral: The Birth of Modern Science and the Death of Faith: An Interview with A. N. Wilson." *Science and Spirit* 11 (March–April 2000): 44–45; "God's Funeral: A Conversation with A. N. Wilson," *Books and Culture* 5 (September–October 1999): 22–23.

64. These include Stephen Jay Gould's *The Lying Stones of Marrakech* (New York: Harmony, 2000); *Leonardo's Mountain of Clams and the Diet of Worms* (New York: Harmony, 1998); *Dinosaur in a Haystack* (New York: Harmony, 1996); *Eight Little Piggies* (New York: Norton, 1994); *Bully for Brontosaurus: Reflections in Natural History* (New York: Norton, 1991); *The Flamingo's Smile* (New York: Norton, 1987); *Hen's Teeth and Horse's Toes: Further Reflections in Natural History* (New York: Norton, 1983); *The Panda's Thumb* (New York: Norton, 1980); and *Ever since Darwin: Reflections in Natural History* (New York: Norton, 1979, 1992).

65. Among Gould's most significant books are: *Questioning the Millennium: A Rationalist's Guide to a Precisely Arbitrary Countdown* (New York: Harmony, 1999); *Rocks of Ages: Science and Religion in the Fullness of Life* (New York: Ballantine, 1999); *The Mismeasure of Man*, rev. ed. (New York: Norton, 1996); *Full House: The Spread of Excellence from Plato to Darwin* (New York: Harmony, 1996); *Wonderful Life: The Burgess Shale and the Nature of History* (New York: Norton, 1989); *Time's Arrow/Time's Cycle: Myth and Metaphor in the Discovery of Geological Time* (Cambridge, Mass.: Harvard University Press, 1988); *Ontogeny and Phylogeny* (Cambridge, Mass.: Belknap, 1985).

66. Part of Gould's cultural cachet comes from his legendary enthusiasm for baseball, which is made all the more interesting by the great historical rivalry between New York—where Gould was raised as a Yankees' fan and maintained a home—and Boston, where he worked just a few minutes away from Fenway Park. When Ken Burns was producing his acclaimed series on baseball for PBS, he used Gould regularly as one of several cultural figures who reflected on what it was like to be raised as a baseball fan. Gould also wrote a fascinating, statistically rich analysis on the disappearance of the .400 hitter. See Gould, *Full House*, 75–132.

67. Gould, "The Late Birth of a Flat Earth," in *Dinosaur in a Haystack*, 38–50.

68. Gould, *Wonderful Life*, 24.

69. Gould, *Wonderful Life*, 24.

70. Gould, *Wonderful Life*, 25.

71. Gould, *Wonderful Life*, 262.

72. Gould, *Wonderful Life*, 289. Though Robert Wright agrees with Gould's argument that there was no "inexorability to the evolution of *Homo sapiens per se*," he suspects that Gould exaggerated the variety and uniqueness of the Burgess Shale animals. Moreover, Wright is strongly opposed to the implications Gould draws about the contingency and aimlessness of evolution. Paleontologist Simon Conway Morris is also highly critical of Gould's celebration of the contingencies of evolution. According to Morris, contingency is "unremarkable" because the forms of life are "restricted and channeled." Underlying the "apparent riot of forms," Morris notes, "there is an interesting predictability." He highlights the constraining role of the evolutionary phenomenon of convergence: animals and other organisms under the scrutiny of natural selection and the physical and chemical constraints of the biosphere "often come to resemble each other despite having evolved from very different ancestors." Morris thinks, therefore, that Gould's metaphor of rerunning the tape of life in an effort to reinforce "the implausibility of humans as an evolutionary end product" fundamentally misses the point. Morris's reasoning is instructive: "Although there may be a billion potential pathways for evolution to follow from the Cambrian explosion, in fact the real range of possibilities and hence the expected end results appear to be much more restricted. If this is a correct diagnosis, then evolution cannot be regarded as a series of untrammeled and unlimited experiments. On the contrary, I believe it is necessary to argue that within certain limits the outcome of evolutionary processes might be rather predictable." See Robert Wright, *Nonzero: The Logic of Human Destiny* (New York: Pantheon, 2000), 272–276; Simon Conway Morris, *The Crucible of Creation: The Burgess Shale and the Rise of Animals* (New York: Oxford University Press, 1998), 13, 138–139, 201–202.

73. Gould, *Full House*, 133–130.

74. Complete randomness in this context means that each step the drunkard takes is unrelated to the direction of his previous step. He may step away from the origin, but his next step is just as like as not to be back toward the origin.

75. Gould, *Full House*, 216.

76. Indeed, that is precisely what Wright argues in *Nonzero*. He objects to the notion that both evolution and human history are aimless. They are not exactly scripted, but they do demonstrate a directionality toward greater complexity.

77. Stephen Jay Gould, "Impeaching a Self-Appointed Judge," *Scientific American* 267 (July 1992): 118–121. We will examine Johnson's work in chapter 9.

78. Gould described the book as an "acrid little puff" and its author as "blinkered" and inadequate even "in his own realm." "[T]he density of simple error is so high," Gould maintains, "that I must question wider competence" (118–121).

79. Gould, "Impeaching a Self-Appointed Judge," 119. It is very curious that Gould used the phrase "do not strongly overlap," suggesting that there may be some overlap. In his later writings, which were mentioned earlier, he argued for complete "nonoverlapping."

80. Gould, *Rocks of Ages*, 4.

81. Gould, *Rocks of Ages*, 3–10.

82. Gould, *Rocks of Ages*, 126–127.

83. These various interpretations of the relationship between evolution and God as creator are known as theistic evolution and will be discussed in some detail in the next chapter.

84. Stephen W. Hawking, *A Brief History of Time: From the Big Bang to Black Holes* (New York: Bantam, 1988).

85. Hawking, *A Brief History of Time*, 136–141.

86. This effect is so small that it can be observed only by using an exotic sort of "atomic clock." The effect becomes much more pronounced when the gravitational fields are much stronger than those on the earth.

87. Technically, it is "mass/energy" that remains constant, but this distinction need not concern us.

88. As we saw earlier with Atkins, however, not all physical chemists do!

89. For example, see John Fix, *Astronomy: Journey to the Cosmic Frontier*, 2d ed. (Boston: McGraw-Hill, 2001), 617.

90. Hawking, *A Brief History of Time*, 46.

91. We caution the reader not to misinterpret the word "imaginary" in this context. In mathematics there are two classes of numbers—"real" and "imaginary." The imaginary numbers are those that are multiplied by the square root of −1; in an analogous, but trivially obvious sense, the "real" numbers are those that are multiplied by +1. Imaginary numbers can be added, subtracted, multiplied, and divided. There is a whole series of operations that can be carried out on imaginary numbers and, once you learn them, they are no harder than similar operations on real numbers. In physics equations describing very ordinary things (like masses on oscillating springs), imaginary numbers often appear. It is a serious mistake—and one made by some of Hawking's critics—to interpret "imaginary" in this context as "a product of the imagination."

92. Hawking, *A Brief History of Time*, 137.

93. Hawking, *A Brief History of Time*, 138.

94. Hawking notes that a proposal "cannot be deduced from some other principle. Like any other scientific theory, it may initially be put forward for aesthetic or metaphysical reasons, but the real test is whether it makes predictions that agree with observation." See Hawking, *A Brief History of Time*, 136–137.

95. Hawking, A *Brief History of Time*, 140.

96. Carl Sagan, introduction to Hawking's A *Brief History of Time*, 10, ellipsis in the original.

97. Tudge, no enemy of science, laments that too frequently science writers make science seem "arrogant, macho, threatening, pompous, but in the end, naive." See Tudge, "Why Science Should Warm Our Hearts."

98. Daniel C. Dennett, *Darwin's Dangerous Idea: Evolution and the Meanings of Life* (New York: Touchstone, 1995), 521.

99. Asimov's reputation was entirely derived from his writing, especially science fiction. He was, however, trained in biochemistry and had a short career on the faculty of Boston University.

100. Crick, *Astonishing Hypothesis*.

101. Both of the models are unique and differ from Hawking's "no boundary" model. Martin Rees argues for a multiple universe model in which our particular universe is just one of many different universes, most of which differ from ours in ways that would rule out the possibility of life. See Martin Rees, *Before the Beginning: Our Universe and Others* (Cambridge, Mass.: Perseus, 1998). Lee Smolin argues for an curious kind of "natural selection" of universes. Universes, via black holes, give birth to other universes. A universe that produces lots of black holes has a higher "fitness." Luckily, black holes and humans thrive in the same kind of universe, so this "evolving" ensemble of universes results in our eminently habitable one. See Lee Smolin, *Life of the Universe* (New York: Oxford University Press, 1999).

102. Paul Davies, *The Mind of God: The Scientific Basis for a Rational World* (New York: Simon and Schuster, 1992).

103. Freeman Dyson, *Disturbing the Universe* (New York: Basic, 1979, 2001), 250. It is interesting to note that this quote and a similar one from Davies's *Mind of God* appear as epigrams in a section of Dennett's *Darwin's Dangerous Idea*, 163.

104. Freeman Dyson, *Infinite in All Directions* (New York: Harper and Row, 1988), 100.

105. Ursula Goodenough, *The Sacred Depths of Nature* (New York: Oxford University Press, 1998), 167–174. Her own religious sentiments are stated more clearly in Thomas Oord, "Leading Biologist Calls for More Science and Religion Dialogue: A Conversation with Ursula Goodenough," *Research News and Opportunities in Science and Theology* 1 (July–August 2001): 54.

106. The Templeton Prize, whose monetary value is pegged just above that of the Nobel Prize, is awarded annually to "a living individual for outstanding originality in advancing the world's understanding of God or spirituality."

107. Dyson's daughter is an ordained Presbyterian minister.

7

◈

Via Media Stances and the Complexity Paradigm: Historical Considerations

Humans have a tendency to oversimplify complex realities and to bifurcate broad spectra into neat, nonoverlapping dichotomies. Americans, in particular, seem especially fond of structuring the world in terms of binary opposites: black or white, night or day, right or wrong, liberal or conservative, Republican or Democrat. There are even some evolutionary theorists who argue that, once upon a time, this "default into dualism" tendency had "survival value" and now persists in the human gene pool as a bit of vestigial philosophical fog. Stephen Jay Gould puts it like this:

> Our minds tend to work by dichotomy—that is, by conceptualizing complex issues as "either/or" pairs, dictating a choice of one extreme or the other, with no middle ground (or golden mean) available for any alternative resolution. (I suspect that our apparently unavoidable tendency to dichotomize represents some powerful baggage from an evolutionary past, when limited consciousness could not transcend "on or off," "yes or no," "fight or flee," "move or rest"—and the neurology of simpler brains became wired in accordance with such exigencies.[1]

So far in this book, we have succumbed to this natural human tendency (or, alternatively, we have failed to escape our primitive genetic proclivities to simplistic bifurcations). In either case, we have been looking primarily at *scientific creationism* and the *naturalistic materialism* of the modern scientific creation story, two species of origins that neatly define opposite ends of the origins spectrum. But, just as there are countless intermediate forms that link disparate species in nature, so are there a great number of intermediate species of origins between these two extremes.

Most scientific creationists, especially those who have been influenced by the approach of Henry M. Morris and the Institute for Creation Research, view origins from a fundamentally religious perspective,[2] accepting only those portions of science with which they are in agreement and challenging the rest on whatever grounds are available. Naturalistic materialists approach origins from a fundamentally scientific perspective and concede nothing to religion that encroaches, or even intersects, with that priority. The dichotomy between these two perspectives is clearly illustrated in the way they deal with origins questions that have not been fully resolved, such as the problem of the origin of life. Creationists, in general, point to such events as clear evidence for the supernatural intervention of God in the course of natural history; materialists point to such events as straightforward scientific problems yet to be resolved. Both positions involve a certain degree of "faith."[3] For creationists, this faith is in the traditional belief that God exists, that he created everything, that his creative processes often transcend human understanding, and that the origin of life was a specifically supernatural act of creation. The reason why science cannot explain the origin of life is, quite simply, because it requires a miracle. For the materialists, the faith is in the all-encompassing power of scientific explanation and its ability eventually to resolve mysteries that presently transcend its explanatory powers. The reason why science has not explained the origin of life is because it is a really hard problem.[4]

Like many dichotomies, this "creationism versus naturalism" categorical scheme is woefully inadequate, submerging what is virtually a continuum of often very interesting species of origins between the two extremes. If scientific creationism is understood as a fundamentally religious–biblical perspective on origins and naturalistic materialism as a fundamentally scientific perspective, the various positions in between them represent different mixtures of these two ingredients.

Eugenie C. Scott, the executive director of the anticreationist watchdog organization—the National Center for Science Education—has developed what she calls the "Creation/Evolution Continuum."[5] Her continuum is designed to illustrate the great number of options available for those who cannot embrace either of the two extremes. Scott starts the continuum with "flat earthers," which derives from "the most extreme biblical literalist theology."[6] This perspective, and its neighbor—geocentrism—are both "insignificant."[7] Next are the "young-earth creationists" (or scientific creationists, as they are more commonly known), followed by a quartet of positions—gap creationism, day-age creationism, progressive creationism, and intelligent design creationism, all of which represent, for the most part, variations on the theme of "old-earth creationism"[8]—one of the oldest and most venerable species of origins, antedating even Charles Darwin, and motivated more by geological discoveries relating to the age of the earth than evolution. The next two positions—evolutionary creationism and theistic evolution—are essentially identical,[9] with the former simply trying to make it clear, at least rhetorically, that the noun is "creation" rather than "evolution."

The final position—naturalistic materialism—is basically that of Richard Dawkins and the science popularizers who were profiled in the previous chapter. For as long as secular thinking and religious thinking have been in contact, there have been serious attempts to reconcile the secular with the sacred perspective on origins. These attempted syntheses generally have names like theistic evolution, evolutionary creationism, progressive creationism, and so on. For our purposes, we will refer to this collection of hybrid positions on origins as "via media," which is Latin for "middle way." In this chapter, we will consider the historical background for those via media positions currently in play. Leading via media positions will be discussed in more detail in the next chapter. Prior to the middle of the twentieth century, we will argue, it was possible at least to harmonize scientific and theological notions of origins without much difficulty. But with the advent of the neo-Darwinian synthesis of the midcentury, this became a much more difficult project. The current American cultural conversation about origins is marked by complexity and finely nuanced positions. There is a bewildering roster of scientific, theological, biblical, and philosophical issues at play in this conversation. Simplicity, however—and a great many Americans— can be found only at the extremes.

BACKGROUND

Simply put, what we are calling via media positions on origins arise from attempts to create models that *combine* scientific and religious elements in precisely the way that Gould said they should not.[10] This approach to origins has a long and venerable tradition within Christianity, a review of which casts some helpful light on current developments.

The basic question is this: How should *theological* affirmations that God is the creator—the originator of all that is—be juxtaposed with *scientific* explanations of origins? How should the *sacred* and *secular* perspectives be reconciled? The significance of these questions has long been recognized. St. Augustine, for example, warned fourth-century Christians not to speak nonsense about the natural world, thinking that somehow their "revelation" short-circuited the need to be informed on secular matters.

> Usually, even a non-Christian knows something about the earth, the heavens, and the other elements of this world, about the motion and orbit of the stars and even their size and relative positions, about the predictable eclipses of the sun and moon, the cycles of the years and the seasons, about the kinds of animals, shrubs, stones, and so forth, and this knowledge he holds as certain from reason and experience. Now it is a disgraceful and dangerous thing for an infidel to hear a Christian, presumably giving the meaning of Holy Scripture, talking nonsense on these topics; and we should take all means to prevent such an embarrassing situation, in which people show up vast ignorance in a Christian and laugh it to scorn.[11]

Pertinent to our discussion here, St. Augustine was also convinced that the six-day creation story in Genesis was an anthropomorphic, poetic device, not to be taken literally.[12] In the thirteenth century, St. Thomas Aquinas developed a famous set of "proofs" for the existence of God, some of which were based on then current scientific understandings of origins.[13] For Aquinas, revelation was combined with secular knowledge to provide what is now called "natural theology." The notorious Galileo affair of the 1630s turned on similar questions—how does one reconcile secular observations of the solar system with biblical and theological claims? Galileo Galilei's simple answer, borrowed from Cardinal Baronius, was that "[t]he Bible teaches us how to go to heaven, not how the heavens go."[14] His longer answer was articulated in his "Letter to the Grand Duchess Christina," wherein he anticipated many of the controversial issues that would emerge much later, once scientific theorizing picked up the question of origins.[15]

For better or worse, mainly worse, the history of the relations between science and religion pivots about Galileo, who in many ways was the first modern scientist.[16] In the arsenal of scientific tools that Galileo brought to his investigations we see, for the first time in history, the power of a fully *secular* approach to nature, one freed from both theological motivations as well as constraints. This trend accelerated throughout the seventeenth century, especially in England. By the time Isaac Newton, who was born in the year of Galileo's death, died in 1727 at the ripe old age of eighty-four, England had developed an active and thriving scientific community and a number of "new" sciences had been born. Most of these sciences were decidedly secular, although certainly not antagonistic to religion. In fact, a great many scientists held deeply religious, if theologically unorthodox, attitudes toward science.[17]

Chief among these new sciences was geology, which was focused on the physical features of the earth and how they had come to be that way. Prior generations had been quite comfortable with the idea that God had made the earth in its present form, more or less, or that the great worldwide Flood of Noah had shaped some of its features. There was general agreement that the world was about six thousand years old.[18] But the steadily growing knowledge of the geology of the earth began to call this history into question. Many geological formations, such as gigantic layers of sedimentary rock, gave every evidence of having developed over vast periods of time. Mechanisms for the slow production of mountains and canyons were discovered. At the same time, fossils of extinct animals were being turned up by the spades of the Industrial Revolution and the emerging fossil record began to raise troubling questions about the traditional biblical account of creation.

Why did the geological evidence point to an age for the earth that was so much larger than that determined by the traditional biblical chronology? Why was there so much fossil evidence for animals that had become extinct? Surely if God, in his wisdom, had created all the animals and then gone to the trouble of protecting them in Noah's ark during the great Flood, he would not have sat idly by and watched them become extinct.[19] And what was the message of the fossil sequence? Why were fossils of *simple* animals and plants found in the *oldest* rocks, which contained no fossil remains from humans, and fossils from more *complex* organisms found in *later* rocks? Were not all the animals and plants created at about the same time, as indicated in Genesis? All of these questions created challenges for the traditional Christian understanding; nevertheless, these challenges were met by creative via media proposals that preserved what were perceived to be essential theological elements while accepting the majority of the findings of the emerging science of natural history.

The great age of the earth could be accounted for in a number of ways. The first two verses of Genesis have technical linguistic ambiguities[20] that make it possible to insert a gap of uncertain duration between them. If the first verse refers to a primordial, original creation and the second refers to the present creation, then there is plenty of room for whatever epochs the geologists dig up. Or, if the "days" of Genesis are long periods of time, one can accomplish the same thing. The first of these strategies is known as the "gap theory" and has enjoyed great popularity right up until the present, having been adopted in the early twentieth century by the influential fundamentalist–dispensationalist biblical scholar Cyrus Ingerson Scofield (1843–1921) and incorporated into a study Bible that sold tens of millions of copies since its publication in 1909.[21] The second of these strategies is known as the "day-age" theory. This interpretive scheme was the one that William Jennings Bryan defended in Clarence Darrow's famous cross-examination during the Scopes trial[22] and remains popular through the efforts of the Christian apologist Hugh Ross.[23] Neither of these attempts to harmonize the Genesis creation story and the findings of geology is particularly problematical in broad outline form, although the details certainly have a bit of the devil lurking in them.

The same is true for the fossil data. If past geological epochs contain records of vanished ecosystems, then perhaps those ecosystems were terminated by catastrophes like Noah's Flood. If the sequence of fossils in the geological record shows an upward progression, then perhaps that record testifies to a series of creative acts by God as he executed the plan of creation in steps, rather than all at once. Enthusiasts for this latter view were quick to point out that there was a rough correlation between the sequence in which animals and plants were created according to Genesis and the sequence in which they were found by the geologists. And so on. Both geology and the Bible possessed sufficient flexibility that creative harmonizers were always able to find some way to bring them together, preserving the essential features of the theological affirmation while heeding St. Augustine's warning about taking secular knowledge seriously.

By the time Darwin embarked on the investigations that were to lead to *The Origin of Species by Means of Natural Selection*, a significant tradition dating back to the very beginnings of Christianity was in place that had as its goal the ongoing reconciliation of the traditional Judeo-Christian creation story and the latest scientific findings on origins, or any other topic that intersected with the biblical record.[24] The general term for this process is "concordism."[25]

Most of the concordist strategies were straightforward. The Bible was an eclectic compendium of writings produced over several centuries by some rather different people; the primary interests of its authors and editors were completely unrelated to esoteric questions like the age of the earth or the origin of fossils. The few comments that the Bible made about such things were cryptic and admitted of multiple interpretations. Similarly, many of the new scientific findings, while perhaps relatively unambiguous at the factual level (sediment is sediment, and bones are bones, after all), did not always demand highly specific theoretical structures for their explanation. Geological "ages" provide a good example. Neither the number, nor the dividing lines between such ages are well defined. If a concordist scheme needs a big gap, a series of catastrophes, progressive creations, or six periods, the data were usually sufficiently flexible to permit such interpolations.

This is not to say, however, that Darwin's age was one in which traditional religious believers calmly adjusted peripheral notions and continued on in the faith of their fathers. Far from it. Victorian England was a time of great religious turmoil, and the faith of a great many intellectuals was simply overwhelmed by the advancing tide of secularism. But ascribing all of this to developments in the natural sciences would be a mistake; of far greater importance was the emerging field of biblical criticism coming from Germany that, more than any fossil or ancient rock, created serious difficulties for traditional Christian understandings.[26]

Christian theologians exhibited a wide range of responses to the challenges posed by Darwinism. On the one hand, many were deeply suspicious of evolutionary theory and tended to view it as a scientific version of atheism. On the other hand, there were those who attempted to interpret the Bible through the lens of evolutionism. Between these two positions a robust theological dialogue emerged, particularly after 1875, that attempted to accommodate traditional Judeo-Christian views on origins to the new understandings of the historical sciences.[27] Creative thinkers, committed to taking both science and religion seriously, constructed viable via media positions that allowed them to embrace with integrity what they believed to be truth, wherever it was found.

There were a number of people who ably represented this position. Perhaps the best example is the Princeton theologian B. B. Warfield (1851–1921). Warfield's credentials as a conservative evangelical were impeccable. A recent scholarly assessment of Warfield's views on science and Christianity notes that during the late nineteenth century—a time when critical views of scripture came to prevail in American universities—"Warfield was more responsible than any other American for refurbishing the conviction that the Bible communicates revelation from God entirely without error." Today, Warfield's position on what is now called "biblical inerrancy" would place him squarely within the ranks of fundamentalism. And yet Warfield was an evolutionist—of sorts. He was staunchly opposed to using evolution as a basis for a scientifically materialistic philosophy of life and rejected any naturalistic reductionism that would banish the supernatural from serious consideration. But Warfield was guardedly open to the possibility that evolutionary mechanisms were operative.[28] Darwin's revolution was thus not some problematical development that overwhelmed a Christianity devoid of intellectual resources with which to respond. There were a great many thinkers who simply continued on in the concordist tradition, finding ways to reconcile Darwin's theory with their religious belief in Creation.

These developments were facilitated by a central ambiguity in Darwin's theory. Darwin's theory of evolution, both at the time he presented it and in its present form, is not a single monolithic idea, like gravity. A great deal of confusion has resulted on the part of those who fail to appreciate this. Harvard biologist Ernst Mayr observes: "The current literature can easily leave one perplexed over the disagreements and outright contradictions among Darwin specialists, until one realizes that to a large extent these differences of opinion are due to a failure of some of these students of Darwin to appreciate the complexity of his paradigm."[29]

Mayr goes on to outline what he calls "Darwin's Five Theories": evolution as such, common descent, multiplication of species, gradualism, and natural selection. We will not go into this complex analysis of Darwin's ideas but will focus instead on a simpler abstraction of two key parts of Darwinism that can be, for the most part, logically and empirically separated from each other, and must be recognized as distinct if one is to understand contemporary Darwinian discourse.

The first part is the "common ancestry" thesis, considered so well established that it has become known as the "fact" of evolution. This thesis claims that all life is descended from a single life-form. Any two species, no matter how disparate, can be traced back to a common ancestor. If the species are closely related, like humans and chimpanzees, the common ancestor is relatively recent. If they are not, like humans and dandelions, the lineages must be traced to a rather distant past to find the common ancestor. The evidence for common ancestry that Darwin presented was considered compelling, and it has grown even more so since then.[30]

The second part of Darwin's theory was his explanation for the origin of species. Supposing common ancestry to be true, there must be some mechanism (or mechanisms) by which these "ancestors" gave rise to new species that eventually differed from them in rather important ways. The ancestor common to humans and dandelions, for example, certainly cannot have been very much like either of these two descendants. How did this remarkable process of change—of speciation—occur?

The first of Darwin's two theories was, to a large degree, "in the air" at the time.[31] The many similarities that had been discovered between organisms combined with a fossil record that suggested change through time had many scientists looking for some comprehensive scheme that would put it all together. The second part of Darwin's theory, however, was vague and incomplete. The change that gives rise to new species, argued Darwin, comes about whenever organisms within the same species differ from each other in ways that are relevant to their ability to leave offspring. If an organism has a trait—such as higher speed, better eyesight, or enhanced sex appeal—that enables it to have more "children," then this trait will be passed down to a disproportionate number of children and spread throughout the population, eventually "taking over" the species. This is the process of natural selection. Recall the full title of Darwin's book—*The Origin of Species by Means of Natural Selection*. That species originate is the *fact* of evolution; natural selection is Darwin's explanation or *theory* for how this occurs.

Clearly, the critical starting point for evolutionary change is the novel trait on which natural selection can act—if one of the baby hawks has been born with better eyesight then, other things being equal, that baby hawk will have more children than its siblings. But from whence cometh this better eyesight? For evolution to work, there must be some wellspring of novelties on which natural selection can act. What was this wellspring—this inexhaustible source of tiny miracles? Darwin's theory was not specific on this point. The relevant science—genetics—had not yet been born, and Darwin was unaware of the seminal work that had been done by the Austrian monk Gregor Mendel (1822–1884).[32] Darwin's theory of evolution required a source of emergent novelty on which natural selection could act, and this remained a complete mystery.

As long as evolution was understood to be facilitated by mysterious emergent novelties that gave rise to ever more complex species, eventually culminating in Homo sapiens, religious believers could, quite naturally, understand the evolutionary process as "God's method of creation." Concordist flexibility simply reinterpreted creation to be something that God performed slowly, a bit at a time, rather than all at once, or in a series of instantaneous acts.

There are two aspects to the response to Darwin that are of critical importance. First, unlike the common ancestry thesis, the mechanisms that Darwin proposed for the origin of species had a vagueness to them that accommodated a variety of interpretations, and thus were *not understood in the same way by all who accepted them*. In particular, many religious believers tended to miss the antiteleological character of Darwin's theory. Oxford historian of science John Hedley Brooke makes this point well: "Among the less acute proponents of theistic evolution there was often a failure to perceive just how damaging the Darwinian mechanism was. Among the more enlightened, the strategy was simply to minimize the scope of natural selection, allowing the process to be controlled by such forces as the direct response of organisms to environmental change, which were more readily compatible with mental agency in a material world."[33]

Peter J. Bowler has pointed out in his now-standard history of evolution that the initial enthusiasm for the classical Darwinian mechanisms quickly began to wane, and by 1900 Darwinism was in a "precarious" state within the scientific community. Evolution itself was not questioned, but the Darwinian mechanisms were. The great geneticist and polymath J. B. S. Haldane observed in 1932 that "Darwinism is dead—any sermon."[34] And while preachers and the William Jennings Bryan fan club may have been the ones rejoicing, the scientists were the ones that had done the deed.[35]

Second, a great many Christians, even very conservative ones, were able to come to terms with Darwinism *as they understood it.* The situation in the decades immediately after the publication of the *Origin of Species* contrasts with the present in which Darwin's mechanism commands near-universal ascent within the scientific community. Bowler observes that "[d]uring the early years of the 20th century, Darwin's theory of natural selection had lost much of its popularity." It was not until the 1940s, long after Bryan's antievolutionary campaign had ended, that Darwinism began to "reemerge as a driving force in biology."[36]

The reemergence of Darwinism, with its emphasis on random mutation and natural selection as the primary mechanism by which it operates, was significant in generating the current, near-universal, hostility to evolution among conservative Christians. Until that time, there were concordist options for even conservative Christians.[37] The question turned on the issue of teleology—if evolution could be understood as purposeful and possessing an overall direction, then it could be the "mechanism by which God creates," and concordists— even conservative ones committed to a strict biblical literalism—could bring it into alignment with the Christian understanding of creation.[38] Only when evolution became understood as a random, directionless process did it pose such a serious challenge to traditional religious understanding, but even then not to everybody.[39]

This state of affairs is clearly illustrated by an interesting episode in the history of creationism. Near the beginning of the twentieth century in America, concern among conservative Christians about the encroaching liberalism within the ranks of the faithful reached a critical juncture. Fearful that "modernism" and evolution were "undermining the Biblical foundations of American civilization," militantly antimodernist Christians launched an effort to identify the "fundamentals" of the Christian faith—understood as elements that Christianity could not compromise without ceasing to be Christian. Evangelical thinkers with impeccably conservative pedigrees were invited to contribute to a series of publications known as *The Fundamentals,* which appeared in twelve paperback volumes from 1910 to 1915.[40] During the 1920s, when the term "fundamentalism" was actually coined, this antimodernist coalition became definitively antievolutionary, particularly under the influence of Bryan. But prior to that, historian Ronald L. Numbers reminds us that while fundamentalists frequently disapproved of the theory of evolution they were not yet stridently antievolutionist.[41] A. C. Dixon, the first editor of *The Fundamentals,* admitted to a "repugnance to the idea that an ape or an orang-outang was my ancestor," but he also confessed a willingness

"to accept the humiliating fact, if proved." Another editor, prominent fundamentalist R. A. Torrey, said that one could "believe thoroughly in the absolute
infallibility of the Bible and still be an evolutionist of a certain type."[42] Of course,
the critical phrase here—"an evolutionist of a certain type"—clearly proscribes
nonteleological evolutionary models such as those that would eventually become common within the scientific community. But that was much later.

    This situation persisted through much of the first half of the twentieth century
with most Christians, even conservatives, finding via media positions that allowed them to accept some variation of evolutionary theory while remaining true
to what they saw as the essence of the historic Judeo-Christian doctrine of Creation. This process was facilitated by ambiguities inherent in evolutionary theory
itself. As long as there was a bit of mystery, there was room for God.

NEO-DARWINISM'S CHALLENGE TO THEISTIC EVOLUTION

Teleological interpretations of evolution became harder to sustain after 1940
when the so-called neo-Darwinian synthesis got underway. This synthesis joined
the work of experimental biologists who had been investigating Mendelian genetics with that of the traditional "field biologists." The details of this crucial
transformation of the science of biology are complex and fascinating [43] but need
not detain us here. What is important for our story is that, by the time this development had run its course, many of the mysterious nooks and crannies in classical Darwinism, where bits of teleology were thought to be hiding, had been
eliminated. Subsequent models for theistic evolution would have to be very specific on exactly what it was that God was supposed to be doing as he "created via
evolution." No longer was it as convincing simply to argue that the whole evolutionary process was somehow directed by God in an unspecified manner that
could not be refuted because nobody knew how the process was supposed to
work in the first place.

    In the years following the Darwinian synthesis, the antievolutionary movement
did not die, but it struggled, unable to persuade the scientific community that evolution was false. The Christian community, more interested in anticommunism,
could also not be convinced that evolution was much of a realistic threat. Antievolutionary sentiment, however, soon received—quite literally—the "boost" it
needed to motivate widespread concern about evolution. In 1957, the Soviet
Union launched its *Sputnik* satellite much to the surprise and consternation of the
American scientific community, which felt upstaged and, in the Cold War environment of the times, threatened. In response, American science teaching was revitalized and federal funds poured into the production of new high school science
texts. One of these projects was the Biological Sciences Curriculum Study
(BSCS) that radically changed the teaching of high school biology. In the decades
since the Scopes trial, biology had undergone a major revolution, and Darwinian

evolution had become the organizing principle that tied the whole field together. While Darwinism was maturing as a science, however, it was paradoxically slowly disappearing from textbooks in the aftermath of the Scopes controversy. This trend was suddenly and dramatically reversed with the BSCS, and parents of high school students across America discovered that their children were receiving heavy doses of Darwinian evolution.[44] Concern began to mount. The result was the near-complete polarization between millions of conservative Christians and the scientific community, which we looked at in previous chapters. The via media voices were frequently drowned out in the ensuing "creation versus evolution" war as "creation" came to be defined as "scientific creationism," and people claiming the generic label "creationist" found all sorts of beliefs imputed to them—biblical literalism, six-day creation, a young earth, literal Adam and Eve, and so on. Evolution came to be understood as a blind purposeless process, and anyone claiming the label "evolutionist" might be perceived, often in total error, as an atheist. For millions of Americans, the choice acquired a remarkable clarity.

Via media positions persisted, nevertheless. And, in fact, they acquired substantial, if often quiet, followings, their continuing vitality nurtured by several different streams. Chief among them was the failure of scientific creationism to develop an academically credible defense of its antievolutionary position. The early promise of John C. Whitcomb Jr. and Henry M. Morris's seminal work *The Genesis Flood*[45] evaporated as the movement failed to produce anything more substantial. And even that important work, while it remained in print and continued to sell, was never even revised despite a number of developments that discredited some of its central claims.[46] From the outset, scientific creationism was presented as a new research paradigm that would, in the hopeful vision of its few champions, guide future research. Other than a few trivial projects, nothing along the lines of a creationist research program ever materialized.[47] At the 1981 Arkansas "creation vs. evolution" trial, creationists claimed that this failure was due to an academic prejudice against their work that prevented its being published. Subsequent testimony revealed that the creationists could not substantiate that they had submitted any manuscripts to established scientific journals.[48] Scientific creationism also tended to alienate anyone who did not subscribe to its literalist interpretation of the Bible. Morris's book *The Long War against God* even suggested that evolution was handed down to Nimrod by Satan at the Tower of Babel—a fanciful notion that strained the credulity of all but the most fundamentalist of religious believers.[49] For better-educated Christians, scientific creationism was like a charged particle that repelled other particles with similar charges. Despite the similarity of the charge, there was an electrical force that kept them apart.

The crystallization of the antiteleological paradigm within the ranks of leading evolutionary thinkers and popularizers created another electrically charged pole that repelled all but the most die-hard of evolutionists. With champions like Dawkins and Peter W. Atkins openly preaching that their atheism was based on the truth of evolution, religious believers, even those completely unsympathetic to scientific creationism, found themselves repelled by this pole of the origins spectrum.

During the last quarter century or so, thinkers unsatisfied with the extreme positions taken by creation scientists, on the one hand, and strict scientific materialists, on the other, have been developing a range of via media positions on origins. In the next chapter, we examine these embattled mediators who struggle to reconcile a seemingly atheistic scientific theory with a belief in a God who creates.

NOTES

1. Stephen Jay Gould, *Rocks of Ages: Science and Religion in the Fullness of Life* (New York: Ballantine, 1999), 50–51.

2. As its name suggests, scientific creationism does understand itself as "scientific" and the writings of its champions, as we saw in chapters 3–5, contain substantial quantities of scientific rhetoric. A careful examination of the writings of the creationists makes it clear, however, that their approach is primarily scriptural and, to varying degrees, antiscience. Some creationists are refreshingly candid on this point. Creationist paleontologist Kurt Wise, for example, applauds a recent creationist textbook for breaking free from the "science-bashing spirit" typical of much creationist literature. See Kurt Wise, foreword to *Faith, Reason, and Earth History: A Paradigm of Earth and Biological Origins by Intelligent Design*, by Leonard Brand (Berrien Springs, Mich.: Andrews University Press, 1997), vii. And we saw in chapter 4 that Paul A. Nelson and John Mark Reynolds are young-earth creationists essentially out of religious and philosophical conviction. They candidly acknowledge that most of the scientific data as *currently interpreted* are against their young-earth creationist stance. See Paul A. Nelson and John Mark Reynolds, "Young Earth Creationism," in *Three Views on Creation and Evolution*, ed. J. P. Moreland and John Mark Reynolds (Grand Rapids, Mich.: Zondervan, 1999), 51, 73.

3. Admittedly, this is a highly loaded statement that must be qualified. At issue is the fact that "faith" is a rich, complex term with a variety of meanings and a quantitative spectrum of relevance for our discussion here. The "faith" of the religious believer is more than simple assent to propositions like: "the origin of life was a supernatural act of God" and "the 'faith' of the materialist is really more of a methodological commitment that promotes a certain problem-solving strategy in science." The collective experience of the scientific community has led to a general intuition that "scientifically posable questions" have "scientifically discoverable answers." Nevertheless, there are similarities that must be taken into consideration. The faith of the scientist that science will be able to answer certain types of questions has metaphysical implications for the character of that universe within which science operates.

4. The question of the origin of life has a fascinating history. For most of recorded history, simple life-forms were thought to be trivially simple—so simple, in fact, that they could arise spontaneously under the right conditions—maggots from meat, flies from human waste, and microscopic "beasties" from warm fluids. The refutation of this "spontaneous generation" by Louis Pasteur (1822–1895) was a major accomplishment, secur-

ing for Pasteur an enduring presence in the history of science and greatly advancing the field of medicine. The growing awareness in the twentieth century that even simple life-forms were enormously complex convinced virtually everyone that such life-forms certainly did not arise "spontaneously," at least on a routine basis. The idea of maggots being generated by decaying meat has to be one of the most far-fetched ideas ever held by scientists, at least in the light of contemporary understanding. The complexity of even the simplest life-form has led creationists to argue that only a supernatural act of God could create something so complex. It is worth noting that for most of the history of the Judeo-Christian tradition there was nothing about life that was thought to require a supernatural acts of origination. Not until science ascertained the complexity of this process was it used as an evidence for the direct involvement of God in natural history.

5. Eugenie C. Scott, "The Creation/Evolution Continuum," NCSE *Reports* (July–August 1999): 16–23.

6. Scott, "Creation/Evolution Continuum," 16.

7. We question Scott's decision to start her continuum with two perspectives that are as far from any mainstream religious notions of creation as astrology is from astronomy. Unfortunately, in her continuum the word "creation" is right next to "flat earthers," perhaps creating what Howard J. Van Till, in a related context, has called "stench by proximity." This juxtaposition also suggests, whether intentional or not, that flat earthism is the "purest" form of creationism. See Howard J. Van Till, "Special Creationism in Designer Clothing: A Response to *The Creation Hypothesis*," *Perspectives on Science and the Christian Faith* 47 (June 1995): 127.

8. Like any categorical scheme, there are ambiguities with Scott's labels. We have argued in this book that these movements are largely cultural, rather than scientific, and thus should be defined—at least partially—in terms of membership, rather than central doctrine. The intelligent design movement, profiled later in chapters 9 and 10, is best understood in this way as it contains within its ranks a cross-section of thinkers, united by their confidence that the theory of evolution is inadequate, rather than acceptance of any particular model for origins.

9. These two positions are so similar that we do not think it is helpful to use both of these labels. "Evolutionary creationism" is little more than a rhetorical mutation of "theistic evolution" and has not achieved any significant currency in the literature.

10. Gould favored maintaining the dichotomy of science and religion, each in its nonoverlapping magisterium. See Gould, *Rocks of Ages*, 4–6.

11. St. Augustine quoted in David C. Lindberg, "Science and the Early Church," in *God and Nature: Historical Essays on the Encounter between Christianity and Science*, ed. David C. Lindberg and Ronald L. Numbers (Berkeley: University of California Press, 1986), 31.

12. John Hedley Brooke, *Science and Religion: Some Historical Perspectives* (Cambridge, U.K.: Cambridge University Press, 1991), 38–39.

13. On Aquinas's five "proofs," see Frederick Copleston, *History of Western Philosophy*, vol. 2, *Augustine to Scotus* (New York: Doubleday, 1950), 336–346. Of course, we must point out that "science" did not have its current distinct status in the thirteenth century; nevertheless, Aquinas was quite clear on the difference between *revealed* knowledge and *secular* knowledge, the latter having just been recovered in the works of Aristotle.

14. This famous quote is more accurately rendered: "That the intention of the Holy Ghost is to teach us how one goes to heaven, not how heaven goes." Galileo Galilei, "Letter to the

Grand Duchess Christina Concerning the Use of Biblical Quotations in Matters of Science, 1615," in *Discoveries and Opinions of Galileo*, trans. Stillman Drake (New York: Anchor, 1957), 186.

15. Galileo, "Letter to the Grand Duchess Christina," 179–216.

16. Anthony Aliota, *A History of Western Science* (Englewood Cliffs, N.J.: Prentice-Hall, 1987), 191–204.

17. See Richard Westfall, "The Rise of Science and the Decline of Orthodox Christianity: A Study of Kepler, Descartes, and Newton," in *God and Nature: Historical Essays on the Encounter between Christianity and Science*, ed. David C. Lindberg and Ronald L. Numbers (Berkeley: University of California Press, 1986), 218–237.

18. Newton, for example, had calculated the date of the creation of the earth to be 3998 BC. He made essentially the same kind of assumptions about the history of the world as the much-ridiculed Bishop James Ussher, who dated the creation at 4004 BC. That scholars tend to quote Ussher's date as the one that was challenged by science, rather than Newton's, reflects the ease with which one can place science and religion at odds by appropriate "selection" of historical episodes. See Timothy Ferris, *Coming of Age in the Milky Way* (New York: Anchor, 1989), 220.

19. Eighteenth-century scholars were enormously troubled by the emerging evidence for extinction. The prevailing paradigm for understanding the natural world was the "Great Chain of Being," which viewed the plan of creation as a carefully organized sequence or "chain" of organisms that represented the realization in nature of God's wisdom. The wisdom of God lay partly in the "completeness" of the chain so that a loss of a species to extinction—a break in the chain—would bring down the whole apologetic structure, thereby mocking the plan of God. Intellectual historian Arthur O. Lovejoy, who has written the definitive work on this subject, quotes the eighteenth-century botanist John Ray on this point. Ray referred to extinction as a "dismembring [sic] of the universe." Ray also believed that the story of Noah's ark provided theological corroboration for this notion. God was "so careful to lodge all Land-Animals in the Ark at the Time of the General Deluge." Ray quoted in Arthur O. Lovejoy, *The Great Chain of Being: A Study of the History of an Idea* (Cambridge, Mass.: Harvard University Press, 1936), 243, 365n.

20. This point involves nuances of Hebrew grammar. Conservative evangelical biblical scholar Robert Young, an important authority for fundamentalists, has attempted to provide a translation of the Bible that does not compromise linguistic faithfulness for editorial clarity. Young renders the first verses of Genesis as: "In the beginning of God's preparing the heavens and the earth, the earth hath existed waste and void, and darkness is on the face of the deep." Such a translation could give license to the assumption of a chronology antedating the traditional "week" of creation. See Robert Young, *Young's Literal Translation of the Bible* (Grand Rapids, Mich.: Guardian, 1976), 1. For a more mainstream scholarly perspective, see Claus Westermann, *Genesis 1–11: A Commentary* (Minneapolis: Augsburg, 1974).

21. Dispensationalism is a form of premillennialism that originated in the late nineteenth century. Dispensationalists divided history into distinct epochs or "dispensations," usually seven in number, that corresponded to the stages of God's progressive revelation. The final dispensation would be the millennium, the one-thousand-year reign of Christ himself on Earth. See George M. Marsden, *Fundamentalism and American Culture: The Shaping of Twentieth-Century Evangelicalism, 1870–1925* (New York: Oxford University Press, 1980), 4–5, 48–62.

22. See Edward J. Larson, *Summer for the Gods: The Scopes Trial and America's Continuing Debate over Science and Religion* (Cambridge, Mass.: Harvard University Press, 1997), 189.

23. Hugh Ross, *The Fingerprint of God: Recent Scientific Discoveries Reveal the Unmistakable Identity of the Creator*, 2d ed. (Orange, Calif.: Promise Publishing, 1991), 146–155.

24. Of course, not all of this "reconciliation" was entirely genuine. In some cases, scientific ideas would be presented in contexts that lent themselves to an "orthodox" interpretation, not because that was the intent, but because that assuaged some of the concern. The great French naturalist Georges-Louis Leclerc de Buffon, for example, cast geological history in seven progressive epochs, not because the data called for seven epochs, but to enable concerned Christians to "read into" his scheme the seven days of biblical creation and rest. Buffon had come up with a way to "date" the earth that yielded an age of about seventy-five thousand years. Since this was incompatible with the age of the earth determined by biblical chronology, he needed to find a way to "make room" for his "old" earth. See, for example, Colin A. Russell, *Cross Currents: Interaction between Science and Faith* (Leicester, U.K.: InterVarsity, 1985), 134; Brooke, *Science and Religion*, 234–238.

25. Concordism is the assumption that the biblical texts, specifically the first chapters of Genesis, are scientifically accurate and can be brought into agreement or "concord" with science by correct (often creative) interpretation. The idea is that scientific knowledge can be used to determine exactly what the biblical texts mean, when such texts admit of a variety of interpretations. This strategy has been used, for example, to "clarify" whether the "days" in Genesis should be interpreted as twenty-four-hour days—the conventional meaning—or whether the days were periods of unspecified duration, in the sense of "in this day and age." Once geologists had determined that the earth was much older than ten thousand years, this result could be brought into concord with Genesis by making the "days" of creation into geological epochs. Concordism continues to be a popular hermeneutical assumption of evangelical Christians. There are evangelical critics of concordism, however. Charles E. Hummel, for example, rejects concordist views because they "strain Genesis by importing concepts foreign to the text." Moreover, "any apparent success in harmonizing the message with 'modern science' guarantees a failure when current scientific theory is revised or discarded." See Charles E. Hummel, *The Galileo Connection: Resolving Conflicts between Science and the Bible* (Downers Grove, Ill.: InterVarsity, 1986), 213. See also Denis O. Lamoureux, "Evangelicals Inheriting the Wind: The Phillip E. Johnson Phenomenon," in *Darwinism Defeated? The Johnson–Lamoureux Debate on Biological Origins*, ed. Phillip E. Johnson and Denis O. Lamoureux (Vancouver, B.C.: Recent College Publishing, 1999), 38n; Howard J. Van Till, "A Partnership Response," in *Science and Christianity: Four Views*, ed. Richard F. Carlson (Downers Grove, Ill.: InterVarsity, 2000), 62–65. Stanley L. Jaki aggressively attacks concordism from a Catholic perspective. He agrees with Hummel that "[c]oncordism could not cope with science, old and new," but suggests that concordism finds its "principal refutation not so much in science as in the plain realism of the Bible in general and of Genesis 1 in particular about things physical." See Stanley L. Jaki, *Genesis 1 through the Ages*, rev. ed. (Royal Oak, Mich.: Real View, 1998), 281.

26. A. N. Wilson, *God's Funeral* (New York: Norton, 1999), especially 3–15; Brooke, *Science and Religion*, 263–270.

27. See Russell, *Cross Currents*, 173–174; Jon Roberts, *Darwinism and the Divine in America: Protestant Intellectuals and Organic Evolution, 1859–1900* (Madison: University of Wisconsin Press, 1988), x–xvi, passim. The political situation in America was rather different from that in England. In England, an entrenched clergy held considerable power, both in politics and in the universities. In that setting, the temptation to fashion evolution into a club to smash on the head of religion was more than some scientists could bear. Thomas Huxley, for example, spent quite a bit of time wielding that club. In the United States, the Christian Church's authority was more cultural. It is significant that one of the leading American evolutionists was Harvard botanist Asa Gray who was also deeply religious and convinced that "Darwin's theory was no more atheistic than Newton's physics." See Adrain Desmond, *Huxley: From Devil's Disciple to Evolution's High Priest* (Reading, Mass.: Perseus, 1994); Peter J. Bowler, *Evolution: History of an Idea*, rev. ed. (Berkeley: University of California Press, 1989), 223.

28. Mark A. Noll and David N. Livingstone, eds., *B. B. Warfield: Evolution, Scripture, and Science: Selected Writings* (Grand Rapids, Mich.: Baker, 2000), 13–44. The quotation is from page 15 of Noll and Livingstone's introductory essay.

29. Ernst Mayr, *One Long Argument: Charles Darwin and the Genesis of Modern Evolutionary Thought* (Cambridge, Mass.: Harvard University Press, 1991), 36. Mayr's book is an authoritative history of Darwin's revolution written from the perspective of one whose own work is an important part of that history.

30. See Steve Jones, *Darwin's Ghost: The Origin of Species Updated* (New York: Random House, 1999), 275–308.

31. The response of Thomas Huxley is the best indicator of this. Presented with Darwin's theory, he said, more or less, "Now why didn't I think of that." The extremely rapid acceptance of the broad outlines of Darwin's theory shows the degree to which many of the ideas that formed the basis for the new paradigm were already widely accepted. Darwin simply showed people how to "see" what they were already looking at. A wonderful introduction to this aspect of evolution is in Jonathan Miller et al., *Darwin for Beginners* (New York: Pantheon, 1990).

32. Aliota, *History of Western Science*, 288.

33. Brooke, *Science and Religion*, 283.

34. Haldane quoted in Bowler, *Evolution*, 246.

35. Bowler, *Evolution*, 246.

36. Bowler, *Evolution*, 307.

37. David N. Livingstone, *Darwin's Forgotten Defenders: The Encounter between Evangelical Theology and Evolutionary Thought* (Grand Rapids, Mich.: Eerdmans, 1987), 100–168.

38. Intellectual historian John C. Greene has noted that while evolutionary theorists like Mayr reject teleology in nature, they continue to use teleological language (e.g., progress, improvement, advance, higher, lower, and fitness) to describe natural processes. See John C. Greene, *Debating Darwin: Adventures of a Scholar* (Claremont, Calif.: Regina, 1999), 181, 220, 244.

39. In the next chapter, we will look at some contemporary theological models for understanding evolution that embrace the Darwinian mechanisms.

40. Marsden, *Fundamentalism*, 3–8, 118–123.

41. Ronald L. Numbers, *The Creationists: The Evolution of Scientific Creationism* (Berkeley: University of California Press, 1993), 38–44.

42. Dixon and Torrey quoted in Numbers, *Creationists*, 39.

43. See Bowler, *Evolution*, 307–308; Ernst Mayr, "Prologue: Some Thoughts on the History of the Evolutionary Synthesis," and Dudley Shapere, "The Meaning of the Evolutionary Synthesis," both in *The Evolutionary Synthesis: Perspectives on the Unification of Biology*, ed. Ernst Mayr and William B. Provine (Cambridge, Mass.: Harvard University Press, 1998), 1–48; 388–398.

44. Larson, *Summer for the Gods*, 230–231, 249.

45. John C. Whitcomb Jr. and Henry M. Morris, *The Genesis Flood: The Biblical Record and Its Scientific Implications* (Philadelphia: Presbyterian and Reformed Publishing, 1961).

46. For example, *Genesis Flood* contains photographs of the Paluxy River Bed in Texas where dinosaur tracks are claimed to be found alongside human footprints. If true, this would be a virtual death blow to evolution since it would imply that humans and dinosaurs were contemporaries. The "human footprints," however, have now been so fully repudiated that even the Institute for Creation Research has withdrawn from circulation its film "Footprints in Stone," which argued that the Paluxy footprint combination refuted the conventional evolutionary time table.

47. Creationist research continues to be primarily the collation of problems within standard evolutionary theory. Creationist books often state explicitly that the choice is between creation and evolution and that evidence *against* the latter constitutes evidence *for* the former. This rhetorical strategy contributes to the highly caricatured nature of America's conversation on origins and, of course, ignores the kinds of via media alternatives discussed in this and the next chapter.

48. See Judge William R. Overton's U. S. District Court Opinion *McLean v. Arkansas*, January 5, 1982, quoted in Michael Ruse, ed., *But Is It Science: The Philosophical Question in the Creation/Evolution Controversy* (Amherst, N.Y.: Prometheus, 1996), 319.

49. Henry M. Morris, *The Long War against God: The History and Impact of the Creation/Evolution Conflict* (Grand Rapids, Mich.: Baker, 1989), 260.

8

◆

The Muddle in the Middle: Via Media Positions on Origins

In the previous chapter, we looked at some historical attempts to construct models by which prevailing scientific theories could be brought into harmony with traditional religious understandings. These concordist enterprises were often successful in blunting the sharper conflicts between the scientific and religious species of origins and, indeed, facilitated their coexistence for a time. The success of these attempts, however, varied greatly. On the one hand, reconciliations of the antiquity of the earth with the abbreviated biblical chronology proved to be quite durable, and this approach still commands a considerable following. On the other hand, attempts to recast Darwinism in a teleological mode have proven to be more problematic. We continue this theme in the present chapter, bringing our discussion and analysis into the present as we examine some of the more sophisticated current attempts to create a species of origins faithful to both science and religion.

Origins discussions are like so many controversial questions that are intensified by incompatible agendas and approaches. In such discussions, clarity will often be found only at the extremes, if at all. The various positions that we call via media exist in the troubled middle ground between scientific creationism, at one end of the spectrum, and scientific naturalism, at the other. These middle positions defy easy definition, are overlapping and ambiguous, and cannot be neatly arrayed along the kind of one-dimensional spectrum that we borrowed from Eugenie C. Scott in the previous chapter. Nevertheless, we will attempt in this chapter to bring some order to this welter of via media positions and outline the primary paradigms under which via media positions tend to cluster.

In the first place, there are a variety of positions that are essentially modified creationism. Their central notion is that God is doing virtually all of the creating via supernatural acts, and any work done by evolutionary mechanisms is minimal at most. In Scott's continuum, this would include gap and day-age creationism, and perhaps intelligent design.[1] These positions share with scientific creationism an often aggressive, antievolutionary agenda and the overwhelming majority of their writings are catalogs of evolutionary theory's perceived flaws and weaknesses.

The second category is theistic evolution, which accepts, for the most part, the central Darwinian notions, including common ancestry. The mechanism of evolution, however, is understood to be teleological rather than blind and purposeless. The "direction" of evolutionary change is determined in one of two ways: (1) a steady "low-level" background activity of God, interacting in unobtrusive ways with the laws of nature, or (2) an initial creation with a "built-in" teleological character that was destined from the start to evolve in the direction of intelligent life-forms.

VARIATIONS ON CREATIONISM

As we have seen in earlier chapters, the primary source for the Judeo-Christian notion of creation is the first chapter of Genesis. The most straightforward interpretation of Genesis is that of the scientific creationists, whose reading of Genesis is as literal as possible. Their distinctive species of origins stands on three key biblical interpretations: (1) the creation described in Genesis 1:1—"In the Beginning God created the heavens and the earth"—was a creation out of nothing on the first day of the creation week; (2) the "days of creation" were literal, consecutive, twenty-four-hour days; and (3) the Flood of Noah was worldwide. All three of these key exegetical points, while faithful to a literal reading of scripture, have inherent difficulties. The first two verses of Genesis, as we have seen, have an ambiguous grammatical construction that could legitimately be translated: "In the beginning *when God began to create* the earth was without form."[2] Another difficulty relates to the length of the days of creation. How should a "day" be defined before the creation of the sun, which comes on the fourth day? And the Bible's use of "worldwide" to describe the flood of Noah is problematical, given that there are other passages in the Bible where "worldwide" clearly means something more local.[3] These and other related problems provide a certain flexibility in the interpretation of the biblical text, even for those remaining within the basic framework of literalism. Indeed, this is exactly how the concordist enterprise has functioned since its inception as creative interpretations have been advanced in an effort to reconcile the biblical account with developments in science. And, perhaps surprisingly, most of these alternate interpretations are still in play, some with considerable support.

Day-Age Model

This was one of the first concordist attempts to reconcile the geological ages with Genesis. In this model, the six days of creation are turned into six geological epochs. Proponents of this position like to quote 2 Peter 3:8: "One day with the Lord is as a thousand years." One of the first proponents of this model was the great French naturalist Georges-Louis Leclerc de Buffon, who used it as a "Trojan horse" to mitigate opposition to his new geological ideas. Buffon's original idea is still around. The influential apologist Hugh Ross, founder and director of the organization Reasons to Believe, is a contemporary advocate of this model.

Gap Model

The first verse of Genesis states: "In the beginning God created the heavens and the earth." The second verse says: "And the earth was without form and void." If a gap of uncertain duration is inserted in between the verses, and the condition of the earth at the end of the interim is "without form and void," then any amount of time can be accommodated. This model became widely known among conservative evangelicals through the enormously popular Scofield Reference Bible, published by Oxford University Press in 1909 and still in print today. This Bible provides study aids that support the gap theory.[4]

Both of these models are capable of accommodating certain aspects of evolution. The fossil record, for example, can be assigned to the "gap." The geological ages, with their record of evolutionary change, can be aligned with the "epochs" associated with the six days or understood as the events described in a series of "revelations." Despite their considerable differences, each of these species of origins shares two common features. In the first place, they are profoundly "concordist," giving considerable weight to the "scientific" content of the biblical creation accounts and avoiding, for the most part, even small details in direct contradiction to the literal statements in Genesis. Second, these models challenge at least some aspects of conventional evolutionary theory such as the actual "order of appearance" of the organisms, common ancestry, the origin of life from natural chemical processes, and so on.

Intelligent Design Model

The last of the antievolutionary models merits considerably more attention, especially from a cultural perspective, and will be treated in some detail as a special case in the next two chapters. This species of origins is unique in being both antievolutionary and, for the most part,[5] nonconcordist. Its fundamental paradigm derives from the conviction that there are a number of things in the natural order that simply could not have come about through the standard evolutionary mechanisms. The favored example is the difficulty of figuring out a way to get even a

simple life-form from random chemicals. Such an event, according to design theorists, could only have arisen through the action of intelligent causes, not undirected natural causes. Moreover, intelligent design is empirically detectable.

As we will see in the next chapter, proponents of intelligent design are not theologically united behind any particular view of creation, nor do they agree on the
broad outlines of how intelligent design has functioned in natural history. They
also do not agree on what, if any, role should be played by the biblical account
of creation. What they do agree on is that the origin and development of life on
this planet could not have occurred without some help from intelligent causes
and that the notion of design can and should be rehabilitated as a mode of scientific explanation.[6]

THEISTIC EVOLUTION

All of the species of origins discussed so far in this chapter have one thing in
common—a hostility toward the philosophy and assumptions of mainstream
science.[7] Their writings are peppered with negative comments about scientists;
their models are defended primarily with attacks on aspects of evolutionary
theory; and most of their arguments are about the philosophy of science, particularly how this or that rule of what characterizes science permits their alternative viewpoint. In fact, a disproportionate fraction of their champions is
drawn from the ranks of philosophers and theologians,[8] rather than practicing
scientists.[9]

A great many religious believers, to the extent that they think about such
things, are generally not hostile to science, however. There is a long tradition going all the way back to Francis Bacon (1561–1626) of understanding science as
another revelation of God—a second "book" to complement the Bible, and not
merely a branch of purely "secular" learning to which religious beliefs must be
accommodated.[10] This is the framework within which proposals for theistic evolution occur—a respect for science as a legitimate source for information about
God. There is a rather substantial literature on theistic evolution that we can but
survey briefly here. We will use the rather common categorical scheme developed by Ian G. Barbour in his 1990 Gifford Lectures, published under the title
Religion in an Age of Science.[11]

The central question for theistic evolution is: How is God involved in the evolutionary process? If the evolutionary scenario disclosed by contemporary science
is basically correct, then where exactly is God and what exactly is God doing? Barbour suggests three possibilities: (1) God controls events that appear to be random;
(2) God designed a system of law and chance; and (3) God influences events without controlling them.[12] All three of these possibilities are complex, highly nuanced
proposals that are defended, not only as models by which creation and evolution
can be integrated, but as models that illuminate other theological issues like the

problem of evil, predestination, or divine foreknowledge and, of course, divine action in general. In what follows, we will focus our discussion on issues related to origins, acknowledging the larger context only where helpful.

God Controls Events That Appear to Be Random

The understanding of the physical world that was developed within the Newtonian paradigm was deterministic. There was a widespread belief among scientists, especially physicists, that all events fit neatly into a "cause–effect" scheme, and that there were no truly random events. The quintessential and hyperbolic statement of this belief was that of Pierre-Simon de Laplace (1749–1827) who is purported to have boasted that if he had knowledge of the "position and velocity of every particle in the universe, he could predict the future for the rest of time."[13] This paradigm made it all but impossible to envision any scenario by which God could interact with the world without intruding in a highly disruptive manner. Such intrusions were suspect for a number of reasons, not the least of which was the extraordinary regularity of nature disclosed in the mechanical laws of physics that came to be seen as all encompassing and inviolable.[14]

The closed mechanical universe, ruled by deterministic forces, collapsed in the twentieth century with the discovery of quantum mechanics and chaos theory, both of which created possible mechanisms by which God could interact with the physical universe without disrupting the natural course of events.[15] Quantum mechanics was an extraordinary revolution in physics that placed genuine randomness into the natural order, a notion that many physicists, most notably Albert Einstein, found exceedingly difficult to accept.[16] Very briefly put, quantum mechanics reveals this about the world: microscopic systems, like atoms, are regularly in situations where they must transition to another state. In an atom, for example, an electron in a "highly excited" orbit must drop into a "less excited" orbit closer to the "ground state" of the atom. In general, there will be several less excited orbits available, and the electron will "choose" its destination orbit in a way that is totally random. There is absolutely no explanation for why an electron will have chosen the particular option that was realized, rather than the others that were available. If the electron is returned to that same excited state, it may "choose" differently the next time around. If ten completely identical atoms are lined up, half of them may do one thing, and the other half something else.

Skeptical readers unfamiliar with quantum theory may respond, as Einstein did, that the "randomness" is really just a function of our ignorance. Just as coin tosses appear random because we cannot identify all the minute causes, the "randomness" of the atom is really just the result of hidden causes that we have not yet identified. The systematic demolition of this very reasonable and natural objection was the challenge to which Niels Bohr rose in his classic debate with Einstein.[17] We will simply affirm, in concert with the collective wisdom of twentieth-century physics, that Bohr was right.[18]

The randomness within nature disclosed by quantum mechanics refutes classical Newtonian determinism and "opens up" the world. The future is not fully determined by the present and cannot be predicted on the basis of present configurations because quantum systems are *intrinsically* unpredictable. Physics stops here, but theology takes the argument one step further. If microscopic systems have "choices" open to them, all of which are allowed within the system of natural law, then a mind—ours or God's—could, in principle, influence such systems. And, since the macroscopic world of ships, shoes, and sealing wax is constructed from microscopic quantum components, God's influence can be "amplified" to accomplish something more interesting than having an electron drop into orbit "A" rather than "B." Quantum mechanics thus transforms the impermeable causal Newtonian network into a porous membrane through which God may interact with the physical world without upsetting the natural order. Quantum mechanics is probably the most "suggestive" of all physical theories, and attempts have been made to relate it to a wide variety of rather disparate things, from free will,[19] to thinking,[20] to Eastern mysticism,[21] to the origin of the anthropic fine tuning of the universe,[22] and to the providential interaction of God with creation,[23] a variation of which is the application that we are presently considering.

Assuming that quantum mechanics provides an "opening" with which God may interact with the world, obvious questions arise: What exactly can God do with this "opening," and what opportunities, if any, does this opening provide to "guide" the evolution of life on this planet? These are very difficult questions—impossible to answer as they belong to that mysterious borderland where science slips over into metaphysics. At best, answers will be little more than suggestive speculations. Nevertheless, for those who take seriously both science and a belief in a God who acts in the world, such questions are critically important and have received considerable attention.[24]

Quantum mechanics renders possible, at least in a speculative sense, that God may drive evolution forward at the level of the mutation. Recall that evolution involves a competition for limited resources among organisms, some of which will turn out to be more "fit" and leave more offspring than their peers. The characteristics of each organism are determined, for the most part, by their specific genes, which are composed of strands of that most well known of molecules: DNA. The "fit" genes that contributed to the birth of the greatest number of offspring are strings of molecules, and molecules are made up of atoms. The molecular genetic sequence of an organism can be altered through what is called a *mutation,* which is a change in the molecular coding of the genes. Since mutations involve changes at the molecular genetic level of the organism, they can be the result of a quantum process and thus have some of the inherent indeterminability of quantum processes. If God wanted to move evolution forward by inducing quantum mechanical changes at the molecular level of the DNA, such interactions would not be detectable as "outside interference"; they would be discerned in the large-scale trajectory of natural history that would have a partially teleological character rather than appearing entirely random. If, as seems to be the case, the world has quantum mechanics as its foundational physical description, then that world is "open" to such direction.

Another possible locus for "physically undetectable divine interaction" is provided by chaos theory, which "opens a window of hope for speaking intelligibly about special, natural-law-conforming divine acts."[25] Traditional examples often used to illustrate chaos theory include a number of large-scale patterns that come in several varieties, such as convective loops in the atmosphere or patterns of oscillation of coupled pendulums. These "chaotic systems" can have entirely different behaviors that result from initial conditions that cannot be distinguished from each other. Take, for example, a large-scale convective wind pattern in the atmosphere. The rising of hot air forces the descent of cold air, and a circulating air mass is often the result, as the reader has no doubt seen modeled many times on televised weather reports. But, whether the circulation is clockwise or counterclockwise is often determined by the most insignificant of initial conditions, which is part of the reason for the sometimes abysmal performance of weather forecasters. In fact, the initial conditions can often be so similar that they cannot be distinguished. Yet they lead to vastly different final results. This is referred to as the "Butterfly effect" — "the notion that a butterfly stirring the air today in Peking can transform storm systems next month in New York."[26] As with quantum theory, we have a situation where an event at the level of the undetectably small can be amplified. And, once again, some find an "opening" where providential interactions of God with the universe may happen without any "violation" of the laws of physics. [27]

Like quantum theory, chaos undermines the notion of a closed deterministic Newtonian universe, within which God could not act without disrupting the natural order. Since chaotic systems are so sensitive to initial conditions, an undetectably small input can be amplified to produce a dramatic result. Quantum and chaos theory thus provide *possible* conduits within the natural order of things for God to influence the course of events.

Clearly, there is much speculation in all of this, and notions about how (and if) God interacts with the world can never be a part of science qua science. Admittedly, only in some "big picture" sense would it become reasonable to speculate that the unfolding course of nature has more going on than is disclosed in the natural laws. After all, any quantum–chaos event whose outcome was determined by God would look identical to an event whose outcome was determined by the randomness inherent in quantum–chaos processes.

But the point is that "science can *never* fully specify whether or not God might be acting in a particular way in a chaotic system."[28] The determinism associated with the Newtonian paradigm was one of the reasons why God's interaction with the world was restricted to simple origination. Now this restriction has been in some sense lifted. Moreover, appeals to quantum and chaos theory create intellectual space wherein those who see through the eyes of faith may hold to ideas of divine action without abandoning science. Australian theologian Denis Edwards, for example, notes that "the unpredictability discovered by contemporary science is highly significant . . . because it provides the basis for a worldview in which divine action and scientific explanation are compatible."[29] And particle physicist turned Anglican-priest John C. Polkinghorne contends that "divine action will always be hidden, for it will be contained within the cloudiness of unpredictable processes." But while divine action will not be demonstrable by experiment, "it may be discernible by the intuition of faith."[30]

God Designed a System of Law and Chance

The second of Barbour's three models for how to get the "theism" into theistic evolution uses an entirely different approach. Rather than God working intimately as an active participant (part of the web of cause and effect) in the evolutionary process, in this model God creates a universe with everything in place, and then that universe simply unfolds. The universe is like a garden with seeds planted in fertilized soil with an automatic watering system in place. The garden will flourish on its own, with no additional help from the gardener.

This species of origins has been promoted vigorously by a number of thinkers, chief among them retired Calvin College physics professor Howard J. Van Till, who is the leading theistic evolutionist within the evangelical Christian camp.[31] He has been a strident critic of the antievolutionary forces within the Christian Church, from scientific creationism to intelligent design, and argues that the Church's rejection of the scientific concept of evolution (as opposed to the worldview of evolutionary naturalism) alienates all but the scientifically uninformed. The following quote captures Van Till's sentiments on this:

> If scientifically knowledgeable persons are led to believe that in order to accept the Christian gospel they must also reject a scientific concept that they have judged, by sound principles of evaluation, to be the best way to account for the relevant observational and experimental evidence, then a monumental stumbling block has, I believe, been placed in their path. I want no part in promoting that false either/or choice between the Christian Gospel and a highly credible scientific concept.[32]

Van Till champions a view that he calls the "fully gifted" or "optimally gifted creation," terms chosen deliberately to get past the now overloaded and controversial term "theistic evolution" and to emphasize the word "creation." Van Till's agenda is not to "Christianize evolution," but to "celebrate the generosity of the Creator and the giftedness of the creation." Consequently, he affirms a "vision that recognizes the entire universe as a creation that has, by God's unbounded generosity and unfathomable creativity, been given all of the capabilities for self-organization and transformation necessary to make possible something as humanly incomprehensible as unbroken evolutionary development."[33]

Those who see evolution as a threat to their religious beliefs have been highly critical of Van Till and others who hold this view, fearing that it is little more than a compromise with a fully naturalistic evolution, one that leads Van Till into a "functional deism."[34] Supporters, however, point to the extraordinary conditions found in the universe that have made life and consciousness possible—a state of affairs so remarkable that it has reinvigorated, within the scientific community and even among scientists without traditional religious beliefs, the long discarded question of design. Whereas nineteenth-century natural theologians like William Paley and contemporary champions of intelligent design like Phillip E. Johnson and Michael J. Behe hold up intricate biological structures as examples of design, a number of thinkers within the mainstream scientific community are looking at the features of the physical universe that possess a "design" that permits the evolution of complex biological structures. Even if Richard Dawkins is correct that the process of evolution is fully random and the Watchmaker is completely blind, the existence and properties of the basic physical material out of which organisms are composed are still unaccounted for.[35]

The collection of insights that science has developed into the remarkable habitability of the universe is known as the "Anthropic Principle." The definitive work in this field is the product of two physicists, John D. Barrow and Frank J. Tipler, both of whom are intrigued by what looks very much like a teleological thread running through cosmic history, revealing itself in a rather large number of surprising physical features of the universe that cooperate to make the universe habitable.[36]

Very briefly, the Anthropic Principle recognizes that certain of the physical features of the universe—the expansion energy of the Big Bang, the absolute strength of gravity, the relative strengths of the gravitational, electromagnetic, strong and weak forces, the contingencies of star and planetary formation, and the emergent complexity of the systems allowed by these physical features do not seem at all obvious. To take some tedious numerical examples that can be found in the tables of a first-year college physics text, the charge of the electron is .00000000000000000016 coulombs, the strength of gravity is .0000000000667 meter^3/kilogram/second^2, and the mass of the proton is .0000000000000000000000001675 kilograms. The tiny numerical values of these physical constants of nature must be determined by painstakingly careful measurement and *cannot* be derived from a mathematical theory.[37] With their values determined exclusively by *experiment* rather than *theory*, there is thus no discernible reason why they have these particular values and not some others. To use philosophical terminology, we say that the numerical values of these physical constants are *contingent* rather than *necessary* properties of the universe. In terms more generally employed by physicists (who tend to have little use for philosophy), such numerical values are often called "brute facts." In Van Till's language, they exemplify the "giftedness" of the creation. Being *contingent*, by definition, they could have been otherwise. If they were otherwise, however, we would not be here, for they play a foundational role in the structure of the universe, determining the size and lifetimes of objects like stars, making planets possible, and providing the raw materials and physical laws that enable the chemistry of life. This very short list only begins to tabulate the extraordinary roster that constitutes the *giftedness* of the creation.[38]

The universe is an amazing symbiosis of law and chance, orderly enough to sustain all manner of stable structures, from stars to people, but not so orderly that the future is nothing but a tired and predictable extrapolation from the present. Our universe, from the moment of the Big Bang to tomorrow's weather, from the first humble living cell to the readers of this book, has developed in complex and surprising ways, often appearing to be exploring built-in potentialities. Is it possible that this amazing universe was created with its "dice already loaded" in such a way that remarkable things, like us, would happen? Several scientists and science writers suggest that this may be so.[39] Perhaps Polkinghorne puts it best: "The actual balance between chance and necessity, contingency and potentiality which we perceive seem to me to be consistent with the will of a patient and subtle Creator, content to achieve his purposes through the unfolding of process and accepting thereby a measure of the vulnerability and precariousness which always characterize the gift of freedom by love."[40]

God Influences Events without Controlling Them

The third and final of Barbour's three models emerges from the work of philosopher Alfred North Whitehead. Known as "process thought," this model argues that every event has three important ingredients—(1) the law and (2) the chance of the previous model, supplemented by (3) God as an active participant, functioning something like a universal catalyst, present and active in every event from the lowliest electronic transition to the largest assemblage of galaxies. Process thought represents a sort of philosophical half-way house between the models mentioned earlier, doing away with certain objections to each while retaining central elements.

Consistent with the quantum–chaos model, the God of process thought is presently active in the universe, influencing the outcome of events. God's role is not confined to the origination and sustaining of a universe unfolding on its own. In contrast to the quantum–chaos model, God, however, is always present and influencing every event, not just those with "opportunity." God also interacts in a fundamentally different way, through "persuasion," encouraging events to unfold in accordance with the divine will but without coercive control. In the quantum–chaos model, the outcomes of many events are completely determined by God, whereas in process thought God's influence is never determinative. Many process thinkers speak of God as a "lure" to which events are "drawn" rather than "pushed."[41]

Consistent with the law–chance model, process thought does not understand God's interaction as disruptive of the natural order in any way. God's persuasive presence is a part of every event, from the orbiting of electrons to the conception of children to the expansion of the universe. But God is not present in a way that has any scientific implications in terms of "experimentally testable proposals."[42]

Process understandings of God's interaction with the world have generated a substantial literature, and there are professional organizations devoted to the exploration and implications of process metaphysics. Process thinkers have an "in-house" vocabulary, in which everything, including God, is described as having a *mental* and *physical* pole and thus being *dipolar*. Jargon like "concrescence," "actual entity," and "lure" figures prominently in their writing. But these terms do not connect directly to anything within science. The "mental pole" of an electron is not something that can be observed or measured, and the "concrescence" that is occurring when something new is arising in the universe cannot be separated out from normal chemical and physical events.[43]

Process thought is, through and through, a comprehensive metaphysics in the most literal sense of that word: "beyond physics."[44] Just as there is a layer of biological description beyond the physics and chemistry of molecules, so process thought provides another layer of description beyond science altogether. God is understood as providing a set of patterns toward which natural systems are drawn. For example, Keith Ward, Regius Professor of Divinity at Oxford and an aggressive critic of his Oxford colleagues Dawkins and Peter W. Atkins, maintains that "God is an agent who is continually seeking to influence physical process in appropriate ways, as physical constraints allow." For Ward, this means that in such processes as

> the organization of quarks to form relatively stable atoms, in the binding of atoms to form enduring chemical substances, in the positioning of a planet in a solar orbit that permits an atmosphere and large masses of water and carbon elements to interact, in the formation of immensely complex self-replicating molecules, in the finely tuned physical interactions that produce mutational changes in DNA, in the structuring of the environment that favours the selection of more complex organic forms, in the organization of living cells into co-operative structures of the body, and in the emergence of central nervous systems that make possible consciousness and action—in all these things God is a causal influence patterning physical events in specific ways, giving them a tendency to complex and consciousness oriented organization.[45]

COMMENT

The three models we have just presented—quantum–chaos, law–chance, and process—are not insular, self-contained, and mutually exclusive. In fact, they share the viewpoint that however God interacts with the world, the interaction does not require that God intrude into the natural order in a way that violates its own integrity.[46] On this they are united against "traditionalists" who prefer a God of signs, wonders, and miracles—who parts seas, floods the globe, and rains fire and brimstone on the wicked. Furthermore, none of the various champions of these three via media views would argue aggressively for the absolute falsity of models other than their own. Such is the humility that must be embraced by those who would speculate about the nature of God's interaction with the world from this middle ground.

Having said that, we still maintain that each of the three has a central distinguishing feature to which its adherents are drawn. The quantum–chaos model attracts those who want a God who can readily perform specific actions in the world. Within this model, God can easily "do" things. God can place a thought in your mind or perhaps heal your grandmother, as well as choreograph the evolution of life on this planet. And God can do all these things within the constraints provided by the openness of the natural order.

The law–chance model attracts those who are uncomfortable with a God who created a world that needs "help along the way" to realize its potential. If God has to constantly "assist" the laws of nature by selecting outcomes, then the creation is perceived as less perfect and not "fully gifted." Surely, an omnipotent, omniscient creator could design a universe that would realize its purposes without so much help.

The process model attracts those who are both unpersuaded and unconstrained by traditional models for God that are often considered to be grounded in ambiguous revelation and originating in a prescientific worldview. Process thinkers seek an understanding in accord with modern science and avoid assigning to God any attributes that are unwarranted by our experience of the world and our desire to understand that experience. They understand God to be finite both in power and knowledge. The God of the process thinkers is subject to the same sort of metaphysical constraints as the rest of the universe. God does not know the future, for example, just as we do not; God is not omnipotent. God's plans are realized in much the same way as ours. Just as we do our best to influence the course of events to unfold in ways that realize our hopes and dreams, always limited by the world-as-it-is, so a loving process God must work within the constraints of the world, vulnerable to the experiences of failure and success, frustration and satisfaction, sorrow and joy.

THEOLOGICAL REFLECTIONS

We have been calling the three positions described earlier via media, since they attempt to find a middle ground between scientific creationism, on the one hand, and atheistic evolution, on the other. A successful via media position must retain some of the traditional theism of the former without its rejection of mainstream science. And it must also embrace the established science of the latter while jettisoning the apparent despair and unwarranted metaphysical claims. As is the case with so many complex debates in history, clarity is generally found at the extremes, where it is always purchased at the price of nuance. The difficult middle road of compromise, however, seems to wind forever uphill and to be constantly forking.

Our focus on the role or lack of a role for God in the various species of origins so far has been concerned primarily with how God's actions come into play in the unfolding history of the universe from the Big Bang to the origin of human beings. Such a discussion is theological. A serious mistake is made, however, by assuming that God's perceived participation in the evolutionary process is the primary criterion that determines the way that God is understood to interact with the world in general. In fact, for most people this consideration recedes into irrelevance when juxtaposed with their personal religious experience.

Someone who believes that God supernaturally healed her grandmother will not be convinced that this belief must be rejected because such a healing would require God to "violate the integrity" of the natural order and interfere with grandma's biochemistry. Someone who accepts the Bible as an accurate accounting of God's action in history will not be convinced that God does not do standard miracles. Those who see the ever-present hand of God guiding them in their daily lives—"opening and closing doors," so to speak—will not be convinced that God is finite, without knowledge of the future, and often frustrated by the natural course of events as, for example, the process thinkers tend to assert. In these people's minds, it is humans who are frustrated because of their inability to be fully open to the leading of an all-knowing God.

In much the same way, someone like Edward O. Wilson, whose childhood faith in God was destroyed by a college-level encounter with science, will resist attempts to smuggle that God back into evolutionary history, whether or not that history makes more or less sense when viewed from a theistic perspective. If belief in God has already been summarily dismissed as a widespread delusion based on wishful thinking, then a possible role for such a "fantasy" in evolutionary history is simply out of the question.

Whatever we may think of the ability of human beings to develop metaphysical schemes that make sense of their experience, we cannot deny that our species certainly has a propensity to engage in such speculative activities. Anthropologists have yet to identify a culture that does not do this. America's cultural conversation on origins is profoundly complicated by the various religious commitments made by people long before they have ever contemplated the question of origins. Present them with a model for how God has acted in evolutionary history and, more often than not, they will evaluate that model based **on their understanding of how they believe God has acted in their lives, in the lives of their friends and family, and in the Bible.**

In a similar way, many scholars attempt to make sense of a world they believe has been created by a God who continues to be relevant. Their speculations are informed, not so much by personal religious experience, although that may play a part, but by a host of larger theological issues such as the nature of revelation, the problems of sin and evil, redemption, eschatology, and so on. A particular model for how God has acted in evolutionary history may draw support from the effective way that it resonates with other religious ideas, like redemption, or mitigates theological difficulties, like the problem of evil. The task of "systematic theology" is to draw together all of these various religious ideas and relate them to each other in a way that makes global sense. And, just as scientific theories often interpret one thing in terms of another in an attempt to create the broadest possible picture,[47] theological schemes try to make "wholes" by juxtaposing "parts."

The relevance of creation for such theological schemes, however, is easily exaggerated. A great many books that attempt to explicate the meaning of Christianity or "systematize" its theological doctrines make virtually no reference to creation other than that it occurred. In those that do address the doctrine of creation in some detail, virtually no mention is made of any scientific insight that might suggest something about the nature of the God that creates and figures so prominently in other Christian doctrines.

Consider Hans Küng's classic *On Being a Christian*.[48] Küng is one of the most prominent and widely read theologians of the latter half of the twentieth century. His writings are broadly based, tackle "big" questions,[49] and boldly challenge traditional ideas when appropriate (and, perhaps, even when inappropriate[50]). He is certainly not intimidated by any controversy that might arise out of his writings. Counting documentation, *On Being a Christian* is over seven hundred pages long and remains in print a quarter century after its first appearance, an enduring statement on the meaning of Christianity from a liberal Catholic perspective. *On Being a Christian*, however, contains no discussion whatsoever of creation, no reference to evolution or any of the particular scientific details of the origins of either the universe or humankind. The thirty-three-page index, with over fifty entries under "Buddhism" and four under "Bach," contains but one for "Darwin" (pointing to a passing comment in the text) and *none* under "creation."

Whether or not Küng's omission of creation from a book about Christianity is justified or not (and some have been critical of him on this point[51]), there is no denying that contemporary professional theologians have very little interest in the scientific picture of the world as a source for theology.[52] Even books that are dedicated to the doctrine of creation, such as *God in Creation*[53] by influential German theologian Jürgen Moltman, do not incorporate scientific insights into their discussion or suggest ways to understand natural history as a creative work of God.

To some degree, the near-complete absence of scientific influence on the writings of theologians is due to the near-complete absence of scientific knowledge among theologians. Science and theology are both esoteric specialties. To work at the cutting edge of either of them is so demanding that it is all but impossible to acquire even basic familiarity with the other. But even those theologians who are not constrained by their lack of familiarity with science do not find science to be an essential resource for theology. For example, early in his career Alister E. McGrath, a professor of historical theology at Oxford University, obtained a doctorate in biochemistry and published some papers in this field. McGrath is also no stranger to the field of science and religion. Two of his books, *Science and Religion: An Introduction* and especially *The Foundations of Dialogue in Science and Religion*, contain considerable discussion of a wide-range of cutting edge scientific ideas and how they might relate to theology.[54] But in literally scores of his other books, an eclectic and substantial bibliography of writings in biblical studies, Church history, and Christian spirituality, science rarely factors into McGrath's work. In his popular textbook *Christian Theology: An Introduction*, which Ward has praised as "a clear and unprejudiced guide to the whole discipline of theology," neither "evolution" nor "Big Bang" is listed in the index. In this book of over five hundred pages, the discussion of creation occupies seven pages in a forty-page chapter on "The Doctrine of God." And no scientific theory of origins appears on those seven pages.[55]

These examples could be multiplied. The overwhelming majority of theologians, rightly or wrongly, do not find much in science of theological relevance. Christian beliefs, as articulated by those who know them best, are only minimally influenced by science. To be sure, certain *interpretations* of a *small* number of doctrines are *nuanced* by scientific theories of origins, but most theological ideas are simply unaffected. When Dawkins claims that "Darwin made it possible to be an intellectually fulfilled atheist,"[56] he was indicating that he really does not appreciate the limited influence that scientific theories have on theological formulations.

As we have seen in this chapter, however, there are some exceptions to this general state of affairs. Currently, there are a number of theologians who consider the scientific picture of origins an important source for theology and whose theological speculations on some topics are both constrained and informed by this picture. For example, many theologians now believe that the evolutionary history of the human race rules out the possibility of a historical "Fall" — a time when a sinless Adam and Eve made a fateful choice to turn from God and a perfect creation became imperfect.[57] With no Fall, however, the source of the creation's imperfection must be relocated or redefined. Furthermore, the nature of redemption, a doctrine that most theologians generally connect tightly to creation, may need to change. In a classic and influential New Testament discussion of redemption (Rom. 5:12-17), the apostle Paul speaks of Christ as a "second Adam" who "undoes" the damage of the original Adam. If the "first Adam" disappears, then one has to speak with care about a "second Adam."

Yet, even something as scientifically well established as the impossibility of a primordial "Adam and Eve" may not be as relevant as it appears at first. The colorful story of Adam and Eve and their sin in the Garden of Eden plays a very specific role in Christian theology. It symbolizes that human nature is profoundly flawed, an empirical observation that hardly needs corroboration from divine revelation![58] McGrath, for example, indicates that the significance of the Fall is that "[t]he present state of human nature is . . . not what it is intended to be by God." There is thus no "body blow" dealt to Christian theology by the disappearance of the "Fall" from history. At some point in history, so the reworked and updated doctrine goes, creatures appeared with moral sensibilities, and there was a "dark side" to those creatures. Whether this dark side originated in a pathological selfishness that emerged from the evolutionary struggle to survive or resulted from a simple decision in the Garden of Eden, the end result for Christian theology is the same — sinful creatures need to be "redeemed."

Another point of intersection between scientific theories of origins and theology occurs with the problem of evil, which loomed large in Darwin's thinking as he was developing the theory of evolution by natural selection. Pre-Darwinian models of the "transmutation of species" had generally assumed that such "transmutations" were somehow a part of God's creative process. As Darwin came to realize that transmutation was accomplished by the ruthless destruction of the less fit (one is tempted to say "less fortunate"), he grew increasingly uneasy about the theological implications of his developing theory. Eventually, he became convinced that evolution could not be reconciled with his understanding of God.[59]

The problem of evil, however, has always been a challenge to traditional models for God. Readers are no doubt familiar with classic efforts like those of the author(s) of the Book of Job and St. Augustine, as well as more popular attempts by contemporaries like Rabbi Harold Kushner,[60] to address the problem of evil. The standard presentation of the theodicy problem found in introductory philosophy textbooks notes that the following three propositions are not reconcilable: (1) God is all-powerful; (2) God is good; and (3) evil exists in the world. Some people conclude that these propositions simply cannot be reconciled and contend that one or more of them must be discarded if theism is to be logical. Others conclude that this is simply an incomprehensible mystery. Still others have suggested a variety of devices to achieve some reconciliation. For example, maybe God is all-powerful but has voluntarily limited his or her power in the act of creation. Or maybe God's definition of "good" differs from ours. Or perhaps evil is illusory, or a means to a "good" end that we cannot see because of our limited perspective. None of these purported resolutions, of course, is entirely satisfactory. Our point here is that while evolution may have added a new twist to the problem of evil, it hardly created the problem, nor did it enlarge it substantially.

Particular models of how God interacts with the world, whether in natural history or the present, are constructed with a variety of considerations in mind and these various considerations interact in some rather complex ways. The via media positions on origins are based on more, and often significantly more, than a simple inspection of natural history combined with a knowledge of where God's intersection with that history might be taking place. The science popularizers who aggressively champion an atheistic interpretation of natural history often fail to understand that the various via media positions that challenge them are not inspired simply by a perceived inability of science to explain adequately the details of natural history. Those via media positions emerge out of an attempt to construct a comprehensive model capable of dealing with all of reality, including religious experience, the existence of the universe, providence, hope, morality, and, of course, our origins.

Process thought, for example, which views God as a finite being, ubiquitously entwined in the organic unfolding of natural history, is attractive to a great many of its adherents because of the way that it deals with the Holocaust. Christopher Southgate, for example, notes that "[t]he massacre of Jews by a country at the heart of European Christendom stands as a devastating critique of images of God acting in power to bring his kingdom in through his chosen Church." Southgate adds: "*Process schemes subvert the notion of the omnipotence of God, and therefore escape some of these tensions.*"[61]

While process theologies may mitigate the problem of evil, some critics object that these benefits were purchased at too great a price. Process theology, by these lights, compromises the central Christian notion of hope. Polkinghorne, for one, is not persuaded that "the God of process theology . . . [offers] an adequate ground of hope." This is no small thing for him since he believes that hope is "central to an understanding of what is involved in a Christian view of God's reality." Process notions of God as "the fellow-sufferer who understands" comprehend "only part of the Christian understanding" that "wishes also to speak of a time when 'God himself will be with them; he will wipe away every tear from their eyes, and death shall be no more, neither shall there be mourning nor crying nor pain any more, for the former things have passed away' (Revelations 21:3–4)"[62] Polkinghorne prefers a more traditional view in which God has voluntarily limited himself in the act of creation and thus only *appears* to be unable to prevent things like the Holocaust. Just as God does not thwart the autonomy of human beings by routinely interfering with the execution of their free choices, so God does not interfere with the "free" processes of nature. But this "self-limited" God is indeed omnipotent in the traditional sense, so the Christian notion of "hope"—that it all works out in the end—remains secure.

CONCLUSION

We have provided only a sketchy introduction to this complex and highly nuanced discussion[63]—a conversation that has been going on continuously for as long as human beings have believed in God (or gods). But even our brief overview demonstrates both the ambiguity and complexity of the issues. How are laypersons to make their way through a thicket that confounds even those who choose to live there? Bohr and Einstein debated for a quarter century on whether or not "chance" was truly a part of the quantum world and never did come to an agreement. How are we to decide whether the "chance" of quantum mechanics is indeed the locus of divine action in the world and the way God manipulated natural history to make it go God's way? Newton, Laplace, and a number of outstanding mathematical physicists of the nineteenth century completely missed the fact that there was a "chaotic" dimension to the physical world. How, then, are we to decide whether God works through chaotic processes? The meandering paths of natural history from the Big Bang to human beings are filled with dead ends and apparent randomness, and yet here we are—looking for all the world like the winners of some glorious cosmic lottery. How are we to decide what role, if any, God played in that process?

On the one hand, less than one in ten Americans have been able to make themselves at home in a universe without any God at all. Such a universe has no *problem* of evil at all; in fact, it doesn't really even have evil. But then it doesn't have good either. It has atoms and molecules. The Holocaust, as ghastly as it was on a human level, from this point of view *ultimately* was a matter of atoms and molecules, as was Aunt Martha. Of course, we don't know why there is something rather than nothing. And it appears that it is all going to end rather badly, in a great thermodynamic funeral. However, the small minority of people who prefer this universe tend, for the most part, to be rather bright. Despite the fact that they have Ph.D.s, write books, and work at famous universities, it all seems so depressing!

On the other hand, about half of all Americans like the traditional Bible account. God created us perfect, in an idyllic setting. To be sure, our ancestors messed things up royally, but it is all going to work out in the end. As for evil, that remains a problem, but there is also a lot of good in the world, and maybe they go together. The Holocaust was dreadful, but the promise remains that good will triumph in the end. And Aunt Martha, while we miss her deeply, has gone to heaven where we plan to join her someday. This hopeful view has sustained Western Civilization since its inception, and most of us learned it from our parents. But despite the comfort it brings, for many people in this scientific age it all seems so incredible and believing it is just too difficult.

Human beings like stories with happy endings. For every Hollywood blockbuster that chronicles a disaster and leaves the audience depressed, there are many more in which the hero saves the day, gets the girl, and rides off into the sunset. Forced to choose between a depressing story and one that is too-good-to-be-true, most Americans will buy tickets for the latter. America's great contemporary struggle over origins, we believe, needs to be seen in the tension between these two views. The atheistic materialism of the science popularizers is a simple view. Everything is nicely empirical. Science has promised to answer any questions that we might have. The traditional biblical view is also very simple, with the added benefit that God wrote down the details in the Bible, saving us a lot of hard work figuring out how it all happened.

But it seems very unlikely that the world is going to be explained so simply, and that is why the via media conversation is so animated and vital, as well as so very complex. The various via media positions are attempting to reconcile viewpoints that are, in their simplest form, contradictory. And in their attempts to find a path between the fantastic forest of biblical creationism and the troubled valley of scientific naturalism, they end up at odds with each other, for nobody can specify the appropriate distance from each of these well-defined markers.

Species of origins are complex things. They answer some questions but always at a price. That price is other questions. To get ahead in the game of explanation requires that you pay less than you receive, that the answers, when they arrive, are bigger than the questions hiding behind them. But how do we measure the "size" of a question? Are we better off with a finite God whom we can't blame for the Holocaust and Aunt Martha's untimely demise? Or do we prefer an infinite God who, for some reason, created a world where such things were either bound to happen as a part of the normal course of events or could happen given human agency and freedom?

Or maybe, as many religious people are quite comfortable affirming, we are simply not supposed to know the answers to all the questions that life throws at us.

NOTES

1. The intelligent design movement provides such a rich and interesting case study of the origins question in America that we have devoted the next two chapters to examining it. Suffice it to say at this point that proponents of intelligent design very much dislike the label "neocreationist" and favor "design theory."

2. For example, Young's translation, originally done in 1898, states: "In the beginning of God's preparing the heavens and the earth, the earth hath existed waste and void." See Robert Young, *Young's Literal Translation of the Bible* (Grand Rapids, Mich.: Guardian, 1976), 1.

3. For example, Genesis 41:57 reads: "All the countries came to Egypt to buy grain"; 2 Chronicles 9:23 reads: "All the kings of the earth sought . . . Solomon." There are many such passages where the text used global language for something considerably less.

4. The Scofield Reference Bible has sold millions of copies in America since its first edition in 1909. In the period from 1967 to 1979 alone, it sold one million copies in America. See Stephen R. Sizer, "Theology of the Land: A History of Dispensational Approaches," in *Land of Promise: Biblical, Theological and Contemporary Perspectives*, ed. Philip Johnston and Peter Walker (Leicester, U.K.: InterVarsity, 2000), 142–171.

5. As we will see in the next chapter, the intelligent design movement is an eclectic coalition of antievolutionists, who embrace a diversity of models of origins but are united in their opposition to evolution and their willingness to subordinate the religious dimensions of their ideas.

6. William A. Dembski, "The Third Mode of Explanation: Detecting Evidence of Intelligent Design in the Sciences," in *Science and Evidence for Design in the Universe: Proceedings of the Wethersfield Institute, September 25, 1999* (San Francisco: Ignatius, 2001), 20.

7. In general, antievolutionary polemicists insist that they are strongly "pro-science" and are simply trying to get science back on the proper footing. If science, however, is understood as the activity of the scientific community rather than a set of activities defined by certain philosophical rules, then there can be little doubt that they are attacking science. Since this debate is primarily waged in the popular press, in televised debates, and in popular writings, rather than in scientific journals, there is often an "extrascientific" dimension to the "scientific" side of the debate.

8. For example, of the twenty-one contributors to the most substantial anthology of intelligent design thought to date, five were philosophers and another five were from fields outside of the natural sciences (law, history of science, journalism, government service, and anthropology). Four of the remaining eleven were trained in either biology or biochemistry. The rest were from mathematics, mechanical engineering, physics, astrophysics, and chemistry. See William A. Dembski, ed., *Mere Creation: Science, Faith and Intelligent Design* (Downers Grove, Ill.: InterVarsity, 1998), 460–464.

9. The significance of "practicing scientists" cannot be overestimated in our opinion. A practicing scientist does creative productive work, either in the lab or in the field, enlarging the scientific storehouse of knowledge. The practicing scientist develops powerful intuitions about the way the world works and masters the central ideas that lead to progress in his or her field of specialization. Of course, practicing scientists also imbibe the prejudices, but this does not appear, under normal circumstances, to create any problems. Philosophers of science, however, are frequently spectators, watching scientists and trying to figure out what they are doing.

10. Charles E. Hummel, *The Galileo Connection: Resolving Conflicts between Science and the Bible* (Downers Grove, Ill.: InterVarsity, 1986), 165.

11. Ian G. Barbour, *Religion in an Age of Science* (San Francisco: Harper and Row, 1990). In 1999, Barbour won the Templeton Prize for Progress in Religion and is considered by many to be the most important scholar in the field of science and religion. His typologies are widely used by other scholars.

12. Barbour, *Religion in an Age of Science*, 174–176.

13. Laplace cited in James P. Crutchfield et al., "Chaos," in *Chaos and Complexity: Scientific Perspectives on Divine Action*, ed. Robert John Russell, Nancey Murphy, and Arthur R. Peacocke, 2d ed. (Vatican City State: Vatican Observatory Publications, 1997), 36. In their 1995–1996 Gifford Lectures, historians of science John Hedley Brooke and Geoffrey Cantor caution against reading Laplace out of context and thus rendering him an "arch mechanist" and rigid determinist. They argue convincingly that Laplace insisted that "science provides us with limited knowledge of the natural world." Except in special cases like physical astronomy, Laplace understood that at best we deal with probabilities. See John Hedley Brooke and Geoffrey Cantor, *Reconstructing Nature: The Engagement of Science and Religion* (Edinburgh: T. and T. Clark, 1998), 92–93.

14. See the wonderful chapter "Divine Activity in a Mechanical Universe," in John Hedley Brooke, *Science and Religion: Some Historical Perspectives* (Cambridge U.K.: Cambridge University Press, 1991), 117–151. Brooke notes the paradox that the seventeenth-century scientists who did the most to usher in the mechanical metaphors of a clockwork

universe did so with the notion that they were "enriching rather than emasculating conceptions of divine activity."

15. A detailed examination of both is beyond the purview of this book. We refer interested readers to some truly excellent popular works for further discussion. On chaos theory, see James Gleick, *Chaos: The Making of a New Science* (New York: Penguin, 1988). On quantum mechanics, see George Gamow, *Thirty Years That Shook Physics: The Story of Quantum Theory* (New York: Dower Publications, 1985); John C. Polkinghorne, *The Quantum World* (Princeton, N.J.: Princeton University Press, 1984).

16. During the development of quantum theory, Einstein carried on an intense debate with the Danish atomic physicist Niels Bohr about whether or not there was genuine randomness. Einstein rejected this aspect of quantum theory, despite the fact that he had made seminal contributions to the field. The Bohr–Einstein debate is a fascinating part of the cultural history of twentieth-century physics. See Max Jammer, *The Philosophy of Quantum Mechanics: The Interpretation of Quantum Mechanics in Historical Perspective* (New York: Wiley, 1974), 108–158.

17. Jammer, *Philosophy of Quantum Mechanics*, 108–158.

18. There are those who still retain a bit of Einstein's skepticism about the metaphysical significance of quantum randomness. No less an authority on quantum mechanics than Freeman Dyson, who made enormous contributions to the development of quantum theory, has commented that quantum randomness is really a reflection of our ignorance. But Dyson is not suggesting that there are some "hidden variables" the discovery of which will dispel the mysterious quantum randomness; rather, we read Dyson as acknowledging that there may be more to the universe than simply material particles and laws of physics. See Freeman Dyson, *Disturbing the Universe* (New York: Basic, 1979, 2001), 250.

19. Arthur S. Eddington, *New Pathways of Science* (Cambridge, U.K.: Cambridge University Press, 1935).

20. Roger Penrose, *The Emperor's New Mind: Concerning Computers, Minds, and the Laws of Physics* (New York: Oxford University Press, 1989).

21. Fritjof Capra, *The Tao of Physics: An Explanation of the Parallels between Modern Physics and Eastern Mysticism*, rev. ed. (Boston: Shambhala Publications, 1991).

22. John D. Barrow and Frank J. Tipler, *The Anthropic Cosmological Principle* (New York: Oxford University Press, 1986), 22.

23. Karl W. Giberson and Donald A. Yerxa, "Providence and the Christian Scholar," *Journal of Interdisciplinary Studies* 11 (1999): 123–140.

24. For example, see Robert John Russell, Nancey Murphy, and Arthur R. Peacocke, eds., *Chaos and Complexity: Scientific Perspectives on Divine Action* (Vatican City State: Vatican Observatory Publications, 1997), which is a collection of papers from conferences cosponsored by the Center for Theology and the Natural Sciences and the Vatican Observatory. Some of the papers are: "Chaos and Complexity"; "Quantum Cosmology and the Laws of Nature"; "Evolutionary and Molecular Biology"; and "Neuroscience and the Person."

25. Wesley J. Wildman and Robert John Russell, "Chaos: A Mathematical Introduction with Philosophical Reflections," in *Chaos and Complexity: Scientific Perspectives on Divine Action*, ed. Robert John Russell, Nancey Murphy, and Arthur R. Peacocke (Vatican City State: Vatican Observatory Publications, 1997), 86.

26. Gleick, *Chaos*, 8.

27. John C. Polkinghorne, *Quarks, Chaos and Christianity* (New York: Crossroad, 1994), 57–58, 66–71. Wildman and Russell caution against an uncritical and overly enthusiastic use of chaos theory to assert a metaphysical openness in nature. Chaos theory does, however, disclose a limitation in how compelling a case can be made in favor of metaphysical determinism. See Wildman and Russell, "Chaos," 84–86.

28. Denis Edwards, "The Discovery of Chaos and the Retrieval of the Trinity," in *Chaos and Complexity: Scientific Perspectives on Divine Action*, ed. Robert John Russell, Nancey Murphy, and Arthur R. Peacocke (Vatican City State: Vatican Observatory Publications, 1997), 173.

29. Edwards, "Discovery of Chaos," 172–174. Edwards also warns that it is not possible or appropriate to attempt to identify the "causal joint" between divine action and natural processes.

30. Polkinghorne, *Quarks, Chaos and Christianity*, 71–72.

31. An accessible summary of Van Till's thought is found in his "The Fully Gifted Creation," in *Three Views on Creation and Evolution*, ed. J. P. Moreland and John Mark Reynolds (Grand Rapids, Mich.: Zondervan, 1999), 159–218.

32. Van Till, "Fully Gifted Creation," 179–180.

33. Van Till, "Fully Gifted Creation," 162, 173, 240; Howard J. Van Till, "Intelligent Design: The Celebration of Gifts Withheld?" in *Darwinism Defeated? The Johnson–Lamoureux Debate on Biological Origins*, ed. Phillip E. Johnson and Denis O. Lamoureux (Vancouver, B.C.: Regent College Publishing, 1999), 87–89.

34. See the responses to Van Till by John Jefferson Davis and Vern S. Poythress in *Three Views on Creation and Evolution*, ed. Moreland and Reynolds, 228, 239.

35. The subtitle of Dawkins's *The Blind Watchmaker—Why the Evidence of Evolution Reveals a Universe without Design*—contains such an egregious logical fallacy that one wonders whether the marketing department at Norton was thinking about anything other than marketing. (We are assuming that Dawkins is not the source of the subtitle, since it does not appear in the original British publication.) Concluding from the lack of design in life-forms that there is a lack of design in the physical universe as a whole is to commit the fallacy of "composition."

36. See Barrow and Tipler, *Anthropic Cosmological Principle*. This massive (seven-hundred-page) scholarly work, with over fifteen hundred endnotes, is an essential starting point for discussions in this area. Unfortunately, in some chapters Barrow and Tipler presume a substantial and wide-ranging background in physics; nevertheless, there is much that is accessible to the layperson. And the presence of rigorous scientific arguments makes the case all the more compelling. The authors are both leading (and currently productive) members of the scientific community.

37. This contrasts with the speed of light (300,000,000 meters per second), which is determined from the theory of electromagnetism to be the ratio of other constants. The numerical value of the speed of light is thus *necessary* rather than *contingent*. The speed of light is not a fundamental constant. One of the goals of theoretical physics is to make the number of fundamental constants that must be empirically determined as small as possible. It is a dream (probably unrealizable) to have the values for *all* of the constants emerge naturally out of some all-encompassing theory.

38. A convenient list of twenty-five such contingencies essential for life is provided in Hugh Ross, "Astronomical Evidences for a Personal, Transcendent God," in *The Creation Hypothesis: Scientific Evidence for an Intelligent Designer*, ed. J. P. Moreland (Downers

Grove, Ill.: InterVarsity, 1994), 160–163. Ross's list contains some speculative elements that are open to challenge (like the decay rate of the proton), but the list is a compact and impressive summary. A similar list of thirty-six contingencies appears with discussion of each in Michael Corey, *God and the New Cosmology: The Anthropic Design Argument* (Lanham, Md.: Rowman and Littlefield, 1993), 42–116. Some of Corey's contingencies are open to challenge.

39. See, for example, Kenneth R. Miller, *Finding Darwin's God: A Scientist's Search for Common Ground between God and Evolution* (New York: Cliff Street/HarperCollins, 1999), 224–259; Robert Wright, *Nonzero: The Logic of Human Destiny* (New York: Pantheon, 2000), 301–334.

40. John C. Polkinghorne, *One World: The Intersection of Science and Theology* (Princeton, N.J.: Princeton University Press, 1987), 69. Polkinghorne's views here seem a bit more deistic than those he has expressed in works like *Quarks, Chaos and Christianity*, where he has suggested that chaos theory provides a way for God to influence events in the present.

41. See John Sanders, *The God Who Risks: A Theology of Providence* (Downers Grove, Ill.: InterVarsity, 1998).

42. Christopher Southgate, ed. *God, Humanity and the Cosmos: A Textbook in Science and Religion* (Harrisburg, Pa.: Trinity Press International, 1999), 201.

43. See, for example, David Ray Griffin, *Religion and Scientific Naturalism: Overcoming the Conflicts* (Albany: SUNY Press, 2000), 221–225, 298–299.

44. The term originated with Aristotle whose discussion of such things occurred in writings that came, quite literally, after his discussion of physics. If he had discussed literary criticism here instead of the nature of ultimate reality, then perhaps literary criticism would now be known as "metaphysics."

45. Keith Ward, *God, Faith and the New Millennium: Christian Belief in an Age of Science* (Oxford: Oneworld Publications, 1998), 106–107.

46. This debate is charged with rhetorically powerful language. Adherents to the various theistic evolution models often talk about God's restraint in not "violating" the "integrity" of nature. In their minds, a God who would set a burning bush ablaze without having it be consumed (Exod. 3:2) is "violating" the laws of combustion and being "inconsistent." Yet, the "God of the Bible" or the "God of Abraham, Isaac, and Jacob" as he is often described, regularly "violates" the laws of nature. Obviously, the Bible records a great many such traditionally understood "miracles."

47. For example, physicists believe that the gravitational force between two objects is mediated by a hypothetical particle called the graviton. There is no direct evidence for this particle, and such a particle is not suggested by the current theory for how gravity works, general relativity. Physicists believe, however, that there probably is a hypothetical particle that mediates the gravitational force because there are particles that mediate the other forces—electromagnetism and the nuclear forces. If we did not know about these other force-carrying particles, then we would have no reason to suggest that gravity has a force-carrying particle.

48. Hans Küng, *On Being a Christian* (Garden City, N.J.: Doubleday, 1976).

49. Some of Küng's other works include: *Why I Am Still a Christian* (Edinburgh: T. and T. Clark, 2000); *Christianity: Essence, History, and Future* (New York: Continuum, 1996); *Great Christian Thinkers* (New York: Continuum, 1995); *Does God Exist?: An Answer for Today* (New York: Crossroad, 1994); *Eternal Life?: Life after Death As a Medical, Philosophical, and Theological Problem* (New York: Crossroad, 1991).

50. Kung's "boldness" brought him into conflict with the Roman Catholic Church, and he lost his status as an "official" Roman Catholic theologian in 1979. See Leonard Swidler, *Kung in Conflict* (New York: Doubleday, 1981).

51. See, for example, John C. Polkinghorne, *The Faith of a Physicist: Reflections of a Bottom up Thinker* (Princeton, N.J.: Princeton University Press, 1994), 86n.

52. The Templeton Foundation's program in science and religion is making an aggressive (and well-funded) attempt to change this with a variety of initiatives that are bringing science and theology (and scientists and theologians) into a closer dialogue. However, despite a number of fascinating opportunities for dialogue, many professional theologians remain committed to their in-house conversation and show little interest in the emerging field of science and religion.

53. Jürgen Moltman, *God in Creation: An Ecological Doctrine of Creation* (London: SCM Press, 1985).

54. Alister E. McGrath, *Science and Religion: An Introduction* (Oxford U.K.: Blackwell, 1999); Alister E. McGrath, *The Foundations of Dialogue in Science and Religion* (Oxford, U.K.: Blackwell, 1998).

55. Alister E. McGrath, *Christian Theology: An Introduction* (Oxford, U.K.: Blackwell, 1994). Ward's comments appear on the back cover.

56. Richard Dawkins, *The Blind Watchmaker: Why the Evidence of Evolution Reveals a Universe without Design* (New York: Norton, 1986, 1996), 6.

57. Polkinghorne considers the Fall to be one of the most difficult problems that science has created for traditional Christian doctrine. See John C. Polkinghorne, *Reason and Reality: The Relationship between Science and Theology* (Valley Forge, Pa.: Trinity Press International, 1991), 99–104.

58. Pundits frequently cite G. K. Chesterton and occasionally Reinhold Niebuhr for the observation that original sin is the only empirically verifiable (Chesterton's phrase was "directly observable") Christian doctrine.

59. His infamous "loss of faith," however, may have had more to do with the death of his beloved daughter Annie in 1851 than the corrosive effects of his scientific theorizing. See Mark A. Noll and David N. Livingstone, eds., *B. B. Warfield: Evolution, Scripture, and Science: Selected Writings* (Grand Rapids, Mich.: Baker, 2000), 69; James R. Moore, "Of Love and Death: Why Darwin 'Gave up Christianity,'" in *History, Humanity and Evolution: Essays for John C. Greene*, ed. James R. Moore (New York: Cambridge University Press, 1989), 195–229.

60. Harold S. Kushner, *When Bad Things Happen to Good People* (New York: Avon, 1997).

61. Southgate, *God, Humanity and the Cosmos*, 202, emphasis in the original.

62. Polkinghorne, *Faith of a Physicist*, 65.

63. The complexity in this whole question is such that even the major "players" in this discussion often appear not to understand each other. Polkinghorne, for example, appears to disagree with Anglican biochemist Arthur R. Peacocke's understanding of his own view. See Arthur R. Peacocke, *Theology for a Scientific Age: Being and Becoming—Natural, Divine, and Human* (Minneapolis: Fortress, 1993), 369–370n.

9

❖

Intelligent Design:
A New Approach to
the Origins Debate?

We have reached the point in our analysis of the origins conversation in America where we need to make sense of a very recent development that does not neatly fit into the categorical scheme that we have been using so far: intelligent design. This is the first "origins coalition" to emerge on the American scene that is self-consciously political in a major way. The "intelligent design movement," as it is coming to be called, has an agenda and a plan for implementing it—a plan that its leaders hope will allow the movement to succeed where others have failed. Before we move into our discussion of the intelligent design movement, however, we will revisit briefly those species of origins encountered thus far with an eye toward identifying the problematical aspects of those positions that the politically savvy leaders of the intelligent design movement hope to mitigate.

Scientific creationism, as a species of origins, is popular among conservative evangelicals for whom the Bible is the primary authority in all areas, not just those directly related to religion. Creationists are happy to subordinate science to scripture and delight in finding authority figures with scientific credentials who attempt to refute contemporary science and replace it with an alternate science that dovetails with the Genesis accounts of Creation and the Flood. In order to make this move, however, the creationists have been forced to defend a number of highly problematical ideas, particularly the belief that the earth is no more than ten thousand years old. Unfortunately for the creationists, practically the entire scientific community believes that the five-billion-year estimate for the age of the earth is completely reliable. Some pundits have even suggested that the age of the earth is as well established as its shape. The earth is not flat, it is round. The earth is not young, it is ancient. It is all but impossible to find a credentialed geologist who will defend the

193

proposition that a scientific determination of the age of the earth will yield a number as low as ten thousand years (or even ten million, for that matter).

Paul A. Nelson and John Mark Reynolds, two bright and well-educated creationists that we encountered earlier, are noteworthy in that they both believe that the earth is young but also recognize that it may not be possible to make a strong scientific case for this viewpoint. To their credit, they are candid enough to admit that they are subordinating compelling scientific evidence to a particular reading of Genesis. However, given their assumptions and a priori commitments, this is not an unreasonable thing to do.

Honest assessments by creationists like Nelson and Reynolds, and the universal affirmation of the scientific community, converge on the position that there is something scientifically suspect, if not preposterous, in believing that the earth is a mere ten thousand years old. The sheer magnitude of this discrepancy has invited much ridicule and lampooning. The end result has been a general humiliation of the creationists within the academy, where they have made virtually no inroads and where they are often portrayed as intellectual Neanderthals. This, of course, contrasts rather remarkably with their great success at the grassroots level, where they have won millions to their point of view.

Scientific creationism, despite its large popular appeal, flourishes only in a scientific backwater. The movement has had no success in establishing itself within the ranks of legitimate science. Creationist books are not read by scientists, nor reviewed in scientific magazines. They are not published by mainstream publishers, despite the popular demand for them. Whatever success creationists have had—and they have had some—they have not succeeded in getting themselves taken seriously by the intellectual elites of America. There is no reason to anticipate that creationism is on any sort of trajectory that will land it in the curriculum of America's great universities, despite the tireless efforts of its leaders to debate leading evolutionists on their own turf. The most scientific creationism can hope for is to flourish within a very large subculture—and it is doing that very well. But, to the degree that America's cultural agenda is set by the ideas emerging from its great universities and political institutions, creationism will have no place at the table. It is not inconceivable that it will gradually atrophy until it reaches the culturally emaciated form that it possesses in Europe.

By contrast, the species of origins that we whimsically titled the "Council of Despair" has exactly the opposite problem. The harsh, almost nihilistic views of people like Richard Dawkins and Peter W. Atkins are attractive only to a very small percentage of Americans, most of them well educated and easily warmed to a worldview that does away with anything that smacks of traditional religion. Their books are published by major presses and reviewed in leading publications; they lecture at prestigious universities; and they are, for the most part, comfortably within the mainstream of the best of contemporary science. In postreligious cultures of the sort flourishing in Europe, they articulate a vision of a radically secular worldview that is widely accepted.

In our discussion of their worldview, we paid particular attention to the "council's" general apathy, even hostility, to the idea that God might actually have had something to do with the origin of the universe, the earth, life, and human beings. This quasi-theological concern, however, is actually only a small part of what they are doing in their voluminous writings, and it is a mistake to overemphasize this aspect of their work. An overwhelming fraction of their writing is devoted to the straightforward explication and popularization of scientific ideas. Writers like Dawkins and Edward O. Wilson are missionaries for science, as was the late Stephen Jay Gould. They love science and want everyone to share their excitement. Gould, for example, wrote countless essays for *Natural History* magazine that have absolutely nothing to do with origins. His agenda was not "origins," it was "science." Dawkins and Wilson want their readers to be captivated by science, as did Gould, and there are indeed a great number of Americans who have grown to appreciate science through their books. While "origins" plays but a small role in most of their writings, it does play a role. And when their musings run beyond the boundaries of science into the arena of ultimates, there is no God to be found there.

Stark worldviews with no place for God do not play well in mainstream America, where almost everyone believes in God. Most people think prayer really works. Most people think that morality is firmly grounded in God. The world is supposed to make sense, to be at least approximately the way that we experience it. There is something profoundly wrong with claims that human beings are nothing but selfish genes, that minds are but pieces of meat, and that meaning is at best an illusion. Such harsh notions run counter to the folk philosophy and conventional wisdom of Main Street America.

The Council of Despair confronts a problem that is, quite remarkably, a photographic negative of the problem confronted by the creationists. They have, to a degree, captured the academy and some fraction of the intellectual elites in America, but they have made very little progress on Main Street America. The typical school board in America, regardless of what it might think about creationism, is certainly not going to embrace the stark materialism of the Council of Despair. It is hard to imagine, for instance, Dawkins's books appearing on very many public high school required reading lists. Like creationism, scientific materialism has had some success, but only within a subculture. It is inconceivable that a deeply religious nation like America will ever be won over by the Council of Despair.

Between these two well-defined and powerful extremes, each with its important constituency, lie the via media positions, which we reviewed in the previous two chapters. As we concluded, via media positions on origins are problematical because of their inherent complexity. The challenge of creating a species of origins through the union of mainstream science and traditional theology is daunting, to say the least. As is the case with about all one-dimensional spectra, the linear "space" in the middle is rather large and diverse, in contrast to the ends of the spectrum that can be well defined and often simple. Scientific creationism, for example, has the virtue of simplicity; the science portrayed in its books is often so diluted and oversimplified that it would not appear to challenge even a first-year college student. The ideas are accessible, coherent, and resonate rather nicely with the idea that the Bible is God's revelation. (Evaluating the arguments, however, requires a level of scientific acumen generally absent from among the creationist constituencies.) The purely scientific account, in the same way, possesses its own simplicity although its texts tend to be more complicated. A few key ideas—such as the Big Bang, origin of life, and Darwinian evolution—are brought to bear on the rich complexity of the world and are able to explain much of it. What is left unexplained is optimistically viewed as "work in progress."

Alas, there is nothing even approaching simplicity within the via media stances. There is no center toward which ideas gravitate. There is no recognized primary authority to adjudicate ambiguities. There is no consensus on which elements to import from religion and which from science. The result has been a number of problems in building a consensus and even some rancor and disagreement within the ranks of those who share the view that there must be an explicitly theological dimension to any species of origins. The conversation is animated, to be sure, but the conversation partners are drawn from that rather limited pool where both science and religion are taken seriously and neither is to be subordinated to the other.

The challenges that arise from this complexity are perhaps best illustrated by simply noting that no "standard" via media texts exist. Readers who want a clear exposition of scientific creationism can find several texts listed in our bibliography. The same is true for the purely scientific accounts. But there is nothing even approaching a standard text for the via media species of origins.

It is hard to see any of these species of origins winning the day in America. Any twelve-person jury that was a reasonable representation of the American populace would most certainly contain a few members who would get "hung up" on some idea. No amount of clever argumentation by the creationists will convince scientifically informed jurors who are not biblical literalists. No carefully crafted purely evolutionary account of origins will convince jurors for whom belief in a God who creates is foundational. And few of those jurors will have the patience to sort through the complex hybrids defended by the via media. In the great public courtroom where such questions are debated, the jury remains hung.

This stalemate on origins is unlikely to be broken by a fresh presentation of creation, evolution, or some novel hybrid. There are some thoughtful commentators who are starting to point this out.[1] If the jury that is America is ever to get itself "unhung," it will be only after hearing a different kind of argument, one framed specifically in recognition of the fact that America is both deeply religious and deeply scientific. These two perspectives can have, at best, some kind of uneasy truce. They can never be reconciled.

Such an argument is now under construction in America. It goes by the name of "intelligent design" and is the subject of this and the next chapter. Its champions are being very careful with their strategy, avoiding the potholes that have sent their less careful predecessors careening off the highway. Their presentation of ideas is sophisticated and nuanced in ways that resemble the eloquent arguments that Americans have come to enjoy on popular televised "lawyer" shows.

Intelligent design is a coalition of thinkers, who have, for the most part, subordinated their considerable differences in order to create a "movement" or at least the appearance of a movement, under the banner of intelligent design. The leaders of this "design movement" are almost all deeply religious and some of them are even biblical fundamentalists. But specific religious considerations are noticeably absent from their presentations, which instead speak only of "design" that is specifically decoupled, at least rhetorically, from any consideration of a "designer." Of course, almost everyone who hears a case made for "design" assumes that design implies "designer." But, by being careful not to say too much about this designer, proponents of design theory are freeing people to infer their own particular theological notion, with or without the baggage of biblical literalism.

The design movement achieves further strength in numbers by uniting everyone who believes in design *of any sort*, even people who reject the particular notions held by other design advocates! People who accept biological evolution but believe that the "laws of physics" are designed are welcomed under the intelligent design umbrella by thinkers who reject evolution and believe that individual species were designed. Scientific creationists are included, as long as they don't call themselves creationists, since that label is a liability. Anyone who can frame an argument that there is too much design to be accounted for by naturalistic theories of evolution becomes, de facto, a "design theorist."

By casting the net so widely, a broad coalition has been formed—one that includes scientifically informed experts from almost every field. What is carefully kept out of sight is the fact that the design movement really shares one belief and one belief only, namely that current theories of origins cannot account for all the design in the world. Moreover, the majority of the work of the design movement consists of an assault on the adequacy of evolutionary theories of origins. Although most of the design people share a strongly antievolutionary perspective, this is a negative criterion for membership, uniting people in a tenuous alliance against a common enemy. In the unlikely event that they should defeat this enemy, the various factions within the design movement would most likely find themselves at war with each other.

To maximize the strength of their coalition, design theorists have been careful not to articulate any replacement species of origins, beyond the somewhat vague notion that there is design in the world. There is thus nothing to criticize or react to. There is no preposterous young-earth notion to lampoon.[2] Just as a lawyer can get a suspect freed without having to provide a replacement culprit, so the design movement is having considerable success in challenging naturalistic evolution without having to put anything in its place. People are free to choose their own replacement species of origins.

The strategy of the design movement is intriguing on a number of counts, not the least of which is the interesting way the design theorists have built their coalition; also of note is their remarkable success in avoiding the pitfalls that have caused others to stumble. None of this strategic cleverness should surprise us, however, when we note that the leader of the intelligent design movement is not a scientist, nor a philosopher, but a prominent lawyer. He is, in his own words, "trying a case before the culture."[3] And he is doing a very good job.

The story of the intelligent design movement really begins in 1991, when a brilliant Berkeley law professor entered America's origins conversation. His book *Darwin on Trial*[4] was a surprise best-seller and, within a year or two after its publication, Phillip E. Johnson had become a controversial fixture within American intellectual culture. More than any one person he set the agenda for the origins debate in the 1990s, and his influence shows no sign of waning. In most respects, the species of origins he championed was not new.[5] Contemporary intelligent design theory[6] has a pedigree that goes back to St. Thomas Aquinas, perhaps further. And yet in the late 1980s and early 1990s this "species" was revitalized by a cadre of talented advocates who viewed themselves as harbingers of a Kuhnian paradigm shift, ushering in a new way to conceptualize, not just origins, but science itself.

THE BIRTH OF THE INTELLIGENT DESIGN MOVEMENT

By the mid-1980s, the neo-Darwinian synthesis that had emerged at midcentury in the work of Theodosius Dobzhansky, Ernst Mayr, Wilson, and others came under attack in two books. While these books had negligible impact in the broader scientific community, they provided the impetus for a new approach in the creation–evolution debate. Charles B. Thaxton (a chemist), Walter L. Bradley (a materials scientist), and Roger L. Olson (a geochemist) wrote *The Mystery of Life's Origin*, which cast doubt that "simple chemicals on a primitive earth did spontaneously evolve (or organize themselves) into the first life." Moreover, they concluded that "the undirected flow of energy through a primordial atmosphere and ocean" is a "woefully inadequate explanation for the incredible complexity associated with even simple living systems." The authors noted that DNA is information or intelligence encoded in the biological structure. Such intelligence implies an intelligent agent.[7] The authors' argument was not entirely novel; Henry M. Morris and A. E. Wilder-Smith had anticipated parts of it already.[8] What is noteworthy about this book, however, is that the authors, while themselves Christians, attempted to argue against evolution not from biblical authority, but rather on *exclusively* scientific grounds.

The *Mystery of Life's Origin* was followed in 1986 by Michael Denton's *Evolution: A Theory in Crisis*. Denton, an Australian molecular geneticist and a religious agnostic, provided further ammunition for those whose objections to evolution were as much philosophical and cultural as scientific. He presented a controversial antievolutionary thesis that, rather than a continuum, life might very well be a "discontinuous phenomenon." Denton was well aware that this assertion challenged the whole thrust of modern biological thought. But he concluded that the fundamental axioms of macroevolution—the idea that there is a "functional continuum of all life forms linking all species back to a primitive cell" and the belief that blind random processes are the authors of biological design—have never been substantiated by direct observation or empirical evidence and remain matters of scientific faith.[9] Invoking Thomas Kuhn's *The Structure of Scientific Revolutions*, Denton charged the scientific community with embracing the evolutionary paradigm to the exclusion of mounting contrary evidence in his field of molecular biology. The reasons for this are clear, he argued: there are no scientific alternatives to Darwinism; it has dominated biology more by default than merit. More importantly, evolution is the keystone of the entire modern worldview. Consequently, evolution holds tremendous cultural importance as "the centrepiece . . . of the naturalistic view of the world."[10] Darwin's theory of evolution has become the foundation for the materialism of the twentieth-century West. And it now served as a "great cosmogenic myth" satisfying modern humanity's need for an explanatory species of origins. Denton's conclusions clearly warmed the hearts and emboldened the spirits of those who had been looking for an approach other than scientific creationism with which to combat Darwinism.[11]

Before the *Mystery of Life's Origin* and *Evolution: A Theory in Crisis* were written, a group at the University of California at Santa Barbara founded Students for Origins Research (SOR) in 1977 as "an alternative viewpoint" to that of Morris's Institute for Creation Research (ICR) and the prevailing science establishment. The founders of SOR disagreed with the ICR and other creationist groups primarily over the issues of authority and style. In addition to its marriage to only one model for the age of the earth, the ICR argued on the basis of the authority of scripture. This stance would never permit a genuine dialogue over origins, since biblical authority was not accepted in the secular academy. Too frequently, creationists were attempting to advance "a fiat creation alternative" without sufficient attention to the type of scientific evidence needed to engage the academic and scientific communities. Beyond that, SOR founders wanted to be less polemical and to adopt a stance marked more by dialogue than debate. *Origins Research*, SOR's newsprint journal, was founded as a forum for proponents of both sides to put forth their best arguments and "leaving readers to draw their own conclusions."[12] While *Origins Research* attempted to focus attention on the scientific evidence and major arguments in the literature of the evolution–creation debate, SOR was self-consciously engaged in the "struggle of world views between the theist and the materialist" that was at the heart of the "large scale 'world view' war in our society."[13]

What this "neocreationist" perspective wanted and needed was credibility in the marketplace of ideas. Clearly, the ICR had no standing in the academy, and the newer, more irenic stance of the SOR needed some way to break out of the creationist ghetto.

Enter Phillip E. Johnson, an almost messiah-like figure, who quickly became the spokesperson for the new approach. "Things really came together in the early [19]90s with the emergence of Phillip Johnson, a strong, recognized voice in the secular university who was a strategic thinker and able to focus the discussion around a few key issues."[14] Within a couple of years, Johnson had galvanized various elements into a self-proclaimed "movement," rallying under the banner of the intelligent design argument. Books and articles began to appear in increasing numbers, an institutional infrastructure was created, and bright young scholars were brought into the fold. In short, it was the birth of a movement. Johnson was both its messiah and midwife. Understanding his role in all of this is critical to making sense of America's origins conversation for the past decade.

PHILLIP E. JOHNSON

In the late 1980s, Johnson was a recognized authority in criminal law and a tenured professor at Boalt Hall, the prestigious law school of the University of California at Berkeley. He was a member of America's academic elite, with credentials and an educational pedigree that made it impossible for critics to dismiss him as some sort of marginal crank. Johnson had a J.D. from the University of Chicago and had clerked for U.S. Supreme Court Chief Justice Earl Warren, hardly the credentials of a hillbilly from a cultural backwater.

In the late 1980s, while a visiting professor at University College in London, Johnson encountered Dawkins's influential polemic *The Blind Watchmaker*, which he read carefully through the eyes of a lawyer. He became convinced that Dawkins's argument, while clearly stated, was not founded on the kind of secure empirical evidence that was supposed to undergird legitimate scientific theories. In fact, Dawkins's argument seemed to Johnson to be carried by the sort of brilliant rhetorical devices that gifted lawyers employ to overcome insufficient evidence. Struck by this, Johnson began devouring other popular scientific accounts of evolution by writers like Denton, Gould, and John Maynard Smith.

Three years later, Johnson published *Darwin on Trial*, which quickly became the manifesto of the emerging intelligent design movement. During his year in England, Johnson met Stephen C. Meyer, an American working on a doctorate in philosophy at Cambridge University. Not only was Meyer writing a thesis analyzing methodological issues in origins sciences, but he was affiliated with a group that had coalesced around the ideas in the *Mystery of Life's Origin*. In

1990, Meyer invited Johnson to Oregon and introduced him to this group, which would form the nucleus of the Discovery Institute. Johnson won the group over[15] and was soon the public voice of the neocreationist/intelligent design movement.

On a scientific level, Johnson agreed with both the scientific creationists and the emerging "neocreationists" that the fossil evidence did not substantiate the claims of Darwinism. But he challenged the notion that this was essentially a scientific problem. Rather, Johnson advocated the strategy of an assault on what he saw as the "materialist philosophy" underpinning the scientific theorizing. In his own words, he brought a "big case litigation point of view" to the issue. Neocreationists must not fool themselves into thinking that evolutionists would welcome an open exchange about the scientific evidence. Their minds were already set, Johnson claimed.[16]

Darwin on Trial, published in 1991, aggressively critiqued Darwinian science and charged that Darwinism was essentially *applied materialist philosophy*. The book sold hundreds of thousands of copies, after having been rejected by a major trade publisher, who believed that evolution was a dead issue in America, and has since been translated into several languages.[17] Johnson was evolving into a national celebrity.

In the decade following the publication of *Darwin on Trial*, the design movement developed an infrastructure of funding and public awareness. SOR became Access Research Network and upgraded *Origins Research* into the glossy *Origins and Design*, the new title reflecting the special interest in what would soon be known as "the design inference." The first issue of *Origins and Design* sported a masthead with the central players of the fledgling design movement: Paul A. Nelson, William A. Dembski, Stephen C. Meyer, and Jonathan Wells; the editorial board included Johnson, Michael J. Behe, Michael Denton, Dean Kenyon, J. P. Moreland, Charles B. Thaxton, and Hubert Yockey. The journal's first editorial reflected the design movement's chief concerns, which would remain at the center of its agenda: "Can there be a theory of design—understood, very roughly, as intelligent causation—that serves as a proper explanation in the historical sciences? If so, what would the content of that theory be? Or must science adopt the principle of methodological naturalism, to avoid being swallowed up by a 'God of the gaps'? These are questions for which *Origins and Design* seeks answers."[18]

In 1996, design theory found an institutional home when the Discovery Institute officially launched a subsidiary branch, the Center for the Renewal of Science and Culture (CRSC), whose mission was to "challenge materialism on specifically scientific grounds." The CRSC was specially linked to "design theory"—a "new scientific research program based upon recent developments in the information sciences and many new evidences of design." Design theory, according to the CRSC's home page, seeks "to detect intelligent causes in natural systems, as well as apply the explanatory power of intelligent design to empirical problems in scientific research." CRSC's fellows, directors, and advisers include virtually all of the leaders in the intelligent design movement, including Johnson, Meyer, John West, Jay Richards, Dembski, Nelson, Wells, Behe, Moreland, Reynolds, David Berlinski, John Angus Campbell, William Lane Craig, Nancy Pearcey, and Thaxton.[19]

After *Darwin on Trial*, Johnson and like-minded academics and writers appeared everywhere with symposia, essays, debates, and books. Johnson clearly struck a chord that galvanized an existing concern. *Darwin on Trial* was the focus of a 1992 conference at Southern Methodist University (SMU) titled "Darwinism: Scientific Inference or Philosophical Preference."[20] The centerpieces of that symposium were addresses by Johnson and the noted Canadian philosopher Michael Ruse, a religious agnostic, followed by a Johnson–Ruse debate. The SMU symposium was followed by other conferences where design theory was a major focus: "The C. S. Lewis Summer Institute" at Queens' College, Cambridge University (1994), "The Death of Materialism" in Seattle (1995), "Mere Creation: Science, Faith and Intelligent Design" at Biola University (1996),[21] "Naturalism, Theism and the Scientific Enterprise" at the University of Texas at Austin (1997), "The Nature of Nature" at Baylor University (2000), "Design and Its Critics" at Concordia University (2000), "Science and Evidence of Design in the Universe" at Yale University (2000), and several of the annual meetings of the American Scientific Affiliation.[22]

Throughout the 1990s, Johnson and a growing group of young design scholars, most of them CRSC fellows, published a flood of essays and reviews.[23] A favorite venue for Johnson was a published exchange with a noteworthy proponent of either Darwinism or theistic evolution. Johnson took on noted Darwinists like Ruse and William Provine, but he also challenged the coherence of theistic evolutionists like Howard J. Van Till and Denis O. Lamoureux.[24]

To date, Johnson has written four additional books after *Darwin on Trial*. By far the most important was *Reason in the Balance* published in 1995.[25] Johnson considers this his magnum opus,[26] since he provides a sustained critique of "metaphysical naturalism" as the dominant underwriter of the contemporary intellectual American worldview. Darwinian evolution, by these lights, is significant less as a scientific theory than as "a culturally dominant creation story." Johnson takes no comfort in public opinion polls suggesting that metaphysical naturalism is far from dominating average Americans' sensibilities about origins. The humanities, law, indeed, most of the institutions of the elite culture, he argues, have been infected with predictably pernicious results: metaphysical naturalism and its epistemological ally, methodological naturalism, lead "inexorably to relativism in ethics and politics," despite the best efforts of many sincere naturalists.[27]

As the design movement gathered momentum, Johnson adopted a strategy he called the "Wedge" that likens the contemporary intellectual world to a "thick and seemingly impenetrable log." Great logs, of course, can be split by inserting a wedge into a crack and pounding. Johnson describes himself as the "sharp edge of the Wedge." His writing and speaking provide the initial penetration of the "log" by contesting the dominant naturalistic creation story and the assumption that the empirical evidence endorses the prevailing materialist philosophy of science. Johnson claims success, not by winning the debate, but by legitimating a line of inquiry and drawing into the discussion an increasing number of significant thinkers. But further blows must be applied frequently and forcefully to the Wedge by a cadre of philosophically and scientifically sophisticated thinkers who explore in greater detail the implications of materialism and its alternatives, thus opening the crack in the log wider and wider.[28] The Wedge, then, includes a group of generally younger scholars, with impressive academic credentials, although not all in science, who have dedicated their careers to attacking Darwinism and advocating design theory. The most significant of these are Behe, a Lehigh University biochemist, and Dembski, a Baylor University philosopher and information theorist, both of whom have published major design theory books by respected secular publishers. And both have immeasurably more credibility in the academy than anyone associated with creation science.

MICHAEL J. BEHE AND THE BLACK BOX

Johnson's Wedge strategy took a major step forward in 1996 when the Free Press published Behe's *Darwin's Black Box*.[29] Here was a credentialed and well-published research scientist — a recipient of funding from the National Science Foundation and the National Institutes of Health — questioning how the gradualism of evolution, most often employed at the level of gross anatomy, could account for the astounding complexity revealed at the molecular level of life. Behe's "black box" metaphor is used by scientists to describe a system that does interesting things, but whose inner workings remain mysterious. Behe contends that, when Darwin wrote, the cell was a black box. But recent developments in biochemistry show that the cell is far from being Darwin's simple glob of "protoplasm." Scientists now have illuminated several ultrasophisticated "molecular machines" within the cell. Behe believes that the gradualism of evolutionary processes cannot account for the emergence of such complex and interdependent structures and processes.[30]

At the core of Behe's argument is the notion of "irreducible complexity," a phrase he coined to describe a "single system composed of several well-matched, interacting parts that contribute to the basic function, wherein the removal of any one of the parts causes the system to effectively cease functioning." He uses the simple mousetrap with great effect to illustrate this. The standard household mousetrap has several component parts: a wooden platform, a metal hammer, a spring, a catch mechanism that releases when jarred, and a metal bar that holds the hammer back. All of the components of the mousetrap have to be in place before it is functional. Remove one part, and it doesn't work.[31] The mousetrap is irreducibly complex.

Behe uses a series of case studies to demonstrate the surprising complexity of life at the molecular level. One example here will suffice. Microscopic cilia are hair-like structures on the surface of many animal and lower plant cells that move liquids over the surface of the cell or "row" single cells through a fluid. Behe notes that cells lining the human respiratory tract have about two hundred cilia whose synchronized beating sweeps mucus toward the throat for elimination. In fascinating detail, with prose reminiscent of the best science writers, Behe illustrates the incredible complexity of the "simple" cilium with its accompanying ciliary motion. The larger point he makes is that evolutionary explanations for the emergence of such complex molecular structures and processes are incoherent. According to the model of evolutionary gradualism, an irreducibly complex system of cilia capable of coordinated motion would develop by means of "slight, successive modifications of a precursor system." But any precursor to an irreducibly complex system that is missing a part is by definition nonfunctional.[32] "Ominously for Darwinian theory," Behe asserts, "the cell contains many irreducibly complex systems."[33]

Behe is not denying the explanatory power of evolution. Random mutation and natural selection are observable on the microevolutionary (intraspecies) level, and Behe believes, contra Johnson and almost everyone else in the design movement, that the evidence strongly supports the common descent of all living things. But Behe contends that no scientist has ever offered a detailed explanation of how mutation and natural selection could create the complex intricate molecular structures revealed by biochemists. There is nothing to substantiate the idea of Darwinian molecular evolution in the scientific literature other than mere assertion.

How can we account for this? Behe contends that many biochemical systems reveal strong evidence of purposeful, intentional design by an intelligent agent. Like Johnson, Behe sidesteps the issue of the identity of the designer. He argues that the conclusion of intelligent design "flows naturally from the data itself—not from sacred books or sectarian beliefs." Design can be inferred when "a number of separate, interacting components are ordered in such a way as to accomplish a function beyond the individual components." What emerges in Behe's analysis is a view of life that combines evolutionary mechanisms and design. Some features of the cell are no doubt the result of simple natural processes, but others can be explained only by design. As a scientist, he has no problem assigning a significant role to the laws of nature: namely, biological reproduction, mutation, and natural selection. But by themselves those natural laws peculiar to life cannot explain biological systems. The hurdles over which gradualism must leap become increasingly formidable as it encounters more complex and interdependent structures.[34]

WILLIAM A. DEMBSKI AND THE DESIGN INFERENCE

In exploring the design implications of biochemistry, Behe relies on the work of another member of Johnson's Wedge: William A. Dembski. *Darwin's Black Box* appeared in the same year that Dembski completed a doctoral dissertation in philosophy at the University of Illinois at Chicago: "The Design Inference: Eliminating Chance through Small Probabilities."[35] By this time, Dembski was already a highly visible contributor to the intelligent design movement. His essays had appeared in all of its important collections.[36] In 1998 and 1999, however, Dembski exploded into print. Christian publisher InterVarsity Press released *Mere Creation*, a Dembski-edited anthology of intelligent design papers from a Biola University conference.[37] Cambridge University Press published his doctoral dissertation: *The Design Inference*;[38] and InterVarsity published *Intelligent Design*, a systematic treatment of design theory.[39] Almost overnight, Dembski had become the most important design theorist and, next to Johnson, the major spokesperson for the design movement. The Wedge strategy was proceeding just as Johnson had hoped. The crack in the log of naturalism was being forced wider.

The importance of Dembski to the intelligent design movement is hard to overestimate. He is attempting to expand design theory from a mere anti-Darwinism argument to a full-fledged ("robust") scientific research program. The basis for this is his contention that design is empirically detectable. That design is empirically detectable is not in the least remarkable, and common sense design inferences are made all the time. When on the one hand we inspect a landscape with neat hedges, shaped shrubs, and clipped grass we infer design; on the other hand, the pattern of trees and plants in a forest, while often very beautiful, does not suggest design. This is common sense. What is not common sense is how to detect design that is not so obvious. Just how do we infer design?

Dembski suggests that we apprehend design by the detection of *specified complexity*: highly improbable events that fit some independently identifiable pattern (i.e., specification). Take the case of the first plane that hit one of the World Trade Towers in September 2001. That event is highly improbable but does not fit into any pattern, so many people immediately inferred that the event was simply a terrible accident. However, as soon as the second plane hit the other Tower, a pattern was immediately apparent and the first "accident" was reinterpreted.[40] The challenge is how to "prove" the validity of the design inference in such cases; and the problem is even more complicated when the phenomenon under investigation does not involve actions that follow familiar human logic, as is the case with the proposal that DNA is "designed."

On one level, Dembski's design inference is little more than a restatement of the classic argument from design, historically applied to complex living things. This argument is thought to have been toppled by Darwin. Dembski's project is to reinvigorate this style of argument using information theory so that "design should be admitted to full scientific status."[41]

To elevate design to the level of scientific explanation, Dembski must establish a criterion that provides an alternative to explanations that appeal to chance (the numbers that show up on dice), to necessity (the falling of bodies in a gravitational field), or to a combination of the two (the winding of a stream as it makes its way down the side of a mountain). In order to detect design, three things must be present: contingency, complexity, and specification. Contingent events are events that don't have to occur. Planes do not have to hit buildings. That is a contingent event. But luggage dropped from planes must fall to the ground; this is a law of nature and is not contingent. For something to have complexity, in layperson's terms, it must have high improbability. But improbability by *itself* is not enough to eliminate chance; luggage from a plane may fall on your house, but this would not be design, even though it would be overwhelmingly improbable. Purely chance events can be highly improbable, as everyone who plays the lottery knows only too well.

Dembski argues that to eliminate chance, we need to know whether an event conforms to a pattern. Here, he invokes the concept of specification, that is, the relation between patterns and events. Specification is a pattern that, in the presence of events of small probability, allows us to say that these events are not the result of chance. It guarantees the "right sort of pattern associated with intelligent causes." Chance is effectively ruled out if a sequence of low-probability events occurs according to a preexisting or otherwise independent pattern. An example of specification would be an archer's painting of a bull's-eye target on the side of a barn. When the archer shoots at it, she specifies hitting the bull's-eye; when she hits the target repeatedly, we are warranted in attributing her success to skill and intention, not luck. Contingency, complexity, and specification (i.e., "specified complexity") are combined by Dembski into a conceptual "explanatory filter" that can be used to establish when design can be inferred. This filter infers design by eliminating regularity and chance.[42] (On an every day level, we use an informal version of this filter all the time without realizing it.) The filter is powerful enough, Dembski claims, to advance what he calls the Law of Small Probability, namely that "specified events of small probability do not occur by chance."[43]

To carry the design inference to the next level, we should recall that the sinister "design" inferred in the terrorist attacks on the World Trade Center clearly pointed to a "designer" and, sure enough, America's armed forces were soon in hot pursuit of that designer. To what "designer" does the design uncovered by Dembski's explanatory filter point? Does the filter point to God? Dembski is careful to note in the *Design Inference* that there is no logical necessity for linking the design inference to any particular metaphysical notion of intelligent agency. To be sure, the design inference is frequently a first step in the identification of an intelligent agent (God), but the design inference does not logically entail an intelligent agent. Design, emphasizes Dembski, is a mode of explanation and not a causal category. Nevertheless, the explanatory filter is well suited for recognizing intelligent agency. Intelligent agents choose, actualizing one among several competing possibilities, ruling out the others, and specifying the one actualized. So, while the primary task of the design inference is to limit explanatory options, it can help to identify a cause, though invariably more information is needed.[44]

The design inference is all about information—its detection and measurement. For Dembski, intelligent design is a theory about information. To infer design by means of his explanatory filter is equivalent to detecting complex specified information (CSI), which is the great mystery of life's origin. Dembski concludes that law and chance together cannot generate CSI and so cannot be the basis for the origin of life. The only known source for the sort of CSI that is found in the simplest living cell, according to Dembski, is intelligence. He even goes so far as to suggest that he has uncovered a dramatic new law of nature, the Law of Conservation of Information, which states that natural causes are incapable of generating complex specified information.[45]

The implications of Dembski's Law of Conservation of Information for the origins debate are obvious. The information needed to account for life's origin had to come from somewhere as there are no natural mechanisms by which it can be created. Either the information (the complex, specified, information) in a closed system of natural causes has been in the system eternally or was added from outside.[46]

Based on his own analysis and the previous work of Behe, Dembski criticizes evolutionary theory for its failure to account for the information hurdles that organisms need to jump in the course of natural history. Darwinian mechanisms of selection and inheritance with modification fail to account for the full diversity of life. Evolutionary mechanisms are adequate for conserving, adapting, and honing already existing biological structures (microevolution), but they lack the information resources to account for the appearance of "irreducibly complex biological structures." Consequently, evolutionary biology needs to be reconceptualized in terms of information. Coming to grips with information theory compels evolutionary biology to trace information pathways. For example, to establish common descent the informational pathways that connect all organisms must be demonstrated.[47] We emphasize that these are Dembski's ideas, which depart in some important ways from the conventional scientific approach to these problems.

The publication of *Darwin's Black Box, Mere Creation, Design Inference,* and *Intelligent Design* in rapid succession in the late 1990s illustrated Johnson's Wedge strategy in advancing increasingly sophisticated intelligent design arguments. We will analyze the influence of the intelligent design movement on the origins debate in the next chapter. But before we do that we need to address two extremely controversial aspects of the contemporary design argument.

Near the end of *Intelligent Design*, Dembski notes that the scientific picture of the world crafted since the Enlightenment is "massively wrong."[48] Such rhetoric

indicates that design theory is much more than just the Behe–Dembski irre-
ducible/specified-complexity argument regarding the inadequacy of chance and
law to account for biological origins. At the heart of the intelligent design movement is a sustained critique of the naturalism that has resided at the core of the
modern Western worldview since the Enlightenment. We have noted already that
Johnson has selected naturalism, which he sees as the reigning metaphysical assumption of our time, as the specific target of the intelligent design movement.
Naturalism assumes that what is ultimately real is nature. And what is nature but
an amalgam of fundamental particles and the natural laws that govern their behavior, a permanently closed system of material causes and effects that is fundamentally purposeless and mindless?[49] Dembski calls naturalism a "disease," "the
intellectual pathology of our age."[50]

Naturalism, however, comes in two varieties: (1) the metaphysical or worldview notion suggested earlier by Johnson and Dembski that accounts for all of
reality using only undirected natural causes, and (2) the methodological assumption that science has limited competence to treat only questions related
to natural phenomena.[51] Design theorists vigorously challenge the near-
universal assumption of the scientific establishment that science must deal exclusively with naturalistic explanations. While the overwhelming majority of
scientists conclude that all talk about transcendent purpose and design is beyond the purview of science and that science possesses only tools appropriate
for naturalistic exploration, design theorists argue that such methodological
naturalism unfairly restricts the dialogue and rules design out of court at the
outset. Dembski states clearly that as long as methodological naturalism sets
the ground rules for science, intelligent design has no chance of gaining a
hearing. Given this state of affairs, many design theorists want to dump
methodological naturalism for "theistic science"—which they argue can be simultaneously rigorous in its investigation of nature but open to design arguments.[52] So the intelligent design movement—perhaps predictably—has generated a corollary debate on the very definition of science—something that
resonates deeply with those religiously conservative sectors of American culture that see well-known scientists systematically attacking cherished notions of
humanity, creation, and the Creator.

The quarrel over methodological naturalism and theistic science does not engage the average scientist in a lab coat—even the 40 percent that believe in an
afterlife and a God who answers prayers.[53] It is essentially a debate among
philosophers and historians of science. In particular, three Christian philosophers have led the charge against methodological naturalism and in favor of
theistic science: Alvin Plantinga,[54] Moreland,[55] and Meyer.[56] As a group, they
contend that in pursuing science, we should use all that we know. If God exists,
then that should be taken into consideration as a possible cause or explanation
for things that we encounter in the natural world. "Theistic science" is an-
chored in the belief that Christians must not limit themselves to science as cur-

rently defined when explaining things in nature or assessing various scientific hypotheses. Theological propositions should also be consulted; otherwise, science will be saddled with hopelessly false and inadequate naturalistic speculations about origins and existence.[57] Methodological naturalism unduly restrains human understanding by limiting itself to the natural order. What we really need, Plantinga argues, is "a scientific account of life that isn't restricted by . . . methodological naturalism," one "that takes into account what we know as Christians." Consequently, Christians should employ their understandings of sin, human nature, and creation in their *scientific* work.[58]

Perhaps the most sophisticated attack on methodological naturalism comes from Meyer. He notes that efforts to discredit intelligent design as unscientific do not take into account the overall failure of "demarcation arguments" to distinguish science from pseudoscience. (Demarcation arguments are attempts to find some boundary that separates science from nonscience.) Relying heavily on the work of philosopher of science Larry Laudan, Meyer argues that there is no overall agreement as to what the scientific method really is.[59] Indeed, there are several scientific methods that have been proposed by philosophers, so the attempt to exclude intelligent design using a single set of methodological criteria (such as falsifiability, observability, repeatability, and the use of law-like explanation) will fail or else some disciplines already considered to be scientific will fail the test as well. Indeed, Meyer argues, there is a methodological equivalence between intelligent design and naturalistic evolutionary theories. As Laudan argues, the question of whether a theory is scientific is really a red herring; what is at stake is whether a theory is *true* or worth believing. If the label of "scientific" is to be guarded jealously, then Meyer suggests that intelligent design be called a "quasi-scientific historical speculation with strong metaphysical overtones." But if so, the same designation must be applied to evolutionary theory.[60]

With regard to the origins debate, advocates of theistic science contend that the belief that God designed the world for a purpose can "appropriately enter into the very fabric of the practice of science." Indeed, they claim, design theory is providing *evidence* that various features of the biological world bear the characteristics of intelligent design. But advocates of methodological naturalism, so the argument goes, invoke the rules of science to rule out design as unscientific and unable to meet "objective standards of scientific method and practice."[61] So, in the name of science, the best explanation of the scientific evidence is dismissed.[62]

All this gets complicated because, in the context of the origins debate, some design theorists charge that *methodological* naturalism is *metaphysical* naturalism "in disguise"[63] or "the functional equivalent of a full-blown metaphysical naturalism."[64] Johnson asserts that the distinction between methodological and metaphysical naturalism collapses because science insists on explaining the entire history of the cosmos and presumes that naturalistic answers are available for every problem.[65]

Critics of theistic science pounce on this line of thinking. Science has limits, they admit. It is not the only way of understanding, but it is a particularly effective way of understanding the natural order, as witnessed by the spectacular advances in medicine and communication. Science cannot entertain transcendent wild cards. In the oft-quoted words of Nobel laureate physicist Steven Weinberg, the "only way that any sort of science can proceed is to assume that there is no divine intervention and to see how far one can get with this assumption."[66] While many prominent science writers are vocal in their atheism, methodological naturalism eschews appeals to theistic interventions, not because of some special distaste for God, but because such appeals are by definition beyond natural laws and not subject to observational testing. According to philosopher Robert T. Pennock, "[s]cience is godless in the same way that plumbing is godless." Science adopts a stance of methodological naturalism, because without it, science loses its "empirical evidential touchstone"[67] and would no longer be science.

A number of Christian philosophers and scientists, including Richard H. Bube, Lamoureux, Van Till, Keith B. Miller, and Robert C. O'Connor, have also taken on the design theorists' critique of methodological naturalism.[68] They do not accept the notion that science's adoption of a methodology that is limited to descriptions in natural categories entails an embrace of the atheistic worldview of naturalism. Nor do they believe there is a distinctively Christian way of doing science. Miller, for example, notes that methodological naturalism simply places boundaries around "what science can or cannot say."[69] O'Connor considers methodological naturalism necessary and proper in order to establish constraints on science. Moreover, attempting to interject notions of divine agency into science compromises the considerable value of a purely natural science.[70]

Since its inception in the early 1990s, the intelligent design movement has attracted so much attention that it has succeeded in dominating the origins debate. By this we do not mean that it is triumphant. Far from it. While design has made some modest inroads in the academy, it is frequently seen, much to the chagrin of its advocates, as a more attractively packaged variety of creationism. But design has succeeded in setting the agenda for much of the debate. We now turn to an assessment of the impact of the design movement on America's search for a creation story.

NOTES

1. For example, see Del Ratzsch, *The Battle of Beginnings: Why Neither Side Is Winning the Creation–Evolution Debate* (Downers Grove, Ill.: InterVarsity, 1996), 196–198. See also Paul K. Conkin's observations about how out of step contemporary intellectual culture is with traditional religious belief in *All the Gods Trembled: Darwinism, Scopes, and American Intellectuals* (Lanham, Md.: Rowman & Littlefield, 1998), 169–175.

2. We have already noted that Paul A. Nelson and John Mark Reynolds subscribe somewhat tentatively to a young-earth position. They are also active in the design move-

ment, but they are voicing a decidedly minority position within the design camp and are careful not to make any necessary linkage between intelligent design and their young-earth stance.

3. Phillip E. Johnson, interview by the authors, 24 March 1999.

4. Phillip E. Johnson, *Darwin on Trial* (Washington, D.C.: Regnery Gateway, 1991).

5. See the appendix for a brief history of design theory.

6. Nomenclature is a very contentious issue in the origins debate. The species of origins under consideration in this chapter is known by its detractors as "the new creationism" or "intelligent design creationism" (see Robert T. Pennock, *Tower of Babel: The Evidence against the New Creationism* [Cambridge, Mass.: MIT Press, 1999], xiv, 28–29) and by its advocates as "design theory" or "intelligent design theory" (Jay Richards, senior fellow and program director of the Discovery Institute's Center for the Renewal of Science and Culture, to Donald A. Yerxa, 4 November 1999). The authors have opted for the term "neocreationism" to refer to the cluster of viewpoints circulating in the 1970s and 1980s that were no longer content with approaching the origins debates from a position based primarily on biblical authority. We will use "design theory" and "intelligent design" interchangeably to refer to the movement that coalesced in the 1990s around Johnson and his associates. According to author Larry Witham, the term "intelligent design" first appeared in 1989 in book written by Percival Davis and Dean H. Kenyon, *Of Pandas and People: The Central Question of Biological Origins* (Dallas: Haughton, 1989).

7. Charles B. Thaxton, Walter L. Bradley, and Roger L. Olsen, *The Mystery of Life's Origin: Reassessing Current Theories* (Dallas: Lewis and Stanley, 1984, 1992), 186–187; Nancy Pearcey, "The Evolution Backlash: Debunking Darwin," *World* 11 (March 1997).

8. See, for example, Henry M. Morris, *Many Infallible Proofs: Practical and Useful Evidences of Christianity* (San Diego: Creation-Life Publishers, 1974, 1996); A. E. Wilder-Smith, *Man's Origin, Man's Destiny: A Critical Survey of the Principles of Evolution and Christianity* (Wheaton, Ill.: Shaw, 1968).

9. Michael Denton, *Evolution: A Theory in Crisis* (Bethesda, Md.: Adler and Adler, 1986), 344–347.

10. Denton, *Evolution*, 355–357. Denton here echoes in part the pathfinding work of historian John C. Greene in *The Death of Adam: Evolution and Its Impact on Western Thought* (Ames: University of Iowa Press, 1959).

11. Denton, *Evolution*, 358. Denton later lamented the misuse of his work. To be sure, he finds the Darwinian model inadequate. But he considers himself a "philosophical naturalist" who flatly rejects special creationism and fully accepts that evolution is "driven entirely by natural processes and by natural law." Where he differs from many evolutionists is his teleological view that the naturalistic evolutionary process is "a designed whole with mankind as its end and purpose." See Michael Denton, "Comments on Special Creationism," in *Darwinism Defeated? The Johnson–Lamoureux Debate on Biological Origins*, ed. Phillip E. Johnson and Denis O. Lamoureux (Vancouver, B.C.: Regent College Publishing, 1999), 152–153.

12. Dennis Wagner, "Put Another Candle on the Birthday Cake," *Origins Research* 10 (spring–summer 1987): 3; personal correspondence, Dennis Wagner to Donald A. Yerxa, 13 May 1999.

13. Wagner, "Put Another Candle on the Birthday Cake," 3.

14. Wagner to Yerxa, May 13, 1999.

15. See Stephen C. Meyer, "Darwin in the Dock," *Touchstone* 14 (April 2001): 57.

16. Johnson, interview.

17. Johnson, interview.

18. Editorial, "Welcome to an Evolving Publication," *Origins and Design* 17 (winter 1996): 4.

19. Jay Richards to Donald A. Yerxa, 4 November 1999; Discovery Institute–CRSC at www.discovery.org/crsc (6 April 2002).

20. The symposium proceedings were published as: Jon Buell and Virginia Hearn, eds., *Darwinism: Science or Philosophy* (Richardson, Tex.: Foundation for Thought and Ethics, 1994).

21. The conference proceedings were published as: William A. Dembski, ed., *Mere Creation: Science, Faith and Intelligent Design* (Downers Grove, Ill.: InterVarsity, 1998).

22. The American Scientific Affiliation (ASA) is an organization of scientists with evangelical religious commitments. The ASA tends to embrace theistic evolution, and some creationist organizations have formed in reaction to their failure to convince the ASA that young-earth creation is the only viable species of origins for Christians.

23. Consult the bibliography for a more complete listing of these, but among the more significant essay-length publications were: Stephen C. Meyer, "The Origin of Life and the Death of Materialism," *The Intercollegiate Review* 31 (spring 1996): 24–43; Alvin Plantinga, "Methodological Naturalism?" *Origins and Design* 18 (winter 1997): 18–27; Alvin Plantinga, "Methodological Naturalism? Part 2," *Origins and Design* 18 (fall 1997): 22–34; Phillip E. Johnson, "The Unraveling of Scientific Materialism," *First Things* 77 (November 1997): 22–25; William A. Dembski, "Science and Design," *First Things* 86 (October 1998): 21–27.

24. See, "The Johnson–Ruse Debate," in *Darwinism: Science or Philosophy?* ed. Jon Buell and Virginia Hearn (Richardson, Tex.: Foundation for Thought and Ethics, 1994), 41–58; Howard J. Van Till and Phillip E. Johnson, "God and Evolution: An Exchange," *First Things* 34 (June–July 1993): 32–41; Phillip E. Johnson and Denis O. Lamoureux, eds., *Darwinism Defeated? The Johnson–Lamoureux Debate on Biological Origins* (Vancouver: Regent College Publishing, 1999); see also Jonathan Wells, John Mark Reynolds, and Howard Van Till, "Debate: The Ideas of Howard Van Till," *Origins and Design* 19 (summer 1998): 16–35.

25. Phillip E. Johnson, *Reason in the Balance: The Case against Naturalism in Science, Law and Education* (Downers Grove, Ill.: InterVarsity, 1995); *Defeating Darwinism by Opening Minds* (Downers Grove, Ill.: InterVarsity, 1997); *Objections Sustained: Subversive Essays on Evolution, Law and Culture* (Downers Grove, Ill.: InterVarsity, 1998); *The Wedge of Truth: Splitting the Foundations of Naturalism* (Downers Grove, Ill.: InterVarsity, 2000).

26. Johnson, interview.

27. Johnson, *Reason in the Balance*, 7–17.

28. Phillip E. Johnson, "The Wedge: Breaking the Modernist Monopoly on Science," *Touchstone* 12 (July–August 1999): 23–24; Johnson, *Wedge of Truth*, 14–17.

29. Michael J. Behe, *Darwin's Black Box: The Biochemical Challenge to Evolution* (New York: Free Press, 1996); see also Michael J. Behe, "Intelligent Design Theory As a Tool," in *Mere Creation: Science, Faith and Intelligent Design*, ed. William A. Dembski (Downers Grove, Ill.: InterVarsity, 1998), 177–194; Michael J. Behe, "Intelligent Design As an Alternative Explanation for the Existence of Biomolecular Machines," *Rhetoric and Public Affairs* 1 (winter 1998): 565–570; Michael J. Behe, "Darwin's Breakdown: Irre-

ducible Complexity and Design at the Foundation of Life," *Touchstone* 12 (July–August 1999): 39–43.

30. Behe, *Darwin's Black Box*, 6–10.

31. Behe, *Darwin's Black Box*, 42–43.

32. Behe, *Darwin's Black Box*, 39, 59–69. Behe also explains the irreducible complexity of bacterial flagellum, the coagulation cascade (how blood clots at the molecular level), the intermolecular transport of waste proteins within the cell, various molecular features of the immune system, and the regulation of AMP biosynthesis.

33. Behe, "Intelligent Design As an Alternative Explanation," 567.

34. Behe, *Darwin's Black Box*, 193–194, 203–204.

35. This was Dembski's second earned doctorate. He received a Ph.D. in mathematics (probability theory) at the University of Chicago in 1988.

36. See, for example, William A. Dembski, "The Incompleteness of Scientific Naturalism," in *Darwinism: Science or Philosophy?* ed. Jon Buell and Virginia Hearn (Richardson, Tex.: Foundation for Thought and Ethics, 1994), 79–94; William A. Dembski, "On the Very Possibility of Intelligent Design," in *The Creation Hypothesis: Scientific Evidence for an Intelligent Designer,* ed. J. P. Moreland (Downers Grove, Ill.: InterVarsity, 1994), 113–138.

37. Dembski, *Mere Creation.*

38. William A. Dembski, *The Design Inference: Eliminating Chance through Small Probabilities* (Cambridge, U.K.: Cambridge University Press, 1998).

39. William A. Dembski, *Intelligent Design: The Bridge between Science and Theology* (Downers Grove, Ill.: InterVarsity, 1999).

40. We would like to thank our friend professor Ted Davis of Messiah College for this example.

41. Dembski, *Intelligent Design,* 23, 106–107; Michael Behe, foreword to *Intelligent Design: The Bridge between Science and Theology,* by William A. Dembski (Downers Grove, Ill.: InterVarsity, 1999), 10.

42. Dembski, *Intelligent Design,* 17; Dembski, *Design Inference,* 3–5, 39, 62, 153.

43. Dembski, *Design Inference,* 5. In *Design Inference,* Dembski devotes a chapter each to how probability and complexity theory undergird his Law of Small Probability. These are very technical chapters that illustrate how probability theory measures the likelihood of an event and complexity theory measures the difficulty of a problem.

44. Dembski, *Design Inference,* 8–9, 62–66; Dembski, *Intelligent Design,* 144–146, 226.

45. Dembski, *Intelligent Design,* 167–170.

46. Whether CSI was present from the very beginning of the creation of the cosmos or whether it was the result, infusion (the direct introduction of novel information) forms a major distinction between intelligent design advocates and theistic evolutionists. Moreover, scholars who decide in favor of the former option differ as to the cause of CSI. Some like Hubert Yockey consider CSI a "brute fact" and "frozen accident," while others adopt a theistic approach. See Dembski, *Intelligent Design,* 175.

47. Dembski, *Intelligent Design,* 176–183.

48. Dembski, *Intelligent Design,* 224.

49. Johnson, *Reason in the Balance,* 37–38.

50. Dembski, *Intelligent Design,* 120. Naturalism is self-defeating, according to Plantinga. Naturalism, Plantinga argues, renders the beliefs produced under it unreliable,

including the belief that naturalism itself is true. See chapter 12 of Plantinga's *Warrant and Proper Function* (New York: Oxford University Press, 1993) and his *Warranted Christian Belief* (New York: Oxford University Press, 2000), 227–240, 350–351.

51. See Howard J. Van Till, "The Fully Gifted Creation," in *Three Views on Creation and Evolution*, ed. J. P. Moreland and John Mark Reynolds (Grand Rapids, Mich.: Zondervan, 1999), 200–201.

52. Dembski, *Intelligent Design*, 119. Recently, Dembski appears to be distancing himself from notions of theistic science. See Donald A. Yerxa, "Questioning Darwin: William Dembski Discusses *Intelligent Design*," *Research News and Opportunities in Science and Theology* 2 (November 2001): 13.

53. Edward J. Larson and Larry Witham, "Scientists and Religion in America," *Scientific American* 281 (September 1999): 89–90.

54. Alvin Plantinga, "When Faith and Reason Clash: Evolution and the Bible," *Christian Scholar's Review* 21 (September 1991): 27–29; Plantinga, "Methodological Naturalism," 18–27; Plantinga, "Methodological Naturalism? Part 2," 22–34.

55. J. P. Moreland, "Theistic Science and Methodological Naturalism," in *The Creation Hypothesis: Scientific Evidence for an Intelligent Designer*, ed. J. P. Moreland (Downers Grove, Ill.: InterVarsity, 1994), 41–66; J. P. Moreland, "Complementarity, Agency Theory, and the God-of-the-Gaps," *Perspectives on Science and Christian Faith* 49 (March 1997): 2–14.

56. Stephen C. Meyer, "The Methodological Equivalence of Design and Descent," in *The Creation Hypothesis: Scientific Evidence for an Intelligent Designer*, ed. J. P. Moreland (Downers Grove, Ill.: InterVarsity, 1994), 67–112; Stephen C. Meyer, "The Use and Abuse of Philosophy of Science: A Response to Moreland," *Perspectives on Science and Christian Faith* 46 (March 1994): 14–18.

57. Paul A. Nelson and John Mark Reynolds, "Young Earth Creationism," in *Three Views on Creation and Evolution*, ed. J. P. Moreland and John Mark Reynolds (Grand Rapids, Mich.: Zondervan, 1999), 46.

58. Plantinga, "When Faith and Reason Clash," 29; Plantinga, "Methodological Naturalism," 25, 27, 32.

59. This is potentially a very dangerous maneuver. Laudan is a very creative thinker who holds to an antiessentialist view of science. Consequently, there are no methods or aims that necessarily delimit the boundaries of science. The scientific community at any given time establishes the methods and aims of science. So when Meyer invokes Laudan, he risks undermining the epistemic validity of theistic science in order to gain its acceptance as scientific. Moreover, Meyer must be careful not to endorse a "methodological anarchism," whereby any conceivable account is deemed scientific. See Robert C. O'Connor, "Science on Trial: Exploring the Rationality of Methodological Naturalism," *Perspectives on Science and Christian Faith* 49 (March 1997): 21–23.

60. Meyer, "Methodological Equivalence," 72–75, 98–99; Meyer, "Use and Abuse," 14–18.

61. Meyer, "Methodological Equivalence," 70.

62. J. P. Moreland and John Mark Reynolds, introduction to *Three Views on Creation and Evolution*, ed. J. P. Moreland and John Mark Reynolds (Grand Rapids, Mich.: Zondervan, 1999), 18–23.

63. See Van Till, "Fully Gifted Creation," 202.

64. Dembski, *Intelligent Design*, 119.

65. Phillip E. Johnson, "Reflections," in *Three Views on Creation and Evolution*, ed. J. P. Moreland and John Mark Reynolds (Grand Rapids, Mich.: Zondervan, 1999), 271–272.

66. Steven Weinberg, *Dreams of a Final Theory: The Search for the Fundamental Laws of Nature* (New York: Pantheon, 1992), 247.

67. Pennock, *Tower of Babel*, 196, 282–291.

68. Richard H. Bube, "Reflections," in *Three Views on Creation and Evolution*, ed. J. P. Moreland and John Mark Reynolds (Grand Rapids, Mich.: Zondervan, 1999), 257–261; Denis O. Lamoureux, "Evangelicals Inheriting the Wind: The Phillip E. Johnson Phenomenon," in *Darwinism Defeated? The Johnson–Lamoureux Debate on Biological Origins*, ed. Phillip E. Johnson and Denis O. Lamoureux (Vancouver: Regent College Publishing, 1999), 70; Howard J. Van Till, "Intelligent Design: The Celebration of Gifts Withheld?" in *Darwinism Defeated? The Johnson–Lamoureux Debate on Biological Origins*, ed. Phillip E. Johnson and Denis O. Lamoureux (Vancouver: Regent College Publishing, 1999), 84–88; Van Till, "The Fully Gifted Creation," 201–203, 245; Howard J. Van Till, "When Faith and Reason Cooperate," *Christian Scholar's Review* 49 (September 1991): 44–45. See also Notre Dame philosopher Ernan McMullin's defense of methodological naturalism: "Plantinga's Defense of Special Creation," *Christian Scholar's Review* 49 (September 1991): 57.

69. Keith B. Miller, "Design and Purpose within an Evolving Creation," in *Darwinism Defeated? The Johnson–Lamoureux Debate on Biological Origins*, ed. Phillip E. Johnson and Denis O. Lamoureux (Vancouver: Regent College Publishing, 1999), 110–114.

70. O'Connor, "Science on Trial," 15–30.

10

❖

The Reception
of Intelligent Design

On August 8, 2000, the *Wall Street Journal* ran a piece by respected journalist Gregg Easterbrook entitled "The New Fundamentalism." In it, *The New Republic's* senior editor indicated that, while intelligent design "may or may not be correct," it is a "sophisticated theory" worthy of being taught in public schools as an alternative to the reigning "evolutionary fundamentalism."[1] Less than a year later, the *Los Angeles Times* ran a story in its Sunday edition about a Burlington, Washington, high school biology teacher who decided to do just that. According to the story, Roger DeHart asked his students to consider whether life was the result of "random, meaningless events" or "designed by an intelligent force." After years of permitting DeHart to teach intelligent design for one day out of a two-week module on evolution, school authorities ordered him "to drop references to design and stick to the textbook."[2] Two weeks after the *Los Angeles Times* piece, the *New York Times* ran a front-page story on the intelligent design movement that, according to leading journalist and prominent science writer Robert Wright, "granted official significance to the latest form of opposition to Darwinism."[3] Ten years after Phillip E. Johnson published *Darwin on Trial*, design theory was making headlines, all but replacing scientific creationism in the public discussion of origins.

Not all of the headlines have been positive. In the fall of 2000, William A. Dembski became embroiled in a nasty squabble at Baylor University, which spilled onto the pages of Texas newspapers and national opinion journals. A year earlier, Baylor president Robert B. Sloan created the Michael Polanyi Center for Complexity, Information, and Design and appointed Dembski to be its director. Many on the Baylor faculty were miffed that Sloan did this by administrative fiat and were somewhat embarrassed that Baylor, the largest Baptist university in the world, was now associated with what they considered a scientifically suspect "research program." The grumbling intensified in the wake of a Polanyi Center conference on naturalism in April 2000 that featured an impressive array of scientists and scholars who spoke to both sides of the issue. Having scholars like Steven Weinberg sharing the program with design theorists like Dembski was certainly evidence that the intelligent design movement had achieved a measure of credibility far beyond anything ever accorded scientific creationism. Nevertheless, the Baylor faculty was up in arms.

Days after the conference, the faculty senate voted by an overwhelming margin to close the Polanyi Center. Sloan refused and even cited his reasons in a *Houston Chronicle* editorial, though he did call for the creation of a nine-member peer review committee of scholars, several from outside Baylor, to look into the matter. This committee recommended that Baylor set up an advisory committee to keep an eye on the center, but essentially endorsed the legitimacy of the intelligent design research program to contribute to the broader science-and-religion dialogue.

Dembski, who felt unfairly attacked, was greatly relieved and issued an ill-advised press release, which included the following: "Dogmatic opponents of design who demanded the Center be shut down have met their Waterloo. Baylor University is to be commended for remaining strong in the face of intolerant assaults on freedom of thought and expression."[4]

Apparently, Dembski was asked to retract his aggressive comments, and when he refused he was removed as the director of the center, though he retained his five-year appointment as a Baylor research professor. An unrepentant Dembski promptly issued an even more scathing press release, which included the bitter assertion that "[i]ntellectual McCarthyism has, for the moment, prevailed at Baylor."[5]

The Baylor episode is interesting not only because of the high drama that such confrontations generate, but also because it moved design theory further into the national spotlight. Journalist Lauren Kern's sympathetic account of the Dembski affair was featured in both the *Houston Press* and the *Dallas Observer*.[6] But the Baylor incident was more than a regional matter among the Southern Baptists of Texas. Editorials and essays appeared in a number of periodicals, including *Christianity Today, The American Spectator, Research News and Opportunities in Science and Theology*, and the *Newsletter of the American Scientific Affiliation*.[7] And it is clear that while Dembski paid a high personal price for his efforts on behalf of intelligent design at Baylor, the overall "Wedge strategy" of keeping intelligent design in the media spotlight was enhanced.

Near the end of her account of Dembski's struggle, Kern noted that "[a]cademia may not be embracing intelligent design, but the general public, it seems, is primed for it." We know of no recent poll that would specifically corroborate Kern's hunch, though Michael Shermer, publisher of *Skeptic* magazine, has released the results of a 1998 poll that he and Massachusetts Institute of Technology social scientist Frank Sulloway conducted to learn about the public's religious attitudes.

They received one thousand survey responses (from a list provided by "the same organization used by the most notable political, social, and cultural surveys conducted by social scientists and the media"). The respondents were highly educated: 12 percent had earned doctorates and 62 percent were college graduates. Shermer reports that 64 percent responded they believed in God and that the most frequently cited reason for their belief (29 percent) was their acknowledgment of "arguments based upon good design/natural beauty/perfection/complexity of the world or universe."[8] Obviously, this survey is not conclusive, but it does at least suggest, as we have been arguing, that the design argument resonates intuitively with religious people.

While we cannot offer a quantitative evaluation of the public's receptivity to design theory, we can assess the reaction to the intelligent design movement in the academy and public square. Entire issues of academic and opinion journals have been devoted to explorations of intelligent design and related issues.[9] Articles and essays addressing intelligent design appear regularly in numerous professional and opinion journals, such as *First Things, Books and Culture, Zygon,* and *Perspectives on Science and Christian Faith.* Although these four journals feature religious topics, they do indicate that a diverse cross-section of American religious thinkers is slowly embracing design in some form. In 1998, PBS stations aired a two-hour *Firing Line* debate on evolution and intelligent design, featuring Johnson. And in the past few years, several book-length assessments of intelligent design have appeared. Not surprisingly, design theory has generated a very mixed reaction, ranging from sneering dismissal to welcome embrace.

In the early 1990s, *Darwin on Trial* was greeted with a flurry of negative reviews that essentially dismissed Johnson's antievolutionary argument as scientifically illiterate. Among the harshest was Stephen Jay Gould's stinging review in *Scientific American.* Gould's review was noteworthy on two counts: his resort to aggressive ad hominem argumentation and the fact that *Scientific American* viewed Johnson's book as important—or dangerous—enough to warrant a review by one of the premier evolutionary theorists.[10] No creationist book had ever received this kind of notice.

"Intelligent design is nothing more than creationism dressed in a cheap tuxedo."[11] This dismissive sound bite, attributed to Leonard Krishtalka, the director of the University of Kansas's Natural History Museum and Biodiversity Research Center, appeared in the *New York Times* in April 2001. While Krishtalka's verbal swipe is certainly colorful, it does capture the sentiment of numerous prominent scientists and science writers that design theory is little more than a rhetorically sophisticated creationism.[12] Niles Eldredge, for example, considers the intelligent design argument merely a variation of creationism that eschews biblical argumentation in favor of challenging the naturalistic assumptions underlying science as a whole, and evolutionary biology in particular. Eldredge is especially unimpressed with design theory because it "pose[s] no novel testable hypotheses and make[s] no predictions or observations worthy of the name." In short, despite the protestations of its advocates, design theory is "nothing but that good, old-time religion." Eldredge, moreover, is irked that the design theorists "impugn the integrity and intelligence of thousands of honest souls who have had the temerity to believe that it is both fitting and proper to try to understand the universe, the Earth, and all its life in naturalistic terms."[13] Robert Wright concedes that intelligent design theory has been fairly effective in challenging Darwinism and getting its message across to Americans. But he agrees with Eldredge that design theory is "just a fresh label, a marketing device." Wright concludes that the major components of design theory are "either not new, not significant, or just wrong."[14]

Design theory does have its admirers, however. Johnson and intelligent design arguments have received a warm welcome in several journals sympathetic to traditional religious thought and expression. These include *First Things*, *Touchstone*, and *Christianity Today*. One of the most enthusiastic supporters of design theory is Charles Colson, a former Richard M. Nixon aide convicted in the Watergate conspiracy and founder of the Prison Fellowship ministry. He is one of the most popular and respected evangelical Christians in America today, and has written several influential books and contributes a column for *Christianity Today*. In 1993, Colson received the prestigious Templeton Prize for Progress in Religion. Recently, he wrote *How Now Shall We Live?* which he considers his most important book, with coauthor Nancy Pearcey, herself a Discovery Institute fellow. Colson argues for the importance of understanding Christianity as a comprehensive worldview, and it is significant that he devotes several chapters in the book to sketch out intelligent design arguments.

Colson concludes—Gould, Eldredge, and virtually the entire mainstream scientific establishment to the contrary notwithstanding—that "[w]hen it comes to the origin of life, science is squarely on the side of creation by an intelligent agent."[15] This is all part of a "titanic struggle between opposing worldviews— between naturalism and theism." Drawing from Johnson and Michael J. Behe, rather than from Henry M. Morris and Duane T. Gish, Colson contends that Darwinism functions as "the cornerstone propping up a naturalistic worldview." And this naturalistic worldview "stands in stark opposition to Christianity."[16]

Beyond the more or less blanket dismissals and embraces, there is a growing body of serious literature assessing intelligent design. Most of this literature is quite critical, and the rest is produced by identifiable design theorists.[17] We select from this literature assessments from Kenneth R. Miller, a team of University of Wisconsin philosophers of science led by Elliott Sober, and long-time participants in the origins debate Del Ratzsch and Howard J. Van Till.

Miller, the reader will recall, is a Brown University cellular biologist and a Roman Catholic. In *Finding Darwin's God*, he offers a strong critique of both design theory and the notion that Darwinism must always be wedded to a naturalistic-materialistic worldview.[18] In a swipe at Johnson's credentials and methods, Miller concedes that "[a]s a purely rhetorical alternative to evolution, intelligent design serves the defense team well. It raises the specter of reasonable doubt."[19] Miller contends that the scientific community has had "Darwin on trial" long before Johnson's book. Darwinism is robust today not because of some naturalistic conspiracy but on account of its ability to explain the data. In Miller's view, so strong is the evidence for evolution that "the imposition of intelligent design on the facts of natural history requires us to imagine a designer who creates successive forms that mimic evolution."[20] Moreover, Miller raises the old question of bad or imperfect design: Why cannot the designer get it right? He appears to be incompetent.

Miller next turns to Behe. Citing a variety of studies (including a 1997 investigation in which a team of scientists in California verified the evolution of a new interface between two proteins; a study that came out just after Behe's book that provides a Darwinian explanation for the origin of the Krebs cycle; and work on the evolution of the clotting mechanism), Miller argues that Darwinian evolution can indeed explain the development of complex biochemical machines.[21] Consequently, Miller boasts, "[i]n the real world of science, in the hard-bitten realities of lab bench and field station, the intellectual triumph of Darwin's great idea is total."[22]

If this is so, then are the design advocates simply dull-witted? Not at all. According to Miller, the problem is that the appeal of various species of origins is not just a rational matter; it is often based on deep prior emotional commitments.[23] This is not just evident in the intelligent design community, but, as we noted in chapter 6, prominent scientists in their popular writings do at times go "well beyond any reasonable *scientific* conclusions that might emerge from evolutionary biology."[24] In support of this, Miller offers a variety of quotes, none more striking than that of Harvard geneticist Richard Lewontin, who in a 1997 review of Carl Sagan's *The Demon-Haunted World* in the *New York Review of Books* stated:

> We take the side of science in spite of the patent absurdity of some of its constructs, in spite of its failure to fulfill many of its extravagant promises of health and life, in spite of the tolerance of the scientific community for unsubstantiated just-so stories, because we have a prior commitment, a commitment to materialism. It is not that the methods and institutions of "science somehow compel us to accept a material explanation of the phenomenal world, but, on the contrary, that we are forced by our a priori adherence to material causes to create an apparatus of investigation and a set of concepts that produce material explanations, no matter how counterintuitive, no matter how mystifying to the uninitiated. Moreover, that materialism is absolute, for we cannot allow a Divine foot in the door."[25]

Miller joins design theorists in calling such rhetorical flourishes "intellectual aggressions."[26] So, while he argues that the design theorists have gotten the science all wrong, he agrees that they have accurately detected a decidedly antireligious bent in the academy. As Miller puts it, "[t]he prospect of an educated person who sincerely believes in God, who prays and fasts, or who is naive enough to think that there is actually such a thing as sin, is just not taken seriously." While many scientists think of their work as "objective and value-free," they fail to take into account that this antireligious bias—whether expressed crudely or as veiled condescension—fuels the fires of antievolutionist camps like intelligent design. "The backlash to evolution," Miller admits, "is a natural reaction to the ways in which evolution's most eloquent advocates have handled Darwin's great idea, distilling from the raw materials of biology an acid of hostility to anything and everything spiritual."[27]

Miller, of course, is convinced beyond doubt that the data support evolution. But he is also mindful that some attempts to craft a scientifically compatible version of religion end up diluting religion to the point of meaninglessness. So he concludes *Finding Darwin's God* with an extended and eloquent via media argument. Interestingly, Miller frequently leaves biology for physics at this point and joins scholars like John C. Polkinghorne in suggesting that the very orderliness and regularities of nature do not exclude the possibility of the divine. In fact, at the quantum level of investigation the "*true* materialism of life is bound up in a series of inherently unpredictable events that science, even in principle, can never master completely." Whereas critics of evolution tend to interpret this indeterminacy as randomness and mere chance, Miller sees it as a "key feature of the mind of God."[28]

Miller's God, then, creates an orderly universe that at its bedrock level allows for contingency. At the evolutionary level, the game is not foreordained in the sense of being rigged. God does not need to intervene, for example, to ensure the success of mammals. But any God that Miller finds worth believing in must also retain the ability to perform miracles. His own Catholic faith proclaims some rather astounding ones, like the virgin birth of Christ, but he argues that they are by definition beyond science. Moreover, God's miracles are not "routine subversions of the laws of nature"; rather, they are rare events that "reflect a greater reality, a spiritual reality, and they appear in a context that makes religious, not scientific sense."[29]

Where does this all lead? In Miller's own words:

> By any reasonable analysis, evolution does nothing to distance or to weaken the power of God. We already know that we live in a world of natural causes, explicable by the workings of natural law. All that evolution does is to extend the workings of these natural laws to the novelty of life and to its changes over time. A God who presides over an evolutionary process is not an impotent, passive observer. Rather, He is one whose genius fashioned a fruitful world in which the processes of continuing creation is woven into the fabric of matter. He retains the freedom to act, to reveal Himself to His creatures, to inspire, and to teach. He is the master of chance and time, whose actions, both powerful and subtle, respect the independence of His creation and give human beings the genuine freedom to accept or reject His love.[30]

Leaving Miller, we turn to Branden Fitelson, Christopher Stephens, and Elliott Sober—philosophers at the University of Wisconsin at Madison—who have offered a very different and highly technical critique of design theory in an article that appeared in the journal *Philosophy of Biology*.[31] They argue that Dembski's attempt to coax out the design inference via his explanatory filter is deeply flawed and that it offers no hope for those who would use it to detect design in nontheological contexts. Dembski's filter places design in a "special position" as the only alternative once regularity and chance have been rejected. Moreover, these philosophers question Dembski's maneuver to correlate design to information and intelligent agency.

Design theory, these philosophers argue, has yet to make the case that it is truly scientific. It is not enough, they argue, to make the plausible case for design primarily by criticizing evolution.[32] Design theorists have failed to demonstrate that design represents the only alternative to evolution. And design, as developed by Dembski, is too vague and deductive and offers no empirical predictions:

> To test evolutionary theory against the hypothesis of intelligent design, you must know what *both* hypotheses predict about observables. The searchlight therefore must be focused on the design hypothesis itself. What does *it* predict? If defenders of the design hypothesis want their theory to be scientific, they need to do the scientific work of formulating and testing the predictions that creationism makes. Dembski's Explanatory Filter encourages creationists to think that this responsibility can be evaded. However, the fact of the matter is that the responsibility must be faced.[33]

Thus far, we have discussed thoughtful critique that challenges not only the antievolutionary assumptions and empirical bases of design theory, but also its theological implications. Before we assess the overall impact of the intelligent design movement in both the origins debate and in American intellectual culture, it will help to look at two additional analyses of design theory—both by professors at Calvin College, one of the academically strongest of America's many evangelical Christian colleges.

We have already introduced physicist Howard J. Van Till as the champion of the notion of the "fully gifted" or "optimally gifted creation." In many respects, his views mirror those of Miller, but he makes the case even more forcefully than Miller that intelligent design theorists commit the "God-of-the-gaps" fallacy. In general, the gap argument claims that the attempt, especially by creation scientists, to find a place for God in the gaps of our current scientific knowledge has been and continues to be an unmitigated disaster. Not only does it restrict God's actions to the gaps, but it runs the very real risk of embarrassment when science plugs a gap with a naturalistic explanation, as it has done on multiple occasions in the past. Specifically with regard to intelligent design, critics like Van Till contend that design theorists place too much emphasis on epistemological gaps. They assume that these *epistemological* gaps are sufficient warrant for believing in *ontological* gaps. This becomes an appeal to ignorance taking the form of: "Given our present understanding, we do not know how X could have been formed by natural means, nor do we think it is likely that we can ever know this; therefore, X must have been assembled by extra-natural means."

All scientific theories are necessarily underdetermined by the empirical data, and gaps in our scientific knowledge are "permanent features of the scientific landscape." Van Till contends that Behe and Dembski should not, then, enlarge gaps in our knowledge to make them appear uncrossable. Science does not consider it appropriate to consider a declaration that a problem is insoluble to be a valid explanation, as design theorists do when they invoke irreducible and specified complexity. The scientific community operates on the assumption that further research will provide more adequate theories that will, in effect, close the gaps.[34] There is a certain pragmatism in this view, borne of long experience in the lab and in the field, that has cemented a near universal intuition among scientists that scientifically posable questions can be answered in standard scientific ways. This intuition is acquired through experience and is not effectively communicated through philosophical arguments about how one should go about doing science. This may account for the paucity of practicing scientists within the intelligent design movement, and the complete absence of any scientists actually working within its paradigm.

Ratzsch, another Calvin College professor, takes a very different stance on the gap argument. In *Nature, Design, and Science*,[35] his philosophical exploration of the concept of design, he notes that in current discourse the mere labeling of an argument as a God-of-the-gaps explanation generally renders it scientifically illegitimate and is "often taken to constitute an unanswerable refutation to it." He cautions that scientific *legitimacy* should not be conflated with *rationality*. Moreover, there is nothing inherently unscientific about the idea of gaps in nature; science "is littered with impossibility claims," such as perpetual motion, acceleration across the light-speed barrier, and the simultaneous determination of the energy and the position of certain particles to "arbitrary degrees of precision." Ratzsch argues that "if God-of-the-gaps explanations are *scientifically* illegitimate, it will have to be solely due to their reference to the supernatural—not because their logical structure violates any other canon of science or rationality."[36] While one could certainly make the case that in the past people have tended to underestimate nature's capabilities and have made unwarranted jumps to supernatural activity and design, Ratzsch contends that should serve as a cautionary safeguard against such tendencies and not become a rigid barrier used "to override any possible solidly empirical cases to the contrary."[37]

Ratzsch moves on to explore possible positive contributions of design in the scientific context. He posits that commitment to design might fuel the effort to find "deeper patterns underlying cases of apparent randomness." He gives as an example the possibility that a design stance might suggest that the so-called Copenhagen interpretation of quantum mechanics was embraced too quickly by physicists, who might have been better off not to have given up so soon in the search for a less counterintuitive interpretation of quantum mechanics.[38] Somewhat contradictory to this speculation, Ratzsch argues that design could contribute to a "general openness to the recognition of the possibility of naturalistic explanatory dead ends—of gaps." This, in turn, would affect the "'flavor' of science," freeing it "to abandon persistently failing naturalistic research programs." His intriguing example here is based on a musing of the rather profound work of Ilya Prigogine and Isabelle Stengers who state that "[s]ince there is no one to build nature, we must give to its very 'bricks'—that is, to its microscopic activity—a description that accounts for its building process."[39] Ratzsch again speculates that a design stance would allow the scientist "both to acknowledge [what] message nature might be trying to display—'tain't how it is—and to move the explanatory search into the right region—mind-correlative agent involvement."[40]

Throughout his provocative book, Ratzsch evidences an affinity for "the correlation to mind" argument that, put crudely, acknowledges the meshing that occurs between mind and phenomena. This pattern-finding faculty played a key role in the rise of science and is a core concept of design theory.[41] In his conclusion, Ratzsch reminds his readers that the structure of science and its conceptual underpinnings, indeed the structure of reality, contain "echoes of mind correlativity." So what? Ratzsch suggests that Darwinian evolution has been such an attractive theory because it provided "a framework within which a significant number of scientifically relevant considerations could coalesce into a larger, integrated system." Similarly, "[g]iven the pervasiveness of the echoes of mind correlativity," design may have potential as an integrating framework.[42]

Based on these and other lines of reasoning, Ratzsch concludes that "there is no compelling conceptual basis for any blanket prohibition on exploring applications or implications of the idea of supernatural design within the scientific context." He acknowledges that the attempt to develop design theories in a scientific context may in fact end up empty, but he does not see that in and of itself as an adequate basis for ruling design out of bounds. Every scientific research program faces the possibility that it will be unsuccessful.[43]

As long ago as the 1950s, the staunchly Christian British chemist C. A. Coulson stated that "[w]hen we come to the scientifically unknown, our correct policy is not to rejoice because we have found God; it is to become better scientists."[44] Coulson's perspective is shared by most of the current critics of intelligent design. Miller notes that design theorists are certainly within the bounds of acceptable science if all they want to do is "calculate probabilities." But beyond that, adopting intelligent design would likely depress motivation for further pursuit of naturalistic explanations. The design theorists run the risk of invoking irreducible or specified complexity at the expense of continuing research into natural causes.[45] Robert C. O'Connor agrees. While the question of origins may never be settled in strictly natural terms, we should never cut short the relentless pursuit of natural explanations. Citing philosopher John Searle in another context, O'Connor asserts that, methodologically, we must adopt the stance that we can understand everything. Otherwise, how do we know the limits of knowledge?[46]

Of course, the design theorists disagree sharply with what they call the "science stopper" argument. Behe asserts that intelligent design theory "promises to reinvigorate a field of science grown stale from a lack of viable solutions to dead-end problems." Design theory will lead to a research program that seeks to identify those systems that were designed and those that arose by other mechanisms.[47] And Dembski bristles at the suggestion that design is a sterile science-stopper. Design can only enrich science. It will not replace any of the scientific explanatory tools; rather, it will "foster inquiry where traditional evolutionary approaches obstruct it." He lists "junk DNA" and vestigial organs as examples of how design would encourage scientists "to look for function where evolutionary science discourages it." In addition, design theory raises a new set of research questions. Determination of design prompts further questions about how something was produced, to what extent the design was optimal, and what was the purpose of the design. Indeed, barring design distorts science and limits science to an inadequate set of conceptual and methodological categories.[48]

Design critic Robert T. Pennock observes that beneath the scientific argumentation, what fuels intelligent design is "a deep philosophical concern about the loss of purpose." Pennock sees this as an expression of existential angst: If evolution is true, then the belief in a benevolent, personal God is jeopardized, and we risk sliding down the slippery slope toward the view that the universe is amoral and supremely indifferent to humans.[49] While we believe he tends to minimize the degree to which science popularizers make startling pronouncements about the purposeless, dysteleological nature of evolution and the cosmos, Pennock is certainly correct.

Respected scholar of world religions Huston Smith argues that "no one can fault believers for finding in Intelligent Design a resource for their faith." While he is disposed to favor the design hypothesis, Smith admits, as a nonscientist, that any pronouncement he might make on the matter would just reflect his beliefs.[50] Pennock and Smith are addressing a very important matter: What are the legitimate scientific claims of design theory and to what extent has design been coopted by other agendas?

Design theory fits nicely with those who combat "modernity's march against traditional cultural and religious values."[51] With its credible spokespeople and rhetorical sophistication, intelligent design offers an attractive alternative to "thinking Christians" who are embarrassed by creation science, but who are also alarmed by what they see as a systematic assault by prominent scientists on cherished notions of God, humanity, and creation. But the danger exists that design theory will be so intertwined with Christian apologetics and "Christian 'cultural renewal,'"[52] that its scientific claims will be inappropriately inflated by supporters and categorically dismissed by critics.

Design theorists repeatedly suggest that intelligent design has "no prior commitment to supernaturalism." Johnson claims that advocates of intelligent design "talk only of scientific evidence," and that it is the "Darwinists" who "want to bring the Bible into the discussion." Dembski seconds Johnson: "Intelligent design is a strictly scientific theory devoid of religious commitments."[53] Furthermore, Dembski has stated that the intelligent design theorists' opposition to Darwinism "rests in the first instance on strictly scientific grounds." To be sure, he admits, design theory has important theological and cultural implications, but they are operative because "Darwinism is on its own terms an oversold and overreaching scientific theory."[54]

The theological implications certainly have not been lost on Behe, who has noted that "the scientific evidence of design means a lot for Christians." He believes that an appreciation for the "planning, precision, and detail required for the creation of life" enables the believer to take greater pleasure in God's creation and to place greater trust in the Creator. Moreover, to the extent that design can undermine the credibility of materialism, the "reasonableness of the [Christian] faith is made easier." Behe concludes that while "Christianity can live with a world where physical evidence of God's action is hard to discern, materialism has a tough time with a universe that reeks with design."[55]

So while design theory itself may be technically devoid of religious commitments, it is surely loaded with theological implications.[56] This distinction between the theory and its implications is often lost on critics and supporters alike. And part of the fault lies with the design advocates themselves, who rarely miss an opportunity to link apologetics to discussions of design and anti-Darwinism. Dembski himself has coedited a book on Christian apologetics, which includes two chapters he wrote on intelligent design. In one of them, he discusses the question of whether God's interaction with the world is empirically detectable. He argues that if science is permitted to investigate intelligent causes, "then God's interaction with the world, insofar as it manifests the characteristic features of intelligent causation, becomes a legitimate domain for scientific investigation." While Dembski would note the qualification—"insofar as it manifests the characteristic features of intelligent causation"—the reader will no doubt make the linkage between design and God.[57] When the design theorists' audience is evangelical Christians, the "God-talk" is everywhere.[58] Certainly, the apologetic dimension is central to the appeal of design theory and accounts for its rapid spread throughout America's conservative religious subculture.[59]

Design theorists are nothing if not ambitious. Considering themselves to be the harbingers of a scientific revolution,[60] their research program challenges not just Darwinism but the whole enterprise of contemporary science (its metaphysical basis as well as its methodological assumptions). Natural science, however, is just the beginning. Design, according to Behe, not only extends deep into nature, but it "promises to be a clarifying lens" that has implications "for virtually all humane studies, including philosophy, theology, literary criticism, history, and more."[61] Dembski concurs. He concludes that since the "scientific picture of the world championed since the Enlightenment is . . . massively wrong," entire fields of inquiry "will need to be rethought from the ground up in terms of intelligent design."[62]

The academy, influential as it is, is not the only objective. One design theorist, political scientist John G. West Jr., suggests that the real stakes are the regeneration of culture itself. Scientific materialism, according to West, inflicted incredible damage, infecting nearly every aspect of our culture. Its claims that all human thoughts and actions are dictated by either biology or the environment undermined traditional theories of human freedom and responsibility. Its assertions that our moral beliefs were merely the products of heredity or environment laid the groundwork for moral relativism. And its argument that man should take control of the material processes that produced him to remake society promoted a "virulently coercive strain of utopianism." While West concedes that it is still in its infancy, he suggests five general implications of intelligent design: (1) it can help reinvigorate the case for free will and personal responsibility, with enormous implications for public policy; (2) it can assist in the defense of traditional morality; (3) it will buttress the sanctity of life and gain new currency for the idea of the nonmaterial soul; (4) it can assist in the debunking of postmodernism and help restore the integrity of science;[63] and (5) because intelligent design is not monocausal, it will support free inquiry.[64]

The cultural renewal argument confirms fears that design theory may have been "hijacked as part of a larger cultural political movement," says design theorist Bruce Gordon.[65] Gordon was Dembski's lieutenant at Baylor's Polanyi Center, and—after Dembski's removal—the interim director of the Baylor Science and Religion Project. Yet, he laments that design theory has been prematurely drawn into discussions of public science education prior to its having demonstrated that it is "making a worthwhile contribution to our understanding of the natural world." Only after a long process of research and publication can design theory ever become "part of the standard discourse of the scientific community." Gordon warns that if design theory is ever to be accepted as a legitimate science, "it must be worth pursuing on the basis of its own merits, not as an exercise in Christian 'cultural renewal,' the weight of which it cannot bear."[66]

As a species of origins, intelligent design brings together many themes in the contemporary origins debate: the nature of the evidence for and against evolution, the benefits and limitations of scientific inquiry, and especially the philosophical (worldview), theological (apologetical), and public policy (science education and cultural renewal) implications of a seemingly arcane species of origins. As such, design has all the ingredients required for making this species of origins a major source of discussion and debate in American intellectual culture, a culture that is dedicated to a thoroughly scientific outlook but remains firmly rooted in its deeply religious traditions.

For now, it is clear that Johnson's Wedge strategy has succeeded in obtaining a foothold for intelligent design. Design is gathering grassroots support while it is slowly, even begrudgingly, entering the academy as a serious, albeit controversial, topic of discussion—something that would have been utterly impossible for scientific creationism. Now that design has gotten itself placed on the agenda of American intellectual culture, how will it fare? Can intelligent design move from desks of the philosophers of science, where it has made modest headway, to the lab benches of the empiricists, where it is all but nonexistent? We are unaware of any current scientific research program dedicated to design theory or, for that matter, any empirical research making even token use of design theory.[67] Whether design theory has enough scientific rigor to warrant a viable ongoing scientific research program remains to be seen. What is certain is that its long-term success depends on this.

NOTES

1. Gregg Easterbrook, "The New Fundamentalism," *Wall Street Journal*, 8 August 2000.

2. Teresa Watanabe, "Enlisting Science to Find the Fingerprints of a Creator," *Los Angeles Times*, 25 March 2001.

3. James Glanz, "Evolutionists Battle New Theory on Creation," *New York Times*, 8 April 2001; Robert Wright, "The 'New' Creationism," *Slate* (2001), slate.msn.com/Earthling/01-04-16/Earthling.asp (3 March 2001).

4. William A. Dembski, "Polanyi Center Press Release," 2000, at www.meta-list.org (5 March 2001).

5. Dembski, "Polanyi Center Press Release."

6. Lauren Kern, "In God's Country," *Houston Press*, 14 December 2000; Lauren Kern, "Monkey Business," *Dallas Observer*, 11 January 2001.

7. John Wilson, "Unintelligent Designs," *Books and Culture Corner* (2000), at www.christianitytoday.com/ct/2000/143/11.0.html (7 March 2001); Tony Carnes, "Design Interference," *Christianity Today Online* (2000), at www.christianitytoday.com/ct/2000/014/18.20.html (7 March 2001); Fred Heeren, "The Lynching of Bill Dembski," *The American Spectator* (2000), at www.gilder.com/amspec/classics/Nov00/heeren0011.htm (8 March 2001); Fred Heeren, "The Deed Is Done," *The American Spectator* (2000–2001), at www.gilder.com/amspec/classics/Dec00–Jan01/heeren0012.htm (11 July 2002); Angela Swanson, "Dembski Removed," *Research News and Opportunities in Science and Theology* 1 (December 2000): 35; Bruce L. Gordon, "The Polanyi Center Controversy at Baylor University: A Response," *Research News and Opportunities in Science and Theology* 1 (December 2000): 34; American Scientific Affiliation, "Dembski, Baylor U. Aftermath," *Newsletter of the American Scientific Affiliation* 43 (January–February 2001): 1, 3.

8. Michael Shermer, *How We Believe: The Search for God in an Age of Science* (New York: Freeman, 2000), 84.

9. William Hasker, ed., "Special Issue: Creation/Evolution and Faith," *Christian Scholar's Review* 21 (September 1991); Roger Olson, ed., "Theme Issue: Creation, Evolution and

Christian Faith," *Christian Scholar's Review* 24 (May 1995); Martin Medherst, ed., "Special Issue on the Intelligent Design Argument," *Rhetoric and Public Affairs* 1 (winter 1998); Jefferson M. Thompson, "Science and Religion," *The Canadian Catholic Review* 17 (July 1999); James Kusminer, ed., "Intelligent Design," *Touchstone* 12 (July–August 1999).

10. Stephen Jay Gould, "Impeaching a Self-Appointed Judge," *Scientific American* 267 (July 1992): 118–121. Johnson's reply to Gould's review was apparently refused by the editors of *Scientific American* and was published in *Origins Research*. See Phillip E. Johnson, "Response to Gould," *Origins Research* 15 (spring–summer 1993): 10–11.

11. Leonard Krishtalka quoted in Glanz, "Evolutionists Battle New Theory on Creation."

12. This dismissal is evident in the common practice of labeling intelligent design theory as "new creationism." See, for example, Robert T. Pennock, *Tower of Babel: The Evidence against the New Creationism* (Cambridge, Mass.: MIT Press, 1999), ix–6; Shermer, *How We Believe,* 109–116. No doubt another reason for the dismissal lies with the fact that both Gould and Richard Dawkins wrote books in the 1980s (Gould, *The Panda's Thumb* [New York: Norton, 1980], and Dawkins, *The Blind Watchmaker: Why the Evidence of Evolution Reveals a Universe without Design* [New York: Norton, 1986, 1996]) that had already addressed elements of the design argument.

13. Niles Eldredge, *Triumph of Evolution and the Failure of Creationism* (New York: Freeman, 2000), 134–147.

14. Wright, "The 'New' Creationism."

15. Charles Colson and Nancy Pearcey, *How Now Shall We Live?* (Wheaton, Ill.: Tyndale House, 1999), 79.

16. Colson and Pearcey, *How Now Shall We Live?* 90–99.

17. In addition to the footnoted sources, this literature includes: William A. Dembski, "Conservatives, Darwin and Design," *First Things* 107 (November 2000): 23–31; Edward T. Oakes et al., "An Exchange on Intelligent Design," *First Things* 112 (April 2001): 5–13; William A. Dembski and James M. Kushiner, eds., *Signs of Intelligence: Understanding Intelligent Design* (Grand Rapids, Mich.: Brazos, 2001); Michael Ruse, *Can a Darwinian Be a Christian? The Relationship between Science and Religion* (Cambridge, U.K.: Cambridge University Press, 2001), 111–128; Michael J. Behe, William A. Dembski, and Stephen C. Meyer, *Science and Evidence for Design in the Universe* (San Francisco: Ignatius, 2000); John F. Haught, *God after Darwin: A Theology of Evolution* (Boulder, Colo.: Westview, 2000); William A. Dembski, "Intelligent Design Coming Clean," *Access Research Network* (2000), at www.arn.org/docs/dembski/wd_idcomingclean.htm (9 March 2001).

18. Kenneth R. Miller, *Finding Darwin's God: A Scientist's Search for Common Ground between God and Evolution* (New York: Cliff Street/HarperCollins, 1999). In July 2000, Dembski indicated that Miller's is "currently the best critique of intelligent design in book form." For Dembski's response to Miller, see "Finding Ken Miller's Point," *Access Research Network* (2000), at www.arn.org/docs/dembski/wd_findingdarwinsgod.htm (10 March 2001).

19. Miller, *Finding Darwin's God,* 93.

20. Miller, *Finding Darwin's God,* 99.

21. Miller, *Finding Darwin's God,* 129–164.

22. Miller, *Finding Darwin's God,* 165.

23. Miller, *Finding Darwin's God,* 172–174.

24. Miller, *Finding Darwin's God,* 185, emphasis in the original.

25. Lewontin quoted in Miller, *Finding Darwin's God,* 186.

26. Miller, *Finding Darwin's God,* 186. Of course, Lewontin's comments have been used by design theorists to corroborate their argument that behind many of the specific scientific claims for evolution lies an aggressively naturalistic worldview. See, for example, William A. Dembski, "What Intelligent Design Is Not," in *Signs of Intelligence: Understanding Intelligent Design,* ed. William A. Dembski and James M. Kushiner (Grand Rapids, Mich.: Brazos, 2001), 22; Phillip E. Johnson, *The Wedge of Truth: Splitting the Foundations of Naturalism* (Downers Grove, Ill.: InterVarsity, 2000), 140; Colson, *How Now Shall We Live?* 96.

27. Miller, *Finding Darwin's God,* 189.

28. Miller, *Finding Darwin's God,* 208–213.

29. Miller, *Finding Darwin's God,* 232–240.

30. Miller, *Finding Darwin's God,* 243.

31. Branden Fitelson, Christopher Stephens, and Elliott Sober, "How Not to Detect Design—Critical Notice: William A. Dembski, *The Design Inference,*" *Philosophy of Biology* 66 (September 1999): 472–488.

32. Dembski objects to the characterization of intelligent design as a form of antievolutionism. He bases this on the distinction between evolution and Darwinism, the latter being a "historical claim (common descent) and a naturalistic mechanism (natural selection operating on random variations)." Intelligent design throws common descent into question, he argues, because it demonstrates that the Darwinian mechanism "cannot bear the weight of common descent." See William A. Dembski, "Teaching Intelligent Design: What Happened When?" *Access Research Network* (2001), at www.arn.org/docs/dembski/wd_teachingid0201.htm (10 March 2001).

33. Fitelson, Stephens, and Sober, "How Not to Detect Design," 487. In-text footnotes have been removed from this quote. It should be noted that in *Intelligent Design,* Dembski cited Sober's *Philosophy of Biology* to support his contention that the design argument is an inference to the best explanation. See Elliot Sober, *Philosophy of Biology* (Boulder, Colo.: Westview, 1993), 34–36; William A. Dembski, *Intelligent Design: The Bridge between Science and Theology* (Downers Grove, Ill.: InterVarsity, 1999), 271–276. For Dembski's response to the Fitelson, Stephens, and Sober's review, see "Another Way to Detect Design?" *Access Research Network* (2000), at www.arn.org/docs/dembski/wd_responsetowiscu.html (10 March 2001).

34. Howard J. Van Till, "The Creation: Intelligently Designed or Optimally Gifted?" *Theology Today* 55 (October 1998): 351–356; see also Pennock, *Tower of Babel,* 163–172. Design theorists have a battery of responses to the God-of-the-gaps argument. J. P. Moreland and John Mark Reynolds note that merely postulating about the action of an agent/designer is not an appeal to a gap. Stephen C. Meyer objects to the charge that design theory is an argument from ignorance. Design is an inference to the best explanation and, as such, it is no different from other scientific explanations that employ negative or proscriptive generalizations. And Dembski questions whether or not science can recognize the limits of its own explanatory power. Citing the example of alchemy, he asks how long do we fund and continue a scientific search for something when the very object of that search is nonexistent? It is not, he claims, blocking legitimate inquiry to put forth a proscriptive generalization that asserts that natural causes are incapable of filling a particular gap. "Not all gaps are created equal," he quips, and "[t]o assume that they are is to presuppose the very thing that is in question, namely, naturalism." See J. P. Moreland and

John Mark Reynolds, introduction to *Three Views on Creation and Evolution*, ed. J. P. Moreland and John Mark Reynolds (Grand Rapids, Mich.: Zondervan, 1999), 22–23; Stephen C. Meyer, "DNA by Design: An Inference to the Best Explanation for the Origin of Biological Information," *Rhetoric and Public Affairs* 1 (winter 1998): 545–547; Dembski, *Intelligent Design*, 244–245.

35. Del Ratzsch, *Nature, Design, and Science: The Status of Design in Natural Science* (Albany: SUNY Press, 2001).

36. Ratzsch, *Nature, Design, and Science*, 47–48.

37. Ratzsch, *Nature, Design, and Science*, 118–120.

38. Ratzsch, *Nature, Design, and Science*, 142.

39. Prigogine and Stengers quoted in Ratzsch, *Nature, Design, and Science*, 142.

40. Ratzsch, *Nature, Design, and Science*, 142–143.

41. Ratzsch, *Nature, Design, and Science*, 14–15, 61–67.

42. Ratzsch, *Nature, Design, and Science*, 150–151.

43. Ratzsch, *Nature, Design, and Science*, 149–151.

44. Coulson quoted in Dembski, *Intelligent Design*, 244.

45. Keith B. Miller, "Design and Purpose within an Evolving Creation," in *Darwinism Defeated? The Johnson–Lamoureux Debate on Biological Origins*, ed. Phillip E. Johnson and Denis O. Lamoureux (Vancouver: Regent College Publishing, 1999), 113.

46. Robert C. O'Connor, "Science on Trial: Exploring the Rationality of Methodological Naturalism," *Perspectives on Science and Christian Faith* 49 (March 1997): 20, 28n.

47. Michael J. Behe, *Darwin's Black Box: The Biochemical Challenge to Evolution* (New York: Free Press, 1996), 230–231; Michael J. Behe, "Intelligent Design Theory As a Tool for Analyzing Biochemical Systems," in *Mere Creation: Science, Faith and Intelligent Design*, ed. William A. Dembski (Downers Grove, Ill.: InterVarsity, 1998), 193–194.

48. Dembski, *Intelligent Design*, 150–151.

49. Pennock, *Tower of Babel*, 312.

50. Huston Smith, *Why Religion Matters: The Fate of the Human Spirit in an Age of Disbelief* (New York: Harper San Francisco, 2001), 177–178.

51. Haught, *God after Darwin*, 28.

52. Bruce Gordon, "Intelligent Design Movement Struggles with Identity Crisis," *Research News and Opportunities in Science and Theology* 1 (January 2001): 9.

53. Phillip E. Johnson, "The Rhetorical Problem of Intelligent Design," *Rhetoric and Public Affairs* 1 (winter 1998): 587; Dembski, *Intelligent Design*, 252, 259.

54. Dembski, "What Intelligent Design Is Not," 12–17. Recall that Dembski objects to the characterization of intelligent design as a form of antievolutionism.

55. Michael J. Behe, "Tulips and Dandelions," *Books and Culture* 4 (September–October 1998): 35.

56. See Dembski, *Intelligent Design*, 187.

57. William A. Dembski and Jay Wesley Richards, eds., *Unapologetic Apologetics: Meeting the Challenges of Theological Studies* (Downers Grove, Ill.: InterVarsity, 2001), 222–223.

58. A prime example is Dembski's *Intelligent Design*, chapter 8.

59. Van Till contends that intelligent design functions primarily as an apologetical reaction to naturalism. Rather than appealing to scriptural authority, design theory utilizes empirical evidence and sound reasoning to engage the contemporary intellectual culture.

He is critical of the foundational theological propositions on which the evidentialist apologia of design is constructed and considers it "a tragedy of major proportions" that design theorists seem to be betting the apologetic farm on the demonstration of a need for occasional episodes of "divine creative action of the extra-natural assembly variety." See Van Till, "The Creation," 352–361.

60. See J. P. Moreland, introduction to *The Creation Hypothesis: Scientific Evidence for an Intelligent Designer*, ed. J. P. Moreland (Downers Grove, Ill.: InterVarsity, 1994), 37; Dembski, *Intelligent Design*, 119; Pennock, *Tower of Babel*, 206–214; Karl W. Giberson, "Intelligent Design on Trial," *Christian Scholar's Review* 24, no. 4 (1995): 459.

61. Michael J. Behe, foreword to *Intelligent Design: The Bridge between Science and Theology*, by William A. Dembski (Downers Grove, Ill.: InterVarsity, 1999), 10–12.

62. Dembski, *Intelligent Design*, 224.

63. Interestingly enough, design critics worry about the coziness with which some design theorists invoke Thomas Kuhn and Larry Laudan, who while not postmodern constructivists, do not advocate the kind of scientific realism that West seems to endorse.

64. John G. West Jr., "The Regeneration of Science and Culture," in *Signs of Intelligence: Understanding Intelligent Design*, ed. William A. Dembski and James M. Kushiner (Grand Rapids, Mich.: Brazos, 2001), 60–69.

65. See Bruce Gordon, "Is Intelligent Design Science? The Scientific Status and Future of Design–Theoretic Explanations," in *Signs of Intelligence: Understanding Intelligent Design*, ed. William A. Dembski and James M. Kushiner (Grand Rapids, Mich.: Brazos, 2001), 193–216.

66. Gordon, "Intelligent Design Movement," 9. Dembski's response to this criticism can be found in Donald A. Yerxa, "Questioning Darwin: William Dembski Discusses Intelligent Design," *Research News and Opportunities in Science and Theology* 2 (November 2001): 13.

67. As his book was in its final editing stages, Dembski announced the launching of the International Society for Complexity, Information, and Design (ISCID). The ISCID is a web-driven professional society created to pursue "the theoretical development, empirical application, and philosophical implications of information- and design-theoretic concepts for complex systems." It appears that the ISCID is a step toward solidifying the empirical and theoretical foundations of intelligent design along the lines Gordon suggested.

Conclusion

◆

The High Cost of Clarity

To ask how life originated and what kind of respect for life we ought to have mixes questions from biology and philosophy. They are not unrelated questions, because how we value life could depend, to some extent, on our picture of how life originated.

—Thomas Cech, Nobel laureate[1]

We have attempted to show some of the reasons for the enduring intensity of America's search for a creation story and to describe the major players in that highly animated conversation. We conclude with a somewhat pessimistic prognosis for the future of this discussion, suggesting that there is little evidence for any convergence, and little hope for any change in the current trajectory of the discussion. The origins debate in America is not going away.

Human beings are inherently pattern-finding creatures. Our brains appear to be particularly adept at "connecting the dots" that make up the complex mosaic of our experiences and inferring patterns from those connections. Such patterns may or may not actually be there. The creatures that populate the Zodiac most assuredly are not; water molecules most certainly are; and the abstraction that we call a "species" is somewhere in between. Just as the construction of the Zodiac, with its rich panorama of creatures, was a highly imaginative process, the development of the concept of a species was also a highly imaginative act, as subtle similarities in things like relative skeletal patterns were deemed of greater relevance in organizing the natural world than more obvious characteristics like size and color. Is it all that obvious that Beagles and St. Bernards belong in the same biological grouping?

The patterns that human beings find in the world cry out for explanation. And it matters not whether those patterns are real or imaginary; we have a deeply

235

rooted need to believe in the reality of our explanatory patterns, the imaginary lines connecting the dots of our experience.

Perhaps the most compelling category of explanation needing to be filled is that of purpose—the universal "why" behind the unfolding of the human story, whether individual, familial, tribal, cultural, or universal. How common is the anguished cry of parents as they struggle in vain to understand "why" their child was taken from them? Alternatively, people who survive accidents often conclude that they were saved for a "purpose" and sometimes go on to live dramatically changed lives, transformed by the conviction that they were saved from death for a reason. In the same way, individuals driven to suicide often travel that road fueled by the demoralizing conviction that their lives have lost all meaning and purpose.

The creation stories at play in America, and in other cultures, of course, are these kinds of stories writ large. The search is for a reason why things are the way they are, an attempt to find an underlying purpose to existence. This is a profoundly spiritual quest and one at the heart of all the world's great religions. And, as we saw in an earlier chapter, when traditional religious explanations are rejected, secular alternatives take their place. But these alternatives, despite their secular origins, are usually recast in quasi-religious terms, as we saw in chapter 6. Edward O. Wilson is something of an archetype for the human need for purposeful lives. His childhood evangelical faith was not so much abandoned as it was transformed into something else. Rare is the person who is truly content with a completely barren picture of the world.

Even Peter W. Atkins, who seems to delight in puncturing religious hopes and aspirations, is quite unable to refrain from turning science into something of a surrogate religion. In his strongly antireligious essay "The Limitless Power of Science," Atkins states: "My scientific world-view is bleak in terms of its origins, its motivations, and it future. Yet, unless it can be explicitly demonstrated otherwise, it should be the sparse working hypothesis to account for our existence."[2] He celebrates that "[s]cience can perform its elucidation without appealing to the shroud of obscurity of man-made artifice, including that supreme artifice, the presumption of purpose."[3]

However, Atkins's rhetoric throughout the essay suggests that he is in no way doing away with the "supreme artifice of purpose" that animates traditional religions; he is simply replacing one purposeful foundation with another. His apologia for science is filled with religious metaphors. Science is "limitless."[4] Science "liberates."[5] Science can "blow back the fog that shrouds the minds of those who have not yet seen."[6] While it may indeed be the case, as Atkins suggests, that scientific explanations need not employ purpose as a part of their explanatory scheme, it is manifestly not the case that Atkins's world is without purpose. That purpose is the search for and evangelistic communication of the scientific understanding of the world. Atkins, despite his claims to the contrary, seems quite unable to do without purpose.[7]

We have raised this point to illustrate the central concern of our conclusion—human beings are constitutionally possessed with an overwhelming need to locate their existence in a framework that provides meaning and purpose. And this need is filled most naturally and powerfully with religion. Wilson and Atkins may indeed be able to worship at the evolutionary cathedral, but most people cannot.

Furthermore, in what has to be the ultimate irony, recent research on the physiology of religious experience—research purporting to "reduce" religion to biochemistry—appears to indicate that human beings are "hardwired" for intense and meaningful religious experiences.[8] Some have suggested that we have a sort of "god module" in our brains that can be aroused through prayer, meditation, worship, or other religious practices. And, no doubt, the god module can be aroused in certain individuals as they celebrate the reductionist glories of science.

Such research is highly ambiguous in terms of what it says about the "reality" of religious experience. Those seeking to explain the ubiquity of religion point in this direction and knowingly tell us that this is why religion, despite its self-evident falsity, retains so much of its vigor. But religious believers counter that these findings are exactly what they would have expected. If God created human beings with the capacity for worship, then we should not be surprised to discover that we have some "circuitry" that appears to serve that purpose.[9] We will not pursue this tendentious issue. We mention it only to support our contention that the surprising endurance of religious belief may not be so surprising after all.

We have argued that America's traditional approaches to religion provide powerful sources of meaning that compete successfully with their scientific challengers. When scientific, or even pseudoscientific, claims about the world are infused with the power of religion, their power is greatly enlarged. That is why there can be very well-educated fundamentalists, competently trained in science, who are quite content to let the Bible rule on the age of the earth or the relationship of human beings to the rest of the natural world. Scientifically weak evidence that accords with the Bible becomes very strong precisely because of that concordance, through a sort of "religious amplification of scientific truth claims."

A compelling illustration of this "religious amplification" can be found in religious prohibitions of smoking and drinking. There are a number of religious groups—like the Seventh Day Adventists or the Mormons—who have long maintained that it is morally wrong and sinful to smoke tobacco or drink alcohol. The arguments that circulate in those communities are not particularly compelling for anyone who does not share their central religious convictions. But these groups are astonishingly successful. Virtually none of their members smoke or drink. Contrast this with the widespread failure of the "scientific message." There is overwhelming evidence that smoking, for example, is "hazardous to one's health," and this message is inescapable, often visible in huge letters on billboards advertising cigarettes. But millions of people still smoke and more are starting all the time. The power of the "scientific" message pales in comparison to the power of the identical religious message.[10] If we really want people to stop smoking, we should convert them to Mormonism, at which time they will accept that smoking is morally wrong and stop! Paradoxically, and along these same lines, science has now established that drinking wine in moderation is good for heart disease, but a great many people refuse to consider this because of religious prohibitions.

These examples illustrate, in a compelling way, the sheer power of religious belief for those who take it seriously. The species of origins under discussion in America, though ostensibly scientific, are at a fundamental level *religious* beliefs. For most people, belief in how the world, life, and human beings originated is a part of the religious framework by which they order their lives. The scientifically specious argument that the earth is only a few thousand years old gains its power from the conviction that God has revealed this truth about the world in the Bible. Carbon dating is hardly an effective challenger.

In 1835, Alexis de Tocqueville noted that "America is . . . still the place in the world where the Christian religion has most preserved genuine powers over souls."[11] While some contemporary scholars suggest that Christianity is now even more influential in parts of Africa and Latin America than in the United States,[12] Americans, nevertheless, remain a "spectacularly religious" people,[13] especially in contrast to the "post-Christian" culture that characterizes much of Europe.[14] As long as this remains the case—and there is scant evidence that it is changing—there will be an intense conversation about origins. Various species of origins, whether scientific creationism, intelligent design, or theistic evolution, will continue to be placed within powerful religious frameworks and will, simply by virtue of this placement, themselves become powerful.

America is not simply a deeply religious society. It is also an advanced scientific and technological culture. Many authors have noted this, but none more perceptively than theologian Langdon Gilkey. He reminds us that while science is central for America's intellectual and academic elites, it is also "thoroughly *established* in our common life." Science permeates all of American society, from top to bottom. Even literalistic creationists are compelled to package their arguments with scientific terminology and see them as scientifically valid.[15] The rub comes when the scientific elite wields its cultural dominance irresponsibly and carelessly identifies "scientific knowledge of origins" with an "exhaustive knowledge or understanding of origins" and thereby dismisses religious views as "primitive and therefore false."[16]

The approach that takes scientific explanations as total explanations is, Gilkey argues, essentially a philosophical stance not warranted by science itself. "[I]t is part of the 'religious aura' of science, not a part of its theoretical structure." Science has become the predominant mode of knowing in contemporary American culture, but Gilkey sees a real danger, not only to religious awareness but also to artistic expression, literary discourse, and philosophical speculation, if we hold that scientific inquiry is the only road to truth.[17]

Similarly, religious groups have a responsibility to appreciate that this is an advanced scientific culture and deal with the tough questions that emerge. Origins, particularly the origin of life, is one of the most persistent and difficult of these questions, involving both scientific and religious modes of speech and ways of knowing.[18] The stubbornness of this issue is apparent when we consider that the belief that the universe, our world, life, and humans were created by a purposeful deity is at the very foundation of Christianity, not to mention Judaism and Islam. And several prominent evolutionists make it clear that "[s]cientific evolutionism as usually understood stands in conflict with any significant religious view of the world."[19] If this is true, then no species of origins that takes religion seriously, be it creationism, intelligent design, or theistic evolution, will succeed in bridging the gap and reconciling the conflict.

So the origins debate in America is not likely to go away. At the close of this book, we need to reflect on whether it is even a good thing for the origins debate to go away, especially if its disappearance comes as the result of a victory from either end of the spectrum. The price of such a victory would indeed be great, for it would probably mean that a really deep question had been given a really shallow answer—a simplistic clarity had diverted the search for a profound truth.

There is perhaps an important relationship between truth and clarity, in that one seems often to come at the expense of the other, in a complementarity reminiscent of quantum theory. Complementarity was one of the deep mysteries that came out of quantum theory, a mystery that was never resolved but merely embraced. Somehow there exists a profound relationship between certain things in nature such that increased knowledge of one can only be had at the expense of the other. The most familiar version of this deals with the relationship between the position and speed of a particle like an electron. If we wish to measure the position of an electron more accurately, we can do so only in a way that reduces our knowledge of its speed and vice versa. Articulating this relationship (and getting Albert Einstein to accept it!) was one of the great challenges faced by the quantum physicists. Eventually, the overwhelming success of quantum theory provided ample reason for people to accept the reality of a deep complementarity in nature, at least within the world of the quantum. But was it possible that quantum complementarity was but one manifestation of an even deeper principle with implications that went way beyond physics?

In the years following the establishment of quantum theory, a very general exploration of the applicability of complementarity to fields outside physics convinced many that complementarity was at least a very useful heuristic, and possibly a profound and general philosophical principle. Niels Bohr, one of the primary architects of quantum theory, was convinced that this was the case and wrote and lectured widely on the topic; at times it appeared that complementarity could illuminate just about any mystery. In 1949, Bohr, who was by then recognized as one of the great minds of the century, was asked: "What is complementary to truth?" Bohr's answer, after some reflection, was: "Clarity."[20]

In the closing paragraphs of a book on origins, we are certainly not going to try to adjudicate the epistemological virtues of complementarity. Nevertheless, as a practical matter, we do suggest that Bohr's assertion that "truth" and "clarity" are complementary sheds some helpful illumination on America's origins debate. If indeed truth and clarity are complementary in the same sense as position and speed (admittedly an odd proposition!), that would imply that clarity can only be achieved at the expense of truth and vice versa. Our analysis of the spectrum of positions on origins has indicated that clarity, despite its seductive attractions, is only to be had at the extremes. There is great clarity in the belief that God created the world in six days and then told us about it in Genesis. There is great clarity in the belief that everything is the result of mindless matter and blind chance. But how much real truth lies in either of these positions? Science has established beyond a reasonable doubt that the world was not created in six days, but science has not established that there is no basis for believing that there might be a mind or purpose behind the universe. And surely human experience, which includes, of course, religious experience, testifies with comparable competence that the world contains more than mindless matter and blind chance. Religion certainly cannot dispute the reality of both matter and chance, but it does suggest that the world has more in it than this.

Neither of the extreme positions at play in the origins debate is completely false in any simple sense. But, in their simplistic reductionism they surely lose much that is important. And this is the intuition that galvanizes concerned parents to oppose the teaching of evolution in our high schools, courageously if misguidedly challenging an intimidating scientific and educational establishment.

Perhaps, in time, a common creation story can emerge, somehow bringing together elements that now seem intrinsically disparate. But perhaps not. There is great mystery in the human experience and in that small portion of the external world that we have penetrated—mystery that has not really been dispelled by science despite its marvelous explanatory accomplishments, for scientific progress rarely occurs without the concurrent discovery of additional mystery. Is the world disclosed by contemporary science, after centuries of rapid scientific advance, any less complex and mysterious than the tidy garden that the medievals took to be their cosmic home?

Truth and clarity balance on the fulcrum of the mystery that lies at the heart of our existence. Perhaps the lesson to be drawn from our analysis of America's troubled origins conversation is that this mystery should be embraced with humility—not ridiculed by those with an overly optimistic view of science, nor wielded like a club by those who believe they have some sort of divine "shortcut" to the truth or privileged filters to remove error.

NOTES

1. Thomas Cech, "The Origin of Life and the Value of Life," in *Biology Ethics, and the Origins of Life*, ed. Holmes Rolston III (Boston: Jones and Bartlett, 1995), 18.

2. Peter W. Atkins, "The Limitless Power of Science," in *Nature's Imagination: The Frontiers of Scientific Vision*, ed. John Cornwell (Oxford, U.K.: Oxford University Press, 1995), 131.

3. Atkins, "Limitless Power of Science," 128.

4. Atkins, "Limitless Power of Science," 122.

5. Atkins, "Limitless Power of Science," 123.

6. Atkins, "Limitless Power of Science," 124.

7. For an interesting exchange on the religious role of metaphor in evolutionary biology, see the correspondence between historian of science John C. Greene and prominent geneticist Theodosius Dobzhansky. Greene contends that leading Darwinians illegitimately use teleological and vitalistic figures of speech in describing the evolutionary process they hold to be mechanistic, blind, and purposeless. He suggests that the evolutionary literature is full of words and figures of speech smuggled into the discourse—like "progress," "improvement," "advance," and "higher"—that clearly suggest striving, purpose, and achievement. The exchange with Dobzhansky reveals a fault line that still divides many Christian and even some secular intellectuals today. See John C. Greene, *Debating Darwin: Adventures of a Scholar* (Claremont, Calif.: Regina, 1999), 91–113.

8. Steven Pinker, *How the Mind Works* (New York: Norton, 1997), 554–558.

9. Carol Rausch Albright and James B. Ashbrook, *Where God Lives in the Human Brain* (Naperville, Ill.: Sourcebooks, 2001).

10. This example comes from Philip Hefner, *The Human Factor: Evolution, Culture, and Religion* (Minneapolis: Fortress, 1993), 188–189.

11. Alexis de Tocqueville, *Democracy in America*, vol. 1, part 2, trans. Harvey C. Mansfield and Delba Winthrop (Chicago: University of Chicago Press, 2000), 278.

12. Missiologist Andrew F. Walls, for example, concludes that the great fact of the twentieth century was the "demographic and cultural shift in the center of gravity of the Christian faith." Christianity must be viewed as a non-Western religion. See Andrew F. Walls, *The Missionary Movement in Christian History: Studies in the Transmission of Faith* (Maryknoll, N.Y.: Orbis, 1996), xiii–xix; Donald A. Yerxa, "On the Road with Christianity: A Conversation with Missiologist Andrew Walls," *Books and Culture* 7 (May–June 2001): 18.

13. Michael A. Ledeen, *Tocqueville on American Character* (New York: St. Martin's, 2000), 71–72.

14. See Gertrude Himmelfarb, *One Nation, Two Cultures* (New York: Vintage, 1999), 93–95.

15. Langdon Gilkey, *Creationism on Trial: Evolution and God at Little Rock* (Charlottesville: University of Virginia Press, 1985, 1998), 161–171.

16. Gilkey, *Creationism on Trial*, 164.

17. Gilkey, *Creationism on Trial*, 175–179.

18. Gilkey, *Creationism on Trial*, 184.

19. William Provine cited in David Ray Griffin, *Religion and Scientific Naturalism: Overcoming the Conflicts* (Albany: SUNY Press, 2000), 243.

20. Bohr quoted in Abraham Pais, *Niels Bohr's Times, in Physics, Philosophy, and Polity* (Oxford, U.K.: Clarendon, 1991), 511.

A Concluding
Unscientific Postscript

We have argued that America's search for a creation story has exposed some rather profound cultural undercurrents that, at least at the present time, do not seem amenable to resolution. Like other controversial issues, familiar to us from both history books and the daily newspaper, the origins conversation in America is a profoundly polarizing topic—not unlike slavery and women's rights in the past, or abortion and multilingualism in the present. Sometimes divisive issues are such that a resolution *must* be achieved, at almost any cost. Utah was not allowed to join the United States, for example, until polygamy was outlawed within its borders. Arkansas was not allowed to educate its black children in different schools than its white children. On the one hand, there are indeed a great many topics on which it is to the benefit of society to find a common viewpoint that can be shared by all and, in the absence of such, to enforce such a position through the courts. On the other hand, sometimes a diversity of opinions and ways of life are to be embraced simply because diversity is often culturally enhancing. Are not regional accents, cuisines, and architectures something to be treasured? Do we want to force Santa Fe or Nantucket to change building codes they enacted to protect local architectural traditions?

In between differences that must be eliminated at all cost and those we celebrate lie more complex sorts of differences—those that are not necessarily culturally enriching, that are, in principle, resolvable, but are somehow intractable. We suggest that the origins debate in America is one such difference; indeed we have argued that it is both unresolvable and inescapable. We are concerned about America's capacity at present to engage in a vigorous and productive debate over something so bedrock as the origins of the universe, of life in general, and over human life in particular, which is to say: what it means to be a human being.

America's search for a creation story should be placed in the context of a whole cluster of contentious issues like abortion, sexual preference, funding of controversial artistic projects, and so on. The intense cultural disagreements on such divisive topics have been called the "culture wars" by sociologist James Davison Hunter. As one seemingly endless facet of the culture wars, the origins debate imposes a particular burden not only on our educational institutions, but also on our democracy as a whole.[1] Hunter poses a critical question, of immediate relevance to our discussion in this book: Is our democratic system capable of sustaining a genuine pluralism in which debates about such ultimate things as origins can continue, even flourish?

Hunter's analysis of the culture wars is very helpful in this context. He introduces two sober notes to any consideration of this question, notes that should give everyone pause before they glibly lampoon or demonize their putative debate partners. First, cultural conflict necessarily entails an "antidemocratic impulse."[2] In the case of the origins debate, this is evident in the tendency of the contending camps to either shut down the discussion altogether by declaring themselves the winners (although they don't go home) or consign the opposing position(s) to the margins or even the flames. Second, genuine debate presupposes a willingness to actually talk to each other. But, as with so many of the controversial issues within American society, the origins debate frequently descends into dismissive rhetoric that only fuels discord and misunderstanding. In one of the rare instances in which he mentions the origins debate, Hunter provides an egregious example. In 1986, a syndicated editorial cartoon depicted five brains of various sizes: "The largest was identified as the 'brain of man'; those in the middle were identified as the brain of a Neanderthal, a Homo erectus, and an ape; and the last, the size of the head of a pin, was identified as the 'brain of a creationist.' The caption read, 'Proof of Evolution.'"[3]

And, as we saw earlier, Henry M. Morris would link evolutionists with a great satanic conspiracy hearkening back to ancient Babylon and including virtually all of the evils in subsequent history—hardly a stance that invites civil discourse!

This is not to suggest that the middle ground of compromise is necessary or even desirable, though it is broadly where our sympathies lie in the origins debate. Hunter asks us to consider the importance of common ground over middle ground, a common ground "in which rational and moral suasion regarding the basic values and issues of society are our first and last means to engage each other. This is the democratic imperative."[4] To advance such common ground, he provides the outline of a framework for public argument in a genuinely pluralistic democracy based on a position paper called the Williamsburg Charter. Its applicability to the origins debate, which we strongly affirm, should be obvious:

First, those who claim the right to dissent should assume the responsibility to debate.

Second, those who claim the right to criticize should assume the responsibility to comprehend.

Third, those who claim the right to influence should accept the responsibility not to inflame.

Fourth, those who claim the right to participate should accept the responsibility to persuade.[5]

The focus on responsible debate is significant because the origins question clearly has a very definite political dimension: public education. As Hunter argues, all too often we resort to political action and the courts to resolve difficult matters.[6] A "principled pluralism" must recognize that political and legal action, while sometimes necessary, are inherently coercive and attempt to resolve issues by a resort to power. Of course, there are instances (e.g., outlawing polygamy as a condition for Utah statehood) when such coercion is deemed a necessary and appropriate exercise of power. But we must recognize the limits of political action in the collective search for a creation story, for beneath the rhetorical salvos that are launched at those with whom we disagree lie deeply personal beliefs about who we are. The war is not about what happened long ago, whether molecules combined to make life, or whether the Big Bang was a random event; the war is very much about what is the case right now. Are human beings made in the image of God with all that is entailed by that venerable belief? Is reality ultimately just elementary particles? Is our perception of meaning and purpose an illusion, a curious by-product of our evolutionary ancestors' need to survive?

When concerned parents in Kansas rallied to reduce the role of evolution in the public schools, they were not motivated by a concern that Charles Darwin's theory was not scientifically accurate, although they would have believed this to the degree they understood it. They were motivated by a belief that learning evolution would erode some important beliefs they had passed on to their children. Yet, when the scientific community responded there was, for the most part, nothing but ridicule for those poor ignorant hicks who dared to criticize evolution. Very little effort was expended in trying to understand why those Kansans felt the way they did. On the flip side, when Morris describes evolution as a great satanic conspiracy and evolutionary biologists as unwitting agents of the devil, what is he saying about the millions of religious people in America who have made their peace with evolution? This is not the kind of civilized discourse—the "principled pluralism"—that is so desperately needed.

The origins debate is not going to end any time soon. America is still searching for a creation story and probably will be for some time. It may never find one. In the meantime, as the intellectual ecosystem continues to be populated by so many species of origins, a commitment to a more civil discourse is in order.

NOTES

1. See James Davison Hunter, *Culture Wars: The Struggle to Define America* (New York: Basic, 1991; James Davison Hunter, *Before the Shooting Starts: Search for Democracy in America's Culture War* (New York: Free Press, 1994). Curiously, Hunter gives the origins debate only scant attention in these books.

2. Hunter, *Before the Shooting Starts*, 5.

3. Hunter, *Culture Wars*, 153.

4. Hunter, *Before the Shooting Starts*, 13.

5. Hunter, *Before the Shooting Starts*, 239–240.

6. Hunter, *Culture Wars*, 320.

Appendix

◈

A Brief History of
Design Arguments

Design arguments have been around for a long time and a great number of them have enjoyed "a robust life."[1] Plato, Aristotle, and Cicero employed the argument from design in their philosophies, but intellectual historians most frequently point to St. Thomas Aquinas's thirteenth-century version as a practical starting point for modern design arguments. In his *Summa theologiae*, Aquinas's classic cosmological proof for the existence of God, design is embedded in a family of arguments. His aim is to prove the existence of a First Cause or Sufficient Reason for the existence of the cosmos. Aquinas depicts the world as a vast teleological edifice manifestly revealing divine purpose.[2] In his famous fifth way or proof, Aquinas clearly posits the purposive design of the cosmos. That natural bodies move toward an end suggests both design and intelligence, much "as the arrow is directed by the archer." "Therefore," Aquinas concludes, "some intelligent being exists by whom all natural things are directed to their end; and this being we call God."[3]

Though the design argument came under critical scrutiny by scholars ranging from Francis Bacon (1561–1626) to René Descartes (1596–1650) and Gottfried Leibniz (1646–1716), versions of it flourished in the early modern period, particularly in England. Key thinkers who subscribed to it included Robert Boyle (1627–1691), Isaac Newton (1642–1727), and Samuel Clarke (1675–1729).[4] The Scottish skeptic David Hume (1711–1776), however, attacked the logical structure of the design argument in his *Dialogues Concerning Natural Religion*, published three years after his death. He concluded that the design argument is inherently unscientific, uses weak and subjective analogical reasoning, and conveniently neglects all contrary evidence. While many, if not most, contemporary philosophers believe that Hume completely demolished the design argument

247

and its notion that "a knowledge of the nature of God can be obtained from rational inference from the natural order,"[5] in fact it would take Charles Darwin
to do that.

Ironically, the period between the publication of Hume's *Dialogues* in 1779
and Darwin's *The Origin of Species by Means of Natural Selection* in 1859 witnessed the heyday of the design argument and natural theology, particularly in
England. By far the most influential work was the best-selling *Natural Theology*
(1805) by William Paley, the archdeacon of Carlisle. He attempted to demonstrate why an intelligent designer is a more plausible explanation than random
physical forces for the fact that organisms are both intricate and well adapted.[6]
He did this in his memorable opening lines that use the familiar Enlightenment
analogy of the clock and the world. Suppose as you are walking across a heath
and you find a watch. You open it and observe the how the intricate interrelat-
edness of all its wheels, teeth, and springs make it well suited to the task of time-
keeping. How would you explain this? Either, Paley claimed, the watch was designed by a watchmaker, or it was the result of random physical processes acting
on a lump of metal. He concluded that the former explanation is vastly more
plausible: "[T]he inference . . . is inevitable: . . . the watch must have had a
maker; . . . there must have existed, at some time and at some place or other, an
artificer or artificers, who formed it for the purpose which we find it actually to
answer; who comprehended its construction, and designed its use."[7] He then asserted that if you agree with his assessment about the watch being designed, you
must draw the same conclusion from the complexity and adaptedness of living
things, that they are designed.[8]

Paley's *Natural Theology* was very popular and became a "minor classic."
Other works on natural theology followed. In the 1830s, a talented group of
British scientists and philosophers articulated a sophisticated version of the design argument in a remarkable series of volumes known collectively as the
Bridgewater Treatises. While they were essentially derivative in argument,
the *Bridgewater Treatises* were extremely popular and went through many editions.[9] By midcentury, the argument for design had matured and diversified,
largely as a result of developments within science itself. Indeed, there may have
been four distinguishable variations of the design argument circulating at the
time Darwin wrote his *Origin of Species*.[10]

In the second half of the nineteenth century, British natural theology—and
with it the design argument—went into a precipitous decline with the triumph
of the positivist view of science that stressed the uniformity of nature, the regularity of natural law, and the sufficiency of physical causes. By the end of the century, references to divine design were essentially absent from scientific texts.[11]
This process, of course, was aided tremendously with the appearance of Darwin's
Origin of Species, which Richard Dawkins has captured with his oft-quoted line:
"Darwin made it possible to be an intellectually fulfilled atheist."[12] What Darwin
did was to provide an alternative explanation that resided comfortably in the

space between design and randomness, effectively synthesizing them. His evolution via natural selection required no intelligent design, but neither was natural selection a completely random physical process. And while the mutations that play an important role in evolution may be largely random events, not every possible outcome has the same probability. Furthermore, the environmental response to organisms with new characteristics derived from such mutations is orderly and predictable at a statistical level.[13]

Although most scholars contend that Darwin and positivism dealt a "death blow" to traditional design arguments, the design argument has had tremendous resiliency. Paley-type design arguments retained wide currency among ordinary Americans who viewed them as commonsensical. And while they largely went out of vogue in the intellectual culture of North America, at least among scientists, even here design arguments that were framed around nonbiological phenomena went largely untouched.[14] Design also reemerged in modified form in post-Darwinian natural theology, which ditched the artisan, clockmaker God in favor of God the artist. In this view, nature became a magnificent canvas on which creative strokes could be discerned. Vestiges of design remain even in the most strident of Darwinians, like Dawkins and Daniel C. Dennett, who frequently use the language of design while they adamantly deny the existence of a designer.[15]

In the latter half of the twentieth century, the design argument was rejuvenated by a collection of insights in astronomy and cosmology, labeled the "Anthropic Principle." As we noted in chapter 8, the Anthropic Principle suggests that the universe seems to have been designed for life, although not necessarily human life. The existence of creatures like us is possible only because the universe has a very special structure and, within the flexible constraints of that structure, some very special things occurred to make human existence possible. Life in general, and human life in particular, is so complex and depends in so many critical ways on the precise details of the universe and its history that it appears overwhelmingly improbable that life could exist in any imagined universe different from this one.

The Anthropic Principle brought design notions back into the conversations of mainstream science. It is true that many prominent science writers like Atkins, Dawkins, Stephen Jay Gould, Carl Sagan, and Steven Weinberg have found the Anthropic Principle an underwhelming tautology: things are as they are because we are. But leading scientists like Freeman Dyson, Paul Davies, John C. Polkinghorne, and George Ellis are intrigued with the design features of the universe. Ellis, a professor of cosmic physics and a former colleague of Stephen W. Hawking, has gone so far as to state that cosmology explores the possibility that "there is an underlying structure of meaning beneath the surface appearances of reality, most easily comprehended in terms of deliberate Design."[16] Another important support to notions of design is the "tantalizing mystery" of the intelligibility of the universe. Why is it that the universe is even open to scientific understanding?[17] While the scientific evidence certainly does not compel one to draw a design conclusion from the Anthropic Principle, the intelligibility of the universe and its finely tuned structure are at least compatible with, and perhaps even suggestive of, the belief that the cosmos was designed for a purpose.

Design arguments derived from the Anthropic Principle, however, are almost exclusively cosmological arguments. They do not suggest, or even hint, that the trajectory of biological evolution contains indications of design. A universe has to be just this way in order for the chemistry of life to work. But given that the universe is fully gifted in "just this way," biological evolution is capable of accomplishing its task of populating the earth with all manner of interesting creatures, including human beings.

NOTES

1. Elliott Sober, *Philosophy of Biology* (Boulder, Colo.: Westview, 1993), 30.

2. William L. Rowe, *The Cosmological Argument* (New York: Fordham University Press, 1998), 7, 10–23; Konstantin Kolenda, *Philosophy's Journey: From the Presocratics to the Present*, 2d ed. (Prospect Heights, Ill.: Waveland, 1990), 74–75; William Lane Craig, "Design and the Cosmological Argument," in *Mere Creation: Science, Faith and Intelligent Design*, ed. William A. Dembski (Downers Grove, Ill.: InterVarsity, 1999), 332–333.

3. *Summa theologiae* 1a, 2, 3. Theologian Anna Case-Winters maintains that "the argument from design should be distinguished from its close relative, the cosmological argument." She notes that an argument for the existence of God may be made on the basis "*that* something exists," whereas the argument from design "works from *what* exists." See Anna Case-Winters, "The Argument from Design: What Is at Stake Theologically?" *Zygon* 35 (March 2000): 69–70.

4. John D. Barrow and Frank J. Tipler, *The Anthropic Cosmological Principle* (New York: Oxford University Press, 1986), 48–68.

5. Barrow and Tipler, *Anthropic Cosmological Principle*, 69–72; John Hedley Brooke, *Science and Religion: Some Historical Perspectives* (Cambridge, U.K.: Cambridge University Press, 1991), 181–189; Sober, *Philosophy of Biology*, 33–36.

6. Sober contends that Paley's argument is in fact a sophisticated "inference to best explanation"—a term that best describes the scientific approach. Sober believes, however, that Darwin's later inference is superior. See Sober, *Philosophy of Biology*, 30–31.

7. William Paley, *Natural Theology: Or Evidences of the Existence and Attributes of the Deity Collected from the Appearances of Nature* (Philadelphia: Johnson and Warner, 1814), 6.

8. Sober, *Philosophy of Biology*, 30–31; Barrow and Tipler, *Anthropic Cosmological Principle*, 76–83.

9. Written by Thomas Chalmers, John Kidd, William Whewell, Sir Charles Bell, Peter Mark Roget, William Buckland, William Kirby, and William Prout, the *Bridgewater Treatises* were published in the 1830s under the terms of the will of the Reverend Francis Egerton, the eighth earl of Bridgewater. Anticipating on a smaller scale the current pa-

tronage of science and religion by Sir John Templeton, the earl of Bridgewater left £8,000 for a series of scientific works that would show that there was a unity of purpose in the physical world that was the result of the work of a beneficent and superior Creator. Shortly thereafter, Charles Babbage published on his own his so-called *Ninth Bridgewater Treatise*. See Barrow and Tipler, *Anthropic Cosmological Principle*, 82.

10. John Hedley Brooke and Geoffrey Cantor, *Reconstructing Nature: The Engagement of Science and Religion* (Edinburgh: T. and T. Clark, 1998), 160–161.

11. William A. Dembski, *Intelligent Design: The Bridge between Science and Theology* (Downers Grove, Ill.: InterVarsity, 1999), 70–93; Brooke and Cantor, *Reconstructing Nature*, 162.

12. Richard Dawkins, *The Blind Watchmaker: Why the Evidence of Evolution Reveals a Universe without Design* (New York: Norton, 1986, 1996), 6. The impact of higher biblical criticism may have been even more corrosive to traditional faith in God than the work of Darwin. Evolution and biblical criticism together, however, generated an intense crisis of faith for many, though certainly not all, Victorian-era intellectuals. See A. N. Wilson, *God's Funeral* (New York: Norton, 1999).

13. Sober, *Philosophy of Biology*, 36. We must note that for a few decades Darwin's notions of natural selection were by no means universally accepted within the science community. But the major alternatives to Darwin were naturalistic rather than design arguments. See Brooke and Cantor, *Reconstructing Nature*, 162.

14. Barrow and Tipler, *Anthropic Cosmological Principle*, 109.

15. Brooke and Cantor, *Reconstructing Nature*, 163–167; John C. Greene, *Darwin and the Modern World View* (Baton Rouge: Louisiana State University Press, 1961), 72–87.

16. George Ellis, *Before the Beginning: Cosmology Explained* (New York: Marion Boyars, 1993), 106.

17. Paul Davies, *The Mind of God: The Scientific Basis for a Rational World* (New York: Simon and Schuster, 1992), 20–21; Case-Winter, "Argument from Design," 77–78.

Bibliography

Alberts, Bruce. Preface to *Science and Creationism: A View from the National Academy of Sciences.* 2d ed. Washington, D.C.: National Academy Press, 1999.

Albright, Carol Rausch, and James B. Ashbrook. *Where God Lives in the Human Brain.* Naperville, Ill.: Sourcebooks, 2001.

Aliota, Anthony. *A History of Western Science.* Englewood Cliffs, N.J.: Prentice-Hall, 1987.

American Scientific Affiliation. "Baylor U. Aftermath." *Newsletter of the American Scientific Affiliation* 43 (January–February 2001): 1, 3.

Ankerberg, John, and John Weldon. *Darwin's Leap of Faith: Exposing the False Religion of Evolution.* Eugene, Ore.: Harvest House, 1998.

Arny, Thomas T. *Explorations: An Introduction to Astronomy.* 2d ed. Boston: McGraw Hill, 2000.

Ashton, John F., ed. *In Six Days: Why Fifty Scientists Choose to Believe in Creation.* Sydney: New Holland, 1999.

Atkins, Peter W. *The Creation.* Oxford, U.K.: Freeman, 1981.

———. "The Limitless Power of Science." In *Nature's Imagination: The Frontiers of Scientific Vision,* edited by John Cornwall. Oxford, U.K.: Oxford University Press, 1995.

———. *Physical Chemistry.* 6th ed. Oxford, U.K.: Freeman, 1997.

———. "Science and Religion: Rack or Featherbed: The Uncomfortable Supremacy of Science." *Science Progress* 83 (2000): 28–31.

Ayala, Francisco J. "The Difference of Being Human." In *Biology, Ethics, and the Origins of Life,* edited by Holmes Rolston III. Boston: Jones and Bartlett, 1995.

Barbour, Ian G. *Religion in an Age of Science.* San Francisco: Harper and Row, 1990.

———. *When Science Meets Religion: Enemies, Strangers, or Partners.* New York: Harper San Francisco, 2000.

Barrow, John D. *Theories of Everything: The Quest for Ultimate Explanation.* Oxford, U.K.: Clarendon, 1991.

———. *The Universe That Discovered Itself*. New York: Oxford University Press, 2000.

Barrow, John D., and Frank J. Tipler. *The Anthropic Cosmological Principle*. New York: Oxford University Press, 1986.

Barzun, Jacques. *From Dawn to Decadence: 500 Years of Western Cultural Life, 1500 to the Present*. New York: HarperCollins, 2000.

Beem, Kate. "Kansas Board of Education's Science Standards Continue to Draw Controversy." *Kansas City Star*, 14 March 2000.

Behe, Michael J. *Darwin's Black Box: The Biochemical Challenge to Evolution*. New York: Free Press, 1996.

———. "Darwin's Breakdown: Irreducible Complexity and Design at the Foundation of Life." *Touchstone* 12 (July–August 1999): 39–43.

———. Foreword to *Intelligent Design: The Bridge between Science and Theology*, by William A. Dembski. Downers Grove, Ill.: InterVarsity, 1999.

———. "Intelligent Design As an Alternative Explanation for the Existence of Biomolecular Machines." *Rhetoric and Public Affairs* 1 (winter 1998): 565–570.

———. "Intelligent Design Theory As a Tool for Analyzing Biochemical Systems." In *Mere Creation: Science, Faith and Intelligent Design*, edited by William A. Dembski. Downers Grove, Ill.: InterVarsity, 1998.

———. "Tulips and Dandelions." *Books and Culture* 4 (September–October 1998): 34–35.

Behe, Michael J., William A. Dembski, and Stephen C. Meyer. *Science and Evidence for Design in the Universe*. San Francisco: Ignatius, 2000.

Bergman, Jerry. "The Attitude of Various Populations toward Teaching Creation and Evolution in Public Schools." *CEN Technical Journal* 13 (1999): 118–123.

———. "Censorship in Secular Science: The Mims Case." *Perspectives on Science and Christian Faith* 45 (March 1993): 37–45.

———. "Forrest Mims Responds." *Origins Research* 14 (spring–summer 1991): 12.

Berry, R. J. "Science and Religion: Friends or Foes?" *Science Progress* 83 (2000): 13–14.

Blume, Harvey "Edward O. Wilson: Aliens, An Interview." *Boston Book Review* (1995), at www.bookwire.com:80/bbr/interviews/edward-wilson.html (11 October 2000).

Bowler, Peter J. *Evolution: The History of an Idea*. Rev. ed. Berkeley: University of California Press, 1989.

Boyer, Pascal. *Religion Explained*. New York: Basic, 2001.

Brockelman, Paul. *Cosmology and Creation: The Spiritual Significance of Contemporary Cosmology*. New York: Oxford University Press, 1999.

Brockman, John. *The Third Culture*. New York: Simon and Schuster, 1995.

Brooke, John Hedley. *Science and Religion: Some Historical Perspectives*. Cambridge, U.K.: Cambridge University Press, 1991.

Brooke, John Hedley, and Geoffrey Cantor. *Reconstructing Nature: The Engagement of Science and Religion*. Edinburgh: T. and T. Clark, 1998.

Broom, Neil. *How Blind Is the Watchmaker? Nature's Design and the Limits of Naturalistic Science*. Downers Grove, Ill.: InterVarsity, 2001.

Brown, Andrew. *The Darwin Wars: The Scientific Battle for the Soul of Man*. London: Simon and Schuster, 1999.

Brunner, Emil. *Man in Revolt: A Christian Anthropology*. Philadelphia: Westminster, 1947.

Bube, Richard H. "Reflections." In *Three Views on Creation and Evolution*, edited by J. P. Moreland and John Mark Reynolds. Grand Rapids, Mich.: Zondervan, 1999.

Buell, Jon, and Virginia Hearn, eds. *Darwinism: Science or Philosophy?* Richardson, Tex.: Foundation for Thought and Ethics, 1994.

Cairns-Smith, A. G. "The First Organisms." *Scientific American* 252 (June 1985): 90–100.

Campbell, Neil A., Jane B. Reece, and Lawrence G. Mitchell. *Biology.* 5th ed. Menlo Park, Calif.: Benjamin Cummings, an Imprint of Addison Wesley Longman, 1999.

Capra, Fritjof. *The Tao of Physics: An Explanation of the Parallels between Modern Physics and Eastern Mysticism.* Rev. ed. Boston: Shambhala Publications, 1991.

Carnes, Tony. "Design Interference." *Christianity Today Online* (2000), at www.christianitytoday.com/ct/2000/014/18.20.html (7 March 2001).

Cartwright, John. *Evolution and Human Behavior.* Cambridge, Mass.: MIT Press, 2000.

Case-Winters, Anna. "The Argument from Design: What Is at Stake Theologically?" *Zygon* 35 (March 2000): 69–81.

Casti, John. *Paradigms Lost: Images of Man in the Mirror of Science.* New York: William Morrow, 1989.

Cavalieri, Paolo, and Peter Singer, eds. *The Great Ape Project: Equality beyond Humanity.* New York: St. Martin's, 1994.

Cech, Thomas. "The Origin of Life and the Value of Life." In *Biology, Ethics, and the Origins of Life,* edited by Holmes Rolston III. Boston: Jones and Bartlett, 1995.

Chaisson, Eric, and Steve McMillan. *Astronomy: A Beginner's Guide to the Universe.* 3d ed. Upper Saddle River, N.J.: Prentice-Hall, 2001.

Colson, Charles, and Nancy Pearcey. *How Now Shall We Live?* Wheaton, Ill.: Tyndale House, 1999.

Conkin, Paul K. *When All the Gods Trembled: Darwinism, Scopes, and American Intellectuals.* Lanham, Md.: Rowman & Littlefield, 1998.

Copi, Irving, and Carl Cohen. *Introduction to Logic.* 10th ed. Upper Saddle River, N.J.: Prentice-Hall, 1998.

Copleston, Frederick. *History of Western Philosophy.* Vol. 2, *Augustine to Scotus.* New York: Doubleday, 1950.

———. *History of Western Philosophy.* Vol. 8, *Bentham to Russell.* New York: Doubleday, 1966.

Corey, Michael. *God and the New Cosmology: The Anthropic Design Argument.* Lanham, Md.: Rowman & Littlefield, 1993.

Council for Secular Humanism. "Religious Belief in America: A New Poll." *Free Inquiry* 16 (summer 1996): 36–37.

Craig, William Lane. "Design and the Cosmological Argument." In *Mere Creation: Science, Faith and Intelligent Design,* edited by William A. Dembski. Downers Grove, Ill.: InterVarsity, 1999.

Craig, William Lane, and Peter W. Atkins. "Craig–Atkins Debate: What Is the Evidence for/against the Existence of God." 1998, at leaderu.com/offices/billcraig/docs/craig-atkins.html (15 November 2000).

Crick, Francis. *The Astonishing Hypothesis: The Scientific Search for the Soul.* New York: Scribner, 1994.

———. *What Mad Pursuit: A Personal View of Scientific Discovery.* New York: Basic, 1988.

Croce, Paul Jerome. "Beyond the Warfare of Science and Religion in American Culture—and Back Again." *Religious Studies Review* 26 (January 2000): 29–35.

Crutchfield, James, P. J. Doyne Farmer, Norman H. Packard, and Robert S. Shaw. "Chaos." In *Chaos and Complexity: Scientific Perspectives on Divine Action,* edited by

Robert John Russell, Nancey Murphy, and Arthur R. Peacocke, 2d ed. Vatican City State: Vatican Observatory Publications, 1997.

Davies, Paul. *The Mind of God: The Scientific Basis for a Rational World.* New York: Simon and Schuster, 1992.

Davis, Percival, and Dean H. Kenyon. *Of Pandas and People: The Central Question of Biological Origins.* Dallas: Haughton, 1989.

Dawkins, Richard. *The Blind Watchmaker: Why the Evidence of Evolution Reveals a Universe without Design.* New York: Norton, 1986, 1996.

———. *Climbing Mount Improbable.* New York: Norton, 1996.

———. *The Extended Phenotype: The Long Reach of the Gene.* Rev. ed. New York: Oxford University Press, 1999.

———. "Ignorance Is No Crime." *Free Inquiry* (2001), at www.secularhumanism.org/fi/index.htm (15 November 2000).

———. *River out of Eden: A Darwinian View of Life.* New York: Basic, 1995.

———. *The Selfish Gene.* 2d ed. New York: Oxford University Press, 1989.

———. *Unweaving the Rainbow: Science, Delusion and the Appetite for Wonder.* Boston: Mariner, 1998.

de Duve, Christian. *Vital Dust: Life As a Cosmic Imperative.* New York: Basic, 1995.

Dembski, William A. "Another Way to Detect Design?" *Access Research Network* (2000), at www.arn.org/docs/dembski/wd_responsetowiscu.htm (10 March 2001).

———. "Conservatives, Darwin and Design." *First Things* 107 (November 2000): 23–31.

———. *The Design Inference: Eliminating Chance through Small Probabilities.* Cambridge, U.K.: Cambridge University Press, 1998.

———. "Finding Ken Miller's Point." *Access Research Network* (2000), at www.arn.org/docs/dembski/wd_findingdarwinsgod.htm (10 March 2001).

———. "The Incompleteness of Scientific Naturalism." In *Darwinism: Science or Philosophy?* ed. Jon Buell and Virginia Hearn. Richardson, Tex.: Foundation for Thought and Ethics, 1994.

———. *Intelligent Design: The Bridge between Science and Theology.* Downers Grove, Ill.: InterVarsity, 1999.

———. "Intelligent Design Coming Clean." *Access Research Network* (2000), at www.arn.org/docs/dembski/wd_idcomingclean.htm (9 March 2001).

———. "On the Very Possibility of Intelligent Design." In *The Creation Hypothesis: Scientific Evidence for an Intelligent Designer,* edited by J. P. Moreland. Downers Grove, Ill.: InterVarsity, 1994.

———. "Polanyi Center Press Release." 2000, at www.meta-list.org (5 March 2001).

———. "Science and Design." *First Things* 86 (October 1998): 21–27.

———. "Teaching Intelligent Design: What Happened When?" *Access Research Network* (2001), at www.arn.org/docs/dembski/wd_teachingid0201.htm (10 March 2001).

———. "The Third Mode of Explanation: Detecting Evidence of Intelligent Design in the Sciences." In *Science and Evidence for Design in the Universe: Proceedings of the Wethersfield Institute, September 25, 1999.* San Francisco: Ignatius, 2001.

———. "What Intelligent Design Is Not." In *Signs of Intelligence: Understanding Intelligent Design,* edited by William A. Dembski and James M. Kushiner. Grand Rapids, Mich.: Brazos, 2001.

———, ed. *Mere Creation: Science, Faith and Intelligent Design.* Downers Grove, Ill.: InterVarsity, 1998.

Dembski, William A., and James M. Kushiner, eds. *Signs of Intelligence: Understanding Intelligent Design*. Grand Rapids, Mich.: Brazos, 2001.

Dembski, William A., and Jay Wesley Richards, eds. *Unapologetic Apologetics: Meeting the Challenges of Theological Studies*. Downers Grove, Ill.: InterVarsity, 2001.

Dennett, Daniel C. *Darwin's Dangerous Idea: Evolution and the Meanings of Life*. New York: Touchstone, 1995.

Denton, Michael. "Comments on Special Creationism." In *Darwinism Defeated? The Johnson–Lamoureux Debate on Biological Origins*, edited by Phillip E. Johnson and Denis O. Lamoureux. Vancouver, B.C.: Regent College Publishing, 1999.

———. *Evolution: A Theory in Crisis*. Bethesda, Md.: Adler and Adler, 1986.

Desmond, Adrian. *Huxley: From Devil's Disciple to Evolution's High Priest*. Reading, Mass.: Perseus, 1994.

de Tocqueville, Alexis. *Democracy in America*. Vol. 1. Pt. 2. Translated by Harvey C. Mansfield and Delba Winthrop. Chicago: University of Chicago Press, 2000.

Devlin, Bernie, Stephen E. Fienburg, Daniel Phillip Resnick, and Kathryn Roeder, eds. *Intelligence, Genes, and Success: Scientists Respond to The Bell Curve*. New York: Copernicus, 1997.

Diamond, Jared. *The Third Chimpanzee: The Evolution and Future of the Human Animal*. New York: HarperCollins, 1993.

Discovery Institute. "A Scientific Dissent from Darwinism." *New York Review of Books* 48 (November 2001): 23

Dobzhansky, Theodosius. "Nothing in Biology Makes Sense Except in the Light of Evolution." *American Biology Teacher* 35 (March 1973): 125–129.

Dyson, Freeman. *Disturbing the Universe*. New York: Basic, 1979, 2001.

———. *Infinite in All Directions*. New York: Harper and Row, 1988.

Easterbrook, Gregg. "The New Fundamentalism." *Wall Street Journal*, 8 August 2000.

Eddington, Arthur S. *New Pathways of Science*. Cambridge, U.K.: Cambridge University Press, 1935.

Edwards, Denis. "The Discovery of Chaos and the Retrieval of the Trinity." In *Chaos and Complexity: Scientific Perspectives on Divine Action*, edited by Robert John Russell, Nancey Murphy, and Arthur R. Peacocke. Vatican City State: Vatican Observatory Publications, 1997.

Eldredge, Niles. *Reinventing Darwin: The Great Debate at the High Table of Evolutionary Theory*. New York: Wiley, 1995.

———. *The Triumph of Evolution and the Failure of Creationism*. New York: Freeman, 2000.

Ellis, George. *Before the Beginning: Cosmology Explained*. New York: Marion Boyars, 1993.

Evolution. Produced by WGBH/Nova Science Unit and Clear Blue Sky Productions. Seven shows, 2001. Videocassette.

Ferris, Timothy. *Coming of Age in the Milky Way*. New York: Anchor, 1989.

———. *The Whole Shebang: A State of the Universe Report*. New York: Simon and Schuster, 1997.

Fitelson, Branden, Christopher Stephens, and Elliott Sober. "How Not to Detect Design—Critical Notice: William A. Dembski, *The Design Inference*." *Philosophy of Biology* 66 (September 1999): 472–488.

Fix, John. *Astronomy: Journey to the Cosmic Frontier*. 2d ed. Boston: McGraw-Hill, 2001.

Floyd, Chris. "A Trick of the Light: Richard Dawkins on Science and Religion." *Science and Spirit* 10 (July–August 1999): 24–25.

Fountain, John W. "Kansas Puts Evolution Back into Public Schools." *New York Times,* 15 February 2001.

Frair, Wayne, and Gary D. Patterson. "Creationism: An Inerrant Bible and Effective Science." In *Science and Christianity: Four Views,* edited by Richard F. Carlson. Downers Grove, Ill.: InterVarsity, 2000.

Fraser, Steve, ed. *The Bell Curve Wars: Race, Intelligence, and the Future of America.* New York: Basic, 1995.

Futuyma, Douglas. *Science on Trial: The Case for Evolution.* New York: Pantheon, 1983.

Galilei, Galileo. "Letter to the Grand Duchess Christina Concerning the Use of Biblical Quotations in Matters of Science, 1615." In *Discoveries and Opinions of Galileo,* translated by Stillman Drake. New York: Anchor, 1957.

Gallup Organization. "Creationism versus Evolution." *The Gallup Poll* 24 (September 1993): 158.

Gamow, George. *Thirty Years That Shook Physics: The Story of Quantum Theory.* New York: Dower Publications, 1985.

Geisler, Norman L. *The Creator in the Courtroom: Scopes II.* Milford, N.J.: Mott Media, 1982.

Giberson, Karl W. "The Anthropic Principle: A Postmodern Creation Myth?" *Journal of Interdisciplinary Studies* 9 (1997): 63–90.

———. "Intelligent Design on Trial." *Christian Scholar's Review* 24, no. 4 (1995): 459.

———. *Worlds Apart: The Unholy War between Religion and Science.* Kansas City: Beacon Hill, 1993.

Giberson, Karl W., and Donald A. Yerxa. "God's Funeral: The Birth of Modern Science and the Death of Faith: An Interview with A. N. Wilson." *Science and Spirit* 11 (March–April 2000): 44–45.

———. "God's Funeral: A Conversation with A. N. Wilson." *Books and Culture* 5 (September–October 1999): 22–23.

———. "Inherit the Monkey Trial: An Interview with Edward Larson." *Christianity Today* 44 (May 22, 2000): 50–51.

———. "Providence and the Christian Scholar." *Journal of Interdisciplinary Studies* 11 (1999): 123–140.

Gilbert, James. *Redeeming the Culture: American Religion in an Age of Science.* Chicago: University of Chicago Press, 1997.

Gilbert, Scott F. *Developmental Biology.* 5th ed. Sunderland, Mass.: Sinauer Associates, 1997.

Gilkey, Langdon. *Creationism on Trial: Evolution and God at Little Rock.* Charlottesville: University Press of Virginia, 1985, 1998.

———. *Nature, Reality, and the Sacred: The Nexus of Science and Religion.* Minneapolis: Fortress, 1993.

Gish, Duane T. *Evolution: The Challenge of the Fossil Record.* El Cajon, Calif.: Creation-Life Publishers, 1985.

Glanz, James. "Evolutionists Battle New Theory on Creation." *New York Times,* 8 April 2001.

———. "Poll Finds That Support Is Strong for Teaching 2 Origin Theories." *New York Times,* 11 March 2000, A1.

Gleick, James. *Chaos: The Making of a New Science.* New York: Penguin, 1988.

Godfrey, Laurie R., ed. *Scientists Confront Creationism.* New York: Norton, 1983.

Goodenough, Ursula. *The Sacred Depths of Nature.* New York: Oxford University Press, 1998.

Gordon, Bruce. "Intelligent Design Movement Struggles with Identity Crisis." *Research News and Opportunities in Science and Theology* 1 (January 2001): 9.

———. "Is Intelligent Design Science? The Scientific Status and Future of Design–Theoretic Explanations." In *Signs of Intelligence: Understanding Intelligent Design,* edited by William A. Dembski and James M. Kushiner. Grand Rapids, Mich.: Brazos, 2001.

———. "The Polanyi Center Controversy at Baylor University: A Response." *Research News and Opportunities in Science and Theology* 1 (December 2000): 34

Gould, Stephen Jay. *Bully for Brontosaurus: Reflections in Natural History.* New York: Norton, 1992.

———. "Darwinism Defined: The Difference between Fact and Theory." *Discover* 8 (January 1987): 64–70.

———. *Dinosaur in a Haystack.* New York: Harmony, 1996.

———. *Eight Little Piggies.* New York: Norton, 1994.

———. *Ever since Darwin: Reflections in Natural History.* New York: Norton, 1979, 1992.

———. *The Flamingo's Smile.* New York: Norton, 1987.

———. *Full House: The Spread of Excellence from Plato to Darwin.* New York: Harmony, 1996.

———. *Hen's Teeth and Horse's Toes: Further Reflections in Natural History.* New York: Norton, 1983.

———. "Impeaching a Self-Appointed Judge." *Scientific American* 267 (July 1992): 118–121.

———. *Leonardo's Mountain of Clams and the Diet of Worms.* New York: Harmony, 1998.

———. *The Lying Stones of Marrakech.* New York: Harmony, 2000.

———. *The Mismeasure of Man.* Rev. ed. New York: Norton, 1996.

———. *Ontogeny and Phylogeny.* Cambridge, Mass.: Belknap, 1985.

———. *The Panda's Thumb.* New York: Norton, 1980.

———. *Questioning the Millennium: A Rationalist's Guide to a Precisely Arbitrary Countdown.* New York: Harmony, 1999.

———. *Rocks of Ages: Science and Religion in the Fullness of Life.* New York: Ballantine, 1999.

———. *Time's Arrow/Time's Cycle: Myth and Metaphor in the Discovery of Geological Time.* Cambridge, Mass.: Harvard University Press, 1988.

———. *Wonderful Life: The Burgess Shale and the Nature of History.* New York: Norton, 1989.

Greene, Brian. *The Elegant Universe: Superstrings, Hidden Dimensions, and the Quest for the Ultimate Theory.* New York: Norton, 1999.

Greene, John C. *Darwin and the Modern World View.* Baton Rouge: Louisiana State University Press, 1961.

———. *The Death of Adam: Evolution and Its Impact on Western Thought.* Ames: University of Iowa Press, 1959.

———. *Debating Darwin: Adventures of a Scholar.* Claremont, Calif.: Regina, 1999.

Griffin, David Ray. *Religion and Scientific Naturalism: Overcoming the Conflicts.* Albany: SUNY Press, 2000.

Gugliotta, Guy. "Black Sea May Hold Mystery of Flood." *Boston Globe,* 13 September 2000, A21.

Guttman, Burton S., and Johns W. Hopkins III. *Biology.* Boston: McGraw Hill, 1999.

Ham, Kenneth A. *The Lie: Evolution.* El Cajon, Calif.: Master, 1987.

Harrison, Peter. *The Bible, Protestantism, and the Rise of Natural Science.* Cambridge, U.K.: Cambridge University Press, 1998.

Hasker, William, ed. "Special Issue: Creation/Evolution and Faith." *Christian Scholar's Review* 21 (September 1991): 7–109.

Haught, John F. *God after Darwin: A Theology of Evolution.* Boulder, Colo.: Westview, 2000.

Hawking, Stephen W. *A Brief History of Time: From the Big Bang to Black Holes.* New York: Bantam, 1988.

Hawley, John F., and Katherine A. Holcomb. *Foundations of Modern Cosmology.* New York: Oxford University Press, 1998.

Heeren, Fred. "The Deed Is Done." *The American Spectator* (2000–2001), at www.gilder.com/amspec/classics/Dec00–Jan01/heeren0012.htm (11 July 2002).

———. "The Lynching of Bill Dembski." *The American Spectator* (2000), at www.gilder.com/amspec/classics/Nov00/heeren0011.htm (11 July 2002).

Hefner, Philip. *The Human Factor: Evolution, Culture, and Religion.* Minneapolis: Fortress, 1993.

Herrnstein, Richard J., and Charles Murray (contributor). *The Bell Curve: Intelligence and Class Structure in American Life.* New York: Free Press, 1994.

Himmelfarb, Gertrude. *One Nation, Two Cultures.* New York: Vintage, 1999.

Horgan, John. *The End of Science: Facing the Limits of Knowledge in the Twilight of the Scientific Age.* New York: Broadway, 1997.

———. "In the Beginning . . ." *Scientific American* 254 (February 1991): 121–122.

Hoyle, Sir Fred, and Chandra Wickramasinghe. *Evolution from Space: A Theory of Cosmic Creationism.* New York: Simon and Schuster, 1981.

Hoyle, Sir Fred, et al. *A Different Approach to Cosmology: From a Static Universe through the Big Bang towards Reality.* Cambridge, U.K.: Cambridge University Press, 2000.

Hummel, Charles E. *The Galileo Connection: Resolving Conflicts between Science and the Bible.* Downers Grove, Ill.: InterVarsity, 1986.

Hunter, James Davison. *Before the Shooting Starts: Search for Democracy in America's Culture War.* New York: Free Press, 1994.

———. *Culture Wars: The Struggle to Define America.* New York: Basic, 1991.

Jaki, Stanley L. "Cosmology: An Empirical Science?" In *The Limits of a Limitless Science and Other Essays.* Wilmington, Del.: ISI Books, 2000.

———. *Genesis 1 through the Ages.* Rev. ed. Royal Oak, Mich.: Real View, 1998.

———. *God and the Cosmologists.* 2d ed. Fraser, Mich.: Real View, 1998.

Jammer, Max. *The Philosophy of Quantum Mechanics: The Interpretation of Quantum Mechanics in Historical Perspective.* New York: Wiley, 1974.

John Paul II. "Theories of Evolution: An Address to the Pontifical Academy of Sciences, October 22, 1996." *First Things* 71 (March 1997): 28–29.

Johnson, George. *Fire in the Mind: Science, Faith, and the Search for Order.* New York: Vintage, 1995.

Johnson, Phillip E. *Darwin on Trial*. Washington, D.C.: Regnery Gateway, 1991.

———. "Darwinism: The Faith and the Facts." September 1989.

———. *Defeating Darwinism by Opening Minds*. Downers Grove, Ill.: InterVarsity, 1997

———. "Memorandum to Campion Center Participants." November 1989.

———. *Objections Sustained: Subversive Essays on Evolution, Law and Culture*. Downers Grove, Ill.: InterVarsity, 1998.

———. *Reason in the Balance: The Case against Naturalism in Science, Law and Education*. Downers Grove, Ill.: InterVarsity, 1995.

———. "Reflections." In *Three Views on Creation and Evolution*, edited by J. P. Moreland and John Mark Reynolds. Grand Rapids, Mich.: Zondervan, 1999.

———. "Response to Gould." *Origins Research* 15 (spring–summer 1993): 10–11.

———. "The Rhetorical Problem of Intelligent Design." *Rhetoric and Public Affairs* 1 (winter 1998): 587–591.

———. "Science and Scientific Naturalism in the Evolution Controversy." August 1988.

———. "The Unraveling of Scientific Materialism." *First Things* 77 (November 1997): 22–25.

———. "The Wedge: Breaking the Modernist Monopoly on Science." *Touchstone* 12 (July–August 1999): 18–24.

———. *The Wedge of Truth: Splitting the Foundations of Naturalism*. Downers Grove, Ill.: InterVarsity, 2000.

Johnson, Phillip E., and Denis Lamoureux, eds. *Darwinism Defeated? The Johnson–Lamoureux Debate on Biological Origins*. Vancouver, B.C.: Regent College Publishing, 1999.

"The Johnson–Ruse Debate." In *Darwinism: Science or Philosophy?* ed. Jon Buell and Virginia Hearn. Richardson, Tex.: Foundation for Thought and Ethics, 1994.

Jones, Steve. *Darwin's Ghost: The Origin of Species Updated*. New York: Random House, 1999.

———. "Evolution, Creation, and Controversy." In *The Cambridge Encyclopedia of Human Evolution*, edited by Steve Jones, Robert Martin, and David Pilbeam. Cambridge, U.K.: Cambridge University Press, 1992.

Kardong, Kenneth V. *Vertebrates: Comparative Anatomy, Function, and Evolution*. 2d ed. Boston: WCB McGraw-Hill, 1998.

Kauffman, Stuart. *At Home in the Universe: The Search for the Laws of Self-Organization and Complexity*. New York: Oxford University Press, 1995.

———. *The Origins of Order: Self-Organization and Selection in Evolution*. Oxford, U.K.: Oxford University Press, 1993.

Kern, Lauren. "In God's Country." *Houston Press*, 14 December 2000.

———. "Monkey Business." *Dallas Observer*, 11 January 2001.

Kitcher, Philip. *Abusing Science: The Case against Creationism*. Cambridge, Mass.: MIT Press, 1982.

Kolenda, Konstantin. *Philosophy's Journey: From the Presocratics to the Present*. 2d ed. Prospect Heights, Ill.: Waveland, 1990.

Kuhn, Thomas S. *The Structure of Scientific Revolutions*. 3d ed. Chicago: University of Chicago Press, 1996.

Kung, Hans. *Christianity: Essence, History, and Future*. New York: Continuum, 1996.

———. *Does God Exist?: An Answer for Today*. New York: Crossroad, 1994.

——. *Eternal Life?: Life after Death As a Medical, Philosophical, and Theological Problem.* New York: Crossroad, 1991.

——. *Great Christian Thinkers.* New York: Continuum, 1995.

——. *On Being a Christian.* Garden City, N.J.: Doubleday, 1976.

——. *Why I Am Still a Christian.* Edinburgh: T. and T. Clark, 2000.

Kushner, Harold S. *When Bad Things Happen to Good People.* New York: Avon, 1997.

Kusminer, James, ed. "Intelligent Design." *Touchstone* 12 (July–August 1999): 18–94.

Lamoureux, Denis O. "Evangelicals Inheriting the Wind: The Phillip E. Johnson Phenomenon." In *Darwinism Defeated? The Johnson–Lamoureux Debate on Biological Origins,* edited by Phillip E. Johnson and Denis O. Lamoureux. Vancouver, B.C.: Regent College, 1999.

Larson, Edward J. *Summer for the Gods: The Scopes Trial and America's Continuing Debate over Science and Religion.* Cambridge, Mass.: Harvard University Press, 1997.

Larson, Edward J., and Larry Witham. "Leading Scientists Still Reject God." *Nature* 394 (July 1998): 313.

——. "Scientists and Religion in America." *Scientific American* 281 (September 1999): 88–93.

——. "Scientists Are Still Keeping the Faith." *Nature* 386 (April 1997): 435–436.

Laudan, Larry. *Beyond Positivism and Relativism: Theory, Method, and Evidence.* Boulder, Colo.: Westview, 1996.

Layzer, David. *Cosmogenesis: The Growth of Order in the Universe.* New York: Oxford University Press, 1990.

Leakey, Richard E., and Roger Lewin. *Origins: What New Discoveries Reveal about the Emergence of Our Species and Its Possible Future.* New York: Dutton, 1977.

Ledeen, Michael A. *Tocqueville on American Character.* New York: St. Martin's, 2000.

Levitt, Norman. *Prometheus Bedeviled: Science and the Contradictions of Contemporary Culture.* New Brunswick, N.J.: Rutgers University Press, 1999.

Lightman, Alan, and Roberta Brawer. *Origins: The Lives and Worlds of Modern Cosmologists.* Cambridge, Mass.: Harvard University Press, 1990.

Lindberg, David C. "Science and the Early Church." In *God and Nature: Historical Essays on the Encounter between Christianity and Science,* edited by David C. Lindberg and Ronald L. Numbers. Berkeley: University of California Press, 1986.

Lindberg, David C., and Ronald L. Numbers, eds. *God and Nature: Historical Essays on the Encounter between Christianity and Science.* Berkeley: University of California Press, 1986.

Lindley, David. *The End of Physics? The Myth of a Unified Theory.* New York: Basic, 1993.

Livingstone, David N. *Darwin's Forgotten Defenders: The Encounter between Evangelical Theology and Evolutionary Thought.* Grand Rapids, Mich.: Eerdmans, 1987.

Livingstone, David N., and Mark A. Noll. "B. B. Warfield: A Biblical Inerrantist As Evolutionist." *Isis* 91 (June 2000): 283–304.

Livingstone, David N., D. G. Hart, and Mark A. Noll, eds. *Evangelicals and Science in Historical Perspective.* New York: Oxford University Press, 1999.

Lovejoy, Arthur O. *The Great Chain of Being: A Study of the History of an Idea.* Cambridge, Mass.: Harvard University Press, 1936.

Marsden, George M. *Fundamentalism and American Culture: The Shaping of Twentieth-Century Evangelicalism, 1870–1925.* New York: Oxford University Press, 1980.

Mayr, Ernst. "Darwin's Influence on Modern Thought." *Scientific American* 282 (July 2000): 79–83.

———. *One Long Argument: Charles Darwin and the Genesis of Modern Evolutionary Thought*. Cambridge, Mass.: Harvard University Press, 1991.

———. "Prologue: Some Thoughts on the History of the Evolutionary Synthesis." In *The Evolutionary Synthesis: Perspectives on the Unification of Biology*, edited by Ernst Mayr and William B. Provine. Cambridge, Mass.: Harvard University Press, 1998.

———. "Some Thoughts on the History of the Evolutionary Synthesis." In *The Evolutionary Synthesis: Perspectives on the Unification of Biology*, edited by Ernst Mayr and William B. Provine. Cambridge, Mass.: Harvard University Press, 1980, 1998.

———. *This Is Biology: The Science of the Living World*. Cambridge, Mass.: Belknap, 1997.

Mayr, Ernst, and William B. Provine, eds. *The Evolutionary Synthesis: Perspectives on the Unification of Biology*. Cambridge, Mass.: Harvard University Press, 1998.

McElroy, Doug. "Evolutionary Biology." In *Encyclopedia of Genetics*, vol. 1, edited by Jeffrey A. Knight. Pasadena, Calif.: Salem, 1999.

McGrath, Alister E. *Christian Theology: An Introduction*. Oxford, U.K.: Blackwell, 1994.

———. *The Foundations of Dialogue in Science and Religion*. Oxford, U.K.: Blackwell, 1998.

———. *Science and Religion: An Introduction*. Oxford: Blackwell, 1999.

McMullin, Ernan. "Plantinga's Defense of Special Creation." *Christian Scholar's Review* 49 (September 1991): 55–79.

Medherst, Martin, ed. "Special Issue on the Intelligent Design Argument." *Rhetoric and Public Affairs* 1 (winter 1998): 469–637.

Meyer, Stephen C. "Darwin in the Dock." *Touchstone* 14 (April 2001): 57.

———. "DNA by Design: An Inference to the Best Explanation for the Origin of Biological Information." *Rhetoric and Public Affairs* 1 (winter 1998): 519–556.

———. "The Methodological Equivalence of Design and Descent." In *The Creation Hypothesis: Scientific Evidence for an Intelligent Designer*, edited by J. P. Moreland. Downers Grove, Ill.: InterVarsity, 1994.

———. "The Origin of Life and the Death of Materialism." *The Intercollegiate Review* 31 (spring 1996): 24–43.

———. "The Use and Abuse of Philosophy of Science: A Response to Moreland." *Perspectives on Science and Christian Faith* 46 (March 1994): 14–18.

Midgley, Mary. *Science As Salvation: A Modern Myth and Its Meaning*. London, U.K.: Routledge, 1994.

Miller, Jonathan, et al. *Darwin for Beginners*. New York: Pantheon, 1990.

Miller, Keith B. "Design and Purpose within an Evolving Creation." In *Darwinism Defeated? The Johnson–Lamoureux Debate on Biological Origins*, edited by Phillip E. Johnson and Denis O. Lamoureux. Vancouver, B.C.: Regent College Publishing, 1999.

Miller, Kenneth R. *Finding Darwin's God: A Scientist's Search for Common Ground between God and Evolution*. New York: Cliff Street/HarperCollins, 1999.

Milner, Richard. *The Encyclopedia of Evolution: Humanity's Search for Its Origins*. New York: Facts on File, 1990.

Milton, Richard. *Shattering the Myths of Darwinism*. Rochester, Vt.: Park Street, 1997.

Moltman, Jürgen. *God in Creation: An Ecological Doctrine of Creation*. London, U.K.: SCM Press, 1985.

Moore, David W. "Americans Support Teaching Creationism As Well As Evolution in Public Schools." *Gallop Poll Releases* (1999), at www.gallup.com/poll/releases/pr990830.asp (12 November 2000).

Moore, James R. "Of Love and Death: Why Darwin 'Gave up Christianity.'" In *History, Humanity and Evolution: Essays for John C. Greene*, edited by James R. Moore. New York: Cambridge University Press, 1989.

———. *The Post-Darwinian Controversies: A Study of the Protestant Struggle to Come to Terms with Darwin in Great Britain and America, 1870–1900*. Cambridge, U.K.: Cambridge University Press, 1979.

Moreland, J. P. "Complementarity, Agency Theory, and the God-of-the-Gaps." *Perspectives on Science and Christian Faith* 49 (March 1997): 2–14.

———. "Theistic Science and Methodological Naturalism." In *The Creation Hypothesis: Scientific Evidence for an Intelligent Designer*, edited by J. P. Moreland. Downers Grove, Ill.: InterVarsity, 1994.

———, ed. *The Creation Hypotheses: Scientific Evidence for an Intelligent Designer*. Downers Grove, Ill.: InterVarsity, 1994.

Moreland, J. P., and John Mark Reynolds. Introduction to *Three Views on Creation and Evolution*, edited by J. P. Moreland and John Mark Reynolds. Grand Rapids, Mich.: Zondervan, 1999.

Morris, Henry M. "The Battle for True Education." *Institute for Creation Research: Vital Articles on Science/Creation* (1995), at www.icr.org/pubs/btg-a/btg-081a.htm (10 April 2001).

———. *The Genesis Flood*. Green Forest, Ark.: Master, 1976.

———. *The Long War against God: The History and Impact of the Creation/Evolution Conflict*. Grand Rapids, Mich.: Baker, 1989.

———. *Many Infallible Proofs: Practical and Useful Evidences of Christianity*. San Diego: Creation-Life Publishers, 1974, 1996.

———. *The Twilight of Evolution*. Grand Rapids, Mich.: Baker, 1964.

———. ed. *Scientific Creationism*. 3d ed. Grand Rapids, Mich.: Baker, 1998.

Morris, Henry M., and John D. Morris. *The Modern Creation Trilogy*. 3 vols. Green Forest, Ark.: Master, 1996.

Morris, Henry M., and Gary E. Parker. *What Is Creation Science?* Rev. ed. Green Forest, Ark.: Master, 1987.

Morris, Henry M., and John C. Whitcomb. *The Genesis Flood*. Philadelphia: Presbyterian and Reformed Press, 1961.

Morris, Richard. *The Evolutionists: The Struggle for Darwin's Soul*. New York: Freeman, 2001.

Morris, Simon Conway. *The Crucible of Creation: The Burgess Shale and the Rise of Animals*. New York: Oxford University Press, 1998.

National Academy of Science. *Teaching about Evolution and the Nature of Science*. Washington, D.C.: National Academy Press, 1998.

Naye, Robert. "An Inconstant Constant." *Astronomy* 28 (March 2000): 54.

Neff, David. "You Talk about an Evolution." *Christianity Today* 44 (May 2000): 7.

Nelson, P. A. "Welcome to an Evolving Publication." *Origins and Design* 17 (winter 1996): 4.

Nelson, Paul A., and John Mark Reynolds. "Young Earth Creationism." In *Three Views on Creation and Evolution*, edited by J. P. Moreland and John Mark Reynolds. Grand Rapids, Mich.: Zondervan, 1999.

Newman, Robert C. "Progressive Creation." In *Three Views on Creation and Evolution*, edited by J. P. Moreland and John Mark Reynolds. Grand Rapids, Mich.: Zondervan, 1999.

Noll, Mark A., and David N. Livingstone, eds. *B. B. Warfield: Evolution, Science, and Scripture: Selected Writings*. Grand Rapids, Mich.: Baker, 2000.

Noonan, Peggy. *On Values: Talking with Peggy Noonan: Faith*. Produced and directed by Michael Epstein. Sixty min. Films for the Humanities and Sciences, 1995. Videocassette.

Numbers, Ronald L. *The Creationists: The Evolution of Scientific Creationism*. Berkeley: University of California Press, 1993.

———. *Darwinism Comes to America*. Cambridge, Mass.: Harvard University Press, 1998.

Oakes, Edward T., et al. "An Exchange on Intelligent Design." *First Things* 112 (April 2001): 5–13.

O'Connor, Robert C. "Science on Trial: Exploring the Rationality of Methodological Naturalism." *Perspectives on Science and Christian Faith* 49 (March 1997): 21–23.

O'Hear, Anthony. *Beyond Evolution: Human Nature and the Limits of Evolutionary Explanation*. New York: Oxford University Press, 1997.

Olson, Roger, ed. "Theme Issue: Creation, Evolution and Christian Faith." *Christian Scholar's Review* 24 (May 1995): 379–458.

Oord, Thomas J. "Leading Biologist Calls for More Science and Religion Dialogue: A Conversation with Ursula Goodenough." *Research News and Opportunities in Science and Theology* 1 (July–August 2001): 54–56.

Orr, H. Allan. "Darwin v. Intelligent Design (Again)." *Boston Review* 21 (1996–1997), at bostonreview.mit.edu/BR21.6/orr.html (12 April 2001).

Pais, Abraham. *Niels Bohr's Times, in Physics, Philosophy, and Polity*. Oxford, U.K.: Clarendon, 1991.

Paley, William. *Natural Theology: Or Evidences of the Existence and Attributes of the Deity Collected from the Appearances of Nature*. Philadelphia: Johnson and Warner, 1814.

Peacocke, Arthur R. *Theology for a Scientific Age: Being and Becoming—Natural, Divine, and Human*. Minneapolis: Fortress, 1993.

Pearcey, Nancy. "The Evolution Backlash: Debunking Darwin." *World* 11 (March 1997).

———. "We're Not in Kansas Anymore." *Christianity Today* 44 (May 2000): 43–49.

Pennock, Robert T. *Tower of Babel: The Evidence against the New Creationism*. Cambridge, Mass.: MIT Press, 1999.

Penrose, Roger. *The Emperor's New Mind: Concerning Computers, Minds, and the Laws of Physics*. New York: Oxford University Press, 1989.

People for the American Way. "Press Release." 2000, at www.pfaw.org/news/press//show.cgi?article=952702330 (7 November 2000).

Perloff, James. *Tornado in a Junkyard: The Relentless Myth of Darwinism*. Arlington, Mass.: Refuge, 1999.

Pinker, Steven. *How the Mind Works*. New York: Norton, 1997.

Plantinga, Alvin. "Methodological Naturalism?" *Origins and Design* 18 (winter 1997): 18–27.

———. "Methodological Naturalism? Part 2." *Origins and Design* 18 (fall 1997): 22–34.

———. *Warrant and Proper Function*. New York: Oxford University Press, 1993.

———. *Warranted Christian Belief*. New York: Oxford University Press, 2000.

———. "When Faith and Reason Clash: Evolution and the Bible." *Christian Scholar's Review* 21 (September 1991): 8–32.

Polkinghorne, John C. "Creation and the Structure of the Physical World." *Theology Today* 44 (April 1987): 53–68.

——. *The Faith of a Physicist: Reflections of a Bottom up Thinker*. Princeton, N.J.: Princeton University Press, 1994.

——. *One World: The Intersection of Science and Theology*. Princeton, N.J.: Princeton University Press, 1987.

——. *The Quantum World*. Princeton, N.J.: Princeton University Press, 1984.

——. *Quarks, Chaos and Christianity*. New York: Crossroad, 1994.

——. *Reason and Reality: The Relationship between Science and Theology*. Valley Forge, Pa.: Trinity Press International, 1991.

——. *Scientists As Theologians*. London, U.K.: SPCK, 1996.

Ratzsch, Del. *The Battle of Beginnings: Why Neither Side Is Winning the Creation–Evolution Debate*. Downers Grove, Ill.: InterVarsity, 1996.

——. *Nature, Design, and Science: The Status of Design in Natural Science*. Albany: SUNY Press, 2001.

Raven, Peter H., and George B. Johnson. *Biology*. 5th ed. Boston: McGraw-Hill, 1999.

Raven, Peter H., Ray F. Evert, and Susan E. Eichhorn. *Biology of Plants*. 6th ed. New York: Freeman, 1999.

Raymo, Chet. *Skeptics and True Believers: The Exhilarating Connection between Science and Religion*. New York: Walker, 1998.

Rees, Martin. *Before the Beginning: Our Universe and Others*. Cambridge, Mass.: Perseus, 1998.

Riordan, Michael. *The Hunting of the Quark*. New York: Simon and Schuster, 1987.

Roberts, Jon. *Darwinism and the Divine in America: Protestant Intellectuals and Organic Evolution, 1859–1900*. Madison: University of Wisconsin Press, 1988.

Rolston, Holmes III, ed. *Biology, Ethics, and the Origins of Life*. Boston: Jones and Bartlett, 1995.

——. *Genes, Genesis and God: Values and Their Origins in Natural and Human History*. Cambridge, U.K.: Cambridge University Press, 1999.

Rose, Steven. *Lifelines: Biology beyond Determinism*. Oxford, U.K.: Oxford University Press, 1997.

Ross, Hugh. "Astronomical Evidences for a Personal, Transcendent God." In *The Creation Hypothesis: Scientific Evidence for an Intelligent Designer*, edited by J. P. Moreland. Downers Grove, Ill.: InterVarsity, 1994.

——. "Big Bang Model Refined by Fire." In *Mere Creation: Science Faith and Intelligent Design*, edited by William A. Dembski. Downers Grove, Ill.: InterVarsity, 1998.

——. "Facing up to Big Bang Challenges." *Facts for Faith* (2001): 5, 44.

——. *The Fingerprint of God: Recent Scientific Discoveries Reveal the Unmistakable Identity of the Creator*. 2d ed. Orange, Calif.: Promise Publishing, 1991.

Rowe, William L. *The Cosmological Argument*. New York: Fordham University Press, 1998.

Rue, Loyal. *Everybody's Story: Wising up to the Epic of Evolution*. Albany: SUNY Press, 2000.

Ruse, Michael, ed. *But Is It Science: The Philosophical Question in the Creation/Evolution Controversy*. Amherst, N.Y.: Prometheus, 1996.

——. *Can a Darwinian Be a Christian? The Relationship between Science and Religion*. Cambridge, U.K.: Cambridge University Press, 2001.

——. "Evolutionary Ethics: A Defense." In *Biology, Ethics and the Origins of Life*, edited by Holmes Rolston III. Boston: Jones and Bartlett, 1995.

———. *Taking Darwin Seriously: A Naturalistic Approach to Philosophy.* Amherst, N.Y.: Prometheus, 1998.

Russell, Colin A. *Cross Currents: Interaction between Science and Faith.* Leicester, U.K.: InterVarsity, 1985.

Russell, Robert John, Nancey Murphy, and Arthur R. Peacocke, eds. *Chaos and Complexity: Scientific Perspectives on Divine Action.* Vatican City State: Vatican Observatory Publications, 1997.

Sagan, Carl. Introduction to *A Brief History of Time: From the Big Bang to Black Holes,* by Stephen W. Hawking. New York: Bantam, 1988.

Sanders, John. *The God Who Risks: A Theology of Providence.* Downers Grove, Ill.: InterVarsity, 1998.

Sarfati, Jonathan. *Refuting Evolution: A Response to the National Academy of Sciences' Teaching about Evolution and the Nature of Science.* Green Forest, Ark.: Master, 1999.

Schroeder, Gerald. *The Science of God: The Convergence of Scientific and Biblical Wisdom.* New York: Free Press, 1997.

Scott, Eugenie C. "The Creation/Evolution Continuum." *NCSE Reports* (July–August 1999): 16–23.

———. "Reply to an Open Letter of February 1998 Addressed to the National Association of Biology Teachers, the National Center for Science Education, and the American Association for the Advancement of Science." 1998, at fp.bio.utk.edu/darwin/Open%20letter/scott%20reply.htm (5 April 2001).

Segerstrale, Ullica. *Defenders of the Truth: The Battle for Science in the Sociobiology Debate and Beyond.* New York: Oxford University Press, 2000.

Shapere, Dudley. "The Meaning of the Evolutionary Synthesis." In *The Evolutionary Synthesis: Perspectives on the Unification of Biology,* edited by Ernst Mayr and William B. Provine. Cambridge, Mass.: Harvard University Press, 1998.

Shermer, Michael. *How We Believe: The Search for God in an Age of Science.* New York: Freeman, 2000.

Singer, Peter. *A Darwinian Left: Politics, Evolution and Cooperation.* New Haven, Conn.: Yale University Press, 1999.

———. *Rethinking Life and Death: The Collapse of Our Traditional Ethics.* New York: St. Martin's, 1995.

Sizer, Stephen R. "Theology of the Land: A History of Dispensational Approaches." In *Land of Promise: Biblical, Theological and Contemporary Perspectives,* edited by Philip Johnston and Peter Walker. Leicester, U.K.: InterVarsity, 2000.

Smith, Huston. *Why Religion Matters: The Fate of the Human Spirit in an Age of Disbelief.* New York: Harper San Francisco, 2001.

Smith, John Maynard. *The Theory of Evolution.* Cambridge, U.K.: Cambridge University Press, 1958, 1997.

Smith, Robert L., and Thomas M. Smith. *Elements of Ecology.* 4th ed. Reading, Mass.: Benjamin Cummings, an Imprint of Addison Wesley Longman, 2000.

Smolin, Lee. *Life of the Universe.* New York: Oxford University Press, 1999.

Snow, C. P. *The Two Cultures: And a Second Look.* Cambridge, U.K.: Cambridge University Press, 1964.

———. *The Two Cultures and the Scientific Revolution.* New York: Cambridge University Press, 1961.

Sober, Elliott. *Philosophy of Biology.* Boulder, Colo.: Westview, 1993.

Southgate, Christopher, ed. *God, Humanity and the Cosmos: A Textbook in Science and Religion.* Harrisburg, Pa.: Trinity Press International, 1999.

Spier, Fred. *The Structure of Big History: From the Big Bang until Today.* Amsterdam: Amsterdam, The Netherlands. University Press, 1996.

Sterelny, Kim, and Paul E. Griffiths. *Sex and Death: An Introduction to Philosophy of Biology.* Chicago: University of Chicago Press, 1999.

Sullivan, Lawrence. *Inchu's Drum: An Orientation to Meaning in South American Religions.* New York: Macmillan, 1988.

Swanson, Angela. "Dembski Removed." *Research News and Opportunities in Science and Theology* 1 (December 2000): 35.

Swidler, Leonard. *Kung in Conflict.* New York: Doubleday, 1981.

Swimme, Brian, and Thomas Berry. *The Universe Story: From the Primordial Flaring Forth to the Ecozoic Era—A Celebration of the Unfolding of the Cosmos.* New York: HarperCollins, 1992.

Tattersall, Ian. "Human Evolution: An Overview." In *An Evolving Dialogue: Theological and Scientific Perspectives on Evolution,* edited by James B. Miller. Harrisburg, Pa.: Trinity Press International, 2001.

Thaxton, Charles B., Walter L. Bradley, and Roger L. Olsen. *The Mystery of Life's Origin: Reassessing Current Theories.* Dallas: Lewis and Stanley, 1984, 1992.

Thompson, Jefferson M. "Science and Religion." *The Canadian Catholic Review* 17 (July 1999): 2–73.

Tipler, Frank J. *The Physics of Immortality: Modern Cosmology, God and the Resurrection of the Dead.* New York: Archer, 1995.

Transnational Association of Christian Colleges and Schools. "Foundational Standards: Biblical Foundation." at www.tracs.org/foundstandards.pdf (5 April 2001).

Trefil, James, and Robert Hazen. *The Sciences: An Integrated Approach.* New York: Wiley, 1999.

Tudge, Colin. "Why Science Should Warm Our Hearts." *The New Statesman* (2001): 6–40, at www.consider.net/forum_new.php3?newTemplate=OpenObject&newTop=200102260015&newDisplayURN=200102260015 (3 March 2001).

Van Till, Howard J. "The Creation: Intelligently Designed or Optimally Gifted?" *Theology Today* 55 (October 1998): 344–364.

———. "The Fully Gifted Creation." In *Three Views on Creation and Evolution,* edited by J. P. Moreland and John Mark Reynolds. Grand Rapids, Mich.: Zondervan, 1999.

———. "Intelligent Design: The Celebration of Gifts Withheld?" In *Darwinism Defeated? The Johnson–Lamoureux Debate on Biological Origins,* edited by Phillip E. Johnson and Denis O. Lamoureux. Vancouver: Regent College Publishing, 1999.

———. "A Partnership Response." In *Science and Christianity: Four Views,* edited by Richard F. Carlson. Downers Grove, Ill.: InterVarsity, 2000.

———. "Special Creationism in Designer Clothing: A Response to *The Creation Hypothesis.*" *Perspectives on Science and the Christian Faith* 47 (June 1995): 123–131.

———."When Faith and Reason Cooperate." *Christian Scholar's Review* 49 (September 1991): 33–45.

Van Till, Howard J., and Phillip E. Johnson. "God and Evolution: An Exchange." *First Things* 34 (June–July 1993): 32–41

Wagner, Dennis. "Put Another Candle on the Birthday Cake." *Origins Research* 10 (spring–summer 1987): 3.

Walls, Andrew F. *The Missionary Movement in Christian History: Studies in the Transmission of Faith.* Maryknoll, N.Y.: Orbis, 1996.

Ward, Keith. *God, Faith and the New Millennium: Christian Belief in an Age of Science.* Oxford, U.K.: Oneworld Publications, 1998.

Watanabe, Teresa. "Enlisting Science to Find the Fingerprints of a Creator." *Los Angeles Times,* 25 March 2001.

Watson, James. *The Double Helix: A Personal Account of the Discovery of the Structure of DNA.* New York: Athenaeum, 1968.

Weinberg, Steven. *Dreams of a Final Theory: The Search for the Fundamental Laws of Nature.* New York: Pantheon, 1992.

———. *The First Three Minutes.* Rev. ed. New York: Basic, 1988.

———. "The Future of Science, and the Universe." *New York Review of Books* 48 (November 2001): 58–63.

Wells, Jonathan. *Icons of Evolution: Science or Myth?* Washington, D.C.: Regnery, 2000.

Wells, Jonathan, John Mark Reynolds, and Howard Van Till. "Debate: The Ideas of Howard Van Till." *Origins and Design* 19 (summer 1998): 16–35.

West, John G., Jr. "The Regeneration of Science and Culture." In *Signs of Intelligence: Understanding Intelligent Design,* edited by William A. Dembski and James M. Kushiner. Grand Rapids, Mich.: Brazos, 2001.

Westermann, Claus. *Genesis 1–11: A Commentary.* Minneapolis: Augsburg, 1974.

Westfall, Richard. "The Rise of Science and the Decline of Orthodox Christianity: A Study of Kepler, Descartes, and Newton." In *God and Nature: Historical Essays on the Encounter between Christianity and Science,* edited by David C. Lindberg and Ronald L. Numbers. Berkeley: University of California Press, 1986.

Whitcomb, John C., Jr. and Henry M. Morris. *The Genesis Flood: The Biblical Record and Its Scientific Implications.* Philadelphia: Presbyterian and Reformed Publishing, 1961.

White, Andrew Dickson. *A History of the Warfare of Science with Theology in Christendom.* 2 vols. New York: Appleton, 1896.

White, Jerry. "Kansas Board of Education Removes Evolution from Science Curriculum." 1999, at www.wsws.org/articles/1999/aug1999/kan-a13_prn.shtml (6 April 2001).

Wilder-Smith, A. E. *Man's Origin, Man's Destiny: A Critical Survey of the Principles of Evolution and Christianity.* Wheaton, Ill.: Shaw, 1968.

Wildman, Wesley J., and Robert John Russell. "Chaos: A Mathematical Introduction with Philosophical Reflections." In *Chaos and Complexity: Scientific Perspectives on Divine Action,* edited by Robert John Russell, Nancey Murphy, and Arthur R. Peacocke. Vatican City State: Vatican Observatory Publications, 1997.

Wilson, A. N. *God's Funeral.* New York: Norton, 1999.

Wilson, Edward O. *The Ants.* Cambridge, Mass.: Belknap, 1990.

———. *Biophilia.* Cambridge, Mass.: Harvard University Press, 1984.

———. *Consilience: The Unity of Knowledge.* New York: Knopf, 1998.

———. *The Diversity of Life.* Cambridge, Mass.: Belknap, 1992.

———. *The Insect Societies.* Cambridge, Mass.: Harvard University Press, 1971.

———. *Naturalist.* New York: Warner, 1995.

———. *On Human Nature.* Cambridge, Mass.: Harvard University Press, 1978.

———. *Sociobiology: The New Synthesis, Twenty-Fifth Anniversary Edition.* Cambridge, Mass.: Harvard University Press, 2000.

Wilson, Edward O., and Michael Ruse. "The Evolution of Ethics." *New Scientist* 108 (October 17, 1985): 52.

Wilson, John. "Unintelligent Designs." *Books and Culture Corner* (2000), at www.christianitytoday.com/ct/2000/143/11.0.html (7 March 2001).

Wise, Kurt. Foreword to *Faith, Reason, and Earth History: A Paradigm of Earth and Biological Origins by Intelligent Design,* by Leonard Brand. Berrien Springs, Mich.: Andrews University Press, 1997.

———. "The Origin of Life's Major Groups." In *The Creation Hypothesis: Scientific Evidence for an Intelligent Designer,* edited by J. P. Moreland. Downers Grove, Ill.: InterVarsity, 1994.

Wright, Robert. "The Accidental Creationist: Why Stephen Jay Gould Is Bad for Evolution." *New Yorker* 75 (December 1999): 56–65.

———. "The 'New' Creationism." *Slate* (2001), at slate.msn.com/Earthling/01-04-16/Earthling.asp (3 March 2001).

———. *Nonzero: The Logic of Human Destiny.* New York: Pantheon, 2000.

———. *Three Scientists and Their Gods: Looking for Meaning in an Age of Information.* New York: Times Books, 1988.

Yerxa, Donald A. "On the Road with Christianity: A Conversation with Missiologist Andrew Walls." *Books and Culture* 7 (May–June 2001): 18–19.

———. "Questioning Darwin: William Dembski Discusses Intelligent Design." *Research News and Opportunities in Science and Theology* 2 (November 2001): 12–13.

Young, Davis A. *The Biblical Flood: A Case Study of the Church's Response to Extrabiblical Evidence.* Grand Rapids, Mich.: Eerdmans, 1995.

Young, Robert. *Young's Literal Translation of the Bible.* Grand Rapids, Mich.: Guardian, 1976.

Index

About the Authors

Karl W. Giberson is a professor at Eastern Nazarene College where he teaches physics, astronomy, and history of science. He is the editor of *Research News and Opportunities in Science and Theology*, a monthly science and religion newspaper, and is a contributing editor of *Books and Culture* where his essays on science appear regularly. He is the author of two books and numerous articles on science and religion.

Donald A. Yerxa is a professor of history at Eastern Nazarene College. He is the assistant director of The Historical Society, an editor of *Historically Speaking*, and a contributing editor of *Books and Culture*. He is the author of two books and numerous articles on a variety of historical subjects.